1930.

How and cynical will find any refreshment in the account, published in the Vienna newspapers on the tenth anniversary of the Austrian Republic's foundation, of the present whereabouts and occupations of various members of the Habsburg family. Strange are the shifts to which some of them have been put in search of accommodation among a harsh democracy. One is a film actor at Hollywood; another is a messenger in the cinema business; a third paints pictures and tries to sell them; a fourth and a fifth have gone into the banking and building trades. The PRINCESS WINDISCHGRAETZ has divorced her former husband, married a Socialist schoolmaster, and become a local force in the Labour movement.

Few things can be harder than this business of adaptation for such as have been nurtured in an atmosphere of luxury and authority and been kept sequestered from the rough-and-tumble of a competitive world. When we contemplate the far origins of the Habsburg Dynasty and its mighty history and tradition, there is something a little terrifying about the Archduke turned film actor. Here is the wheel turned full circle with a vengeance, and royalty exposed to a new and unfamiliar limelight. 1928 Dec 7

JAN-1940

A LINK WITH SARAJEVO

From Our Own Correspondent

BELGRADE, Sunday.

The father of Gavrilo Princip, the man responsible for the assassination of the Archduke Ferdinand at Sarajevo on June 28, 1914, an event which precipitated the Great War, has just died in Bosnia.

EMPEROR FRANCIS JOSEPH
OF AUSTRIA

THE MACMILLAN COMPANY
NEW YORK · BOSTON · CHICAGO · DALLAS
ATLANTA · SAN FRANCISCO

MACMILLAN & CO., Limited
LONDON · BOMBAY · CALCUTTA
MELBOURNE

THE MACMILLAN CO. OF CANADA, Ltd.
TORONTO

EMPEROR
FRANCIS JOSEPH
OF AUSTRIA

A Biography

BY

JOSEPH REDLICH

Ὡς ἄνθος μαραίνεται καὶ ὡς ὄναρ παρέρχεται
καὶ διαλύεται πᾶς ἄνθρωπος.

Like a flower Man withers and like a dream
he passes away and vanishes.

MACMILLAN AND CO., LIMITED
ST. MARTIN'S STREET, LONDON
1929

COPYRIGHT

TO MY DEAR WIFE

GERTRUD REDLICH

IN LOVE AND GRATITUDE

INTRODUCTION

THE life of Emperor Francis Joseph can only be understood in close connection with the political transformation of Europe and the progressive shift in world power that went on during the century between the Congress of Vienna and the Treaty of Versailles. It is from that standpoint that it is here written. At the same time the specific content of this description is his human and political personality. On no other terms can any bounds be set or any form given to the vast mass of interconnected historical events covered by the period of Francis Joseph's life and reign.

Since, however, whether as man or ruler, he falls far short of being an embodiment of human greatness, it is in a somewhat limited sense only that he fills the conception of a historic personality. So comprehensive, on the other hand, is the range of countries and peoples over whom he reigned; so extensive is the period of his governance; so mighty and multifarious are the European issues influenced, and deeply influenced, by his action and his character, that, judged by the test of influence on great events, he must be said to have counted for more than any other European monarch of the nineteenth century. Compared with his, the singular and momentous career of Napoleon III is but an entr'acte in Europe. Guardian of an ancient line, inheritor and defender of rights that date far back into medieval times, natural foe of the modern struggle to transform Europe into a series of closed national states, Francis Joseph assumed and maintained for sixty years a position in the Europe that the war destroyed to which that of no other sovereign affords an analogue. What makes him all the more impressive is that there was in him, as in no other European monarch of the past century, a perfect correspondence between the man and his work.

To Francis Joseph and to the Empire that came to an end in 1918 the saying certainly applies which is the veritable title deed of biographical history—History is made by men. Even in a period preoccupied as is our own with research into the development and function of ideas and of institutions, economic, social and political, history cannot omit personality, since it is the instrument through which the will of a nation or a state has to be exercised. Least of all can this be done where, as with Francis Joseph, the idea of the ruler overpowers that of the man and makes his personal individuality its servant.

This is the special note of the problem in biography here attempted. Its peculiarity lies in the sharpened contrast with which we have here to deal, between the limited mental and spiritual powers of the individual in his individual life, and unexampled pressure upon it of political and national, social and economic, ideas and tendencies in all their national and international complexity and all their permutations and combinations, affecting as they did, now this way, now that, the equilibrium of forces in Europe.

INTRODUCTION

The extent and difficulty of the task which fell to
Francis Joseph in his early youth lends an interest and a
special color to his purely personal story. Here the dominant note is given by the fact that, throughout nearly
seventy-seven years of action and suffering, Francis
Joseph maintained, unaltered, the position he took up on
entering on his inheritance. The whole weight of the
problems, internal and external, of his realm rested on
him; he stood firm. This is his distinguishing mark. Constitutional forms might and did alter, but the Emperor
retained to the end his primitive conception of the ruler
whose will is always the strongest political force in his
realm. Actually Francis Joseph never was a shadow Emperor; down to the day when the World War began, he
was the ultimately deciding will in his wide empire.

A historical survey of European monarchy in the eighteenth and nineteenth centuries shows clearly enough the
roots of the idea of the old right of the ruler. They
strike down to the notion of the right and duty of the
hereditary sovereign and the belief that in the exercise
of the office given him by Providence the Christian ruler
was limited only by his own conscience. For all the princes
of Europe this idea proved an unassailable moral and
spiritual foundation, which persisted even after the
French Revolution set against it, successfully for a time,
the idea of the unlimited sovereignty of the people. It is
the idea repeatedly proclaimed by Frederick William IV
of Prussia and his brother, the German Emperor, William I. It reappears, more or less definitely, in every
prince of the German Empire, as well as in the French

Bourbons, with a specific nationalist admixture, as in the Russian Czars, and in the rulers of the Habsburg realm. Fundamentally, monarchy in Europe is a uniform product of the thousand-years-old common history of the Continent. Orleans and Napoleans do not belong to it any more than do the Bernadottes in Sweden, Coburgs in Belgium, Karageorgievič in Serbia, or the rulers of United Italy, elected by plebiscite.

This legitimist conception of the ruler, operating from childhood up, inevitably conditions and determines the human personality and its possibilities of development. The individual character of the monarch tends to be subdued to his "ruler personality"; individual traits, while they affect the success or failure of his government, can hardly be detached from his political existence. No clearer case of this exists than Francis Joseph. The life exposed to us over a period of 68 years' rule is almost from the beginning history—and more history; the history of his countries and peoples, the history of Europe, in the last resort, the history of the world.

His biographer must, therefore, attempt to show the person in the politician, the man in the ruler. Despite the extreme difficulty of the task, aggravated as it is by the lack of sufficient data about his personal life, an endeavor will here be made to show the Europe of Francis Joseph's day from the standpoint of his personal activity as ruler. Justice may thus be done to the personality of the most impersonal monarch of the nineteenth century. It must never be forgotten that from the time of his accession at eighteen, the single influence that brought his character to maturity was his position as a ruler. His education from the day he became emperor was not derived from any school or study; only from practical politics. At the same time there was no "favorite" to spare him the burden and responsibility of his duties. On the contrary, the daily demands of his task of maintaining a great old European Empire, of molding its internal and external policy by decisions derived in the last analysis from his own judgment of men and things—this it was that made him what he was, as the men of his day saw him and as he lives on in the recollection of those who knew him.

This is the distinguishing trait in Francis Joseph's life. It was his destiny to be called, on the very threshold of life, to put his own manner of thinking against almost all the great forces and movements of the Europe of his day. It was his own, it was the inviolable tradition of his ancestors; such education as he had received presumed it. And he was an autocrat. In 1848 revolution shook the Habsburg realm to its foundation. He ascended the throne in 1848 as its conqueror. Through nearly seven decades, he had again and again to feel, first in this part of his realm and then in that, the contradiction between his inmost convictions and the political ideas derived from them and the political aims and objects of the day. Again and again he recognized it as his highest duty to overcome this contradiction, and did overcome it, for the sake of the one task that was always before him—the maintenance of his inherited realm. The method of overcoming it was sometimes difficult enough; generally through temporary compromises; generally step by step, though sometimes with astonishing rapidity.

His immovable guiding idea was his duty to maintain his realm intact. To realize it permanently by a creative application of modern ideas to the old Habsburg conception of the realm of the peoples of the West and East, lay beyond his mental scope. But he was strong enough always to impose compromises upon himself and upon his peoples that could only be regarded as temporizing expedients, means of coping with an immediate difficulty. The peoples, on the other hand, were never strong enough to unite and so provide a constructive, positive solution to the problem, growing more momentous year by year, of the continued existence of the old many-nationed realm.

Neither in the past nor in the present has European democracy been able to found lasting realms or create great new human units. Thus it is not astonishing that the contemporary nationalist democracy which attained to full power at the opening of the twentieth century could not achieve this task in Francis Joseph's kingdom. But it was the World War, unleashed by Francis Joseph's ultimatum to Serbia, bringing in its train the active coöperation of the enemy in revolutionizing the Slav and Romanic peoples of the monarchy and the ultimate dissolution of the Austro-Hungarian army, that finally dissolved the realm itself into its historic component parts. Francis Joseph maintained Austro-Hungarian unity throughout his long life. Whether the destruction of that unity was really an act of creative policy for the liberated peoples and for Europe as a whole; whether it signifies lasting peace in the new national states and among their peoples, whether it will produce elevation of the general level of European life—these are questions that the present may put to the future but cannot answer itself.

CONTENTS

CONTENTS

ILLUSTRATIONS

EMPEROR FRANCIS JOSEPH
OF AUSTRIA

EMPEROR FRANCIS JOSEPH
OF AUSTRIA

CHAPTER I

ARCHDUKE FRANZI

(1) *The Dynasty and the 1848 Revolution*

EMPEROR FRANCIS, the last prince of the house of Habsburg-Lorraine to be elected and crowned Roman Emperor over the German nation, and the founder of the new Austrian Empire, was in his sixty-third year when Sophia, wife of the younger of his two sons, the Archduke Francis Charles, gave birth, on August 18, 1830, in the Castle of Laxenburg, to her first child—a boy, who received, in baptism, the name of his father and of his grandfather. It is easy to understand the joy of the aged Emperor in this happy event. At last the succession seemed secured to the Florentine line, founded by Emperor Leopold II, second son of Maria Theresa.

The Crown Prince, Archduke Ferdinand, though tainted with mental defect ever since his tenth year, had married Maria Anna of Savoy: but the marriage was, and was likely to remain, childless. The good-natured, but hopelessly feeble-minded Prince was nevertheless accepted as successor to the throne on his father's death. So the Emperor willed, and Prince Metternich, the chancellor, agreed. Archduke Francis Charles, the second son, was not below the average in competence, but his personality was so insignificant that, on the birth of his eldest son, the hopes of the Vienna court passed him by and settled on the eldest grandson of the reigning monarch. Above all was this true of his mother. Sophia, daughter of the King of Bavaria, gave to her eldest child the physical beauty and strength of the House of Wittelsbach, but, fortunately, nothing of that perilous mental instability which caused so many tragedies in that house in the course of the nineteenth century. She bore her husband three more sons; but the centre of her life, from now on, was the brilliant future of her son Franzi, as the boy was called at court. A woman of strong will, she brought him up and educated him as heir to the throne. She must, very early, have made up her mind to renounce in the interest of her son any hopes for her husband, any dream of being Empress herself.

The court in which Archduke Franzi grew up had, from time immemorial, been the centre of the greatest realm in Europe, with the exception of Russia. The Austrian house had endured heavy defeat in the course of its quarter of a century-long struggle with France and Napoleon. Yet, after Napoleon's eventual overthrow by Europe, the Emperor Francis was the first among the sovereigns of the five great powers. And that place was not wholly undeserved. Something in the final success of the Coalition was due to the tenacity of the Emperor himself and the statesmanship of his chief counsellor, Prince Clemens Metternich: more to the loyalty of the peoples of whom he was the hereditary ruler.

The return of peace, and, consequently, of comfort, produced in Austria, as in Germany that "era of good feeling" which, much later—about the last decade of the nineteenth century—was called the "Biedermeier" epoch. Europe entered upon a state in its social development in which class distinctions in so far as they continued, appeared to have been transformed into a sort of decorative appendage for public occasions, with a kind of antique flavor about them. Class opposition in its modern form had not yet emerged sufficiently to cause any apprehension in the minds of the new middle class society created by the age of enlightenment. Politically, this epoch found expression, in Austria, in the "popularity" of "good" Emperor Francis and in the legend of his kindliness and staunchness, as in the painting and craftsmanship of the period, in the cultivated and varied civilization of the Viennese middle classes of the time of Schubert, or in the unchanged, old-fashioned habits of the ancient German folk living in the towns or on the farms and small villages of the Alpine valley and heights.

It was in this atmosphere that the genius of Franz Grillparzer matured. Deeply affected as he was by the soft drowsiness that then filled the air, the great poet nevertheless grew up to be the sharpest critic of conditions in his native country, and of the principles of its government. Bitterly he characterizes his beloved and beautiful home as "Vienna, thou Capua of the spirits!"

[3]

Grillparzer saw more clearly than did most of his contemporaries how deeply-rooted were the evils of which the Austria of Emperor Francis and his chancellor, Metternich, were sickening. He was blinded neither by the simplicity and plainness of the Emperor, the prestige of Habsburg power, nor the diplomatic fame of the "coachman of Europe," as the chancellor's intimates liked to call him. Grillparzer knew how lamentably far, for many years past, Austria had lagged behind the technical progress of western civilization, and, above all, of Germany, of which it was a part. There was an abundance of creative talent, artistic and other, among the Germans in Austria; but, as a whole, the German elements in the country were being brought to a standstill, thanks to the "stability" system of the Emperor, that cut them off increasingly from the progressive tendency that was developing itself more and more definitely and powerfully throughout the life of the western nations.

Austrian rulers interpreted victory over "the ideas of the French revolution" as a divine judgment, that gave them a right to block every social and political innovation, repress every attempt to give the smallest scope to the ideals and aspirations of the new middle classes, and forestall any admission into Austria of the notion that the people were now of age and that the time had come for the development of a constitutional state there. Among the non-German peoples in the Empire the Italians had been most strongly seized by the new national idea born of the storms of the Revolution and the struggle against Napoleonic world dominion. It soon spread to the Mag-

[4]

yars and the Southern Slavs. All these peoples felt a double oppression in the central government of Austria, with its foreign language and its police régime, "as citizens and as nationalists." Everywhere it was, of course, the educated classes who first became opponents and then enemies of the government and of the Empire. As yet, throughout the far-flung Habsburg lands, the peasant masses and the settled middle classes in the towns (mostly small) had hardly begun to wake out of their long political sleep. The high standard, both of honesty and efficiency, of the central government (which had both a remarkable technique and a magnificent codification of law in all departments to its credit at the opening of the century) still served to protect the minds of the middle classes from being penetrated by the dissatisfaction with public conditions that stirred, more and more strongly, in the minds of the small band of intellectuals in touch with contemporary ideas. .

Criticism grew, however, when the rigidly bureaucratic absolutism of Emperor Francis was unnaturally prolonged under the nominal rule of the feeble-minded Emperor Ferdinand. Actual administration was in the hands of a triumvirate called the "State Conference," composed of the Archduke Ludwig, Prince Metternich and his old political and personal opponent, Count Kolowrat, who had controlled home affairs for two decades, as the special confidant of the Emperor Francis.

A quite peculiar state of affairs now arose. The State Conference and the government departments under it, which controlled the whole life of Austria through the innumerable offices and officials of the various countries, were the scene of endless intrigues and of strife, overt and covert, between Metternich and Kolowrat, with the Archduke holding the scales, or, as a rule, simply putting off decision on any issue that arose. The day-to-day work of the giant machine that the Emperor Francis had wound up went on like a clock. The police and the censorship operated; officials went through the daily administrative routine; Prince Metternich kept watch and ward over foreign affairs. In the army one or two far-sighted generals succeeded in effecting essential reforms. In finance, a misleading appearance of order was maintained. Baron Kübeck, a highly gifted man with a quite modern point of view, actually incorporated modern improvements, like the railways, into the state system, and secured their future development by excellent legal enactments. Industrial progress indubitably took place in Vienna, in Prague, in Brünn, and in Bohemia generally. The harbor of Trieste was raised. Nevertheless, economic life in Austria remained backward. In the country the peasants were bound to the soil by considerations partly quasi-legal and partly practical. There was no change in the omnipotence of the state, in the tenacity of old institutions, or in the boundless activity of the police, which was the real fountain of state life. But in the rulers of this omnipotent state there was absolutely no initiative, except in the repression of anything new. The rôle assigned to the citizen was purely "vegetative." The departments had a monopoly of state will. If the ministers neither could nor would exercise this monopoly, the state and its power simply disappeared before the eyes of subject millions rigidly shut out from any form of public activity.

No one has given a better description of this period of Austrian history than Prince Metternich, in the letters written after his fall from office, to the faithful friends he left behind. A few weeks after the 1848 Revolution he wrote to Count Hartig, one of the high officials of the "patriarchal" government: "The main evil lay in not governing," and this, in its turn, arose from a confusion between administration and government. Regencies, being brief interludes, have always been exposed to the danger of passivity; but the pre-March Austrian Regency lasted for thirteen years, until the Revolution finished it off.

The trouble was, of course, that the intellectual and political life of the people did not stand still during these years. On the contrary, new social forces, new ideas of law and state, philosophy, education, and science were exercising a stronger and stronger influence in every department of life, cultural and economic. Outside Austria, new conceptions of a civil society were working themselves out, and reacting with increasing force on the people inside of it. Keen observers began to note signs of approaching disintegration in the system of Emperor Francis. A wealth of political criticism poured forth in pamphlets that, printed in Germany, got smuggled across to Austria in spite of the censorship. Opposition to the "system" and to Prince Metternich grew, year by year, among the upper classes, and, above all, among the nobility. In the Diets of Vienna and Prague the main subject

[7]

of the attacks was the incapacity of Austrian statesmen to solve the specific problem of the day—the emancipation of the peasants; among the educated classes first deep dissatisfaction and soon contempt for the government, was caused by the out-of-date arrangements of the universities, and the way in which students and teachers were controlled by the police government. Although externally things were quiet, there was a sufficient degree of unrest among the upper and middle classes, and of doubt as to the possibility of maintaining the police system, to go far to loosen the fetters, apparently so strong, with which the government had restrained individual freedom and obstructed the natural class movement among the various nations. The outworn forms of patriarchical rule were being maintained, in the absence of any effective ruler.

The increasing disintegration of the Conference régime, aggravated by concealment, was accelerated by events in Hungary from 1840 on. The racial pride of the Magyar nobility, spurred to new life by Joseph II, was stimulated to complete revival first among the younger generation of lesser Hungarian nobles, who had been influenced by western liberal ideas, and then among the intelligentsia in the towns, most of them of German foundation. Magyar political imperiousness burst into full flame when the struggle against the young Croation national idea broke out in the Diet at Pressburg. For years Francis II had neglected the constitution, not even summoning the Diet to meet. Now it was visibly struggling to assume the form of a national parliament. Prince Metternich was related, through his third wife, to the Hungarian great houses, and understood the history of a country which had been an aristocracy for a thousand years. Vienna, therefore, was more or less tolerant of the conservative reform movement in Hungary, as represented by Count Stephen Szechényi. Yet there also were minds, and very distinguished minds, in Hungary which responded to the western European liberalism.

It was in these years that Francis Déak, still a young man, and Joseph von Eötvös came forward as leaders of a national reform movement, and Ludwig Kossuth, soon to win European fame as an agitator, gave them the aid of his journalistic pen and his unequalled powers as a popular orator. Soon, Magyar nationalism rose all over the country. Their one object was the restoration of the old constitution of the country, solemnly reaffirmed by Leopold II in 1791, but allowed by the Emperor Francis to fall, so to speak, into disuse. What the young men dreamed of was not the old rule of the Magyar aristocracy, but its transformation into a liberal constitutional state. The essence of the historic constitution, asserted at the point of the sword, again and again in the course of three centuries against Habsburg princes by Magyar nobles under kings of their own, was independence and autonomy. Maria Theresa was clever enough to draw the Hungarian nobles more and more into the circle of the Viennese court, and this policy actually kept the political self-will of the magnates dormant for nearly two generations.

After the days of Joseph II, however, the central bureaucracy in Vienna more and more lost touch with Hungary; it was regarded as one among the many provinces governed from Vienna. The solemn renewal by the kings of the rights of the Diet and the comitats (counties) tended, there, to be looked upon as a piece of empty show, handed down from time immemorial to the advantage of the magnates, but a mere nuisance from the point of view of the imperial government of Hungary. Now, Magyar opposition in its turn reacted on the dissatisfaction in educated Viennese circles, strengthening it and heightening its tempo. There, too, public life, confined as it was in outworn forms, began to be looked upon as an expression, however imperfect, of political freedom.

During the three lustra that followed the old Emperor's death, this gradual process of disintegration went on, while the dynasty, the real *raison d'être* of the whole Empire, remained entirely passive. Emperor Francis had kept his brothers as much out of politics as he could. They molded their lives according to their private interests. Archduke Charles, the one military success of his house, looked after his vast fortune and the art treasures he had inherited. Archduke John, a man of intellectual interests and wide culture, lived in Graz and there promoted scientific and technical studies and general culture. Archduke Ludwig, as has been noted, functioned as "substitute will" for the feeble-minded Emperor, Ferdinand, his nephew, who, as Kübeck puts it in his Memoirs, could serve at best but as "imperial symbol." Archduke Francis Charles amused himself by carrying on the traditional good humor and simple citizen bearing of his father. He liked chatting with all and sundry, was on good terms with many people of the Viennese middle class, and really had a sort of native liberalism, though his will was too weak for it to amount to anything in practice. In the various parts of the Empire, there were other old and young archdukes belonging to the Hungarian and Italian lines. But, as a contemporary observer puts it, among all these "Highnesses" at the court, there was only one man—the Archduchess Sophia. She was the one personality at the court with strength of will to oppose the gray heads of the State Conference.

Too little reliable information exists about the education or personal history of the mother of the Emperor Francis Joseph for anything like a full picture of her. Sophia, however, certainly was a natural ruler. Brought up under strong clerical influence, her education was definitely conservative; her proud and passionate temperament made itself more and more strongly felt in Austrian government under the "state conference" system. Even outside court circles her growing opposition to Metternich, who stood for her as for the rest of the world as the exponent of the "system," was known. Undoubtedly she was in close contact with the opposition in the Vienna Diet from 1847 on, and at least aware of the machinations of Metternich's declared enemy Kolowrat, after the outbreak of the February revolution in Paris, to secure a passive official attitude to the demonstrations against the chancellor which contributed to his fall. That her opposition to Metternich was wiped out by the terrible events of March, 1848, is, however, suggested by a letter sent to the aged chancellor eight days after his flight from Vienna. The Archduchess begins with a notably warm appreciation of Metternich's personality and past achievement:

"Ne m'en veuillez pas, mon cher, bien cher Prince, de ce que je viens vous importuner avec quelques lignes dictées uniquement par le besoin de vous dire combien je vous aime et vous révère, combien je vous suis reconnaissante pour notre pauvre Autriche de tout ce qu'elle vous doit de beau, de grand, d'ineffaçable et combien je vous remercie du bien que vous avez fait à mon fils durant ce dernier hiver, en donnant une si bonne direction à ses idées et à ses sentiments."

Then, the mother's heart overflowing with pride in her son, and emotion at his behavior in the worst days the imperial house had yet seen, she goes on:

"Si vous l'aviez vu, ce cher enfant, lorsque le 13 Mars au soir une générosité et une delicatesse exagérée vous ont engagé à nous quitter; si vous l'aviez vu venir chez moi, le désespoir dans l'âme et sentant tout le poids de ce moment décisif pour la monarchie, vous auriez eu au moins un instant de satisfaction et de douce emotion.

"Mon pauvre Franzi était ma seule consolation dans notre détresse; au milieu de mes angoisses et de mon désespoir, je bénissais le ciel de me l'avoir donné tel qu'il est! Son courage, sa fermété, sa manière de sentir et de juger forte, inébranable, étaient bien au-dessus de son age et pourraient presque nous faire espérer que le bon Dieu veut encore lui accord-

ARCHDUCHESS SOPHIA OF AUSTRIA,
MOTHER OF FRANCIS JOSEPH.

er un avenir; puisqu'il lui a donné les qualités néces-
saires pour en accepter toutes les chances."

This remarkable woman derived her strength from a
deep vein of religion, curiously interwoven into her strong
dynastic sense. From her youth she was full of the romantic Catholicism strongly developed on the Rhine and in
southern Germany from the beginning of the century, but
in Austria, despite the influence of Zacharias Werner and
the saintly Clemens Maria Hofbauer, held back by the
influence of the court and the bishops, over whom the ra-
tionalistic tradition of Joseph II in church problems still
held sway. The explanation for any inclination toward
"liberalism" Sophia showed before the revolution, must
be found in her opposition to Prince Metternich.[1] Anyhow, the visible results of the popular movement, so light-
heartedly espoused by certain court circles, as seen in the
outburst of anti-imperial and anti-religious feeling that
spread through great sections of the population in revolu-

[1] The publication of the portions of the diary of Princess Melanie
Metternich hitherto withheld gives a fuller insight into the relations of
the Chancellor and his wife to the court and to the mother of Francis
Joseph than was previously available. Undoubtedly Sophia blamed Metternich for the accession of the weak-minded Ferdinand, which she felt
as a wrong done to her and her husband. From 1845 she fought against
the paralyzing régime of the Triumvirate with obstinate intensity. She
openly supported Kolowrat, the Minister of the Interior. Indeed Princess
Melanie in her diary bluntly says that the Archduchess and her husband,
who was completely under her thumb, were mainly responsible for the
fall of the Chancellor on the night of March 13. It evidently rankles in
Melanie's passionate heart that Metternich's withdrawal from Vienna,
at the wish of the court, was by them described as a cowardly flight.
When the ex-Chancellor and his family returned to Vienna in 1851,
there was a very frank exchange between Archduchess Sophia and
Princess Metternich, of which a characteristic account is given in the
latter's diary.

[13]

tionary excitement, caused her to react in horror. All her life she felt an intense indignation at the outrage of the Revolution to her and her house. In 1849, she said to General Kempen: "I could have borne the loss of one of my children more easily than I can the ignominy of submitting to a mess of students. In the future the shame of the past will seem simply incredible." These words reveal the depth of hatred felt for the Revolution and its leaders by the mother of Francis Joseph. From now on she devoted herself to gathering together everything and everybody that had stood faithful to the dynasty in the stormy months of 1848. She relied more than heretofore on the counsel of her ecclesiastical friends and supported every political measure designed to strengthen and extend the power and status of the Church. Abbot Rauscher, who became Archbishop of Vienna soon after the Revolution, was her oracle for the time being in all political questions.

There is no recorded instance of her interposition on the side of mercy or reconciliation in the dark years when the iron heel of military reaction was on the necks of the defeated rebels in Austria and Hungary. After, as before, she dominated the court, even after her son's accession. Those about her marveled at her brains and energy and her steady pursuit of her goal. Affection she hardly seems to have excited, even in those nearest to her. Her sons, and above all her eldest, certainly gave her a boundless devotion. He and Max, next to Franzi in age, were her favorites. Certainly none of the heavy strokes Fate was again and again to deal at her house during her lifetime, altered or weakened her temper. She went through life firmly and unalterably fixed in her convictions.

The incalculable consequences that an apparently harmless popular movement was to produce at the opening of the session of the Vienna Diet on March 13, 1848, were, of course, not foreseen by Sophia. The State Conference and the police department of Vienna knew little or nothing of the gathering forces in the city struggling to effect a political and social transformation there. The witless and weak behavior of the ministers and of the court turned a demonstration into a revolution. An impossible thing—but there it was, in flames. Within three days it had overwhelmed the senile organization of the patriarchal government and, subject to the provision that the "imperial symbol" was kindly allowed to continue ruling, attained the complete catalogue of popular demands—freedom of the press and the promise of a constitution. The "man in the street," as we now call him, had defeated the whole historic order. On no one did these events fall with more crushing force than on high-spirited, self-reliant Sophia, who now learned for the first time how deeply detested her name was among the people. The new democratic press of Vienna, growing up in a night and for the moment wholly unrestrained, at once started a campaign against the "Court Camarilla," of which Archduchess Sophia was presented as the soul. After the flight of Metternich on the evening of March 14, and the resignation of Archduke Ludwig and of the State Conference the wrath of the radicals was concentrated in the main on her.

Sophia's was an active nature. The main resolution she derived from the experience of these stormy days was that the sham rule of the good-natured Ferdinand must be ended, and, above all, that men must be gathered at the court who could not merely resist the progress of revolution but plan an organized counter-revolution from above. First of these was Prince Alfred Windischgrätz, the commandant of Prague who, on Sophia's appeal, had functioned for a few hours on March 14 as a dictator, only to withdraw at once. Count Francis Stadion, the Governor of Galicia, accounted the best mind in the higher bureaucracy, was summoned to Vienna by a holograph letter from Archduke Francis Charles. Moral support the Archduchess found in her ecclesiastical friends, above all in Archbishop Otmar Rauscher, her most trusted spiritual counsellor. This group gave life and force to Sophia's grand design of preparing a counter-revolution whose object must be the abdication of the Emperor Ferdinand. He had accepted the Austrian constitution and acceded to the constitutional law drawn up by the Hungarian rebels on Kossuth's lines: in his name the feeble government formed by Pillersdorf, a liberal bureaucrat, was making fresh concessions daily to the democracy of the Vienna streets. Once the revolution had been got under way, Ferdinand was to lay down the crown and be succeeded on the throne by the youthful Archduke Franzi.

Sophia was firmly resolved on sacrificing the rights of her husband and her own imperial ambitions. She had no doubts of her power of persuading her husband. The revolution could be beaten and the Empire reconstructed only by handling the scepter to the strong and uncompromised hand of youth. Then a strong monarchical power would be able to fuse all the peoples and regions of the Empire into a comprehensive whole and make them, as a whole, again amenable to the imperial will. This was the dominating purpose of Sophia; it was also the plan of the men who had gathered round the court since the March days, on whom it could rely. Such were the circumstances under which the narrow path of the seventeen-year-old Archduke was irresistibly widened to become the highroad of the history of the dynasty and its realm. At this point then we must look back over the path which led Sophia's eldest son straight from the nursery and the schoolroom to the throne of the oldest ruling house among the great powers of Europe.

(2) *The Education of the Heir Apparent*

Francis Joseph had a happy childhood and boyhood. Admirably brought up, he had a thorough, many-sided, if anything too well-balanced education. Certainly he had the best of nurseries. Every care was devoted to his physical well-being and he grew up a remarkably handsome boy, with good-looking features, slim and hard of muscle, with beautiful manners and a faultless bearing. Even in boyhood his distinguishing trait was a self-control beyond his years; a fact that by no means prevented his enjoyment of childish pleasures in the company of his younger brothers and the noble youths of his own age selected for his companionship. The plan of studies chosen for him

[17]

covers an extraordinarily wide range. Franzi's native gift for languages was assiduously cultivated: the young Emperor spoke Magyar and Czech tolerably and Italian and French excellently. His sense for his own German language was good; the letters—unfortunately relatively few—which he wrote himself show a genuine talent for the expression of ideas in concise phrases.[2] That he was educated on strict religious lines goes without saying. Not only was his tutor, Count Bombelles, a man of definitely religious outlook; but his mother's strong faith was bound to exercise a profound influence. As Emperor, Francis Joseph was always personally a loyal believer in the Catholic faith, although in the course of his long reign he had to take up very varying positions to the Church and its authority. His attitude to religion was that of almost every Austrian gentleman of old nobility. Catholicism, to him, seems as natural and obvious as the mountains of his country or any of the great given facts in the landscape of his life. One does not talk much about it; nothing is less liked in settled Austrian circles than any sort of talk about faith, whether popular or scientific. Everyone knows that faith is the substance of religion and not any wordy or profound apparatus of proof. What the individual says about dogma does not signify; on the contrary what does signify is what the Church teaches him.

Criticism of and aversion to Protestantism is traditional

[2] More than half a century ago, Alexander von Helfert, the admirable historian of the 1848 Revolution and its aftermath, gave a full description of the education of Francis Joseph, showing the great care with which the future Emperor's mother and the teachers she selected for him carried out their task. That they made many mistakes Helfert does not deny. For instance, he notes the very poor instruction given in history.

in these circles; certainly it was in that of Archduchess Sophia, though only her third son, Charles Ludwig, seems to have inherited her passionate Catholicism. Francis Joseph was never a devotee, nor had he any tinge of deep religious fervor. His whole temper was alien to it, for the basis of his make-up was an unmistakable matter-of-factness, an intelligence that was exceedingly quick in apprehension, but at the same time had a sort of dryness, both in what it took in and in what it gave out. Mysticism was a sealed book to him. He was always unsympathetic to anything vague and misty in personality or expression. Only what was simple and natural seemed real to him. In this he represented one of the best of Austrian traits. He was, moreover, so sure of himself that he could tell a genuine man from a sham. People whose approach was marked by what in Austria is called "play-acting" never got on with him. Further, as soon appeared, his disposition shut him off from any purely spiritual pleasure; he was apt to dismiss anything beyond the average level almost with irritation, as incompatible with an outlook based upon the practical logic of experience in the school of life.

Painting and poetry, like music, played small part in his education. He had a certain natural talent for drawing on which he spent much pains as a boy, deriving real pleasure from its exercise. It is significant that special emphasis should have been laid in the education of the heir to the throne on his military training. This was really a novelty in the Vienna court. It was centuries since an hereditary prince of the house of Habsburg had displayed any ambition to be a military expert before he became Emperor.

An exception perhaps should be made for Joseph II who was certainly more of a Lorrainer than a Habsburg. The atmosphere of the Vienna court was not military. All that was possible was of course done for the standing army; the necessary money for it was always produced, often with the greatest difficulty. Neither Joseph II nor Francis II would have opposed the view that war was the most powerful resource of a king. Emperor Francis indeed went so far as to say that he was at all times ready to engage in war. His ministers, Thugut, Colloredo, and Cobenzl, supported him in that. But he took no personal part in military matters. The heavy defeats of his generals left him calm; victory he took with the same equanimity.

The actual military gifts of Archduke Charles, unusual in the family, did not particularly please Emperor Francis. It was no part of the ambition of the dynasty to have its members military heroes. Their greatest general, Prince Eugène of Savoy, had been borrowed from another dynasty like many of the victorious captains of Maria Theresa who had come from abroad. Archduke Franzi was actually the first heir to the throne to be carefully trained as an officer. Since his military instructor was Colonel Hauslab, a highly educated man, he was not only excellently trained professionally but acquired a lasting interest in all military matters. Native gifts for generalship he did not possess, but he certainly would have been a reliable officer.

Count Coronini, who superintended his military education, impressed military discipline and punctuality upon

him with no light hand, as well as the bearing of a soldier and a high respect for soldierly virtues and duties. So
from childhood up Francis Joseph looked upon the soldier
as the embodiment of the highest qualities in man. Naturally, thus, he conceived of the monarch as first and foremost the supreme war lord. His military guide seems
indeed to have had a suspicion that he had done rather
too much. Anyhow, on December 8, 1848, directly after
Francis Joseph's accession, he accompanied his duty to the
new Sovereign with the following highly characteristic
sentences:

> "Your Majesty's remarkable sense of duty and
> truth will make it easy for you to show enough con-
> descension and pliability to win the hearts of all
> classes; special study devoted to that end will as-
> suredly bear golden fruit.
>
> "Your Majesty possesses physical and even more
> notable moral courage; this will be of the greatest
> utility to your Highness in helping you to give those
> who press upon you those negative answers that
> one has in mind but shrinks from expressing."

In relation to the rank and file Francis Joseph, all
his life, took what is called in Austria the "regimental
point of view." Order, punctuality, uniforms and discipline, strict observance of prescribed forms of promotion and decoration, the whole of the "pipeclay" side
of the service, constituted too exclusively his conception
of looking after the army. Of the vast importance of
making the best use of the higher spiritual and moral

elements in the army as a whole, as was done forty years earlier with such brilliant success by Scharnhorst and Gneisenau in the Prussian army, the imperial youth knew nothing nor did he in this respect ever learn much. For the rest he showed that he was fearless as a soldier when, to the great concern of old Field Marshal Radetzky, he appeared in the Italian camp in May, 1848, and displayed his bravery at the cannon's mouth in the bloody engagement of Santa Lucia.

This circumstance only made the old General the more eager to get the young Archduke back to the court at Innsbruck. But it is a great pity that the scientific military training of the young man only began in 1847, and the great events of the following years hindered its continuation. Francis Joseph was never able to make good this gap in his military knowledge. The same is true of his instruction in politics and jurisprudence, which likewise began in the autumn of 1847. In the winter of that year he was given lectures on statesmanship and politics, every Sunday by Chancellor Metternich. It proved later, however, that his personality had no lasting influence on the Emperor. The influence of two of his other teachers was to be of considerable importance in his later life—Abbot Rauscher who taught him Canon Law and Councillor von Lichtenfels who lectured to him on Civil Law. Both these men later played important parts in his internal policy.

* * * * * * * *

Take it all in all—the eighteen-year-old Archduke, on whom the fate of the dynasty hung when the political

earthquake of February, 1848, in Paris shook the Habsburg realm to its foundations, was mentally and physically a good specimen of the average prince, in whose
make-up tradition must of necessity count for more than
individual faculty. Franzi was certainly not without serviceable gifts for the great position for which he was destined, if yet he lacked any striking special gift. As a
prince just emerging from boyhood he already showed a
marked feeling for personal dignity and exterior bearing, a lack of higher intellectual interests, a notably early
developed sense of fact, and an objective judgment. He
did not strike his contemporaries as particularly amiable.
Naturally enough his boyish emotions were concentrated
in a deep affection and admiration for his mother. The
school bag he took with him as he left boyhood behind,
was no doubt as well, or possibly better, filled than that
of the youthful scions of the nobility who were his sole
companions. His education ceased when he was too young
for him to have acquired any advanced scientific training.

One must always guard against assigning more importance than it deserves to school learning in the case of
men who have to enter very young on an inherited position which compels them before their time to act as
leaders in affairs—whether those of a throne, of a great
fortune, or landed estate. Of course in every such case
the premature assumption of independence or leadership carries a danger to the heir, much as he is apt to be
envied. That Francis Joseph could not escape this danger
is perhaps the first of the tragedies in the life of the
future Emperor. He was not sufficiently ripe to cope with

the indescribably heavy burden to be laid on his young
shoulders by the necessities of his house and the vaulting
ambition of his mother. Therefore, his real, practical education in rulership was in the hands of the men who, in
the early years of his imperial task, both influenced him
personally and through their political decisions marked
a path along which he had to tread. This was the effective schooling of the last great Austrian Emperor.

(3) *The Coronation at Olmütz*

Archduchess Sophia's great design became more and
more definite as revolution gained ground in Vienna. The
May rising, abolishing the constitution issued by the Emperor Ferdinand and compelling the feeble Pillersdorf
government to substitute for it the election of a constitu-
ent assembly based on a democratic franchise, caused the
imperial family to flee from Vienna and seek peace and
quiet in loyal Innsbruck. The court, against the will of the
Empress Maria Anna and of Archduchess Sophia, its
leading personalities, returned to Vienna for the opening
of the Reichstag, in the hope that some change for the
better might be produced by the new government under
the experienced diplomat Baron von Wessenberg. The
growth of parliamentary radicalism, the omnipotence of
the revolutionary committee of safety, and uncertainty
as to the loyalty of the national guard testified that it was
not in the power of the ministry to protect the court or
to count on the moderate elements in the people, though
in a majority, to hold down revolutionary forces gather-

EMPEROR FRANCIS JOSEPH
AT HIS ACCESSION TO THE THRONE

ing in Vienna from all over Europe. The government's
attitude to the demands of Hungary soon forced it into
open war. This proved, in effect, to be the first act in the
counter-revolution. At first Count Jellacic, Ban of Croatia,
got no support in his threats to Hungary, but he was
secretly encouraged in them from Innsbruck. He launched
civil war by crossing the Croatian frontier into Hungary,
this act inevitably affecting the revolutionary forces in
Vienna and in the Reichstag. On October 6 there was a
fresh outbreak in the city. The war minister, Count
Latour, fell a victim in the most horrible way, and there
were not enough troops to save the government from a
complete collapse. Once again the court left the capital. This time they betook themselves to the old Mora-
vian fortress of Olmütz, whither most of the members
of the cabinet soon followed them.

These events ripened the resolve of the group of men
who had put their services at the disposition of the court
at the time of the outbreak of the revolution. First of
these was Prince Windischgrätz. During the summer,
after repressing the rising in Prague, he had gathered a
considerable force there. Windischgrätz was the embodiment of resolute will, of all that was still strong and
capable in the Austrian noble class. An aristocrat of the
old school, he believed firmly that Providence had designed him to be the savior of the Habsburg Empire. At
Innsbruck he had discussed with Empress Maria Anna,
who had the most complete confidence in him, the ways
and means of restoration of imperial authority, but did
not then agree with her desire of having the Emperor's

abdication declared on August 18, the day on which Archduke Franzi would attain his majority.

In his correspondence with the court, Windischgrätz took the view that some new revolutionary blow at monarchical authority should be the occasion of Ferdinand's renunciation. He foresaw the inevitable progress of revolution. Writing to Prince Lobkowitz, whom he had installed as general adjutant to the imperial family, he said: "Above all I make you responsible for seeing that His Majesty makes no further concessions. If you observe any pressure in that direction or any danger threatening the person of the Emperor, assemble all the troops you can and transport His Majesty under the protection of the army, not by way of flight, to Olmütz. I shall then seize Vienna, His Majesty will abdicate in favor of his nephew Archduke Francis and we will then take Ofen." So it happened. The forced journey made a deep impression on the young heir to the throne. Helfert records that at Olmütz everyone noticed that he was visibly abstracted and serious beyond his years. It was the future Emperor's first harsh personal experience. From this time on, the revolution constituted an indestructible element in the thinking of a young man whose political education was to be given him by events.

Even Prince Windischgrätz's sensitive legitimism now saw the great change in the throne as inevitable. The first step towards it was the institution of a new government, capable of putting through a course of action in which the first move was the seizure of Vienna, the second the restoration of imperial power. As head of this government Prince Windischgrätz selected his brother-in-law, Prince Felix Schwarzenberg. Windischgrätz enjoyed the exclusive confidence of the Empress, on whom everything depended since the childish mind of her husband was entirely under her direction. Maria Anna accepted Schwarzenberg simply and solely as his nominee. Abdication could not be delayed since Schwarzenberg was prepared to accept the post of prime minister and Count Francis Stadion that of minister of internal affairs only on that condition.

For six weeks after the October rising in Vienna the aged Baron von Wessenberg continued in office as prime minister, although Schwarzenberg had actually undertaken the formation of a government. The new ministry was not formally announced till November 23. Four days later Prince Schwarzenberg read out the program of the new government to the Reichstag, assembled at Kremsier, in the summer palace of the Archbishop of Olmütz. The great difficulty that had to be overcome was the personality of Empress Maria Anna.

The best account of the remarkable events surrounding Francis Joseph's accession is to be found in a memorandum by Councillor Hummelauer, one of the prominent officials of the old chancellery. "The Empress," says the worthy old man, "was under no illusion as to the capacity of her husband. When the question of forming a government arose after the arrival of the court at Olmütz Prince Schwarzenberg and Count Stadion enjoyed the imperial confidence in full measure. These two gentlemen did not desire to continue service with the

Emperor Ferdinand. They desired him to be removed from the throne, and to have Archduke Francis Charles passed over. The Empress wished the Emperor to abdicate. But her conscience would allow her personally to advise him to take this step only on the condition that action against the revolution and safeguarding the monarchy, action that involved energetic resistance to revolutionary tendencies and attempts, was certainly guaranteed. This *conditio sine qua non* the Empress divulged to Prince Windischgrätz who alone enjoyed her complete confidence.

"But the political views of the two men to whom the destinies of the monarchy were to be confided did not correspond with the Empress's. They wanted to make Austria constitutional; the Empress would not have a constitutional monarchy. The Empress thus represented an obstacle; abdication would of course remove it. But since the new ministry must be formed in the name of Emperor Ferdinand a promise had to be extracted from the Empress to exert no influence on the course of events. She, however, refused to consent to the Emperor's abdication except on condition that this act left his successor completely unhampered by the concessions exacted from his exalted uncle, concessions incompatible with the welfare of the monarchy and the rights of the throne; that this freedom were then used to save the throne, the Emperor having renounced the throne because the acts to which he had given his consent made it impossible for him to reign."

Now, with the help of the men in whom the Empress

reposed confidence, and of the old statesman Baron Kübeck, an Abdication Act was drafted which set out in plain words the events that had compelled Ferdinand to abdicate and condemned the revolution and its leaders in the harshest terms. This was a question of conscience with the Empress and she therefore insisted on hearing from Windischgrätz whether he was satisfied with the document. "You need have no scruple," wrote the field marshal to her, "in inducing the Emperor to abdicate." He assured her in his own name and in that of the new ministers that their policy would entirely correspond with her views. Prince Windischgrätz in fact answered for his brother-in-law, the prime minister, to the Empress.

What the Empress had feared, if not expected, now took place. Prince Schwarzenberg made such alterations both in the Abdication Act and in the proclamation of the young monarch that the effective content of these momentous documents was not the condemnation of the revolution but the promise on the part of Archduke Francis to reign as a constitutional monarch. At the same time he assumed the name of Francis Joseph, with a view to attracting the section of opinion that might see in the name of the popular Emperor Joseph II a promise of a constitutional outlook on the part of the young monarch. Prince Schwarzenberg carried out the abdication of the incompetent Emperor in a manner which blankly broke the promise given to the Empress and at the same time cold-bloodedly effected the first great deception of the people to be perpetrated in the name of Francis Joseph.

Schwarzenberg, of course, had not the faintest intention of making a real constitutional monarch of the young Archduke who now ascended the throne; but he was clever enough to see that, for the moment, the game the court had been playing all the year under cover of "kind" Ferdinand, must be carried on. The spirit of revolution was not laid in Austria; the war begun in September against the revolutionary Hungarian government was far from being successfully terminated. Therefore, in the face of the honest reactionism of the old Empress, the people must have what they had won by the revolution again guaranteed. The object of Schwarzenberg's whole plan was to tranquillize Vienna and the other Austrian towns and lull them into the belief that the government of the new ruler freely accepted the constitutional principle and intended to realize it. The countryside, it was well known, had been won over wholeheartedly for the imperial house and against the revolution by the act of the first Austrian parliament of September 7, 1848, emancipating the peasants from all feudal burdens, promulgated by Emperor Ferdinand. So far as Vienna was concerned, they could rely on the state of siege, the court-martials and the executions of some of the captured leaders of the October rising to keep down the revolutionary spirit there.

When Prince Schwarzenberg and his government met the Reichstag on November 27, he addressed them with his habitual icy calm in words whose inner meaning was known only to himself and his few confidants: "The great task before us and the people is the foundation of a new union comprising all the regions and races of the monarchy in a single *great* state body. The government will not act as a drag on aspirations for free and popular institutions; on the contrary it conceives it as its duty to put itself at the head of this movement. Sincerely and without reserve do we desire a constitutional monarchy; the foundations of our new structure shall be the equality of all citizens before the law, the equality of all nationalities, and openness in every department of administration. The free commune is the basis of the free state!"

In thus solemnly proclaiming his ministry a liberal constitutional government, Schwarzenberg broke his promise to Windischgrätz and the Empress, and accomplished the first conscious deception of the Austrian people and the Reichstag.

Early on December 2, 1848, the imperial family gathered in the Archbishop's palace at Olmütz in ceremonial conference, to hear Prince Schwarzenberg read the solemn declarations, prepared by himself, in which Emperor Francis and Archduke Francis Charles renounced the throne, Archduke Franzi was declared of age, and, finally, his accession as Francis Joseph was announced. The young man had been informed of the plan several weeks before the great act took place and his bearing during the scene was one of calm and modest dignity. At its completion, he deliberately sank on one knee before his uncle to express his gratitude to him. The departing Emperor embraced his young nephew, stroked his face, and said, "Bear yourself bravely; it is all right." With this, the last honorable word of the old Austria, the new epoch was ushered in in true "Biedermeier" style.

The young Emperor's manifesto, published on December 2, composed again with conscious intent to mislead the public, was his first political action, and one for which his prime minister bears full responsibility both to his contemporaries and to history. But in the view of the young Emperor's millions of subjects, he was himself personally and lastingly bound by it. Such an obligation of the new ruler towards his people found no place in Schwarzenberg's plan, nor was it for one moment taken seriously by the eighteen-year-old youth. This is indeed the decisive historic fact that gives the personality of Francis Joseph its peculiar and permanent character. "Convinced"—so began the manifesto of the young Emperor, read in the Reichstag a few hours after his accession to the throne by the prime minister—"convinced, on our own motion, of the need and value of free institutions expressive of the spirit of the age, we enter with due confidence, on the path leading to a salutary transformation and rejuvenation of the monarchy as a whole. On the basis of genuine liberty, on the basis of equality of all the nations of the realm and of the equality before the law of all its citizens, and of participation of those citizens in legislation, our Fatherland may enjoy a resurrection to its old greatness and a new force. Determined to maintain the splendor of the crown undimmed and the monarchy as a whole undiminished, but ready to share our rights with the representatives of our peoples, we count on succeeding, with the blessing of God and in understanding with our peoples, in uniting all the regions and races of the monarchy in one great state."

The natural echo of these words was the president of the Reichstag's cry, "Long live the Constitutional Emperor Francis Joseph." Many of the members who doubted the seriousness of the solemn imperial words—the doubters were not few—may have found their doubt confirmed next day, in the obvious embarrassment with which the young Emperor replied to the president of the delegation that waited on him at Olmütz. Remembering that this inheritor of a mighty empire, this mere lad hardly emerged from boyhood, who had grown up apart from any wrong and altogether apart from the world, now entered on his imperial destiny with a lie which he must have known to be a lie, one realizes the tragedy that fastened on Francis Joseph, innocent up to this hour, and was never after to leave him. Cruelly was the poet's "evil deed that forever bears fresh evil" to be realized in this life of eighty-six years!

No doubt the *mala fides*, the bad faith with which Francis Joseph met his people on the threshold of his rule, was never felt by him as in any way a fault or a sin. But a young man, ripe and reflective beyond his years, cannot be wholly excused because that very youth of his gives us the measure of his grasp of the moral bearing of his deed. True it was not his doing, it was Schwarzenberg's; but something essential in Francis Joseph himself caused him to make the deed his own, instead of feeling or uttering any resistance to it. Schwarzenberg had won his entire confidence. He had taught the young Archduke that he could, under his guidance, attain supreme fame and tread the path to full dominion if he possessed the force, the self-confidence, and the firmness to oppose to the disastrous ideas and aims of European revolution and the folly of western democracy the will of a true ruler who brings happiness to his people. From the first it was on this foundation stone that Francis Joseph erected the philosophy of state by which he sought to solve the multifarious problems presented to him as ruler. Further, Schwarzenberg told him that the utmost foresight was needed if the great aim were to be attained. The greatness and importance of that aim sanctified in advance such means as untruthfulness and conscious deception. The young Emperor understood this doctrine. He accepted it fully. From this hour down to his death sixty-eight years later, Francis Joseph believed in the gospel, first preached to him by Schwarzenberg, of the blessed power of absolutism.

(4) *Prince Schwarzenberg*

Full understanding of these events requires some account of the character and past of the man who, at Olmütz, within the space of a few weeks, by a single shrewd stroke, molded the destiny of the Habsburg monarchy and the life of Francis Joseph.

Prince Schwarzenberg is the strongest and most notable personality raised to power by the storms of 1848 in Austria or Germany. Hitherto there had been nothing extraordinary in his career. Second son of the head of the older line of the richest and most powerful noble family in Bohemia, he was born on October 2, 1800, and received the education usual with young men of his class. After several years in the cavalry regiment commanded by his brother-in-law, Prince Windischgrätz, he rose, with the speed then normal to the sons of princes, to the rank of colonel. This did not prevent his entering the diplomatic branch of the Viennese chancellery at twenty-four, his first post being with the embassy in Petersburg. Within the next twenty years he served under Metternich in St. Petersburg, London, Rio de Janeiro, Turin, Naples.

These were years when Byronism and the romantic movement swept over the young men and women of the European governing classes and deeply influenced their minds. The conception of the hero as an Epicurean who passes, with unruffled mien, from countless dangerous amours to the battlefield or involves himself deep in the risky intrigues of high politics in the interests of his country or his king, was then at its apogee and frequently exemplified in real life. It found a perfect embodiment in this young Austrian aristocrat who enjoyed the reputation of an irresistible lady-killer, the hero of numerous dangerous "affairs" in every social centre in Europe; a reputation which no one could challenge after his inspiring so lively a passion in one of the most famous beauties of English society, Lady Ellenborough, that she left her husband and her palace for his sake and fled with him to Paris. When this bond was broken, some time after the birth of a child, Prince Schwarzenberg was stricken to the heart. He emerged from it, finally, with the cynicism which had been a fundamental trait from youth up, immensely and wilfully exaggerated, though to the last his relation to his friends and men whom he respected was governed by *noblesse oblige*. This dark crisis in his experience caused him to develop himself on the intellectual side, previously badly neglected. For a time he pursued scientific studies at the University of Vienna and revived an old taste for the classics.

Attached to the courts of Naples and Turin, he took his diplomatic profession seriously and won a certain measure of acknowledgment from Metternich. He was in Italy when the news of the European movements of 1848 reached him. He hastened at once to Radetzky's headquarters and took part in the campaign as a major-general, being wounded in the heavy fighting at Curtatone, where he displayed the greatest bravery. He won the sympathetic recognition of old Field Marshal Radetzky, who had such confidence in his political judgments and plans that he sent him to Vienna that he might co-operate there with Windischgrätz. Arriving in Vienna shortly before the October rising, Schwarzenberg showed the same energy he had displayed in Italy in grappling with the very unsatisfactory military conditions; and then departed for Bohemia. Hitherto his relations with his brother-in-law had not been good, either personally or politically; now, however, he made so strong an impression on Windischgrätz that the latter, before moving against Vienna, sent Schwarzenberg to Olmütz, and recommended him expressly to the Empress Maria Anna and

Archduke Francis Charles as prime minister in the new government.

At Olmütz, in the dreary atmosphere, heavy with doubts and apprehensions, in which the imperial family waited anxiously for news from the dictator Field Marshal, Schwarzenberg gave the first proofs of his purposeful energy which no obstacle could bend, and also of his cleverness. From the start he was determined to include in his government declared liberals like Count Stadion, Bruck, and Dr. Alexander Bach. From the first moment, too, he captivated the imperial youth. It was the decisive moment in the lives of both. A question must arise —what can have been the secret points of contact, the inner impulses in Francis Joseph's nature, to produce so complete and instant a mutual understanding and maintain it in lasting force? Of a surety not the passionate romanticism that once held Schwarzenberg in its grip and was legendary in court circles. That was long outworn in him,—Archduke Franzi, despite his youth, had no understanding of and less sympathy for such a trait.

No, what won the young Emperor to Schwarzenberg so swiftly and held him so lastingly was his unbending pride in Austria as a great power and the irresistible force that spoke in every action of his dominant nature. That first: then the daily accumulating proofs of the genuineness and sincerity of his prime minister's attitude to the world. Seeing him at work day by day, Francis Joseph found, in him, the ideal of the great man, formed in his boyish mind, realized with a completeness to which experience affords few parallels. Utter fearlessness, perfect indifference, an authority dominating in fact but absolutely quiet in expression,—characteristics of Schwarzenberg's that can be readily discerned from the admirable reminiscences of his chief assistant, the later Ambassador Hübner; and, above all, complete contempt for the revolution and its low-born promoters and exploiters: such were the qualities that the young Emperor half unconsciously believed that he felt stirring within, half consciously strove to develop in himself and as far as possible strengthen.

For any young man, the qualities which he is afraid he does not fully possess but strives to achieve, are at once his dream and his ideal; it is in riper years that men begin to idealize their own merits or weaknesses. With the instinctive certainty of a soul not yet "cabined, cribbed, and confined" Francis Joseph felt that Schwarzenberg's dynastic patriotism was rooted in the very depths of his being, was the dynamo that now set in motion the whole native will-power of a man who had once wasted it on so many trifling objects, and on adventures that had turned to dead sea fruit in the mouth of the weary and disillusioned libertine. Only the high ambition and the passionate hatred roused in him by the revolution could have stimulated to supreme exertion the burned-out heart of this aristocratic Epicurean who had, in a night, become the director of an empire: ambition to rebuild the great realm up anew and hatred both of the men embodying the revolution and of the aristocratic boobies whose cowardice and weakness had first made revolution inevitable and then quailed before it.

When his brother-in-law wrote informing him of his plans and those of the nobles' party for the necessary formation of an Austrian house of lords in a future imperial parliament, Schwarzenberg replied drily and coldly: "There are not four men of high rank in Austria who possess sufficient capacity to justify the institution of a House of Lords in Austria." Felix Schwarzenberg knew his compeers. Since he also knew the revolution and despised the democracy, his strongest conviction was that the world could only be ruled by the unscrupulous use of force. In the evening of his life, shortly before his death, at the close of a long cabinet meeting in which he had admired the juristic and political ingenuity in tackling stiff problems shown by a bourgeois minister who still passed, outside, as a liberal, he said: "Yes, one ought to have learned more, earlier!" This piece of insight came too late; too late for him; too late, above all, for the youth whom he had taught to be Emperor, Francis Joseph.

CHAPTER II

THE YOUNG EMPEROR

(1) *The Opening of the New Régime*

"GOODBY, youth!" Thus, according to a well-established court tradition, did Francis Joseph greet his elevation to the imperial throne. Whether or no, the young man certainly fully appreciated the burden of his lot. All reports agree on the seriousness and dignity with which he forthwith dedicated himself to his new duty. At the same time, in immediately accepting it he neither denied nor pretended to deny himself the pleasures of youth, once the immediate dangers threatening him and his realm were successfully overcome. Of the sin of hypocrisy he never showed the smallest trace. Not that he in the least deserved—let this be stated at once—the evil reputation of libertinism that was attributed to him in that dark decade by circles—high and low—in Vienna society least in a position to throw stones, and that since has been a standing item in the backstairs bookmaking about European monarchs and courts from which even republican countries are not free.

Naturally the first weeks in Olmütz flew by, filled as they were by his first duties—reception of foreign ambassadors and deputations from the country and, above all, his own initiation into the routine of government. On December 5 he attended the first meeting of the cabinet. For two decades he habitually did this, as proved by the official minutes. The members of his first ministry, who were certainly not courtiers—no one could be less of a courtier than Schwarzenberg—found him a most intelligent auditor. He was soon taking part and, by 1849, the minutes bear many traces of his opinion, generally expressed with great firmness on the matters that came up for discussion. For the rest he went on living with his parents and brothers; there was no change in the simple life of the household of Archduke Francis Charles. "Spanish ceremonial," as a court lady of the day notes down in her diary, vanished at a stroke. The Emperor's mother was and remained the center of the whole court. Beaming with maternal pride, she would often take part in his public activities.

On May 6, 1849, the Emperor moved into the Vienna Hofburg. His own court was then first constituted and he started the way of life continued almost unchanged for almost seventy years. The rigid maintenance of the plan of work devised by the young man in his early years as Emperor expressed both his innate conservatism and his personal individuality. From his boyhood a regular daily task and a plan of ordered work were necessary to him. The strong sense of duty that marked him as a boy, together with native diligence, now induced him, as Emperor, to create the condition of successful work for himself as a monarch—a perspicuous organization of the business he had to transact, reliable assistants in it, and its speediest possible execution. In this he was notably assisted by the excellent memory which was later so often to surprise people. Keen observers of course saw the defects of these qualities: chief among them an inclination to haste to be, externally, finished with a problem and a distaste for persons who would have liked him to consider decisions rather more deeply.

His outstanding intellectual defect was a complete lack of imagination. Such minds are always hostile to any change in an existing order. With that is apt to go a tendency to overestimate the value of forms and practical principles once laid down, which sooner or later must cause respect for tradition and forms to outweigh any consideration of the content of the duty performed. One of his most faithful servants said of old Emperor Francis, who dealt personally at his table with a mass of appeals, decrees, and documents of all sorts every year, that he was his own best "Aulic councillor"; a praise he not infrequently gave himself. His grandson may be said to have inherited this completely bureaucratic conception of his functions. Francis Joseph was, indeed, altogether the successor of Francis, for his uncle, the "Imperial symbol," had never been Emperor in more than name. It was, therefore, natural that the new organization should join, in many respects, on to that of Francis Joseph's grandfather. At the same time some traces of the mighty transformation that 1848 had produced were inevitably reflected even in the intensely conservative sphere of court life.

The young Emperor had been restored to his capital by

the army. He felt himself, therefore, preëminently the War Lord. Thus Francis Joseph's accession meant that the military element was brought to the front. Archduke Franzi's chamberlain, Colonel Count Charles Grünne, was made imperial aide-de-camp. He undoubtedly had the strongest influence on the young monarch. If we are to seek for the individual who had the most lasting effect on his personal character, we must study Charles Grünne. Descended from a noble family living in Lorraine which came to Austria with Maria Theresa's husband, he became, after a long period of service as a cavalry officer, chamberlain to the young Hungarian Palatine, Archduke Stephen. He left him, however, on his becoming the spokesman of the Hungarian independence movement and the means of inducing the court to nominate the Batthyány-Kossuth ministry. This action won Count Grünne the high approval of Archduchess Sophia. She made him chamberlain to her son, thus putting him in a position to act as imperial mentor to the young man. Credit was often given him later for the elegance of the new court service, the admirable reforms in its offices, especially the stables, and all the arrangements for the public appearance of the monarch.

Count Grünne was a representative of the foreign aristocrats who, coming to Vienna, allied themselves by marriage to the great native nobles of Austria, Hungary, and Bohemia, and made their way successfully into the army, the bureaucracy, and above all into the service of the court. These noble families from Lorraine, Belgium, and Italy had always been most warmly welcomed. They took kindly to and affected the speech and habits of Vienna; they soon became Austrians. They in their turn influenced both the life of the court and beyond that social life in general both in Vienna and the other capital cities of the Empire. They of course helped to strengthen the conservative and Catholic impress of the court itself and to give the life of the Hofburg and of the palaces of the great nobles its characteristic form.

About Count Grünne there is almost no documentary information, but opinion in Vienna at the time and for long after saw him as the incarnation of all that was evil in the court. Traditionally he is credited with having been Francis Joseph's evil influence. A more favorable view of him was taken by the nobles. Essentially he was, assuredly, the typical aristocratic cavalry officer of the old Austrian brand, personally brave and strong-willed but supple and adaptable. His views were what the Viennese liked to call "high tory"; the views natural to a soldier. He was one of those men for whom the simple and effective principles of the army suffice for all the complex problems of life; for whom the division of mankind into those who rule and those who obey is part of the order of nature. In addition, Grünne was an experienced man of the world of no mean competence in affairs, who filled his highly exacting and responsible office for more than a decade with great zeal and even self-sacrifice. In the position he created for himself at court, in relation to ministers and generals, he obviously had to use all kinds of means to ward off ambitious persons eager to influence the Emperor. In Francis Joseph's new military empire everything depended on the Emperor; everybody had to deal with the Emperor. The consequence was that private and public interests pushed, often shamelessly enough, into his closet.

The result was to aggrandize the importance of his general aide-de-camp and private secretary. He had to cope with countless intrigues, smooth down innumerable difficulties and conflicts between persons and offices at court and in the government; it was on his skill and tact in doing this that the Emperor depended for smooth running in the business of the cabinet, of the war office, and the court.

Grünne aimed at elevating his own position to all intents and purposes to that of a sort of military cabinet minister, by constituting himself the sole channel through which military questions reached the Emperor. He succeeded, with the most detrimental consequences to the development, technical and personal, of the army administration and of the army itself. He succeeded in the main because his ambition coincided with the desires of the young monarch. From the day of his accession, Francis Joseph saw his monarchical office essentially as a military command. He sought, therefore, to have purely military affairs concentrated in his own hands, and, further, first permitted and then consciously encouraged the mediation of his aide-de-camp as the channel for direct transmission to himself of a great mass of political business. This technique assumed, as was in fact the case, that Count Grünne was personally sympathetic to him. Actually a confidential relation grew up between the young Emperor and the aristocratic officer of more than twice his age such as existed with no other among the officials and officers working with him. Grünne soon became indispensable.

In so far as Francis Joseph had a private life, Grünne was his counsellor and helper. Naturally this mentor's influence determined the views, the decisions, and the actions of his young master more and more as the months passed, in political as well as military matters. The tongue of scandal, which further designated the general aide-de-camp as *maître de plaisir* and credited him with introducing the young Emperor to the pleasures of youth, was not far wrong. Francis Joseph was shy in personal intercourse even at court. His confidant could only be a man whose office brought him into constant and conscientious contact with him; a man who, as used to be said in Vienna, "must know everything about him." At the same time Grünne was not in the strict sense of the word, a favorite. That Francis Joseph never had. Grünne was no more than the Emperor's most useful, skilful, and trustworthy military and political servant. Difference in age at once made confidence easy and set limits to it.

The influence of his aide-de-camp inevitably tended to an overemphasis of military interests and the military point of view, naturally pronounced in Francis Joseph. On his accession, the Emperor sent holograph letters to the field marshals in Italy and Hungary, Windischgrätz and Radetzky, the paladins of 1848. In so doing he recognized the fact that the throne would only be maintained by the support of the army. Natural enough in view of the circumstances of his accession that Francis Joseph should have drawn the conclusion that the throne could only be so maintained in the future. But his advisers entered on a disastrous course in failing to transform this view into a conception of the state and of the monarchy at once more profound and more congruous with the new age. From the start the young Emperor was surrounded by young officers; as a result the limited and one-sided military view of life and politics was stamped upon him in his most impressionable years.

In the picture of the world thus created for the Emperor the citizen was completely in the background. For this Grünne and the young officers can hardly be blamed. The fault lay and lay exclusively with a man who could have foreseen the consequences of such a completion of the Emperor's practical training. This was Prince Schwarzenberg, prime minister and authentic founder of the new empire. His was the really decisive influence. He was, from the day he formed his government to that of his death, the real leader of the whole policy of the empire. He dominated everything at court. The Emperor listened to him as he did to no one else. Schwarzenberg is responsible for the practical education of the young monarch and for the reactions of his own political doings on that young monarch's mind.

The influence of Schwarzenberg began with the day when the young Archduke first met him as general in the field in Italy. The eighteen-year-old lad could not but be deeply stirred by the powerful and self-contained personality of this soldier and diplomat who had risen within a few months to be prime minister. But it was not merely the great prestige he had won in Italy, which automatically opened his path to government in the darkest hour of the dynasty, that captivated the young man; nor can he have spontaneously felt the special aura of this princely Epicurean of European renown. What seized and held him at once and lastingly was the concentrated force and calm of this self-possessed man, who put before him his simple, lucid, and completely self-contained idea of Austria and the necessity of restoring dynastic power there.

Schwarzenberg succeeded in strengthening and deepening the first impression he made on Francis Joseph to such an extent that a relation of complete mutual understanding developed between the prime minister of forty-eight and the young man. If, in this, Francis Joseph was the grateful taker and Schwarzenberg the giver, the latter was aware of a spontaneous gratitude to the young man for a confidence that enabled him to satisfy the deepest ambition of his soul. From the first day the Emperor took part in the daily work of government. He watched Schwarzenberg at work, bold in aim, careful in preparation. He read Schwarzenberg's diplomatic notes, full of pride in the ancient imperial splendour of the Habsburg House, crossed at times by the instinct of domination that moved like a passion in the Bohemian aristocrat.

Schwarzenberg was able to set the feet of his young master unhesitatingly on the road of despotism and a complete break with the political currents of the day, and to help him on it, because he had very quickly formed a correct judgment of his character. The penetration and power of his insight and consequent grasp is evidenced in Schwarzenberg's own words. In a letter addressed on July 29, 1850, to Prince Clemens Metternich, he said:

"The Emperor sees the magnitude and difficulty of his task and his will is firmly set to meeting it. His intelligence is acute, his diligence in business astonishing, especially at his age. He works hard for at least ten hours a day and no one knows better than I how many ministerial proposals he sends back on the ground of faultiness. His mien is dignified, his behavior to everyone exceedingly polite though rather dry. Men of sentiment—and many people in Vienna make claims to kindliness—say he has not much heart. There is no trace in him of that warm superficial good-heartedness of many Archdukes, of the wish to please and make a personal effect. On the other hand he is perfectly accessible, patient, and well disposed to be just to everyone. He has a rooted objection to any kind of lie and is absolutely discreet. But the quality that is most valuable to him in his present position, above all at a time like the present, is his courage. I have never seen it fail for an instant, even in the most difficult situations of whose peril he was entirely aware. Physically and morally he is fearless and I believe that the main reason why he can face the truth, however bitter, is that it does not frighten him. Time will make him more self-reliant: I do my best to assist that good work; then the country will have in him what it needs above everything—a man."

The lucidity of this portrait is admirable. If there are defects in the character of the young Emperor which it does not note, they are in the main the defects of Schwarzenberg's own; and for this reason the portrait contains mainly praise and recognition of the pupil by his master. Schwarzenberg's emphasis on his courage is just. Francis Joseph proved his bravery in his first battle-field in the Italian campaign; again he showed courage when he rode over the half-burning bridge across the Raab in his visit to the army operating against Görgey in the spring of 1849. And his was not merely the physical courage of the young officer.

Francis Joseph had ample opportunities to show "civilian" courage in the days after his accession. These instances, however, in their turn suggest that the basis of his moral courage was really a circumspection beyond his years, united to a sort of cold-bloodedness; an emotional balance which many contemporaries early set down as coldness of heart. In that, too, Felix Schwarzenberg may, almost unconsciously, have set him a model. Nothing in him was so astonishing as the self-control, the icy calm, with which he faced his enemies—and turned his back on many a friend. Schwarzenberg had reached this glacial calm through a life rich in shattering experiences and adventures. It was really more astounding in the young Emperor. In this he struck those about him as wise beyond his years. Thus Czar Nicholas after his first meeting with him on May 23, 1849, writes to his wife:

"Je l'ai trouvé fort grand et dévelopé sans être beau. Il a une charmante et intéressante figure qui prévient en sa faveur, beaucoup de calme et quelque chose de profond et de sévère dans l'expression de sa figure. Plus que je le vois, plus je l'entends, plus je suis étonné de sa raison, de la solidité et de la rectitude de ses idées. C'est une bonheur pour l'Autriche de le posséder."

One thing was plain from the start. The young Emperor would not lack the necessary sense of being a ruler. That, however, he was far from being on his accession. In Italy the revolution and the external enemy—the invading army of Piedmont-Sardinia—had got to be quelled. In Hungary the rebel army which Kossuth and his government had got on its feet with astounding rapidity, and which increased daily, had got to be broken. And both these huge tasks were made more difficult by the great transactions at Olmütz on December 2. According to Hungarian constitutional law, as everyone knew, neither the abdication of Ferdinand and Francis Charles nor the accession of Francis Joseph had any validity.

The basis of the Hungarian constitution, more than eight centuries old, and solemnly confirmed after the death of Joseph II, recognized no king in Hungary as legitimate save one solemnly crowned by Saint Stephen's holy crown with the full coöperation of the Reichstag. Easy, therefore, for Kossuth to rouse the Hungarian masses more effectively than ever to resistance to the imperial army of the new Emperor with the cry that they were fighting for the rights of King Ferdinand, illegally driven from his throne. Worst of all, a division was created within the ranks of the officers' corps of the regiments of the imperial army garrisoned in Hungary. They had taken the oath to the constitutional king of Hungary and were under the orders of the minister of war whom Ferdinand had nominated, now one of Kossuth's most enthusiastic colleagues. They were between the devil and the deep sea; on one side, the Hungarian government and Magyar nationalism, sweeping over the upper classes to which they belonged, drove them to the rebellious army; on the other, they were afraid that, were they actually to serve in that army, Vienna would look upon them as traitors to the imperial army and treat them accordingly. Many sons from the noble families in Hungary were involved in this insoluble conflict; not a few paid for it with their lives; nearly all with their ruin. Some were lucky enough to make their escape and succeed in putting their services at the disposal of the imperial command in Vienna. But the strength of Magyar revolutionary influence on the Hungarian regiments is shown by the fact that only a single infantry regiment in Galicia, among all those recruited from Hungary, remained completely faithful. It was led before the young Emperor in Olmütz in the early days after his coronation. Radetzky's army in Italy suffered far less; the aged field marshal was able to maintain his authority over practically all his troops.

Very soon after Prince Windischgrätz's troops marched into Hungary, the struggle there developed to a veritable war. A pause followed the early successes of the imperial army, and very soon after it the Prince's troops sustained some heavy reverses. The rebels, led by young officers educated in the imperial army, knew how to take advantage of the familiar weaknesses of Austrian generalship. Windischgrätz's strategy was faulty. In addition to possessing no military élan, he was preoccupied, from the start, by political considerations which hampered the entire military action. Windischgrätz did not really want to "conquer" Hungary. He had always been on good terms with the conservative Hungarian nobles who, hitherto, had ruled and administered the country. His idea was to attain his purpose by negotiation with the great lords, the magnates, and the lesser nobles who clung to their skirts.

More the conservative statesman than the general, Windischgrätz hoped to restore Hungary to its old footing, after a few military successes had exorcised the spirit introduced by Kossuth and his radical followers. This view of his was the origin of the severe conflict between him and Schwarzenberg, which now became unavoidable. From the beginning the prime minister represented the exactly opposite standpoint. Neither in Hungary nor in Austria did he want any more of the historic policy of the nobles. He knew that the Hungarian nobility had long ceased to present a closed front to the liberal ideas. He was, further, convinced that the nobles did not possess the power, even if they had had the will, to curb the Hungarian rising.

Schwarzenberg, in direct contradiction to his brother-in-law, regarded military conquest as essential. Every possibility of Hungarian resistance or Hungarian self-government must be eliminated. Schwarzenberg had set out his program on this in brief but lucid words some time back, both in his own first speech to the Reichstag at Kremsier and in the manifesto issued by the young Emperor at his accession. The totality of Habsburg lands must from now on constitute a close unity; a new realm, in which there was no place for the historic constitution, was to be created. For that reason, Hungary had got to be conquered. Schwarzenberg was well aware that even the Hungarian nobles would never consent to this great plan of the fusion of their kingdom in a new empire at the price of the sacrifice of the secular constitution of the Magyar state. He had no idea of negotiating with the great landlords, but only of forcing them, as well as the radical leaders of revolt, to bow beneath the might of a victorious imperial army.

This was the first great problem presented to the young Emperor. Schwarzenberg, who set it, and its solution before him, certainly won him, without much difficulty, to his own view and his own plan. This became abundantly clear, when irritation with the dilatory strategy of his brother-in-law caused him to resolve on sweeping this obstacle to his policy out of the way. He demanded the removal of the Prince. The young Emperor may have found it unpleasant to have to deal such a dishonoring blow at the man who had really saved the dynasty; but he acceded to Schwarzenberg's views and demands and readily signed the order replacing Windischgrätz as general over the imperial forces in Hungary by General von Welden.[1] This new commander proved a disappointment. His caution, evidenced in his evacuation of the capital Budapest, gave a poor impression of the forces of "law and order" throughout Europe, and, above all, to Czar Nicholas whose ambassador stayed with the court in Olmütz.

This raised the second great question and one that was bound to touch the young Emperor deeply. Must the Austrian ruler and his government appeal for aid to the arch-enemy of revolution, the Czar, to finish off the Hungarian rising? And if so, when? The military position in Hungary became worse after Arthur von Görgey, a young man of thirty, who had been an officer of engi-

[1] The removal of the dictator of October, 1848, from his command was the first really bad moment in Francis Joseph's life as Emperor. "I have decided," he wrote to the Prince, "to transfer the command over my troops in Hungary and Siebenbürgen to my General of Ordnance Baron von Welden, and rely on your tried patriotism and self-sacrificing devotion to my house and to Austria to accept this step, which causes me endless pain, as what it really is, namely, the recognition of an imperative military necessity and of a sense of duty as a ruler which compels me to put the welfare of the country before every other consideration." Prince Windischgrätz's absolute devotion to the dynasty enabled him to bear this shattering blow. The proudest aristocrat of old Austria could never forget his humiliation; but there was no danger, here, for Francis Joseph. There was nothing of Wallenstein in his countryman Windischgrätz. He now turned exclusively to politics, and made himself the leader of the extreme Conservatives among the nobles and at court. In that capacity he fought, especially, Schwarzenberg's vigorous measures for the emancipation of the peasants from feudal burdens. Once, when he repeated in the imperial presence his standing complaint of having been sacrificed to the intrigues of his brother-in-law, the young Emperor contradicted him bluntly.

neers in the imperial forces, became commander of the revolutionary army and firmly raised the blockade of Komorn, the strongest fortress in the country. The Russian autocrat was watching these events in his neighboring state with the keenest attention. His letters to his friend, Marshal Prince Paskievitch, the most trusted of his generals, show that Poland was his first care; a great part of the nobility there sympathized with the Hungarians. The formation of a Polish legion in Upper Hungary, with the entry of those dreaded Polish revolutionaries, Generals Bem and Dembinski into Kossuth's army, caused the Czar to see the overthrow of the Hungarian revolution as a primary object of Russian policy.

The fall of Prince Windischgrätz, for whom Nicholas had a high personal esteem, strengthened his sense of the necessity of assisting Austria. Nicholas' idea was to protect Poland against revolution by occupying Galicia, Austria's Polish province. For the moment he would not hear of intervention in Hungary. "The Austrians want someone else to put out the fire for them. Not I!" he wrote to the Czarina early in April. By April 20, however, his ambassador at Olmütz informed him that Austria was about to appeal to him for aid. It was by no means easy for Schwarzenberg to bring himself to this. Only a short time ago he had rejected General von Welden's suggestion of Russian assistance: "For the Austrian government to appeal to Russia for help would constitute a complete moral defeat, an admission of weakness in the face of Europe; it can only be justified in case of extremity, that is to say if the existence of the monarchy is at stake."

This feeling was shared by the Austrian army and, on different grounds, by the mass of the civil population of Vienna and Austria generally. The prime minister knew this. Further, on April 3, Radetzky had smashed the Piedmontese army at Novara; Charles Albert had abdicated in favor of his son Victor Emmanuel. A cry for help from Austria must adversely affect the peace discussions with the new king. Nothing could so plainly reveal how low hopes of crushing the Hungarian revolution had sunk at Olmütz as the fact that, in spite of all this, and in the face of his own strong feeling, Schwarzenberg made up his mind to ask Russia for military support.

In a letter to his prime minister, Francis Joseph says that he is "fully cognizant of Prince Schwarzenberg's feelings and knows well that he would never take this step if our own force were sufficient." Schwarzenberg and Francis Joseph himself tolerated this momentous step because they believed that in fighting the Hungarian revolution they were fighting an international revolutionary movement. In writing to the Czar on April 26, 1849, to thank him for the distinction he had bestowed upon Radetzky on the news of the amazing exploits of the eighty-year-old field marshal, Francis Joseph says:

"In showing this remarkable favor to an old soldier whose devotion has always been as great as his bravery, you, Sire, win a new title to the fame that history cannot deny you. At a period when the pil-

lars of social order are shattered, you have the glory
of having been the true appreciator and guardian of
military honor, the last bulwark of a society that
is about to perish under the blows of ruthless foes.
I ask you to believe, Sire, that in the midst of the
painful trials to which it has pleased Providence to
submit me, I have since the beginning of my reign
found comfort and hopefulness in my happy certainty of being able always to count on the unmistakable friendship of your Imperial Majesty—a
friendship whose precious inheritance has been
transmitted to me by my predecessors."

On May 1, Francis Joseph addressed a holograph letter to the Czar asking him as the "firmest support of the
monarchical principle" for aid against the international
revolution in Hungary. In his reply the Czar recalls
the obligations towards the young Emperor he had assumed at the time of the latter's coronation. In view of
these he will not hesitate a moment in answering his call.
"I should not find it easy," says the Czar, "to express
to you how much moved I was by the openness with which
you set your present situation before me and recall memories always sacred to me. It is but too true that Providence gave you an extraordinarily hard and thorny way
to tread when you were called, so young, to the throne.
At the very moment when your realm seemed to be restored by a brilliant victory abroad it is threatened even
more dangerously by its enemies at home. But the courage with which you have taken up this harsh discipline of

supreme power will, I doubt not, give you the strength to support it." The Czar's legions, in fact, were at once in movement, entering Hungary through Galicia.

Francis Joseph took no personal part in the campaign of the allied armies against the Hungarian revolution. The superiority of the troops of the two Emperors left room for no doubt of their success. Command over the Austrian troops was now assigned to the most reckless and the most gifted of the generals of Radetzky's school, Baron Haynau. There was friction from the start between him and his Russian colleague, Prince Paskievitch. While he drove the rebel troops towards the southeast by a series of methodical manoeuvres, Haynau was successful in defeating the portion of the Hungarian army opposed to him over and over again. On April 13, Kossuth, in the rump of the Hungarian Diet, had taken the momentous step of formally declaring that the old Habsburg dynasty had forfeited their succession to the throne; he was himself elected governor of the country. When he realized the hopelessness of the military position, he handed political and military power over to Görgey, the commander of the revolutionary army and crossed the Danube into Turkey. Görgey showed at once his insight and his humanity by getting into touch with the Russian high command, when he found himself threatened on every side by their columns, and on August 13 entering into an agreement of surrender at Világos on honorable conditions on behalf of his 30,000 men.

Prince Paskievitch sent his own son to bring the news of this success to the Czar. Nicholas, rejoiced and profoundly moved, fell on his knees in a passion of prayer on the receipt of this intelligence. Paskievitch summed up the result of the campaign in these words to the Czar: "Hungary lies at your Majesty's feet." For the Czar, supreme triumph; for Francis Joseph and his generals, supreme humiliation. Indignation in Vienna was the more poignant that the military exploits of the campaign were Austrian. Görgey was guaranteed his full personal freedom by Paskievitch. Paskievitch wrote to the Czar:

"Görgey relies exclusively on the magnanimity of Your Majesty. Could I hand over to the gallows all those whose sole trust is in Your Majesty's mildness of heart, to be all the more severely punished because they surrendered to our troops? I said to Prince Schwarzenberg before that the Hungarian army might perhaps surrender to us, but would not to the Austrians. What was I to do, in the actual case? The fate of the captive army falls, consequently, to Your Majesty to determine. You are the victor. Hungary lies at your feet and the war is at an end."

Paskievitch foresaw what was only too soon to happen. The Austrian commander, Baron Haynau, proceeded to give rein, in the most hideous fashion, to his lust for vengeance on the vanquished rebels and above all on ex-officers of the Austrian army who had left their own colors and at the same time to air strong dislike of the Austrian army for their Russian allies. Without regard for the conditions on which they had laid down their arms, the thirteen captive generals of the Hungarian army were court-martialed and condemned at Arad on October 9. Most of them perished on the gallows, several were shot. Arthur von Görgey alone was protected by the Czar; Vienna banished him to Klagenfurt. A man of fine character as well as a great strategist, he lived another sixty years, writing a valuable and objective account of his military and political work in the year 1848-49. After 1867 he returned to Hungary, but remained morally condemned by the Magyar society; this ban, though mitigated in the two last decades of his life, was never wholly raised.

General von Haynau, clothed with dictatorial power over Hungary, proceeded with his work of vengeance. His courts-martial passed sentence of death on 281 out of the 475 Hungarian officers who had been taken prisoners. This sentence was not carried out, but more than 386 officers were punished with terms of imprisonment from one to twenty years. Haynau undoubtedly was a man of somewhat warped disposition. The effect of his appalling severities was to bring the heaviest odium and disgrace not to the Hungarian nation but to the young Emperor. The Bloody Assize of Arad, recalling as it did to Hungarian patriots the horrible cruelties committed in the seventeenth century by the generals of Leopold I, continued throughout the reign of Francis Joseph to serve as a symbol of the martyrdom to which the Magyars were subjected in Vienna in punishment for their revolution. The blood shed at Arad cried out to all Magyars against Francis Joseph, in whose name Haynau did his work of vengeance. He, rather than Haynau, bore the stigma. That singular individual, whose diseased sensitiveness and overweening self-esteem brought him into constant conflict with his superiors throughout his entire military career, soon after this got into trouble with the government at Vienna on account of subsequent instances of his reckless severity and personal ambition, and was suddenly relieved of his command.[2]

The hideous doings of the Austrian army command in Hungary caused not Hungary only but the entire public opinion of Europe to attribute to the young Emperor who had allowed such things to be, a hardness of heart which a survey of his life does not substantiate. The charge, so the documents make plain, lies in the main against Schwarzenberg. He is reported to have said, when mercy was recommended, "Yes, yes, a very good idea; but we must have a bit of hanging first." It is yet a fact that in the case of the sentences on the thirteen generals the young Emperor personally accepted the arguments of his minister for the necessity of expiation and a terror-striking example.

Another case which roused deep indignation both in

---

[2] At the last Haynau revenged himself on Schwarzenberg by causing the sentence of death on twenty-three former members of the Hungarian Diet, condemned for participation in the decree abolishing the dynasty, to be published, together with his own pardon to them, before the legal formality of confirmation of the sentences by the Emperor had taken place. Haynau's object was to make a display of his personal power as against the government; indeed his naïveté carried him to the point of publishing a statement to the effect that he had by this action earned the thanks of the whole Hungarian nation. This was an example of the peculiar humor of this strange man—who by the way was no Austrian but one of the many illegitimate sons of the Elector of Hesse.

Austria and in Europe was the execution of Count Batthyány, the first Hungarian prime minister after the March
revolution, and this again Francis Joseph did not prevent. This sentence was the more unjust that even the indictment of the unfortunate statesman could cite no action that legally justified the extreme penalty. It was an
act of vengeance on an impassioned Hungarian patriot
who, ever since 1848, had traveled along paths very far
remote from those of his aristocratic friends and relatives. Prince Metternich, who must bear his share of responsibility for frequent acts of cruelty exercised against
Lombards guilty of high treason, and was never given
to excess of mercy to political conspirators, passes the
severest condemnation, in a great number of letters, on
the conduct of the Hungarian courts-martial, and on the
execution of Batthyány.

The sanguinary irony of history is in the picture of
Prince Paskievitch appealing earnestly to the Czar for
mild treatment of the Hungarian officers and men, and
begging Metternich in Vienna to raise his voice on the
side of mercy! There had not been much mercy in Metternich's treatment of the plotting Italian nobles and
intellectuals, or Paskievitch's handling of the Poles after
the suppression of the 1831 revolution. Yet they may well
have been honest enough in their attitude to Haynau's
reign of terror. More or less friendly relations had
grown up between Russians and Magyars in the course
of Paskievitch's campaign; indeed many of the Hungarian revolutionary leaders seriously thought of offering
Nicholas the Hungarian crown for one of his sons!

The bloody régime in Hungary was in the main the work of the half-crazy Haynau. That it was not characteristic of old Austrian militarism is shown by the fact that no such reprisals were taken after the defeat of the Piedmontese army either in Milan or anywhere else in Italy. Radetzky and his generals showed no particular harshness against the rebels in Lombardy. The only case of frightfulness there belongs, again, to Haynau, when he recaptured Brescia. Old Baron Wessenberg wrote to a confidential friend, "The young Emperor is being forced to make his way to power over the scaffold and the bloodbath instead of being given the chance of coming with the olive branch in his hand and so founding a lasting peace in the spirit of conciliation." Again, on September 18, 1848, he wrote, "Hatred seems to rage against Hungary and hatred never brings conciliation. As Napoleon himself once said: 'Il y a quelque chose qui vaut mieux que haïr, c'est pardonner.' "

The men who took the greater part of the burden of government off the young Emperor's shoulders in these difficult years had other views than Wessenberg's, old liberal and true child of the eighteenth century. They believed in terror, which is never more senseless and cruel than when applied in the form of a retribution designed to serve political ends. That Francis Joseph made no serious effort to throw off this tutelage, at least in this case, was bound to remain a difficulty for those who, at the time and later, should seek to clear him of responsibility for the evil work in Hungary on the ground of his youth. There must have been but a small stock of belief in the salutary power of mercy and kindness in him, even at nineteen.

(2) *The Austro-Prussian Rivalry*

The two great successes gained by the army in 1849 in the first eight months of the young Emperor's reign raised the prestige of both in the eyes of Europe to a level that no one could have foreseen at the date of his accession. Prince Schwarzenberg lost no time in taking advantage of this to push on his plans. He was perfectly aware that Europe could not begin to see his new military empire safe until a solution favorable to Austria had been found to the complicated questions of the relations of the hereditary possessions and those of the Bohemian crown to the German confederation as the successor to the Holy Roman Empire. The 1848 revolution had made this German question at once a European problem and a life and death one for the German states, first and foremost Austria and Prussia. The actual suspension of the confederation under the first shock of revolution in Germany, the election of a German democratic parliament to make a constitution, the risings in Berlin, Vienna, Dresden, Munich, Baden, Hesse, as well as in most of the separate German states, with the erection of a provisional central power—Archduke John, the uncle of Francis Joseph, was elected Administrator of Germany—all this showed clearly enough that the entire German nation was much more influenced by an underlying desire for national union than by democratic and constitutional ideas, although these had supplied nationalism with its dynamic force. But the real issue in the Frankfort Parliament was how to devise a constitution that might give Germany as a whole an effective political unity in the sense in which England or France had it.

At Frankfort the principle of division was the rivalry between the two great German powers—Prussia and Austria; between the houses of Brandenburg-Hohenzollern and Habsburg which had borne the imperial crown almost without intermission since 1437. It was this rivalry that created the antagonism between the Great and Little Germans which was the basis of the party organization created in the parliament meeting in the Church of St. Paul at Frankfort. Frederick the Great's elevation of Brandenburg-Prussia to the rank of a first-rate power had lifted what was once a merely dynastic struggle into one involving the fate of the whole German nation. Prince Metternich in letters written to his friends at this time talked of the progressive "fattening" of Prussia. The process seemed to have reached its climax when the Frankfort Parliament, after promulgating a constitution, elected the King of Prussia German Emperor.

Frederick William IV refused the "Crown of Mud." The work of Parliament was smashed to pieces and its consideration ruined in the eyes of the nation. The result was to throw wide the door to the gathering tide of reaction. The German governments now came out openly against the liberal, democratic movement in the towns, and also, to some extent in the country; most of them had counted from the beginning on the help of Prussia. In Prussia, meantime, the national assembly was replaced by a government which used the aid of the army to hold down radicalism in Berlin and, without any notable resistance from the masses, proceeded to revise the constitution in a conservative direction, and restore the authority of the crown and royal administration. At the same time the Prussian government, affirming Prussia's historic mission to unite Germany, enlisted the support of the nobles and of large sections of the middle class for an open effort of its own to realize the idea of German unity through the action of the German princes and governments.

The program of the "Little Germans" was thus proclaimed to the world as the great task of the House of Hohenzollern and the government of Prussia. A German confederate state was envisaged; a "German realm" in which Prussia should combine the leadership of the common army with that of its customs union. The government of this union of German princes and states was to be completed by the establishment of a German parliament and the progressive development of the idea of national unity in great federal institutions. The great plan saw the light of day on May 26, 1849, with the alliance of Prussia and most of the German kings. With that a period of incessant diplomatic negotiation and struggle opened among the five and thirty governments of the German states. The problem of German unity had risen to the lofty regions of cabinet policy—there to be lost in darkness. Once again political forces, watchwords, sympathies and attachments, hopes and fears, centered in the historic issue—Austria versus Prussia.

Prince Schwarzenberg's proclamation of the new Austrian constitution in March, 1849, gave a semblance of encouragement to the Little Germans. In announcing a unitary empire he seemed to be approaching the view of the German question already formulated by Frederick William IV of Prussia in private letters to the court of Vienna—the conception, namely, of a closer bond between himself and Francis Joseph's new military realm, which might call into existence a new central European power of seventy million inhabitants, for whose young sovereign the dreamy spirit of the Prussian king designed the dignity of the imperial crown. Prince Schwarzenberg had from the first rejected all the demands of the Little German party at Frankfort for the exclusion of Austria from the German confederation. Now that Austria's power and prestige had been restored, he came forward boldly with his own scheme. It was quite simple. The old German confederation, which had quietly gone to sleep in the spring of 1848, was to be recalled to life in full conference at Frankfort. This was, of course, a declaration of war on the union of north and central German states which had been created by Frederick William IV and his government.

The open fight of Austria against the German policy of Prussia is Prince Schwarzenberg's life work. Its often dramatic course in the next two years cannot be followed in detail here. The account so far given was necessary merely to indicate the fearful problems with which young

Francis Joseph had to cope in his first years of power. We need concern ourselves further with it here only so far as to show his personal attitude toward Schwarzenberg's effort to restore Austria's ancient primacy in the German Empire.

On this question Schwarzenberg undoubtedly was sure of the absolute agreement of his young pupil from beginning to end. His own great campaign is, in fact, the most important episode in the education of the ruler. Francis Joseph then became acquainted by practical experience with the technicalities of cabinet diplomacy on the one hand and on the other with the robust will power of his prime minister. He had the opportunity of seeing Schwarzenberg's irony, his contempt for average humanity, and his unbending force at close range, day by day, in his duel with von Radowitz, for so long the confidant and for so short a time the prime minister of Frederick William IV.

Radowitz was at heart determined on war with Austria. He let the tension between the two powers reach a crisis at the conference at Olmütz on November 26, 1850, whose result was the collapse of Frederick William's union policy. Then, too, Francis Joseph realized the real power of Czar Nicholas who grumbled at his brother-in-law because he was not ready simply to abrogate the inconvenient Prussian constitution. He came down on Schwarzenberg's side in his struggles with the Prussian statesmen mainly because, on the occasion of his visit to him at Warsaw, Francis Joseph had assured him of his early intention of recalling the constitution of March, 1849, and

[69]

introducing autocratic government. Francis Joseph also formed impressions of the German princes, who, faced with the necessity of choosing between Austria and Germany, swung first to this side and then to that. He received impressions in these two years that sunk deeply. They gave living actuality to the old tradition of inevitable conflict between Habsburg and Hohenzollern.

At bottom Francis Joseph never moved out of the circle of ideas of his eightenth century ancestors on this point. He saw the German problem as purely dynastic; a matter of opposing interests of the two dynastic houses. To him, as to the King of Prussia, there was nothing but revolution and therefore danger in the struggle of the German people as a whole for unity. Schwarzenberg taught him to see in the exploitation by the Hohenzollern house of a national movement to feed its own lust for power, and with a view to finally putting itself at the head of Germany to the exclusion of the Habsburgs, the capital sin of the government of his confused but conservatively-minded uncle. So it was not only the interest and the right of Austria to checkmate this policy but the duty of Francis Joseph to come forward and champion against revolution the ancient right on which the German confederation was based.

Schwarzenberg's fight with Prussia put Francis Joseph in a very difficult position, however. A peculiarly close personal relationship existed between him and the Prussian King, whose wife was his mother's favorite sister. King Frederick William IV from the beginning treated him with the sympathy of a near relative and with singu-

lar deference. For him the Habsburg Emperor was always
the descendant of Charlemagne. From his early youth
Frederick William IV had had a strong historical feeling for the medieval empire; a feeling that caused the
world outside to smile at the Romantic on the throne.
On December 23, 1848, when he heard of the plan for his
own election as German Emperor, he wrote to his friend
Joseph von Radowitz:

> "The ancient legitimate German national crown,
> in abeyance since 1806, which makes its wearer su-
> preme in Germany and obedience an obligation of
> conscience—that crown one could accept if one felt
> the strength to do so and the duties to which one is
> born permitted. But no one can give that crown
> save Emperor Francis Joseph, I, and our peers; and
> woe to the man who seeks it outside of us, woe to
> the man who takes it if the price be the loss of a
> third of Germany and of the noblest race in our Ger-
> man people. God help us! Amen."

In May, 1848, however, Frederick William had himself worked out a reform of the constitution of the German Empire which he sent to the young Emperor shortly
after his accession. In this he proposed that Francis Joseph
should restore the German Empire and he, the King of
Prussia, should be its hereditary commander-in-chief.
Schwarzenberg did not take this seriously, nor Francis
Joseph either. Not that it was easy for a youth of nineteen to come out as clearly against such ideas as Schwarzenberg did to Frederick William's ministers. From this

time on there was a steady exchange of confidential letters between him and his uncle. Frederick William liked to go over his ministers' heads by himself corresponding with other sovereigns, and was particularly addicted to the political use of friends as special ambassadors. The correspondence lying in the Vienna archives shows his genuine sympathy for the young Emperor, strangely crossed by a romantic feeling for German imperialism and a pronounced monarchical sense hostile to any sort of compromise with modern ideas of constitutional or popular rights. Nevertheless the King's vague apprehension of reality induced him again and again to allow his ministers to enter into such compromises.

It was indeed the contradictory personality of Frederick William IV that settled the great struggle between Austria and Prussia. In the late autumn of 1850 first Austria and then Prussia had mobilized; the Austrian ambassador in Berlin, Baron Prokesch, was on the point of asking for his passports, whereupon Frederick William turned his back on his own policy and, with the secret coöperation of the "Bavarian" ladies, his wife, and of Archduchess Sophia, forced a conference at Olmütz between his prime minister and Schwarzenberg which, if its immediate outcome was the humiliation of Prussia, at least made peace secure. This was the first occasion on which Francis Joseph took decisive personal action. He had never hindered Schwarzenberg from putting more acerbity into his diplomatic campaign. But when Schwarzenberg rejected Berlin's urgent appeal for a conference, Francis Joseph, doubtless under pressure from his mother, made a com-

plete volte face by ordering Schwarzenberg to go to Olmütz and have an understanding with Prussia.

Prince Schwarzenberg in his private conversation later
frequently regrets this peaceful issue. In this instance,
thanks no doubt to the influence of his relatives, the Emperor's fundamentally unwarlike temper won a victory
over the hitherto unquestioned authority of his minister.
He was indubitably assisted by the fact that the war with
Prussia which had been preparing since the autumn was
highly unpopular in the Austrian army. No less a person
than Field Marshal Radetzky gave the tone in this to the
other generals.

The history of Austrian policy in relation to the German confederation and to Prussia in the following decades
showed plainly enough that Francis Joseph, though opposed to any attempted decision by force of arms at the
given moment, took quite as serious a view of the historic
rivalry with Prussia as did Prince Schwarzenberg.

CHAPTER III

DICTATING A CONSTITUTION: ABSOLUTISM, TRANSITIONAL AND PERMANENT

BEFORE Francis Joseph appealed to the Czar for aid, an action had been taken which would certainly have alienated him, had he not long been privy to Schwarzenberg's real intentions. On March 4, 1849, the Reichstag was prorogued, by imperial decree. It had spent two months of strenuous work in drafting a constitution, endorsed by the votes of a majority of its members. On the day of its prorogation, a new constitution, derived exclusively from the supreme authority of the Emperor, was issued with a special manifesto. With this legislative work the Schwarzenberg ministry had been silently occupied during the past three months, working in ceaseless consultation, drawing their material to a large extent from the contemporaneous deliberations of the constitution committee of the Reichstag, but, of course, watering down the very democratic ideas of that committee. The constitution now dictated to the people of Austria was, in its broad outline, liberal. Structurally, it differed from that produced at Kremsier mainly in the fact that it did, while the other did not, include Hungary.

Count Francis Stadion, the minister for home affairs, was the member of the Schwarzenberg cabinet to whom this constitution was mainly due. A singular man this: though belonging to one of the oldest feudal families of South Germany he was a liberal from youth up, he counted, in the eyes of the court, almost as a revolutionary. He was the real creator of this thoroughly coherent piece of legislation. Valuable assistance was rendered to him by the minister of justice, Dr. Alexander Bach, who at this time still frequented exclusively liberal circles. Prince Schwarzenberg calmly left them to their work. In April, 1849, Count Stadion was attacked by an incurable disease. For three years he lived on, a helpless paralytic. With him far the strongest, indeed the only, supporter of constitutional and progressive ideas disappeared from the ministry. Alexander Bach, who succeeded Stadion as minister of the interior was, in his own mind, quite prepared to drop the ideas that had made him a revolutionary pioneer in Viennese society, and put himself completely in Schwarzenberg's hands. Stadion's removal left the way free for the adoption of the premier's own views.

He had given his consent to constitution building. More than that, he did everything in his power to remove the obstacle of Prince Windischgrätz's objection in principle to any kind of constitution. The difficulty did not prove great; a few immaterial alterations satisfied the old dictator. So the first legislative work issued by Francis Joseph was promulgated on the rising of the Reichstag. Reasons of domestic policy alone explain why Schwarzenberg not merely permitted this to be done but even accelerated it. He wanted, first, to influence public opinion in Germany, where, at the time, a stiff fight had begun in the Frankfort parliament between the Greater German party, friendly to Austria, and the Little Germans, aiming at the leadership of Prussia. He knew that the promulgation of a liberal constitution would incline the still dominant liberal tendencies in Germany in Austria's favor, and also impose a veto on the plans of those politicians at Frankfort who aimed at dividing the Habsburg monarchy into two and incorporating the western half in the German confederation. Second, he wanted to lay firm bases for his ruling idea, well ahead of the defeat of Kossuth and his rebels.

The reconstruction of the Empire now going busily ahead was to culminate in a completely unitary realm, leaving no room within its comprehensive ambit for the patriarchal constitutions of the hereditary provinces, Austria in its proper old sense, and those of the Bohemian crown as little as for the millenary constitution of the Kingdom of St. Stephen and the historic constitution of the Kingdom of Croatia and Slavonia. As was later to be said, in bitter jest, in Hungary, "The Croats have endured the same fate as the Magyars—namely the loss of their constitution. The punishment of the one was the reward of the others."

The promulgation of the new imperial constitution opens, in Austria, a régime of conscious fraud such as has no analogue even in that period of bold and skilfully concealed reaction. The new unitary monarchy, strictly constitutional on paper, and presented to the world as such, was "provisionally" governed by the Schwarzenberg ministry on purely absolutist lines. In the various areas, innumerable laws were introduced which, devised with the greatest care by the cabinet, were promulgated by the Emperor as "provisional." In this way the whole system of administration, justice, local government, rates and taxes, as well as education, was reorganized on lines that both in detail and as a whole were designed to one end— the construction of a thoroughly unified instrument of power. At the same time the whole thing was expressly provisional; the government announced that all these edicts, issued in the first instance by the supreme authority of the Emperor, were to be scrutinized by the central parliament established under the new constitution and then, and not till then, finally promulgated as laws.

To gauge the range and intention of this supreme piece of political jugglery, one has only to remember that Prince Schwarzenberg openly spoke, in the circle of his friends and colleagues, of the "mis-constitution" which they also called the "dirt-constitution." Hypocrisy, of course, there was none. Everyone knew that Schwarzenberg had no intention of carrying out the constitution he had proclaimed. The drama enacted in Vienna, amid the amazement of both liberals and conservatives in Germany and the world, was by no means transparent. Its close could not be predicted even by Schwarzenberg and his immediate colleagues. No one could foresee that Vienna and the provinces, which at a stroke had become the scene of the hottest and most dangerous revolution in 1848, would prove, in the long run, so completely submissive to the new militarist régime set up by Schwarzenberg after Francis Joseph's accession, as each month that passed showed it in fact to be. The beauty of the drama lay in the fact that Prince Schwarzenberg—the first statesman to apply the modern policy of might in Central Europe—gathered around him a group of prominent liberals, set these men to work for two years constructing a program of modern legislation, and provided for its execution by the appointment of admirable governors, mainly civilians, in the provinces; and, at the same time, maintained a régime of martial law of the most rigid kind in Vienna and Prague, and established throughout Austria a wholly new instrument of imperial and central control—a military gendarmerie finally sixteen regiments strong, whose technical equipment, flawless discipline, and absolute police powers, represented something entirely new in the Empire or in Central Europe itself.

Here was a contradiction baffling to the outside world. A storm of criticism was directed against the régime of "provisional" liberal laws and actual military absolutism, both from the conservative and the liberal sides. The foreign press was open in its violence. The violence was hardly less in the correspondence privately exchanged between leading Austrians of the most various political complexion, or in that of the civil population of Vienna. Vienna was far too frightened to speak. The true temper of the people there came out only in the theatre—that genuine Forum of old Vienna—in the shape of apparently harmless speeches uttered by stage characters whose references to actual circumstances were taken up by the audience with cheers or hisses.

The letters exchanged between old Prince Metternich

and his friend Baron Kübeck show the criticism of Schwarzenberg and his liberalism at its sharpest; the Austrian notes in the Prussian *Kreuzzeitung* reveal the same point of view. It reappears in the letters of a certain member of the Prussian Diet, who was also its representative at the Confederation Diet, Herr von Bismarck-Schoenhausen. He is never weary of running down the "Jewish clique," which is promoting clericalism in Austria under Alexander Bach's direction and, at the same time, strengthening the worst kind of liberalism in economic and other matters. The longer this stupendous comedy of Schwarzenberg's constitutional and responsible government lasted, the more incomprehensible became the actual course of events in the first two years of the young Emperor's reign. The true direction of things in Vienna was shown clearly enough by the dismissal of a moderate liberal of conspicuous honesty, like the Minister of Justice, Anton von Schmerling; by a series of administrative measures; and, above all by the constant strengthening of the police system that dated from the elevation of the military head of the gendarmerie, Baron von Kempen, as minister of police.

Schwarzenberg's organized political bluff was protracted mainly as a consequence of foreign events. From the spring of 1850 on he was in open fight with Prussia on the German question. Once Schwarzenberg's aim, the restoration of the 1815 régime for the German confederation, already referred to, was achieved, it was unnecessary to continue the constitution of March 4, 1849, or to maintain the liberal element in the government and administration. Schwarzenberg had educated his young master so successfully that, by the beginning of 1851, he seemed more impatient than his mentor to cast off the mask.

The decisive circumstance at this juncture was the personality of Baron Kübeck. This statesman had played an important part in arranging the Emperor's accession. He now came forward as the protagonist of stark reaction against the ideas of 1848 and even those of the Stadion constitution of March 4, 1849. Schwarzenberg and Alexander Bach may have gone so far as to play with the idea of trying how some sort of sham liberal régime would work, on lines such as were being adopted by the Manteuffel ministry in Prussia. Baron Kübeck went to the Emperor himself with his own plan of establishing a nakedly autocratic system, and found the young sovereign impatiently straining towards that same end. Kübeck's letters to Metternich are full of unsparing criticism of the Schwarzenberg system. For two years he had been at work on a plan for establishing the young Emperor's absolute rule over the whole of the realm.

What Kübeck (and Metternich) disliked in the régime that had been established since Francis Joseph's accession, was what they saw as the despotism of the bureaucracy, incorporated for them both in the person of Dr. Alexander Bach. They detested Bach's political suppleness, and feared him as a danger to the true idea of conservatism. There is a touch of real drama in the manner in which Kübeck came upon the scene at the moment when his influence was bound to tell on the young Emperor's mind:

the moment when Austrian prestige and its military and diplomatic position seemed to have been fully restored. How apt the moment was is proved by the absolutely excited sympathy with which the young Emperor received him and his plans. The old statesman showed deep knowledge of men and high skill in his selection of a point of attack on the system of responsible government which destroyed it at a stroke. What Kübeck suggested to the Emperor was that rule belonged not to his ministers but to himself; therefore, there must be no talk of the responsibility of ministers to a parliament which, it was to be hoped, would never exist. On the contrary, what ought to be set up was a supreme council of state, absolutely at the Emperor's disposal, whether for legislation, government, or administration. To this end, a few paragraphs only should be retained out of the 1849 constitution, which ought, in general, to be abolished: those modest paragraphs which established the so-called council of the realm, Reichsrat. Over this same council Kübeck was to preside; a post which would at once make him head of a government that, from now on, would be conducted by the Emperor and the Emperor alone. Such was Kübeck's program.

Within a few days, both Prince Schwarzenberg and Alexander Bach learned for the first time of the program and accepted it. They saw, in fact, that if they opposed Baron Kübeck, whom the Emperor had at once nominated president of the council, their power was at an end. The minutes recording the defeat of the man of might, Schwarzenberg, and his trusty colleague, Bach, are extant. Plainly, the impatience of the young sovereign played into the hands of the cunning old baron, reinforced as they were by the strong impression both of his personality and arguments. It is very probable that Archduchess Sophia came in too, though there is no proof of her co-operation. Anyhow, with all the methodical, almost pedantic, thoroughness of old Austrian statesmanship, of which Kübeck was the true ideal, the demolition of the sham liberal constitution and its legislative machinery was now swiftly and systematically accomplished. On August 20, 1851, a decree was promulgated, based on the supreme will of the Emperor, setting out the program of autocracy in juridical form. The establishment of the council and appointment to it of tried bureaucrats of pre-March order, followed. In the program, the essential part was the solemn recantation of the principle of ministerial responsibility. "Ministers," so it was stated, "are solely responsible to the Monarch." The joy expressed by Czar Nicholas in this change must have warmed the young Emperor's heart. But the coup d'état of Louis Napoleon in 1851 stirred him to almost ungovernable impatience.

At "exalted request," the methodical execution of the August decree was accelerated. The memoranda laid by Kübeck before his young sovereign formulated both the main principles of the future plan of absolute government and the method of discussing "revision" of the constitution, i.e., its abrogation. A commission of the council, presided over by Kübeck, prepared drafts of the decrees and of a collection of "principles for the organic institution of Cæsarism"; these "principles" set out a detailed program of government, administration, and law in thirty-six paragraphs. Its basis was the complete exclusion of the citizen from any share in legislation, administration, and law, including jury trials and local government assemblies.

Indubitably Prince Schwarzenberg, who was greatly under Dr. Bach's influence in all domestic questions, was surprised by Kübeck's action, disliked his growing influence over the young Emperor, and endeavored, in cooperation with Dr. Bach, to resist the plan of the new president of the council. Soon, however, they were both compelled to see that opposition was useless in the face of the complete possession of the Emperor's mind by the arguments and ideas of his new counsellor, and his eager zest for the realization of his coup. From first to last, Baron Kübeck was the author of all the decrees necessary for the complete realization of the counter-revolution. It is, indeed, in the aphoristic comments which Kübeck entered in his diary that one can best read the history of the 1851 coup:

January.

9. Call to the Emperor, who becomes more and more open. Great hopes in that fine young man! May they unfold successfully!

18. A change has come over my relation to the Emperor. Prince Schwarzenberg's jealousy has been roused and he is undoubtedly working on his mind.

20. So much is clear: Emperor full of confidence in Schwarzenberg, who depends on Dr. Bach while

imagining he leads him. Dr. Bach pretends to be keen on the Absolutist Régime, because he is keen on power for himself.

February.

8. Bach flatters the young Emperor who desires to be strong, powerful and feared, by suggesting to him that he has already reached this lofty aim.

March.

3. Present at Cabinet meeting, Emperor presiding, on the Statutes of the Council at which the Emperor came forward very decidedly in their favor against the Minister who opposed. (Ministerial machinations about said Statutes.)

June.

3. Pressure from the Emperor for political changes. My request for an interview.

5. Long conversation with the Emperor on our political situation. He asked me to put my proposal on paper and send it to him. The Emperor seemed to be struck and went into everything in detail.

17. Called to the Emperor who declares he wishes to proceed with my proposals but will confer first with Prince Schwarzenberg as is due to him.

23. The Emperor, to whom I am called, is apprehensive of the possible resignation of Prince

Schwarzenberg with expressions of pained concern; but declares that he is nevertheless determined on the step advised.

28. Call to him. The Emperor weakens.

30. Call to the Emperor. His doubts and disquiet.

July.

13. Call to the Emperor. He tells me that he has read the work in question to Prince Schwarzenberg who stated his agreement with it, but asked to have the loan pushed on and certain alterations made in the conditions.

Prince Schwarzenberg does not dare to oppose the Emperor openly; he seeks to gain time to find ways and means to upset the applecart.

19. Call to the Emperor, about the postponement of the regulations. I expressed my views, verbally and in writing to him.

August.

17. Cabinet, Emperor presiding.

The Emperor opened the meeting with a brief address indicating the purpose of the gathering and closed with a demand for support to the monarch at this critical juncture.

Hereupon the Emperor invited Prince Schwarzenberg to read out the clauses as amended. After this reading, during which Finance Minister Krauss kept throwing himself about restlessly in his chair, discussion followed.

[85]

Prince Schwarzenberg: Complete agreement and assurances to the Emperor of his services in all circumstances.

Finance Minister Krauss: He was in a different position from that of other ministers. He had taken an oath under Emperor Ferdinand which his conscience does not allow him to break. He is convinced that the Constitution is unworkable but thinks that an effort should be made to work it and then get the Reichstag to declare the impossibility of continuing this constitution in existence. He recalled his past services, his self-sacrificing devotion, the dangers that he ran, etc., etc., but closed with the declaration that, were the Imperial proposal insisted upon, he could not continue a Minister.

Minister Bach: Complete agreement, supported by reasons, with the Imperial proposal, assurance of his unconditional loyal service.

The readiness of Prince Schwarzenberg and Minister Bach to accept the newest proposals of the Emperor has greatly strengthened their position with him.

27. Call to the Emperor, who received me with a handshake and most hearty expressions of thanks. The handbills appeared yesterday in the *Wiener Zeitung.*

For the moment, at any rate, all the Ministers remain.

This is good, since those who went out must,

even against their will, serve as heroes and as a
rallying flag for the Destructives.

September.

12. Call to the Emperor, to whom I take the opportunity of stressing the urgency, to my mind
of further regulations for carrying out the
Handbills of August 20.

October.

1. Conversation with Prince Schwarzenberg on the
revision of the constitution. After two hours
talk, the Prince accepted my views.

4. Call to the Emperor. Conversation about the
question of constitution revision and the policy to
be adopted in Hungary. He seemed to approve
my ideas.

5. Success of the Imperial effort. Conversation
with Prince Schwarzenberg as to the method of
execution, which, after a long debate, leads to
agreement.

10. At last the ministers are sworn in, their conscientious scruples being overcome by their self-sacrificing love for their places.

November.

10. Imperial banquet in honor of the Grandduke
Constantine and his wife. The Emperor deigned
to present me to the Grandduke, the Archduchess Sophia to the Grandduchess. Fur-

ther she took the opportunity to say some very
friendly words about me.

December.

16. Call to the Emperor. He seemed to be somewhat
changed towards me, as a result of the steady
intrigue on the one hand of the diligence of the
Advocate (Bach) and, on the other, of the ignorance of the Arrogant (Schwarzenberg) who
have united their forces.

30. Session of the Commission. As soon as it was
over I edited the minutes and brought them to
the Emperor, who went through them with me,
and expressed doubts only as to the execution of
the emancipation of the Jews, saying that he
would put them into execution as soon as possible.

31. I found in my office the Emperor's signatures.
With the exception of the Jewish Emancipation
decree he has accepted them all.

To understand the readiness with which Francis Joseph
accepted Kübeck's momentous plan, one must have some
knowledge of the atmosphere surrounding the young man.
It was dominated by the military note. The tone of the
court was given by officers, youngish and not so young,
who had fought in the wars in Italy and Hungary, and
in 1850 made ready for war with Prussia. Count Grünne,
who had never fought a campaign, was all powerful,
despite his unpopularity as general aide-de-camp and

fatherly advisor to the young Emperor. Together with the war minister, Count Gyulai, like him without any military laurels, he busied himself in securing advancement for young officers of noble family. They injured the army by this, and by their superficial contempt for theoretical education as part of military training. A further cause of their unpopularity was their maintenance of the privileges of the aristocratic honorary colonels of most of the regiments, which made still worse the already poor position of the ordinary subaltern, both as to pay and as to promotion. The military circles surrounding the Emperor were permeated to excess by the evil spirit of contempt for the modern civilian mind, called out by Grünne and Gyulai, for the universities and for men of science, whom they regarded as embodiments of political unreliability and promoters of revolution. The ideal dominant in the minds of the members of this world—the world of officers and of the "first and second society" from which they came—ever since the 1848 Revolution and its overthrow, was the permanent establishment of the victory of 1848 by a counter-revolution. Literary expression of the anti-civilian views general throughout the conservative nobility and privileged classes of Austria was given in a pamphlet by one of the Emperor's junior aides-de-camp, Major von Babárczy. Hostility was concentrated on the liberal members of the Schwarzenberg government; Alexander Bach, the strongest head in that government, being singled out on account of his liberal past, although he had long been Schwarzenberg's most useful aid in combating liberal ideas.

A veritable blast of absolutist ideology and of adoration of the purely militarist aspect of the youthful Emperor swept through the generals and the officers' corps, through the court and the nobles attached to it, at this time. It spread thence, in this direction and in that, through the established civil population. The professional code of the soldier—with its emphasis, on one side, on the absolute power of command of the officer and, above all, of the Emperor as commander-in-chief of the army; on the other, on absolute obedience—was simply transferred from the military sphere to that of government and administration. Superficially, at any rate, the idea of absolutism was approved or at worst tolerated by the educated classes, as well as by the press, again severely restricted in Austria. Natural enough that the young Emperor neither could nor would resist the tendencies operative all round him. He was very young, ill prepared for government, totally inexperienced. What he had seen and endured during the revolutionary period had injured his dynastic pride deeply. The idea of a repetition of such experiences was horrible to him. The influence of his mother and of the young Archdukes was all on the side of the dominant tendency at the court. He had no desire to resist them.

Kübeck was a statesman of pre-March days, whom he had been brought up to revere. He accepted his admonitions with complete sympathy, and saw Schwarzenberg as dallying with the task of making an end of the revolution and its child, the constitution of March, 1849. He acted with the military "resoluteness" that seemed to him the first duty of the soldier. At the time he felt himself simply and solely the soldier; he was but twenty years of age. For him, the introduction of absolutism was merely the logical consequence of his position as "supreme war lord." In all this he was perfectly honest. When he heard of the events in Paris of December 2, and of the personal dictatorship inaugurated by President Louis Bonaparte, Francis Joseph remarked: "He is perfectly right. The man who holds the reins of government in his hands must also be able to take responsibility. Irresponsible sovereignty are, for me, words without meaning; such a thing is a mere printing machine for signatures." Here the whole of the young man's theory of the state is expressed —horse and rider, people and Emperor, with the ministers as a machine to produce decrees for the imperial signature.

Francis Joseph had, of course, no adequate conception of the far-reaching consequences of the act to which he affixed his seal on December 31, 1851. All he knew was that, acting on the advice of Count Grünne, he had laid the foundation of his purely personal rule, in the one department in which, hitherto, the government had not been able to advise him—that of the army organization and the supreme command. True, the war ministry was not actually superseded, but it was limited almost exclusively to barrack administration, the commissariat, and the finance department. All really military concerns were transferred to the young Emperor personally, as supreme commander of the army; he had to examine, decide, and organize, throughout the entire realm, everything touching the army in Vienna, in Prague, in Lemberg, as well as in Hungary, under military government, in Lombardy, and in Venetia. He governed the army with the aid of the Quartermaster-General, General Hess, at the head of the strategic division, the general staff, and with that of the imperial military chancellery, with Count Grünne at its head.

Grünne, further, commanded the imperial adjutants corps, and actually settled all military matters, although he had had no military training beyond mere service routine. To this model Francis Joseph thought the government of the "civil" departments ought to be approximated. The ministers, whose number he hoped to reduce, were to submit to him the decisions, laws, decrees, and appointments which made up the real contents of government, preparing them with their officials and then handing them up to him for his signature. He wanted to be sole ruler and sole bearer of responsibility. What does a youth of twenty take upon himself more readily than this —responsibility?

Francis Joseph, further, was not aware that the autocracy created for him by Kübeck was something quite new in Austria; nor that, in combination with the erection of a new unitary realm, it connoted a second revolution, a revolution to the right, conducted from above, carried through in the interest of the imperial person, and constituting a veritable coup d'état. Nor, thanks to the poor education in history that he had "enjoyed," was he aware that this new autocracy did not correspond with the history of the house of Habsburg.

DICTATING A CONSTITUTION: ABSOLUTISM

When Empreor Francis, his grandfather, after the defeat and banishment of Napoleon, ordered that everything in his reconquered realm should be organized anew on its old footing, so as to dam up the ideas of the French Revolution, this, though a reactionary act from the standpoint of those ideas, was a conservative one from that of Austrian history. No historic right of his peoples which Emperor Francis had sworn to respect was violated by him. The estates constitutions in the hereditary provinces remained in force, small as was their political significance; the 800-year-old constitution of Hungary remained intact, inconvenient as it always was to the statesmen of Vienna. But what Francis Joseph did, on the advice of his conservative counsellors, was anything but conservative. He abolished all the rights that had existed from time immemorial between the monarch and his kingdoms and territories by the self-same stroke with which he destroyed the entire achievement his people had won through the revolution.

On one point only was caution shown. There was no tampering with the law by which the Vienna Reichstag had given the peasants ownership of their lands. But, for the rest, everything, old and new, affecting the political life of the many nations of the ancient monarchy, was swept away in the interest of the ruling absolutism of one single man now proclaimed. Austria, of course, remained what it had always been, a "legalistic" State (Rechtsstaat); existing laws remained in force so far as they had not already been "provisionally" repealed. In many instances they were replaced by new decrees, in many more they were to be so replaced. In the relations of the citizen to the state, the idea of the former's political right was extirpated, inasmuch as now the question was purely one of the supreme will in the state, of supreme authority in legislation, taxation, and administration.

Over this entire area the imperial will alone was valid. It alone had free scope, unimpeded by any right in the citizen, who was to be a mere subject: on the one side, peoples with no political rights; on the other, the Emperor, who with his army, his ministers, and his officials, would bring prosperity to the whole realm, through a non-party government simply and solely pursuing the common good. Such was the picture of the future held up to the eyes of Austria by the New Year's patent of 1852. It substituted for the ruinous system of ministerial absolutism the autocracy of a man of one and twenty, who, unhampered by the ugly intrigues and secret liberalism of old ministers, was to be free to exercise all his gifts, all his conscientious benevolence and justice.

A somewhat childish Utopia this, that was staged before the world in the good old city of Vienna; something odd, too, in the fact that of the ministers there described as so dangerous to the common weal all save one, and that the most honorable among them, Finance Minister Krauss, remained in office.

The most fatal point in the basic law of this new autocracy was that, for Hungary, it constituted the last word in permanent subjection to the foreign absolutism of Vienna. Buried, now, all the hopes of understanding with Vienna and restoration of the old Hungarian constitution cherished by the conservative Hungarian nobility, men who had taken no part in the revolution or in the war under Kossuth, but who had actively opposed every liberal or democratic movement. True, these Hungarian "Old Conservatives" had pursued purely class politics and desired nothing more than the restoration to power in Hungary of their old aristocratic régime. At the same time, they were ready to make all the concessions that the experiences of 1848 had caused them to see as necessary, to have the imperial royal monarchy, as symbol of the power of the hereditary house, put upon a new and firm foundation; if only they need not sacrifice the internal autonomy of Hungary as a kingdom. But the horrible "theory of forfeiture," which Alexander Bach had put before the old conservatives as long ago as 1850, was solemnly established as the basis of the new autocracy. Hungary was no longer a "Marian" kingdom. It sank to a mere province of the imperial state, divided into five districts, each to be governed, like the other hereditary provinces, by German, or German-speaking Slav, officials. The law was to be Austrian. The primeval institutions of the country were suppressed, and the Magyar majority, including the nobles, permanently held under by the presence in the country of a great army and of a carefully organized police force, supported by the gendarmerie.

Such was the future which Francis Joseph's coup d'état held out to the Hungarian nation—absolutism, centralization, and a complete equality of dumb obedience to the Emperor, his military and civil instruments. This was the firm and uniform foundation on which a new dynastic patriotism was invited to grow and bloom among all classes and nationalities.

The next and most important step in the direction of carrying out this equalitarian program, was the establishment of the appropriate institutions. The advisers of the young Emperor were clearly of the opinion that, if life was to be infused into the gigantic bureaucratic machine, it must have spiritual forces at its disposal. The tradition of the court, the views of the all-powerful mother of the Emperor, the entrenched habits of thought of the nobility and also of the peasants, as well as of the great majority of the "settled" civilian population implied that it was only in Catholicism that they could be found. The first step towards the alliance of the new autocracy and the Roman Curia had been taken shortly before the establishment of personal absolutism. Imperial rescripts approved the demands made by episcopal conferences of all the dioceses. The supremacy of the state over the church, as established by Emperor Joseph II and never abandoned by Emperor Francis, was now freely surrendered by Francis Joseph. Here, too, the first step went much further than the last ought to have gone. At the same time it was being announced that the great reform was going to bring about a Concordat with Rome.

Three months after Francis Joseph had pronounced himself autocrat, on the fifth of April, 1852, Prince Felix Schwarzenberg died. A stroke carried him so swiftly from the mortal scene that the young Emperor, hurriedly summoned to his side, could only watch the last moments of his political teacher. He wept bitterly over the deathbed of the savior of his house. Soon, however, he recovered, ordered Prince Schwarzenberg's workroom to be locked up, and took the key away with him. The death of Schwarzenberg signalized the young Emperor's majority. The burden of his legacy, in the domain of internal policy, fell on to the shoulders of the man who, from the first, had borne it with him, Alexander Bach. The gigantic mechanism which gave actual form and force to Kübeck's new plan of autocracy, was the "Bach system."

Schwarzenberg's death left Francis Joseph standing alone. With no other of his many subsequent ministers did he stand in any close personal relationship. Despite his youth he remained solitary on the heights to which the coup d'état had lifted him. The most momentous and calamitous circumstance in Francis Joseph's life is that his advisers were guilty of a gross exaggeration of the monarchical idea which set him, at this crisis in his own development, in sharpest opposition to the great political ideas and tendencies of the age to which he belonged.

CHAPTER IV

PRINCE SCHWARZENBERG'S death ended, at a stroke, Francis Joseph's practical education in autocracy. From the first, the young monarch had shown a will consciously set to complete independence of his advisers, both of his ministers and of his immediate entourage. Here was the decisive moment if he were to achieve absolute freedom of action. Prince Schwarzenberg had actually raised him to the throne; his ruthless removal of Windischgrätz, the military fulcrum of that action, had raised Schwarzenberg to a pinnacle of personal power in the eyes both of the monarch and of the outside world, which could only be described as a personal dictatorship, tolerated by the sovereign. The succession of great diplomatic and military successes which marked the Prince's régime had naturally raised the Emperor's confidence in his prime minister to the highest point; attempts, overt or covert, proceeding either from the injured field marshal's circle or from the Hungarian nobility, shattered against it. Gratitude to the statesman who had saved the hereditary house and its rule, was bound to grow in Francis Joseph's heart with the progressive restoration of the imperial authority. Long years after, the Emperor was, indeed, to say that Felix Schwarzenberg was beyond all comparison

[98]

the greatest of his ministers. Foreign diplomats used to refer, jestingly, to Schwarzenberg in their letters as the Austrian "Vizier." The word characterized, aptly enough, the quite special position of a man who, at first, obviously overtopped all other statesmen and generals at the court of Vienna.

What determined Schwarzenberg's relations to the young Emperor and gave him his quite unrivaled position as his instructor in practical statesmanship was not any accident or favor, however, but the serene power of the man himself. Francis Joseph, as has been noted, never had a favorite. A natural dryness, marked even in his early youth, accompanied by a high if never obtrusive self-consciousness, saved him from any such danger, then and later. Prince Schwarzenberg was, moreover, impossible as a favorite, according to Austrian ideas; he was far too much of the grand seigneur. The court and the young Emperor might well see in him a knight sent by the grace of heaven to save the hereditary house. But this first prime minister of Francis Joseph's owed his power solely to his successes and the perfect reliance on his acumen and security inspired in the young monarch and the whole imperial family at the crisis of their fate by his iron decision of character.

The manner in which the offices thus vacated by Schwarzenberg's death were filled was, therefore, of supreme importance both for Francis Joseph's development and for that of his realm. In view of his personal position and his personal significance, it seemed impossible to find a real successor to the man who had so suddenly vanished from the scene. Nor did the Emperor think of doing so. This was shown when he hastily summoned the acting ambassador at the English court, Count Buol-Schauenstein, to act as foreign minister. This hurried summons was due to the fact that Prince Schwarzenberg had nominated Count Buol to act as his representative, in the event of his falling ill. No prime minister was nominated. A few days after Buol's arrival, he was further entrusted with the chairmanship of the cabinet. The appointment of a successor to Schwarzenberg seemed hereby expressly waived; there was to be no second prime minister in Francis Joseph's unitary realm. Well-informed persons saw this momentous decision as signifying that the Emperor intended, from now on, to be his own prime minister, the immediate head of the government, and, of course, his own foreign minister too. That was why he gave this office to one among the considerable range of average diplomats available.

These events made a deep impression on the court and public opinion generally. The aged ex-chancellor, Prince Metternich, wrote indignantly about Buol's appointment, and the hurry with which it had been made. "The Emperor may try out, *ad interim*, the individual who may finally prove right for foreign minister, but not *ex abrupto* definitively summon him." Here was, in fact, the first of many such "*ex abrupto*" decisions of the young Emperor; perhaps the most momentous of them all. For, in calling Count Buol to the Kaunitz Palace on the Ballplatz, this young man of twenty-two consciously inaugurated the era of his autocracy in foreign politics. Buol was the first of the Emperor's ministers from whom he knew, in advance, that he need fear no sort of opposition to his own will and intention, whatever they might be.

Prince Metternich and his friend Baron von Kübeck were the last people in the world to enter any just criticism of Francis Joseph's resolve to exercise autocracy to the full. No men had more often and more openly criticized Prince Schwarzenberg for his pseudo-conservative constitutional policy, or the "Liberal ministerial despotism" by which Schwarzenberg and Alexander Bach filched supreme power from the monarch, than these two survivors of the revolution. Kübeck, it is true, had persuaded the "imperial youth" to accept his imperial council in order to free him from the tutelage of his ministers. His action has already been described. The seed he sowed fell on fruitful soil. Francis Joseph lent a ready ear to Kübeck's doctrine, and, immediately opportunity offered, proceeded to put it into execution. Truly it did not lie with the statesmen of the pre-March epoch, or their "Old Conservative" allies, to complain of the young Emperor's taking the first available opportunity to show his readiness to realize the ideal they had put before him of the monarch who governs as well as reigns.

Thus light-heartedly did Francis Joseph assume the vast burden of responsibility assigned to him by such conservative doctrinaires as Prince Metternich, Baron Kübeck, and Count Hartig. His biographer may well ask what were the internal springs whence he derived the calm assurance revealed at this turning point in his career. For more than three years, now, he had been learning, under the guidance of Felix Schwarzenberg's powerful hand, to understand the machine of government, during the most difficult period his house had had to pass through since the Thirty Years War. The main impression he must have received was that practical statesmanship, and above all, the art of diplomacy, did not present difficulties that he could not master, despite his youth. True, he must have realized, in his inmost soul, how much he still lacked in experience and above all in positive knowledge. Court flattery, though it might please, could not deceive him on this. He was more or less armed against this evil perilous to kings and emperors, for he had a native simplicity and naturalness which his education had done nothing to diminish, that made him almost immune to this poison. He was further assisted by a lively distrust of most of the men with whom he had to do. The terrible events of the revolution no doubt accentuated this mistrust.

Francis Joseph had no innate tendency to "think nobly" of humanity. But his best armor against the court flatterer was a quality inherited by him from his mother, and by her tended—that calm pride, that serene sense of royalty which struck all those who speak of him. "The man who can praise me to my face I must allow to blame me likewise; which however may not be." Here is a view which Francis Joseph maintained throughout life. Therefore, so soon as he had acquired a certain experience of life, he let all men see that no one need hope to get anything from him through flattery; see, too, that, as Emperor, he felt himself above praise or blame from others.

At the same time, his self-consciousness was aggravated by the events of his youth. In so far as he imagined himself to possess the gifts and powers attributed to him by men of such standing as Metternich, Kübeck, and others, he was inevitably bound to overstep the limits set for him by his youth and the narrowness of his personal experience.

Old Baron Kübeck, in his diary, apropos of the struggles between the various parties at court at the time of the Crimean War, reproaches Buol and General Hess in this connection. In so doing, however, he forgets that a far greater responsibility for the creation of an unwholesome self-reliance in the young Emperor rests upon himself, and upon his highly successful effort in 1851 to persuade him to undertake a complete absolutism. Whoever was mainly answerable, however, hardly affects the issue. It may be assumed that young Francis Joseph was no less conscious of his own moral responsibility than any average young man at his entry on an independent career. Politically, his conception of responsibility was that of every European monarch of his day: as a duty to maintain his inherited realm intact; a duty whose most obvious practical expression lies in the responsibility of the head of the dynastic family to the latter for its continuance and that of the realm.

Further, the characteristics of Schwarzenberg's statesmanship were not such as to cause the sense of monarchical responsibility to be one of the strongest impressions he had imprinted on his pupil's mind. He was, of course, by no means one of those professional statesmen who, having reached their position slowly, love to talk of their responsibility and, in so doing, lull their own sense of weakness or insecurity. The marks of Schwarzenberg's diplomacy were a sureness, swiftness, and passion in attack, coupled with a penetration of men and circumstances and a ready adjustment to real political forces that was always keen and often unscrupulous. His was not a school to teach the leader of a state to shrink from personal responsibility.

The Prince was a convinced absolutist, at least so far as the Habsburg realm was concerned. Within two short years, in the teeth of opposition, and with a complete disregard of constitutional promises, he, apparently without effort, restored the Emperor's autocracy. In so doing he inevitably gave Francis Joseph a perilous conception of the nature and premises of statesmanship. These conceptions, in their turn, became the basis of the whole political thinking and action of the young monarch, from the time when Schwarzenberg's death cast him back entirely upon himself. Too young to comprehend or apply an independent, realistically-grounded judgment to the events about him and his throne, he saw only the surface facts and results. So the events of the first years of his reign, down to Schwarzenberg's death, taught him one lesson, and one lesson only—that material might, physical force, in the shape of the standing army and military police, constituted the kernel of the state, at any rate under a monarchy.

As for the human qualities that might be needed for a statesmanship built on this foundation, the Prince, as Francis Joseph saw him, gave him the model of certain qualities necessary for leading and ruling men. This line

[104]

of thought led the young monarch back to the ideal that his education had imprinted so deeply on his mind—that same military conception of statesmanship and its problems which Schwarzenberg, too, had accepted. In his case it was emphasized by the fact that the prime minister invariably appeared in public in uniform. From the first the young Emperor followed this example. His contempt for "civilian dress" was one of the main causes of his lack of popularity with the great masses of Vienna, and was criticised freely in sound monarchist circles. Certain it is that the young monarch went beyond what was good for him in imitating traits in Schwarzenberg's ways of thinking and acting that he found sympathetic. Where he failed was in understanding the immense significance of the organically developed and achieved personality of his first prime minister. That he did not learn during the years of his practical education as ruler under Schwarzenberg's guidance.

The reason for this want of understanding is not far to seek. Francis Joseph lacked the capacity for any deeper insight into the facts and forces of human life. From his youth up he took things and men "as they came," without attempting to penetrate the hidden causes of visible events. No doubt most men are like this, at all events in youth; average men certainly are. They never meditate upon what happens to them; experience teaches them, very slowly, to judge others correctly, and at least to respect the mystery of human personality. Why should Francis Joseph have been different from the great majority? At this period he certainly was far from seeing personality as the strongest force in life; later, too, such a view hardly visited him, although in his riper years he was to show an astonishing understanding of men. For him, as for most rulers, personality as such had no attraction.

This failure in appreciation was to have very serious consequences for him both as man and as ruler. In general, of course, no human being has more difficulty in appreciating the significance of an achieved personality than the young ruler. His position accustoms him to regard men as mere instruments, as "functionaries," to be judged according to their usefulness at the given moment. Strange—in this point sovereign democracy and royal absolutism meet. Each accepts the assumption that any average man will serve as well as any other for any and every given office. Neither the ruling "people" nor the autocrat love personality. Personal values vanish; in the one case before reliance on majority selection, in the other, before the proud belief in the God-granted elevation of the ruler—a belief that is apt to be strengthened by the education of the heir.

We have here perhaps the most harmful results of the sense of personal pride instilled into Francis Joseph from childhood by his mother. A surprising insight into this close contact between mother and son is afforded by a passage in the Diary of Princess Melanie Metternich. She remarks that "This Imperial family never loved Metternich, never appreciated him. The stupid people did not see what he was, and in their period of good fortune he was often a nuisance to them." "I remember," Princess Metternich continues, "Archduchess Sophia saying to me, several years ago, in Nice, that one never ought to regard individuality as having any importance; that she, the Archduchess, has always seen that one man can be replaced by another without its making the smallest difference."

These views of his mother's were thoroughly shared by Francis Joseph, and adhered to by him throughout his life. Even in relation to the highest achievements of statesmanship and the rarest aspects of character he regarded men merely as "functional creatures." For this reason he never looked for strong personalities, or definite individualities in the men he used. On the contrary, he rejected such men; he avoided them in his service or, where that was impossible, remained as aloof as possible from them. This trait was accentuated by the natural tendency of the ruler to keep everyone at a distance—a tendency the more marked in so reserved a character as Francis Joseph's. To this must be referred most of the grave errors and failures he made in his long reign in the choice of ministers, generals, provincial governors, and even high court officials and members of his immediate entourage. His pride contributed, of course, to this.

The good fairy who is supposed to hover over the cradle could bestow no more precious gift on a monarch than the capacity for attracting and holding to the service of the state men of strong individuality, potent intellect, and unbending will, and for supporting the difficulties involved in personal and professional intercourse with such men, difficulties which even a monarch cannot escape. European history shows how rarely that gift has actually been possessed by a sovereign. King William of Prussia did possess a surprising power of tolerating strong individualities and even geniuses, and in that lies the main cause of his amazing rise as a ruler. Love them he did not; at many a moment in his life he had to struggle hard with them, and with himself. But it was this gift of his that made his own career, like the life work of a Bismarck and a Moltke, possible in monarchical Prussia.

Francis Joseph in this respect was the antithesis of the son of Queen Louise of Prussia, and the fact is the key to an understanding of many a grave failure in policy. It will be necessary to return more than once to this fatal flaw in his disposition. Unfortunately for him, his own personality was so strong that, even in his early youth, he was immune to the charm—often a dangerous charm—of strong individuality in others. This immunity was no doubt in part inherited from his grandfather, Emperor Francis, who rated men according to their utility for his own purposes. Pride, in grandfather as in grandson, was the root of the feeling that the ruler, if he is to rule, needs reliable servants, not incalculable individualities.

In the momentous hour of Prince Schwarzenberg's death, Francis Joseph was seized by the conviction that he had now achieved autocracy. The Prince had not prevented the young Emperor from following the advice of Count Grünne, and making his personal supreme command of the army the basis of a complete scheme of military reconstruction. Once actually supreme war lord, Francis Joseph, seeing as he did the army as the sole secure support of the head of the state, felt himself strong enough to take into his own hands—and with a light heart—

the direction of government and above all of foreign policy. In Count Buol he selected an assistant with technical experience, about whose ideas of foreign policy nothing was known at court beyond the fact that, when Austrian ambassador at St. Petersburg, he had felt himself "ill used" by the Czar, since when he had made no secret of cherishing a deep dislike for Nicholas I. It is not certain whether or no Francis Joseph was aware of this trait in the character of his new minister. For any adept it was of evil omen for the future of Austrian policy in the East.

What mattered to Francis Joseph was that Buol promised to be an easy-going minister with no ideas of his own. As a matter of fact foreign policy did not, at the time of Schwarzenberg's death, appear to present any great problems. It was possible to assume that Buol would "function" adequately enough. At the same time most careful handling was needed for the systematic development of Schwarzenberg's new Austrian policy in relation to Prussia and the German confederation. Awkwardly enough, Buol here was quite without practical experience; he had never been employed in German affairs. Anyhow, Francis Joseph took questions of Austria's attitude to Prussia and the whole business of the German federation entirely into his own hands from the start. To his mind it was a sort of family affair. His whole education, as well as his training under Schwarzenberg and Kübeck, caused him to see in the house of Habsburg-Lorraine the old German imperial dynasty, naturally designed by history and distribution of power to be the leader of Germany in the policy of the confederation. Actually the German dynasties did, as a whole, constitute a sort of great princely family. For centuries there had been conflicts of opposing princely and particularist interests within them; there were, to-day. Nevertheless, there was a strong sense of common interest, ready to spring to life on any issue touching the "trade union" of monarchs. Indubitably, too, a certain traditional feeling for the old hereditary house of Habsburg persisted. It was at its strongest in Frederick William IV of Prussia. Just before the March revolution in Berlin, this remarkable monarch said: "I am not the first in Germany, I am not the third, I am the second. Austria comes first, then I."

The quotations already made from the correspondence of Francis Joseph with his uncle show that this feeling lasted on after 1848. Wherever important problems, differences of opinion between the cabinets of the two countries, arose, Francis Joseph dealt directly with his uncle in letters. From his early youth as an Emperor, he was in the habit of handling German matters, i.e., above all, Prussian-Austrian relations, as it were from throne to throne. In the years 1850-51 almost all the German princes visited Vienna, which would then present all the air of the old capital of the one-time Holy Roman Empire. He knew the heads of almost all the great princely families personally: the King of Würtemberg, the Grandduke of Baden, the Duke of Saxony, the Granddukes of Mecklenburg and Oldenburg. His close and various relationship to the Bavarian house made Viennese policy in relation to the most *difficile* member of the confederation something of an intimate family affair; how often in families the closest relationships prove the most delicate and difficult! One deep and genuine friendship, perhaps the only one with another man that Francis Joseph had in all his life, goes back, too, to these early days: his friendship with Prince Albert of Saxony, heir-presumptive of the Saxon throne, and, through his mother, a cousin of the Emperor.

Enough has been said to explain the lack of diffidence with which Francis Joseph set to work, once he had made up his mind to be his own foreign minister. Schwarzenberg's puissant personality had reëstablished Austria as one of the great powers; Radetzky's victories had won respect for the army on which its strength depended. Francis Joseph had, in 1850, served his apprenticeship to the trade of monarch in the difficult business with Germany. From the start he regarded German matters as a department of politics which he could handle best by himself, in virtue of the fact that he felt himself the recognized head of the German princely family.

The object of Schwarzenberg's new Habsburg policy in Germany was to consolidate the chairmanship in Frankfort, reacquired for Austria through the defeat of Prussia in December, 1850, at Olmütz, and develop it carefully but systematically, to a genuine leadership of the trade and foreign policy of Germany as a whole. This was even more to the young Emperor's idea than Schwarzenberg's. When he intervened to prevent Schwarzenberg from smashing Prussia's attempt at German leadership by a stroke of arms, an alternative future policy for Austria in the confederation was adumbrated. This now came to the fore.

Baron Werner, for years assistant to Prince Metternich in his dealings with the confederation, and possessed of an unexampled knowledge of its working, opposed the new policy as contrary to the old traditions of the Vienna chancellery. But Francis Joseph set in the Kaunitz Palace as his counsellors for German affairs, two new advisers, Baron von Gagern and Baron von Biegeleben, both of whom were firm believers in Schwarzenberg's grandiose conception of an empire of seventy millions, comprising a single customs union from the Rhine to the Turkish border, and ruled over by Francis Joseph with the support of a strong central power developed out of the national assembly at Frankfort. Both these men were devout Catholics and Conservatives and Archduchess Sophia and Archbishop Rauscher were undoubtedly ready to devote all their strength to working for their policy.

Certainly, at this time, one of the basic elements in the developing thought of the Emperor was the hope of renewing the German power of the Habsburg house. Again and again he let himself go, in this idea, only to be blocked and forced to retreat before the impenetrable obstacle of the power of Prussia. To this point we shall have to return. For the moment, on Schwarzenberg's death, Francis Joseph held in his hands all the threads between Vienna and Munich, Hannover, Stuttgart, and even Dresden and Darmstadt. To his strong monarchical sense, Germany naturally presented itself as a collection of princes among whom he enjoyed a dominating position as head of the

Arch-House. His first envoy to the restored National Assembly at Frankfort, Count Frederick Thun, was by no means unsuccessful in carrying out the new Austrian policy there.

Another contemporary appointment of Schwarzenberg's was that of Count Prokesch to Berlin. Famed throughout Europe as an orientalist and writer, Prokesch was also one of the most capable diplomats of his day. In Berlin the difficulties were overwhelming and success not great. In Frankfort the Schwarzenberg policy met with opposition from a man who was to embody Francis Joseph's personal destiny in a unique degree. On May 23, 1851, the office of Prussian envoy to the Frankfort Assembly was taken over by a lieutenant in the Prussian Landwehr and member of the Prussian Diet, Otto von Bismarck-Schönhausen.

From this day began Bismarck's unresting fight against the new Austrian policy of making a real position of power out of the chairmanship assigned to Austria in the Act of the Confederation. And this although the Prussian prime minister had nominated Otto von Bismarck to this position to promote the conservative policy of friendship between Prussia and Austria, then the capital item in the program of the Prussian Junkers! Bismarck came to Frankfort as an adherent of this program. The explanation of the change that took place in him, step by step, but irresistibly, and determined the whole course of his future as a statesman, lies deep within the psychology of the man himself. Seen in the light of the knowledge we now possess of his experience, the solution, as with all great things, is very simple.

[113]

The 1848 Revolution had ripened Otto von Bismarck to the perfect embodiment of the Prussian ideal of state might. The deeper the injury to his Prussian feelings caused by the weakness of the king and his ministers, the stronger his conviction that no people and no state in Europe possessed such a concentration of moral and material force as did Prussia in its state and army. He was sent to Frankfort as Prussian envoy, to find Prussia second, always second, second forever. The whole force of his demoniac nature rose in revolt, though externally the proper measure and the most perfect form were preserved, as always, by the power and sagacity of his genius. Under pressure from him, however, the Assembly at Frankfort and the princes there represented by their envoys began to comprehend the profound change that had come over the attitude of Vienna to the German question.

Bismarck taught those who were willing to listen that Vienna was now engaged in an effort to transform the hitherto honorific position of Austria as presiding power into an effective leadership of the German states, and the confederation into an extended Austria. Were this to succeed, then, to quote an admirable student of the history of these years, "the life-threads of Prussian destiny as a great power would be cut." Therefore, Bismarck lost no opportunity, no matter how small, how merely formal it might be, of fighting with every weapon, open and secret, with speeches and with notes, with wit or with coarseness, against the Austria of his vision. Count Thun, and later Count Prokesch, were the exclusive targets of his brilliant sarcasm, his witty diatribes. They were the *corpus vile* on which he exercised an opposition that ranged out far beyond them into the distant future. In the eight years spent at Frankfort Otto von Bismarck grew to be the deadly foe of the confederate organization of Germany. Plans formed in his mind for casting Austria out of Germany, and making Prussia sole sovereign over this reduced Germany. No one made a deeper mark in Francis Joseph's life than this Pommeranian junker-diplomat.

When, in June, 1852, Bismarck was sent to Vienna by his king and, at the court at Ofen, Francis Joseph saw him for the first time in person, he can have had no idea that he was encountering his own destiny, and that of Europe, incarnate. The impression made on the young monarch of two and twenty by the ambassador, at that time seven and thirty, is given in a letter he addressed on June 25, 1852, to his uncle. He writes:

"Your Royal Majesty has given fresh proof of your friendly feelings to me in sending Herrn von Bismarck-Schönhausen here, a proof the more valuable in that you have selected a man already favorably known to me by reputation, whose chivalry and loyal devotion you have thus so handsomely recognized. It has also been a great pleasure to me to be able to receive him here in Ofen, on my return from my excursion into a part of Hungary.

"I have found Herrn von Bismarck an upright and straightforward man, and as such he will doubtless faithfully report to Your Majesty the terms in which I spoke to him of the high value I place on the

[115]

continuance of the many years' friendship between our houses."

To Bismarck, on his side, we owe an excellent picture of the young Emperor, who had in these days just begun acting as his own foreign minister. In a letter of June 25, 1852, to Leopold von Gerlach, aide-de-camp in chief to Frederick William IV, he writes from Ofen:

> "The youthful ruler of this country makes a very agreeable impression on me: the fire of the twenties, coupled with the dignity and foresight of riper years, a fine eye, especially when animated, and a winning openness of expression, especially when he laughs. The Hungarians are enthusiastic about his national pronunciation of their language and the elegance of his riding."

In subsequent years, when Francis Joseph read the reports of his envoys at the Frankfort Federal Diet with their accounts of the unheard-of attacks of the volcanic Prussian envoy and of his incessant intrigues against Austria, the gigantic form of the Pommeranian Junker must often have risen before his eyes; and he may have recalled the terms in which his maternal uncle had introduced his envoy, in a letter in his own hand:

> "He belongs to a knightly family which is settled in our Marches even longer than our own House, and has always retained its ancient virtues, notable in him. To him, and his fearless and energetic labors in

the darkest days of the years just behind us, we owe the maintenance and strengthening of the happy position of our country. I have great satisfaction in the thought that Your Majesty should make the acquaintance of a man whose free and chivalrous obedience and irreconcilable and deep-rooted objection to Revolution have made him honored of many here, and detested of many. He is my friend and faithful servant and brings with him to Vienna the vital and sympathetic impress of my ideas, my plan of action, and my will, and I may add, of my love for Austria and Your Majesty."

Bismarck was thus most warmly commended to the head of the House of Austria. His reception corresponded fully to his high credentials. But a decade had not passed before Francis Joseph was forced to see in his former guest at the Palace of Ofen a serious opponent. And there was to be no doubt of his seriousness!

CHAPTER V

(1) *Francis Joseph's Friendship with Czar Nicholas and Its Breach*

THE governing factor in Austria's international position had, of course, ever since the Emperor's accession, been its relation to Russia. Conservatives throughout the world put their trust and set their hopes on Nicholas, who regarded himself as the God-appointed guardian of the monarchical order in Europe, as restored in 1815, and, for that reason, had been ready to come forward in 1848 and protect the dynastic houses, above all those of the two great German powers, against revolution. The fact that he did render this assistance to the Habsburg dynasty, whereas his brother-in-law, Frederick William IV of Prussia, disappointed him most painfully by his policy of "pacts" with revolution, no doubt strengthened Nicholas' quite genuine sympathy for the young Emperor. He took him completely to his bosom when Schwarzenberg began energetically restoring absolutism and finally suspended the constitution, promulgated on March 4, 1849, but never really put into operation. Friction and tension did, of course, occur between the two powers throughout this period.

[118]

In ordinary life, the giving and accepting of benefits is apt to injure the friendship out of which they arise; it is even more markedly so in the relations of states and governments. The "brotherly aid" rendered by Nicholas' army was, from the beginning, a source of grievance in governing circles both in Austria and Russia. At the time it caused lively irritation among the officers on both sides: on the one, a sense of shame in having to accept aid regarded as superfluous; on the other, the feeling that saviours were insufficiently recognized.

Prince Schwarzenberg was no more popular in Petersburg than Prince Paskievitch in Vienna. It exasperated Austrian generals and statesmen that the heroic Görgey had surrendered to the Russians; the greatest indignation was felt in Russia over Haynau's Bloody Assize on Magyar generals, officers, and revolutionary nobles. This mutual ill-feeling, however, did not disturb the relations of the two emperors, and consequently the contacts of their cabinets, which both regarded as quite subsidiary to themselves, continued to be friendly.

At the same time a source of recurrent irritation, both on the part of Schwarzenberg and his master, existed in the German question, in which the Czar's active and constant interposition annoyed both the Austrian and the Prussian courts. For Schwarzenberg, the Olmütz agreement, brought about by pressure from the Czar, was no friendly service rendered by Russia to Austria, but a calculated obstacle to his policy. To his last day the Prince remained convinced of the necessity of the most absolute resistance to the claims of Prussia to leadership, and openly regretted that he had not been allowed to wage war on Prussia in 1850, as he had desired to do. The dominant feeling both of himself and of Francis Joseph toward the Czar of Russia was well expressed in the words he uttered shortly before his death, about the "magnitude of the ingratitude, by which Austria would astonish the world." Francis Joseph not only knew and understood the feelings of his prime minister; he had experienced in his frequent meetings with Nicholas I, at Olmütz and Warsaw, plenty of petty instances of want of tact or of personal consideration towards himself or towards members of his personal entourage, and had hoarded many an unpleasant recollection.

In general, no outstanding problems awaited Francis Joseph when he took the control of foreign policy into his own hands with Count Buol as assistant. The general situation of Austria in Europe, at Schwarzenberg's death, was by no means unfavorable. Relations to Prussia, after the restoration of the federation, were normal again. In England, the new coalition ministry had brought Austria's old enemy, Lord Palmerston, back to power; but it was known in Vienna that Queen Victoria and her husband regarded him with standing suspicion. Lord "Firebrand" had no respect for the monarchs of Europe; as little for Habsburgs or Hohenzollerns as for Coburgs. With Piedmont-Sardinia Austria lived in a sort of armistice.

The coup d'état of Napoleon III Schwarzenberg had viewed sympathetically, as likely to strengthen the conservative forces in Europe; but in Vienna, as in other European courts, considerable anxiety was felt about the approaching restoration of the empire in France. Its recognition was the first problem Buol had to face: at first in the form of the question, ridiculous enough to-day, whether the three rulers of Austria, Prussia, and Russia were to accord the new French Emperor the address of "My Brother" in their letters. At the last moment, the aloof attitude, on which the three courts had agreed, was dropped, on the occasion of the visit of Francis Joseph to his uncle in Berlin, both by Vienna and Berlin. Nicholas was left alone in his invidious attitude to Napoleon. In St. Petersburg, this result was attributed, correctly enough, to the want of skill and uncertainty of purpose of Count Buol. Napoleon was the more deeply injured by the isolated unfriendliness of the Russian cabinet because Nicholas had hitherto been very gracious to him as the conqueror of revolution. The Czar brusquely characterized his brother-in-law's behavior as "cowardly," and wrote, "c'est pitoyable" on the report sent him by his Vienna ambassador of the "accident" to the Austrian cabinet.

All such diplomatic pin pricks, irritabilities, and slights sank into utter insignificance a few weeks later, when the great courts learned, with a shock of painful surprise, that Prince Menschikoff had been sent from Petersburg to Constantinople with an ultimatum to the Turkish government. Nicholas demanded of the Sultan a solemn admission, in the form of a draft convention, of the Czar's protectorate to be exercised by the Czar's ambassador over all the othodox Christian inhabitants of the Turkish realm. This claim, affecting as it did ten to twelve millions of the Sultan's subjects, meant nothing less than the beginning of the dissolution of Turkish power in Europe—and the Sultan himself was to carry it out! The veil was rudely drawn from the long-cherished plans of conquest that Nicholas had been preparing. He was the first to concern himself seriously with the "sick man" of the Bosphorus, and the division of his inheritance, on his decease. The Czar, indeed, was the inventor of the catchword that was to serve politicians, diplomats, and journalists for a century. At the same time he put the eastern question, in all its extent and all its potential danger to the peace of the world, right in the center of the stage, and kept it there. The revelation of Russian designs led to that complex tissue of military and diplomatic action known as the Crimean War, in which, for the next three years, the whole of central Europe was passionately involved. It was the first great conflagration after the great Napoleon's overthrow; it produced consequences not finally worked out till the World War itself.

This is not the place for even the briefest survey of this fatal period of European history. We are concerned only with the reactions of the crisis on the main lines of Austrian policy, and the personal share of Francis Joseph in its mighty events. What has already been said of his personal responsibility for all important decisions in foreign policy, even in the earliest years of his rule, and more markedly after the appointment of Buol, is true of this period: in the years 1853-59 he directed Austrian foreign policy himself even in its smallest details. Of course, Count Buol remained responsible for the actions of the Vienna cabinet and was, in these years, the standing counsellor and executive organ of the young Emperor. The archives of the Austrian Foreign Ministry prove that this responsibility of his was no light one, as does the testimony of his colleagues, notably Count Hübner, Austrian Ambassador in Paris.

But Austrian policy in the Crimean War was to a peculiar degree the personal affair of the Emperor. Originating in the personal relations between Francis Joseph and Nicholas, it was influenced by them throughout. Moreover, on the other side, the conflict with practically the whole of Europe that developed out of Russia's attack on the Sultan arose, directly, from the political and personal feelings of the Czar. The relation of the aged Nesselrode to Nicholas was that of Count Buol to Francis Joseph: he was the faithful servant and adviser of his master, not a statesman carrying out an independent policy.

So much, in this, for Austria, tragic breach with Russia is a function of the personal contacts of the two rulers, that its decisive points can best be shown through the recently published correspondence between the young Emperor and the Czar, some thirty years his senior. Contrary to the sound tradition of European monarchies since the seventeenth century, the policy both of Russia and of Austria in this great conflict on the eastern question, was, at every turning point, definitely a personal affair between sovereigns. The main action is contained in their (mainly holograph) letters. The notes of the two cabinets serve more or less as the chorus in the Greek tragedy.

On October 11-23, 1851, the Czar, then at the summit of his power in Europe, wrote to the young Emperor, whom he had met at Olmütz in the middle of June:

> "My dear, good friend, I have long felt a real need of saying to Thee how happy I was with Thee in Olmütz and how grateful for the thousand acts of affectionate attention that Thou has showered upon me, and, above all, for the warm and brotherly reception I found with Thee and Thine. Neither Thou nor I care for writing or making phrases, but there is no question of that here, for I speak to Thee from the depths of my heart and thank Thee most sincerely.
>
> "How have I rejoiced, how happy was I made by the great and splendid resolution that the wishes of Thy own lofty soul have prompted Thee to make for the welfare of Thy fatherland: joyfully do I congratulate Thee and pray God to bless Thy efforts.
>
> "It is said that new storms are brewing in France: I trust that they will bring no terrors for us, if the good understanding with Prussia can hold in its present shape, thanks to Thy government and that of Prussia. One must hope that the tragic past has not been in vain, as an example. Were the event to prove otherwise, as may Heaven forfend, Revolution would certainly raise its head again.
>
> "I envy my son that he comes to Thee and should

be happy if I might once again have the opportunity of rendering Thee a service—let me hope I may.

"A thousand greetings to Thy parents, keep me in Thy precious friendship, and believe, my dear, my cherished friend that, in heart and soul, I am ever Thy true brother and friend, Nicholas.

"My wife asks to be remembered to Thee."

Francis Joseph's reply is no less cordial, though no doubt traces of Schwarzenberg's hand can be seen in it. He writes:

"I think with Thee, that Europe is not yet at the end of its trials. Whatever Providence may yet have in store for us I hope, my very dear friend, our united efforts may succeed in overcoming. The object of all my wishes is to gather the scattered powers of Germany into a Confederation and if, thanks to Thy wise and benevolent advice, the Berlin cabinet assists me in this task with loyal coöperation, we shall, I trust, succeed in erecting a powerful barrier to the ideas of revolution in the center of Europe."

The Czar's letter of April 7/19, 1852, shows the continuance of a truly paternal feeling on Nicholas' part to his young friend in Vienna:

"If Thou will permit it, I shall visit Thee this time in Vienna. The hope of embracing Thee again gives me new life, and I feel more than ever the need of telling Thee how I love and prize Thee

[125]

and how greatly I rejoice to see Thee daily more admired and honored, as Thou deservest, as I have perceived from the first moment that brought us together."

Waiving all ceremonies of reception, etc., the Czar goes on:

"Thy friend Nicholas comes simply to embrace his dear Francis Joseph—that is all."

Deploring the loss caused to his friend by the death of Schwarzenberg, he continues:

"This man rendered Thee outstanding services, and his devotion to Thee, like his other great and noble characteristics, compel respect even from his adversaries."

Too many tears were not shed in St. Petersburg over the removal, by death, of the "respected" adversary. Certainly the course of the great war, now approaching, would have been quite different for Austria, had Prince Schwarzenberg controlled its foreign policy.

Francis Joseph's reply, from Vienna, in April, 1852, is brief but warm in tone. Another exchange of letters, towards the end of the same year, shows the continued affection of the two monarchs. Nicholas asked the young Emperor to do him a friendly service in the case of his close relative, Prince Alexander of Hesse (father of that Prince of Battenberg who was to turn up so singularly in the European history of the next period). This Francis Joseph could only promise with certain reservations. In his letter from Vienna, he says:

> "The new year has now opened. Whatever changes it may bring, and whatever trials may be prepared for us, I am happy in being able to hope that Thy friendship will not desert me, and that, with God's help, we may overcome all difficulties between ourselves and with Prussia."

A few weeks later, immediately after Francis Joseph had been wounded by the assassin Libényi, the Czar writes to his good friend in Vienna, and after urging him earnestly to take special precaution in the future says:

> "Thy life does not belong to Thee but to Thy country and us all. Great God, what would become of Thy country if it were to lose Thee, above all at such a moment!"

Then, however, the letter turns to politics. The Czar commissions his aide-de-camp, who is to bring it to Vienna, to say to the Emperor, "that I have just learned of the fruitless result of General Leiningen's mission."

The Czar was mistaken. The sharp intervention undertaken by Francis Joseph, through General Leiningen, in favor of Montenegro, threatened by the Sultan, had been completely successful. Ignorant of this, the Czar goes on, in his letter:

> "I do not know what Thy decisions may be, but whatever they are, if war by Turkey against Thee

should result, Thou mayest be assured in advance that it will be precisely the same as though Turkey had declared war on myself.

"I am instructing Prince Menschikoff to inform Constantinople in this sense. Meantime, I am mobilizing the 4th and 5th Army Corps, and the Black Sea fleet; they will be in readiness. But I deeply regret this sad necessity, since the end might well be the collapse of the Ottoman Empire, and the consequences of that would be incalculable."

Francis Joseph, though perhaps "moved" by the Czar's friendship, must have read this epistle with mixed feelings. He replied briefly:

"The attitude that Thou wast ready to assume in the event of my being inclined to let it come to a breach with the Porte, gives Thee fresh claims to my deepest gratitude. Thank God, Count Leiningen's mission has produced a satisfactory result, which, I am sure, will rejoice Thee as much as it does me."

If he really believed what he wrote, Francis Joseph must have deceived himself. The Czar, completely committed to the subjugation of Turkey to his will, was not over pleased by Francis Joseph's success at Constantinople. Shortly after this exchange of letters, decisive discussions took place between the Divan at Constantinople and the Russian ambassador there, which led to the break-

down of Prince Menschikoff's mission. The crisis precipitated by the Czar developed more and more threaten-
ingly. Francis Joseph felt compelled to put off the visit
he had planned to him in the summer, and "discords"
appeared in the diplomatic correspondence between Vienna
and St. Petersburg. They are indicated in a letter from
the Czar of April 8, 1853, in which he "defends himself
against the assumption" of having "really aggressive designs against Turkey." He says:

"Dear friend, I cannot admit that I have done
more, in this Oriental business, than my duty. I have
never thought of attacking the Ottoman Empire;
its maintenance so long as it can endure, seems to
me far more useful to our two realms than anything
that might replace it. I have always thought so;
but I must retain the possibility of acting in this
sense without compromising the honor and interests
of Russia. If the Turkish Government is so blinded
as not to admit the wrong it has done, and refuse
to make it good by guarantees for the future, I
should be compelled to take up arms. And I should
do it, despite any opposition or obstacles placed in
my way—for it would be my duty. To foretell the
outcome of such a war is impossible. If the Ottoman Empire falls, by its own guilt, I shall, my dear,
good friend, communicate all that I see coming to
Thee, and, together with Thee, we shall avert the
catastrophe that other Powers might precipitate in
such an event, but which in our case will with God's

help be forestalled by our intimate association and the similarity of our aims and interests."

The Czar now proceeded to act on his program, whose first step was the occupation of the Danubian principalities.

On July 3, 1853, without waiting for any understanding with the Austrian government to be reached, Russian troops crossed the frontier into Moldovia. This reckless action annoyed the Emperor greatly. Nevertheless, Count Buol was actively occupied in the next few weeks in an attempt at diplomatic mediation between Russia and Turkey. Nicholas was not entirely pleased by these efforts on the part of Austria to keep the peace. He would, at this juncture, have been satisfied with a purely political success, the more that the entry of the French and English fleets into Besika Bay clearly showed that the Western Powers were bent on blocking further Russian aggression against Turkey. The occupation of the Danubian principalities, and the fear lest revolutionary action among the Christian populations of the Balkan lands might react on the Southern Slavs in Hungary and Croatia, was bound to cause the gravest anxiety to Francis Joseph and his advisers in this preliminary period. The Czar attempted to allay it, by solemn undertakings, given to Vienna, that his troops should not cross the Danube. In order to maintain a good understanding with him, Francis Joseph sent General Count Gyulai, high in his own favor, to St. Petersburg, to transmit a letter dated July 2, 1853. To this Nicholas at once replied. His reply shows him still the fatherly and trustful friend; it also shows the seriousness of the general situation created by his policy.

"With keen delight," writes Nicholas, "have I received Thy admirable letter at the hands of General Count Gyulai. Nothing gives me so much pleasure as the realization that Thou retainest that friendship for me so dear to my heart, and the warm and close relations so happily developed between us. All that Thou hast said to me through Count Gyulai, as well as the action taken by Thee in Constantinople, meets my own wishes so completely that I simply cannot say to Thee how deeply and gratefully I feel it. I shall gladly put it down to Thy good offices if, despite the ill-will and opposition of Lord Redcliffe, we reach a good understanding with the Turks. That may still be, for I fancy the English minister is beginning to come to his senses again and sees, at last, how his ambassador has misled him and worked against the object of the English government, i.e., has done everything to strengthen the Turkish government."

Then comes a passage which reveals the conscious Cæsarism of the writer:

"My own action is determined; I shall not deflect from it. As I said in my last letter, I shall not cross the Danube so long as the Turks do not attack me on the left bank of the river; I shall wait. The loud talk of the English and French alarms me as little as do their fleets in the Dardanelles, and will not prevent my insisting on the satisfaction owed us by the Turkish Government. I have said it, and shall with God's help, put it through in spite of everything. It seems to me that the English and the French begin to perceive that they cannot prevent it; begin to feel the shame put upon them by their impotent presence down there; and will, from now on, do their utmost at least to save appearances— at the expense of the Turks, whom they have forced into this enterprise, they will manage to get off scot-free. They are beginning to be doubtful of the outcome, and, so I am assured, are already becoming disgusted with their so-called friends. This result I have always foreseen—on the assumption that it is not too late, and the Sick Man does not immediately die on their hands. It is pitiable! The sufferings of the Christian populations are well nigh unendurable; the Bulgarians, beside themselves as a result of what they have had to bear, are beginning to flee into the Principalities. Impossible to foresee what may come of it all. Probably they will take to arms: that would be a misfortune, horrible to contemplate. In any event, it will be impossible for me to come to their aid, without driving them back into Turkish bondage. That I have long foreseen. The case is so serious that I implore Thee to consider it, for it is more than possible that the matter will not stop at the Bulgarians, but the other Christians of the same creed will follow their example. We must then be in a position to unite our action in this matter."

The last sentences in the Czar's letter indicate the difficulty of the Vienna cabinet. In his reply of July 21, Francis Joseph expresses his apprehension, if in conciliatory words. He calls the Czar's letter very interesting, and expresses his satisfaction in the friendly frankness with which the Czar approves his, Francis Joseph's, views. The young Emperor is still so polite as to assure the Czar that he is convinced that his first object is peace and the maintenance of the Ottoman Empire. He emphasizes that "the present state of opinion, and the strengthening of revolutionary tendencies everywhere visible, would make the collapse of the Turkish Empire an evil, and lead to most difficult complications. I am firmly convinced," he writes, "that no one desires war, save the enemies of social order." He, therefore, trusts that Austrian mediation may result in the Turks' making acceptable proposals to the Czar.

"In the event, however, of its proving impossible to prevent war and the break-up of the Ottoman Empire, I am entirely of Thy opinion that we must act in the closest union to secure such a future organization of these territories as is demanded by their position on our frontiers and by our mutual relations."

[133]

Francis Joseph then puts forward a very serious consideration:

"Disinterested as is Thy attitude to the exercise of a common protectorate and to the fate of Constantinople, I am visited by doubts too serious not to be submitted to Thy judgment. I sum them up in the two following points: Must there not, contrary to all our wishes, be some danger that the intimate bond between us might be more or less shattered by the difficulties that must arise in practice from the exercise of a common protectorate? Such a break, although transitory and too unimportant in itself to injure the cause for which we stand, would, nevertheless, be so deplorable in my eyes and, in present circumstances, so disastrous, that one ought, in advance, to take all possible precautions to avert it. Second, must not the city of Constantinople, if made a republic, and the weakly-governed Turkish provinces surrounding it, undubitably become the playground for the democratic tendencies of the South Slavs, the focus of all the efforts of our opponents, and just such an opening as they desire for carrying on their intrigues in immediate proximity to our boundaries? Let us recall that we had to make an end of the independence of the city of Cracow on similar grounds although we were near enough to it to keep it under supervision. Events in Switzerland are also of a kind to serve as a warning to us, in this regard."

[134]

The definite tone of this letter must have shown the Czar that he would have to count on the full opposition of Austria if he attempted to carry out his own plans. This troubled him so much that after six days he wrote his young friend in Vienna a very long and remarkable letter, which shows that he had no longer any thoughts of a friendly settlement with the Sultan, but was exclusively occupied with the partition of Turkey. In it he sets his whole plan of attack before the Austrian monarch. He assumes that the Turk cannot hold the field for any length of time, without assistance from outside. Then, in the Czar's opinion, the moment would have come for recognizing the independence of the principalities, proclaiming the Hospodars as Princes, hereditary sovereigns, over their provinces, and inviting all the powers of Europe to recognize this independence.

> "It is highly probable that this example would react on the other Christian populations in Turkish territory, if they have not already risen; the moment then would have come for settling their destiny, too."

He then turns to the doubts expressed by Francis Joseph as to his plans for Constantinople:

> "Tell me," says the Czar, "the alternative Thou wouldst suggest, and I will tell Thee openly what I think of it. Perhaps Constantinople might be made a free city, without territorial rights; the Dardanelles being held by Thee, the Bosphorus by us. I admit

that I see stronger arguments against this than against the removal of all fortifications on the Straits."

Of course, says the Czar, there must be police supervision over Constantinople, in order to prevent emigrants (Polish and Hungarian, no doubt) from settling there. He goes on to emphasize his dislike of any extension of Russia or partition of Turkey:

"Russia does not need that, and I should view it as a misfortune and source of incalculable trouble. If, however, in the interest of Thy country Thou viewest this as necessary, I am ready to hear Thy views, in order that between ourselves, entirely between ourselves, we may arrive at mutual clearness through a frank interchange of opinions."

With the breakdown of the efforts of the Vienna cabinet to induce Turkey to submit to Russia, as the result of the determined war policy of the all-powerful English ambassador in Constantinople, Lord Stratford de Redcliffe, the Czar felt that it was absolutely essential for him to have a personal interview with the Austrian Emperor, and, if possible, secure his friendly attitude in view of the now inevitable war between Russia and Turkey. Francis Joseph had just become betrothed to Elizabeth of Bavaria, and the happy bridegroom-to-be communicates this intelligence to the Czar in a short but affectionate epistle. It is, however, highly characteristic of Francis Joseph that, even at such a time, he by no means forgets his business as ruler. He thanks the Czar for his plan of visiting him at Olmütz, and promises that, should this not come off, he will go and see him in Warsaw. As a matter of fact the meeting took place at Olmütz on September 24. The Czar allayed the apprehensions of Francis Joseph and his counsellors by the express promises that he would not dismember Turkey, that he would carry on the war only in Asia Minor, and that he would not cross the Danube. Francis Joseph expressed his conviction of the Czar's loyalty, but reiterated that any rising of the southern Slavs in the Balkan peninsula would jeopardize the peace and security of Austria, and must, therefore, be excluded. The emphatic moderation of the Czar was in no sense seriously meant, and undoubtedly inspired no conviction in Vienna. At the same time, Francis Joseph went to Warsaw with the Czar, and thither, after refusing at first, the King of Prussia likewise decided to go. The result of this meeting was the initiation of fresh efforts of mediation at Constantinople, on the part of Francis Joseph.

Whatever the mistrust felt at Vienna of the Czar, when the declaration of war against Turkey took place on October 1, 1853, no official diplomatic warning was issued to Russia against the continuation of the plans of conquest thus involved. The semi-darkness in which the foreign policy of Francis Joseph and Buol had been conducted hitherto was thickened by the decision on financial grounds, in October, 1853, to reduce the strength of the Austrian field army. This step seemed to indicate that the apprehensions felt by Francis Joseph and his government about the further development of the war, had been lulled to rest; as a matter of fact, however, those apprehensions mounted constantly. Actually this contradictory step in Viennese policy was the beginning of the whole series of grave errors of which the cabinet was guilty in relation to the European war as it unfolded. Intervention by the great Western Powers became more and more obviously inevitable; but the attitude of Francis Joseph to Russia remained perfectly dark. Yet the clarity with which he foresaw the approaching danger of European conflagration, issuing from the Russo-Turkish War, is evident in the letter he wrote to the Czar on September 15:

"While those who believe in social order everywhere contemplate with gloomy forebodings the possibility of a general conflagration, the subversive party is filled with joy and hope; I have been told that Kossuth has said he is only waiting for the moment when the course of events has dragged Austria into the war to approach the field of action and cause a new rising. The *anguish* caused me by a prospect of being forced to shed blood to destroy the revolution with which we are but now finished, can be understood by no one better than by Thee, dear friend, whose entire life has been dedicated to the welfare of Thy people. Of course I do not doubt for one moment the ultimate triumph of Thy arms, if it comes to a serious war, but I confess with entire frankness that such a victory would seem to me too dearly bought if it proved the occasion of a new flare-up of revolutionary activity in Europe and new upheavals of incalculable outcome."

In subsequent passages in this long document Francis Joseph attempts to prove to the Czar that the guarantees he is asking of the Porte, in the interest of the orthodox populations of the Turkish Empire, actually exist, in the shape of the immense power God has placed in the hands of the Czar. That is far more effective than any formal declarations of the Sultan could be. "What I have most at heart in this Oriental conflict is to prevent religious strife from being carried over into the political sphere." Here, great moderation and self-restraint is requisite on all sides, on the part of the orthodox powers as well as of the Catholic. Having taken this as his own rule of conduct, he believes he is entitled to appeal now to the Czar.

The reply of the Czar shows that he had, by now, fully worked himself into his rôle of protector of the Christians of the east, and that this was to be his line towards the Western Powers. Peace can only be restored if the Sultan makes up his mind to enter into "reasonable negotiation" directly with the Czar, through a plenipotentiary. True, the Czar is ready to show the moderation on which Francis Joseph lays stress, in so far as is consistent with the honor and interests of Russia.

"My hope is in God and in the justice of the cause I am defending, the cause of Christendom. The fanaticism that now dominates the unhappy Turks makes it almost a crusade, in which Russia defends Christianity while France and England are guilty of the infamy of fighting for the Crescent. Is it conceivable that Russia should have no allies in the holy cause it is defending?"

These last words put a very "painful" question to the young sovereign in Vienna. Plainly, the Czar hoped that Austria, as a tried ally, would support him in his orthodox crusade. Long were the discussions between Francis Joseph and Buol as to how they could insure themselves against this crusade, without going to war with Russia! Their dilemma was an evidence of the degree to which Francis Joseph and the diplomacy of his cabinet had misled the Czar as to the true intentions of Austria.

It had, meantime, become obvious to the governments and public opinion of Europe that the Western Powers had practically made up their minds to take up arms against Russia, not so much for the protection of Turkey as for the permanent reduction of Russia's supremacy in Europe, and the promotion of their own interests in the east. As is shown by communications of the Czar and his cabinet with Berlin and Vienna, at this time he still hoped, in the great conflict now imminent, to be able to count at least on the friendly neutrality of his old allies, Austria and Prussia. Because of this confidence he was ready to force an issue with the Western Powers. To Berlin, he sent his ambassador with a personal letter to his brother-in-law, King Frederick William IV, in support of the views that his cabinet had already communicated to the government of Prussia. To Vienna, at this critical juncture, he sent Count Orlow, with a holograph letter of his own to Francis Joseph, and instructions to support the ideas set forth in it by word of mouth.

Although the reply brought to the Czar from Berlin by Baron Budberg was a severe disappointment to him, he did at least receive from Frederick William IV the firm assurance that Russia could count on Prussia's maintaining strict neutrality. Count Orlow's mission to Vienna, on the other hand, was a complete failure. The first reason for this was the character of the letter sent by Nicholas through his special envoy. It crossed with a letter of Francis Joseph's dated January 7, whose contents were calculated to cause the Czar great distress, since this letter was a direct result of the decision arrived at on December 5, by the conference of powers, sitting in Vienna, to address to the Czar an invitation to appear with Turkey in some neutral city, for the purpose of peace negotiations —subject to the preliminary condition that the Danubian provinces be immediately evacuated.

This proposal incensed the Czar to the last degree, the more that it was not accompanied by any promise that the Western Powers would withdraw their fleets. Francis Joseph promised neutrality in the event of an extension of the local war in the east. But, at the same time, he stated that in so doing he was counting on the fulfillment of promises

> "which have been the basis of the line of policy I have laid down from the start. To place the strict neutrality I am determined to observe upon a solid

foundation; to resist successfully the pressure certain to be put upon me by the naval powers, once they are drawn into the fight, to compel me to change my attitude; and, finally, to protect the dignity and the interests of Austria, as is my primary duty, I must receive, on Thy part, the most definite and solemn undertaking that Thou wilst remain on the defensive on this side of the Danube; or that, should military events compel Thee to cross it, that Thou wilt not depart to the smallest degree, from Thy previous declarations, in accordance with which Thou seekest no territorial aggrandizement, no interference in the relations between the Sultan and his subjects, in a word, no rights that do not proceed out of Thy old treaties with the Porte. These declarations, with the addition that Thou wilst make no alterations in the political relatoins of the provinces of European Turkey, I must necessarily have in my hands, in the interest of Austria, which—as Thou wilt understand—must come first with me. I appeal to Thy friendship, proved to me by Thee in more than one critical moment, to accord me these guarantees. Since Thou hast declared from the beginning that Thou hadst no conquests in mind, it cannot be difficult for Thee to repeat this assurance, solemnly, in respect to Turkey in Europe."

This was a language the Czar had never yet heard from any sovereign in Europe, and which he had least of all expected to hear from his friend in Vienna. The subsequent passages in the letter, which pointed out that the maintenance of Turkey had, after all, been the core of the solemn agreement reached between the Czar and Emperor Francis at the Münchengraetz Conferences of 1833, may perhaps be attributed to the diplomatic finesse of Count Buol. They were bound to annoy Czar Nicholas excessively, and strike him as a kind of mockery. Was it not the Münchengraetz conversations that had caused him, the Czar, on his own initiative, without waiting for an appeal for help, to intervene in revolutionary Hungary?

The Czar replied at once on January 16. Despite the politeness of its form, his letter shows the ill humor of the despot, unmistakably. Francis Joseph had caused him a surprise, in which there was an admixture of pain. "Canst Thou believe," he says in his letter, "that a man of honor is double-tongued, or that he could go back upon what he has once declared to be his intention? That established, is there not something hatefully superfluous in permitting oneself a doubt of his word, once given, or asking him to repeat it? After I have bound myself before Thee and before the world, and, what is more important, after I have told my nation, that we need no conquests and seek none, is it permitted to anyone, no matter who he be, to doubt? Thou above all, who must know me, how canst Thou permit Thyself one instant's doubt of what I have once said to Thee?"

At this point in the letter one sees the Czar remembering the youth of the Austrian sovereign, and attacking him with the sharpness that springs from a sense of unjust imputation. Is he, a Czar, proud of his honor and

[143]

his trustworthiness, to take such a suggestion quietly from a Habsburg hardly grown to man's estate? The essential, however, is that the Czar refuses the guarantees Francis Joseph asks for. No reference, therefore, to the next point, the immediate point at issue: the evacuation of the Danubian principalities, which Nicholas by now regarded as conquered ground, and Francis Joseph was not pre-pared to recognize as Russian at any price. When, in his letters, the Czar comes to the Emperor's advice not to cross the Danube, he breaks out into violent attacks on the Western Powers, whose fleets are protecting the Tur-kish Empire. The Czar "will be compelled, if Anglo-French impertinence and folly continue to wax against us, to take extreme measures." Russia will free the Chris-tians of the fetters which to-day repress their natural long-ing for liberty. All the passionate self-consciousness of the universally-dreaded and all-powerful Czar breaks out when he asks whether he is to see a formal ally of the Turk in the young Austrian Emperor whose throne he once saved.

"Art Thou really to make the Turks' cause Thy own? Emperor Apostolical, does Thy conscience per-mit it? If it be so, good; then Russia alone shall raise the Holy Cross and follow its commandments. If Thou wert to range Thyself with the Crescent against me, I say to Thee, that would be a parricidal war."

Now comes the reply to the reference to München-graetz:

[144]

"Thy grandfather of glorious and honored memory never took such views. The act we signed at Münchengraetz on my proposal had quite another purpose. It laid down that so long as Turkey remained what it then was, not Anglo-French, nothing could be more favorable for us than its maintenance, as it then was. . . . This act further laid it down that, as neighbors, and therefore most nearly concerned, we would, in the event of circumstances that might lead to the fall of the Ottoman Empire, do nothing without a thorough agreement between ourselves. Now, my dear friend, that moment is not yet come. And yet I have constantly said openly to Thee what I had in mind to do, at any given moment. Could I treat Thee with more consideration? . . . But if Thou imaginest that I can ever sink to bringing the liberated Christians back under the Moslem yoke, hasten to clear such thoughts out of Thy mind, and go over to my enemies. God will be our judge, but I shall not quail."

Later on in his letter the Czar recommends Count Orlow to the Emperor, saying that he may trust him as he would the Czar himself. But this envoy-extraordinary encountered, from the first, a completely non-committal attitude on the Emperor's part. The Czar's promises did not satisfy him or Count Buol. In the closing words of his letter the Czar described the moment as a very serious one, inasmuch as a decision had to be taken whether or no the alliance between the two empires, which had lasted for over forty years, was now to dissolve. Francis Joseph, therefore, was under no illusion as to the fact that a very grave issue in his foreign policy now confronted him.

The forms of friendliness were maintained; but the request preferred by the Czar through Orlow for unconditional neutrality on the part of Austria was rejected. The imperial cabinet further decided that a policy corresponding with the independent interests of the Danubian monarchy must be pursued throughout in relation to Russia. In a conversation with Count Orlow, Francis Joseph stated plainly that any assertion of Russian suzerainty over the Christian provinces of the Balkan peninsula, in the form of an extended protectorate of the orthodox Czar, would be dangerous to Austria, and, therefore, inadmissible. Throughout he insisted that the Czar carry on the war in Asia only, without crossing the Danube. If the Czar rejected these conditions, Francis Joseph must reserve freedom of action.

The policy that Francis Joseph thus laid down was a bold but realistic one. It certainly completed the breach with Nicholas personally and with the might of Russia. The great question was now, what was to be Francis Joseph's next step? Obviously it was inevitable that Austria should unite with the Western Powers. Buol was unweariedly occupied in conferences with their representatives, working out possible conditions of peace between Russia and Turkey. Here, of course, a purely self-interested policy had to be pursued. The Czar meanwhile himself precipitated declarations of war by France and England. Both Napoleon and Palmerston counted on securing Austria's adherence within a brief space of time. But Austria had, from the start, one great danger before its eyes—Napoleon III, the old ally of the Italian Carbonari, might try to work upon it by the threat of raising revolution in Lombardy and Venetia. It was well known in Europe that the new Cæsar of the French regarded himself as heir to his great uncle, and notably so in the case of Italy. In his writings and speeches he had made self-determination the slogan of the most modern type of radicalism, in France, and above all in Italy. The slogan had been taken up not only in Italy, but by the Magyar emigrés and by the infant south Slav, or as it was then called, Illyrian, nationalist movement. From the beginning, and especially since the breach with Russia, the danger point for Francis Joseph was this weakest section of his realm.

With this we are at the beginning of that unhappy policy of the young Emperor which in detail reveals both his character as a human being and his political thinking. He determined on the action that constitutes the capital error of statesmanship—to seek at one and the same time to be friends with both parties to the war. He sought, therefore, to go half-way to meet each of the opponents between whom he stood. He was and remained set in his resolve to wage war against the Czar. Nor did he ever seriously contemplate a formal alliance with Napoleon. His action followed completely the authentic Habsburg model, characterized, some two decades earlier, by the immortal Grillparzer, in his historical tragedy "The Habsburg Brothers' Feud," in the words

> "Here is the curse upon our noble house,
> On half-trod ways to half-done deeds
> We strive uncertain, with but half our means."

Francis Joseph was by no means, at bottom, a weak character. But he was one of those men who, lacking the resolute drive given by a passionate aspiration, an immovable conviction, a deep belief in some great idea, or even the force of imagination, are inclined to substitute for it the bare calculus of what one may call tangible, immediate need. Now, in his youth, and right on up to his death, Francis Joseph was dominated, spiritually and intellectually, by the notion of maintaining intact the might of the dynasty whose head he had become through his accession to the throne, and preserving the foundations of this might, namely, all the territories of his realm, as a unit. It is only with this in mind that his actions in these days of extraordinarily difficult decision in foreign policy can be rightly appraised. He hoped to attain this end by giving himself *wholly* to *neither* of the two warring parties.

In view of his anxiety about Italy, Napoleon seemed to him the immediate and more dangerous enemy. For he knew that the Czar would not attack him, hardly could attack him. Therefore, he gradually drew nearer to Napoleon, one step at a time, always seeking to keep the threads of friendly understanding with Russia unbroken. This line of action once laid down, he held to it with all his force. He resisted the efforts of both parties at his court and among his own generals, as throughout the world in the years 1853-56, one clamoring for a war against Russia, the other, for alliance with Prussia and Russia against Napoleon.

The next serious step he took was the momentous summons addressed on June 3, 1854, to the Czar, demanding of Russia the speediest possible evacuation of the Danubian principalities, and refusing permission to it to cross the Danube. Francis Joseph further sought to come to an understanding with Prussia, by way of guaranteeing this policy. Thanks to personal correspondence with his uncle, Frederick William IV, and the despatch of General Hess, Radetzky's admirable assistant, to Berlin, the Vienna cabinet succeeded in concluding a defensive alliance with Prussia. Subsequent negotiations widened this to an offensive alliance, in the event of Russian armies occupying the Balkans. An effort was also made to get the German confederation to be a party to these agreements. Russia's isolation in Europe was thus complete, and the breach between the Czar and Francis Joseph irretrievable. In the upshot, Nicholas had to evacuate Moldavia and Wallachia. This was facilitated when, after some delay, the Western Powers, having definitely entered on the war, made the Crimea their point of attack, and, from now on, the centre of action.

The state of tension between Russia and Austria brought about by the increasing bitterness felt in the Russian court and Russian society generally, by the sharpening antagonism of the eastern and western parties at the Vienna court, and the progressive increase in the financial burdens involved in the inevitable mobilization of Austria, was hardly distinguishable from open hostility.

(2) *The European War and Francis Joseph's Mediation*

Francis Joseph's diplomacy made Austrian foreign policy more and more complicated; its position grew more and more difficult. On August 8 he joined in signing the note drawn up in Vienna by the Western Powers, which set out under four heads the necessary conditions to be observed by Russia for the restoration of peace, and at the same time demanded an alteration of the Dardanelles Treaty of 1842. This incensed the Czar and society in Russia against him to the point of fury. The Prussian King attempted to convince the Czar of Austria's love of peace, and to soften his indignation with his young friend, declaring himself ready to answer for Francis Joseph's undertaking no war against Russia. The Czar himself, however, began to perceive that owing, as he believed, to the attitude of Austria, his policy was in grave danger. On August 26, Nicholas wrote to his brother-in-law that every bond between him and Francis Joseph was broken. No change in the Czar's mood was produced by the fact that, in the autumn of 1854, the Danubian principalities were smoothly evacuated and thereupon Austrian troops of occupation held the territory between the Russians and the Turks. Nicholas saw in all this only the working out of

[150]

the Austrian policy of neutrality; it was this that had cheated him of success.

Francis Joseph's policy was so far successful that Russia was compelled to abandon the Czar's plans of overrunning the Balkans and revolutionizing the orthodox peoples in the Turkish Empire. On the other hand, however, the pressure of the Western Powers on Francis Joseph and his minister, Count Buol, to enter into a definite alliance, became more and more uncomfortable and dangerous. Long afterwards, when the tragedies of his family life lay heavy on him, Francis Joseph complained that he had known little happiness. He may well have recalled the difficult and dangerous circumstances that surrounded his realm on the day—April 24, 1854—when he stood with his bride, radiant in youth and loveliness, before the altar of the Augustinian Church in Vienna. The weeks of his honeymoon were darkened by vast military preparations. By the winter of 1853, three army corps had been mobilized in southern Hungary. Further mobilization follows: on May 15, Francis Joseph, as supreme war lord, ordered the formation of a second army, of four army corps, in Galicia, as well as a second extraordinary calling up of conscripts from the realm as a whole. The huge expense of this mobilization—the entire army budget was used up in the first three months of 1854—increased the depreciation of Austrian paper from 108 to 134; the issue of a huge forced loan was considered and, in the summer, actually carried out.

But the troubles and complaints of the finance minister seem hardly to have perturbed the young Emperor or

Count Buol. Francis Joseph showed, for the first time, that complete indifference to the financial distress caused to his ministers by his foreign policy, which belonged to his undeveloped comprehension of civil life in general and his almost total lack of appreciation of economic problems in any form. Although he was, later, to learn to take the representations and warnings of his finance minister far more seriously, he was, in this respect, thoroughly the monarch of the old school. Actually, the huge armaments piled up against Russia in the years 1854 and 1855 created lasting difficulties for Austrian and Hungarian finance; right down to the nineties the economic life of the empire and the country suffered from financial results of Francis Joseph's diplomacy in these fatal years—a diplomacy uncertain in itself and impossible of understanding either by the cabinets of the other powers or the people of Austria. It was the policy that was so expensive; technical faults in the finance itself counted for comparatively little, on balance.

Both in relation to Prussia and to Germany Austria's diplomatic position got steadily worse. In Berlin, despite the erratic policy of the unhappy King, which swayed uncertainly between his love for his brother-in-law and sister in Petersburg, and his ancient, often positively subservient attitude to Vienna, the Russian party had undoubtedly won the upper hand. The hostility of the Junker party to Austria came to the fore there, and, of course, on the floor of the Federal Diet at Frankfort. Now, too, Francis Joseph's policy came for the first time into sharp and definite opposition with Otto von Bismarck-Schönhausen, who had learned to know the young monarch at the time of his visits to Vienna and Ofen in 1852.

Bismarck, and Bismarck's unwearied and cunning campaign among the German princelings of the federation, doomed to failure Buol's attempts to bring the whole military force of the confederation, including Prussia, under Austrian leadership for the event of war with Russia, now the barely concealed aim of his policy. There can be no doubt that, in the summer and autumn of 1854, as the result of the steady aiming of his anti-Russian policy at the idea of war, Buol did make the Emperor, absent at the time, for many weeks, from Vienna, waver in his hitherto firm determination never to take arms against Nicholas. Special envoys were sent to Prussia, and, as the result of their negotiation, the alliance of April 20 was extended. Most important, the renewed efforts of Napoleon III to induce Austria to enter into alliance with the Western Powers, gained a partial success, thanks in the main to the energetic efforts of Hübner, the Austrian ambassador in Paris, a staunch friend of this idea.

Since the summer of 1854, Austrian foreign policy had inclined, suspiciously, to the side of the Western Powers. In the autumn, the Emperor instructed General Hess, commanding the Austrian troops in the Danubian principalities, not to oppose the Turks if they should cross the Danube to open an offensive against Russia. On October 22, he issued orders for the mobilization of the entire imperial army. Within a very short time, 450,000 men were under arms, facing the Russian troops in Galicia as well as in Bukovina and Transylvania.

[153]

When the Russian army sustained a fresh defeat in the Crimea, on November 5, at Inkerman, all Europe expected Austria to enter the war on the side of the Western Powers and so compel Russia to accept the peace conditions that had once again been formulated. Czar Nicholas actually began to divide his army into two portions, one designed to wage war on Austria through Poland and South Russia. It seemed as though a crisis tremendous as that of 1812 were imminent. The Czar in his manifesto to Russia appealed, as then, for the rousing of national resistance to the west. Austria's young Emperor plainly had the decision over his own destiny and that of the whole of Europe in his hands. His action must decide whether Europe were to cast down the semi-Asiatic empire of Czar Nicholas from the pinnacle of power it had attained since the fall of Napoleon I and maintained and consolidated in the last four decades.

Nowhere was the young Emperor's decision awaited with such tension as in London and Paris. The frightful losses of the Allies before Sebastopol and the decimation they had suffered through disease and privation, had compelled both England and France to send constant reinforcements. There was deep resentment among the peoples of both countries over the sufferings of their soldiers. Napoleon III, in personal letters, pressed more and more strongly for the entry of Austria into the war. Buol went so far as to inform the French government that he was ready to conclude an alliance with France and England on the basis of the proposals worked out by Hübner, the Austrian ambassador in Paris.

On November 18, Napoleon received a holograph letter from Francis Joseph which, though very vaguely couched, again put Austrian neutrality in the foreground. At the same time, however, came the news that on November 21 Francis Joseph had ordered the mobilization of his whole army. But when Napoleon, in his reply, practically threatened Francis Joseph with a breach between the Western Powers and Austria, the Emperor wavered again, since the Western Powers' threat to withdraw their ambassadors from Vienna had been followed by the offer of Count Buol's resignation. The upshot was the alliance concluded, on December 2, between Austria and the western belligerents—Buol's diplomatic masterpiece; correctly described by Friedjung as a veritable fox's trap, for it was capable of any number of different interpretations and could be circumvented in innumerable ways.

It is certainly astonishing that Napoleon can still have thought it possible to involve Francis Joseph seriously in war with Russia. The explanation no doubt is that London and Paris took the bends and turns of Austrian policy as proving that it was, in the last resort, capable of anything. If one result was that Viennese policy was more and more distrusted by the West, another was that Francis Joseph drew down upon himself personally the bitter hatred of Czar Nicholas. When he received the news of the conclusion of Austria's alliance with the Western Powers he gave voice to his bitterness by ordering two presents of Francis Joseph's, a statue and a portrait of the Emperor, to be removed from his workroom. The statue he presented to his valet. When he received the

Austrian ambassador, Count Valentine Esterházy, he asked him whether he knew which had been the two stupidest kings of Poland, and answered his own question, saying, "The first was King John Sobieski, who liberated Vienna (1683) from the siege laid by the Turks, the second am I. For both of us . . . saved the House of Habsburg."

Another far from desired result of his policy was presented to Francis Joseph. His uncle Frederick William IV was violently incensed by the alliance of December 2, 1854, concluded without his knowledge. He considered that he had been betrayed by Austria, and, from this time on, gave his ear almost exclusively to the Russophile Junker party and their representatives in his government and at court. The guarantee, received by Francis Joseph on the part of the Western Powers, of Austria's possession of Italy for the duration of the war, was more than offset by the admission of the Kingdom of Piedmont-Sardinia into the western alliance in 1855, on condition that Piedmont bound itself to send an auxiliary corps to participate in the war in the Crimea.

Needless here to follow the divagations of the Viennese cabinet's policy of "half and half" through the year 1855. Count Buol, although in the bad graces of the Emperor, continued unweariedly holding peace conferences with the representatives of England and France and sending out one diplomatic note after another designed to convince all the cabinets of the disinterestedness of Austrian policy, while busy endeavoring to induce the German confederation to prepare to mobilize all the federation troops with a view to entering the war under Austria's leadership. Ultimately all these attempts of Buol's broke on the resistance of the Prussian envoy, Herr von Bismarck, who was able to hold not only Prussia but all the confederation princes aloof from the Austrian alliance with the Western Powers. The unhappy consequences of thus bringing the "German question" into the open, for the first time since 1848, seemed to have been suspected neither by Count Buol nor the young Emperor. Austria's diplomatic defeat in Frankfort was Bismarck's first great victory: moreover, the struggles of this period gave his views of the German question their decisive turn. For the future, this was to be the most important result, for Austria, of Francis Joseph's Crimean policy.

The alliance with the Western Powers entered into by Francis Joseph in December divides Austria's action during the Crimean War into two parts. In the first, Francis Joseph did everything to make a lasting enemy of Russia, inasmuch as he chose a policy of armed neutrality, in order to keep Russia out of the Balkan peninsula, while constantly endeavoring to mediate between the belligerents. In the second, the Austrian cabinet was equally busy evading the pressure of the Western Powers to draw it into active participation in the war, with the object of proving to the Czar the reality of Francis Joseph's friendship for him. If these are the two main strophes in the diplomatic hero-song composed by the young Emperor, its concluding stanza is his rejection of Napoleon III's proposal of a permanent alliance with France.

The way in which Austria slipped out of the alliance of December 2, 1854, after England rejected the peace formula which had been drawn up by Francis Joseph in person and Napoleon's foreign minister, Drouyn de Luys, is perhaps the most characteristic episode in the course of the foreign policy of himself and Count Buol. And there was genuine diplomatic skill in the manner in which Buol succeeded, at the end of 1855, in formulating conditions as between the Western Powers and Russia, on which, at the Paris Congress of March, 1856, the young Czar actually concluded peace. At the same time Francis Joseph and his minister again showed their lack of real foresight for they could not resist making the peace conditions so severe, for Russia, that far from Austria's getting any thanks for the restoration of peace, it earned Russia's increased enmity.

Any plans the Austrian cabinet may have cherished for the acquisition of the Danubian principalities had long been futile, in view of the opposition of both France and England. Austria, indeed, had to consent, immediately after the Peace Congress, to the union of the two principalities in a single state. Here was a heavy defeat for a foreign policy initiated with the slogan of protection for the interests of the realm, and ending with empty hands, the loss of thirty thousand men, sacrificed to disease in the army, and the most appalling financial dislocation.

Austria, indeed, suffered more than Russia did as the result of this uncertain policy of endless mediation between the Western Powers and the Czar. In the course of the kaleidoscopic military and diplomatic changes of the campaign of 1853-56, Francis Joseph and Count Buol succeeded in getting at odds with every one of the great powers.

Russia, allied with Austria ever since the time of Catherine the Great, felt that it had treacherously been brought down by the policy of Francis Joseph at a crisis in its national history. The feelings of Russian society in this regard speak eloquently in the letter in which the new Czar, Alexander II, replied to the condolences of Francis Joseph on the death of Czar Nicholas I on March 17, 1855.

"Tu comprends donc facilement ce que les évènements politiques de cette dernière année ont dû produire sur son cœur—il en a été navré—car au lieu de retrouver en toi l'ami et l'allié fidèle, sur lequel il comptait et qu'il aimait comme son propre fils, il t'a vu suivre une marche politique qui te rapprochait de plus en plus de nos ennemis et qui nous conduira, si elle ne change pas, infailliblement à une guerre fratricide et Tu en rendras compte à Dieu!"

Even at the Congress of Paris the Russian plenipotentiaries formed friendly relationships with France and England—it was Austria that seemed to be their real enemy there. In England Metternich had created a certain feeling of confidence in the House of Austria, that had not been quite lost during Palmerston's struggle against Schwarzenberg; but recent experiences with the Vienna cabinet had created profound ill-feeling in England.

Everyone who knew the mind of Napoleon III knew that he could not get over Francis Joseph's refusal to enter the alliance, so long and earnestly offered him by France, and take part in the war. The Reminiscences of Count Hübner, Austrian ambassador in Paris, prove how much Napoleon took to heart the fact that he had been put off by Francis Joseph with mere promises. The enmity thus roused in Napoleon made itself felt in the many trials and difficulties of treaty-making in Paris. Reconciliation of the Paris and the Vienna cabinets proved a most laborious matter. Worst of all, the Kingdom of Piedmont-Sardinia, the despised foe of 1848, had emerged triumphant from the conflagration, with the enhanced prestige of an ally in war of the great Western Powers, and their friend.

Later, Francis Joseph was to learn how grave a change had come over the relative positions of Austria and Prussia in the German confederation, as the result of the hole-and-corner work of the Vienna cabinet and its mistakes, when, threatened by Napoleon and his ally, Piedmont, he in vain attempted to get Prussia and the German confederation to take part in the war to safeguard Austria's possessions in Italy. Austria and its absolutist Emperor stood completely isolated in Europe, and that at a juncture that left no one in doubt that the two basic problems of its European position—the German question, and the question of Italian unity—must, in the near future, arise again in a form most threatening for the house of Habsburg-Lorraine.

(3) *"Historic Ingratitude," and Its Consequences*

In view of the position of Austria at the conclusion of the Peace of Paris, the question must arise: What was the guiding idea impelling Francis Joseph to pursue, for more than three years, a policy which he must have realized was bound to bring with it the greatest evil, in the loss of friendship with Russia, and could hardly secure the compensating advantage in the west of a consolidation of his Italian possessions? Was it the counsel of Count Buol, indolent, at times excitable, but normally a mere man of routine, satisfied with the superficial aspect of things, which strengthened the Emperor in such a policy? We know that this was not the case. We know, on the contrary, that Count Buol was not sympathetic to the young Emperor, and had no authority with him. Nevertheless, Francis Joseph kept him in office, and this although he must constantly have heard his minister's views and plans criticized on various sides.

He here displayed a strong habit, later to prove often detrimental, of sticking to a minister the more firmly because he was attacked from outside. This peculiarity of his, as a ruler, derives, like so much else, from his readily injured pride and sensitiveness to criticism. As a very young man, he had the naïve idea that no other person could have anything to say as against the view of things taken by him, and by persons working in his name. This is, in the last analysis, a natural deduction from the absolutist idea, which had grown so strong in Francis

Joseph and had to meet its severest test in the fearful difficulties of the European situation.

Events then transformed his entire surroundings into a sort of diplomatic battlefield. Most of the generals, with Marshals Radetzky and Windischgrätz at their head, were hotly opposed to the Russophobe policy of Buol, behind which the Emperor stood with most of his diplomatic resolution, but only half his heart. The more intimate official relations became between Austria and the Western Powers, the more strongly did this group oppose his policy. The Austrian ambassador at Constantinople, Baron von Bruck, later to be minister of finance, strove mainly for the closest coöperation of the Vienna cabinet with Prussia and Germany and openly criticized the diplomatic aims and methods of Buol, which were constantly causing personal offense to King Frederick William IV and strengthening the Russophile Junker party at the Berlin court.

Alexander Bach, the first mind in the Vienna government, sedulously supported—mainly through the Vienna press, thrown open to him for this purpose—rapprochement with France. Essentially, he agreed with Buol, and, like him, was ready to wage war on Russia. In high military circles men would openly say that they would rather resign their commissions than fight the Russians. General Hess, who commanded the mobilized army corps, proved himself a skilful military diplomat in averting armed conflict with Russia. The young Emperor listened to all these contradictory opinions, observed the endless struggle between the two parties which divided his court and government and set army chiefs in opposition to ministers and ambassadors, and sided now with this group and then with the other. His decisions, often over-hasty, kept the diplomacy of Europe on tenterhooks.

From time to time, Francis Joseph met diplomatic reverses. Tenaciously, however, and with a coolness astonishing in a young man in the middle of the twenties, he held fast to the main lines of his foreign policy, i.e., the idea that Austria had interests of its own to protect in the east, and that for that reason he must maintain a position of independence between the two adversaries, between west and east. Since, however, this involved a constant dispersion of diplomatic, financial, and military resources, and prevented his power ever being put behind any single decisive action the result was, finally, that "fatal confusion" of which old Prince Metternich said that "he had never seen anything like it." Yet his chief counsellors were men of ability, like General Hess and Baron von Bruck, not Count Buol, on whom Prince Metternich turned such annihilating criticism. "The consequences of any and every action are hidden from Count Buol. He sees what is right in front of him; of what is coming he sees nothing. He is at the mercy of personal impressions, attraction, and repulsion, and since he has no conception of the need of keeping a plan of action before his mind, he conducts his politics like a forester who has no idea of orderly tree-cutting. One way or the other, wood is felled—but what about the forest?"

This criticism was as applicable to the young monarch as to his minister.

On these three years of the Crimean War, we possess a body of valuable evidence by good observers, which, taken together, gives a distinct portrait of Francis Joseph at this period. All note, as a specially distinguishing trait, that the young man was or appeared self-controlled and self-contained to a notable degree. Hübner, Austrian ambassador in Paris, who himself took a leading part with Napoleon and his ministers in weaving the diplomatic web that led Francis Joseph to break with Russia, was invited, in the spring of 1854, to attend the Emperor's betrothal ceremonies in Vienna. This invitation, characteristically enough, issued not from Francis Joseph himself, but from Count Buol, chief pillar of the government's official policy. Although, as Count Hübner relates, he saw the Emperor every day, he was only once bidden to audience with him. In his reminiscences he gives the following account of this occasion:

"The Emperor viewed the situation from a correct and lofty standpoint. The fact that his sympathies for the person of Czar Nicholas are obviously weakened, does not appear to affect his judgment upon him. Although he speaks with extreme tenderness of his personal relations to the Czar of Russia, he uses the clear, precise and prosaic language of a man of business about the interests involved. He regrets frankly a tension that is equivalent to a break, has not forgotten the great services rendered by Russia through its intervention in 1849, but no exaggerated pricks of conscience will prevent him from doing his duty to his peoples. 'Duty' was the dominant note in this part of our conversation. Again and again the Emperor reverted to the concern caused him by this quarrel with his old friend. Orlow's mission, and the arrogant bearing of this envoy, seem to have offended him, deeply. 'Up to then,' he added with a smile, 'I wanted, like the good boy I was, to believe Russia's assurances; after Orlow's arrival I gave up being a good boy.'"

Here is the young absolutist to the life, "prosaically," and disturbed by no deep sensibility, pursuing the interests of his realm, like a realistic, political man of business. There was, so Hübner relates, no second arranged audience, since it was prevented by the Emperor's going heathcock shooting, a sport to which he was much addicted. In general, Hübner says, the Emperor, in these days, "presented a picture of health, youth, and happiness, and was so obviously in love with his young wife that it was a pleasure to behold."

This description is confirmed by the impressions of Duke Ernest, brother of the husband of Queen Victoria of England, at the time of his visit to Vienna in May, 1854.

"I find," he says in his recollections, "a great change for the better in the Emperor, since I saw him last; he has become much stronger, more free and definite in his movements. Despite the dark outlook and the political frost, one felt a sort of joyful excitement about the bright young monarch: his domestic happiness seemed to have had a most happy effect on his temper. The more I saw of him the more convinced I became that he has a remarkable talent for governing and will give the old Habsburg state a great position. In His Majesty one finds united a passionless and calm judgment of things and a firm resolution in executing decisions once arrived at. In this last respect, particularly, his growth is marked: he has now reached the full height of his consciousness of power.

"Keen and frank as is his entry into discussion of affairs, he seems to have laid down certain quite definite limits beyond which he is personally disinclined to go. Details and specific decisions he tends to remit to his ministers. In this method of handling business, one notes the old tradition of Austrian government in close alliance with natural, personal intelligence."

It is worth noting that Duke Ernest says that the Emperor openly regretted the existence of a very large Russophile party both in Vienna and Berlin. At home, according to Francis Joseph, they knew how little "logic chopping" was likely to influence him. Speaking of Berlin, he said, "They do very odd things, politically, there." Characteristic, too, was his declaration that, as against France, he could count fully on Prussia. "He wished he had many such good Austrians as King Frederick William in his monarchy." But when Duke Ernest spoke about

Napoleon with the Emperor, he saw that the latter became very restless, when, as the "voluntary agent" of Napoleon among the German Princes he told the young Emperor that Napoleon took Austria's acquisition of the Danubian principalities quite for granted, and that, so far as Bosnia and Serbia went, he left the Austrian government a free hand. Francis Joseph's retort is, again, characteristic. He said that all these countries were unproductive, and would be rather an expense than an asset to the state. The Emperor's disquiet became marked when the Duke gave him to understand that Napoleon thought that Milan was even more of a burden for Austria than those eastern provinces could be. Most decidedly did Francis Joseph reject any idea of concessions on Italian soil. Duke Ernest received the conviction, which he communicated to Napoleon in due course, that there was no hope of the realization of his favorite idea of causing Austria to exchange its Italian for eastern possessions.

These accounts show how completely Francis Joseph relied upon himself in the conduct of the destinies of his realm. At this time, however, in sharp contrast to his later practice, he gave attentive ear to every counsellor of weight, and even went so far as to conceal much of what he discussed and did from his minister, Count Buol. Indeed, his self-confidence was so pronounced that he was convinced that he could best form his own judgment as to what ought to be done by listening to a variety of views. This self-confidence he owed to Felix Schwarzenberg. At this time, that model was still before him, in all its freshness, and he tried to imitate it. Schwarzenberg, as depicted by Hübner, the most intimate of his colleagues, was always ready to listen tranquilly to opinions the most opposed to his own, since he was sure of finding his own way at the right moment and then pursuing it, unafraid, to the end. The young Emperor tried to do exactly as his teacher would have done: needless to set out the reasons why success was denied him.

Thus, in foreign policy, the Emperor was, personally, the leader not the led, from the first stage in every transaction. In sharp distinction to his method in domestic politics, he, in this sphere, kept the threads of ministerial action completely in his own hands, and therefore could not be officially deceived as to the real facts and the state of public opinion, as was the case in economic, military, and other departments. Buol, of course, played his part in poisoning relations between the courts of St. Petersburg and Vienna, but it was Francis Joseph himself who gave truth to Schwarzenberg's cynical phrase about the ingratitude of Austria, at which the world should stare.

Schwarzenberg was an excellent prophet because he knew how irksome, not to himself only, but to his young master, was the sense of obligation to the Czar. Francis Joseph's native pride, both personal and dynastic, which his mother had done so much to strengthen, was certainly hurt by this idea of obligation. Frequent meetings with the Czar at Warsaw, Olmütz, and Vienna may well have exacerbated and deepened this wound. Prince Bismarck once, apropos of a criticism of William II, spoke of the danger for princes of frequent meetings between monarchs. Throughout Europe, Nicholas I, despite the *preux chevalier* touch of his external bearing, was hated at every court and feared at most. Young Francis Joseph had to honor him as an affectionate, fatherly friend and firm supporter of his own dominion; but, from the very beginning, the highly self-conscious young Habsburg was here in contact with the *one* man in the world who made complete freedom of movement impossible for him. And, secretly, he resented this.

The Czar's letters to his wife show how little he liked the court of Vienna, and how repugnant the devout Catholicism of the two Empresses and of Archduchess Sophia was to the orthodox demi-God. Further, the Czar had an old grievance against the Viennese court, for the failure—again, on religious grounds—of his favorite plan of marrying his beautiful daughter Olga to the Austrian Archduke Stephen. Of course the Czar, on his side, may often enough have given offense in Vienna; it was hardly avoidable, in view of the heightened sensitiveness of members of old dynasties in mutual intercourse.

Finally, Francis Joseph was a monarch in the twenties. Every trait in him of military and dynastic self-esteem resented the fetters of gratitude which Russia had, as it were, laid upon him in the face of all the world. He may have heard Prince Schwarzenberg say, often enough, that, in the policy of Europe, there never had been gratitude between peoples and rulers, nor ever would be. It is not astonishing that he should have regarded the Czar's occupation of the Danubian principalities as an injury to a vital interest of the Austrian monarchy.

The slogan of Austrian trading interests in the Near

East had just come into force. And, anyhow, the thirties
and forties of the nineteenth century had seen a great development in both Austrian and south German trade with
the Levant and Turkey, both via the lower Danube and
by sea, via Trieste. Both in Vienna and in Ofen-Pest,
Frederick List, in a notable series of lectures, had stressed
the economic importance of trade with the southeast.
There is ample evidence, in the literature published in
southern Germany in these years, that the states bordering
Austria on the east were beginning to be regarded as of
very great significance for the whole future of trade with
Turkey. Austrian policy made it an obvious duty for
Francis Joseph to prevent the Czar from annexing the
Danubian principalities and the lower Danube to Russia.
There he was entirely in the right.

His great mistake was first that, completely informed
as to the Czar's plans, he behaved, both in his correspondence with the Czar and in the action of his cabinet, as
though he did not understand the Czar's real intentions
at all, and second, that he failed to make it quite clear to
the Czar, in advance, that he would use the whole power
of Austria to resist any effort of his to carry his orthodox
crusade against the Turks beyond the borders of the Danubian principalities. Francis Joseph could, moreover, have
counted on the help of Germany, if only he had made it
clear to himself from the outset that Prussian policy could
hardly contemplate a war against the brother-in-law of
Frederick William IV. He, therefore, failed to achieve the
preliminary essenital of a successful policy of self-interest, i.e., the choice of the right moment in which to come

[170]

out clearly against the self-interest of his adversary. Further, he lacked the resolution to reckon, from the start, with the final consequence of the real opposition of states, namely, war.

Apart from the purely personal faults in this policy, which may be excused on the grounds of Francis Joseph's youth and limited experience, there is another, even more important circumstance. It is true that when Nicholas showed his hand against Turkey and thus inevitably drew down the hostility both of England and of France, there was a real possibility of a coalition of the whole of Europe against the Czar, as envisaged in London, as well as in Paris and in Vienna, in the year 1854. More than that, the intolerable arrogance of Russian policy made the policy pursued by Germany and by Austria entirely natural. Natural, however, from the standpoint of those peoples and parties in Europe who found the reason for this arrogance the despotism of the Czar in his own country, and therefore condemned the "rule of the knout" outright from the standpoint of western liberalism.

Germany was the vital point. Here, through family connection, the Czar was supreme in a series of the middling and smaller courts. He further enjoyed a powerful support in the Prussian Junker party and at the Prussian court. But everything in Germany that had been, overtly or covertly, liberal since 1848, that is to say the whole of civilian opinion throughout north and south Germany, loathed the Czar and his régime, and was ready to impose great sacrifices on Germany if only Nicholas I, the head and fount of German reaction, could be cast down from his pedestal. What had made it possible for Prussia and Austria to destroy in 1848 the German national parliament at Frankfort, the Reichstag in Vienna, and the first democratic Diet in Berlin? The fact that the terrible Russian Czar stood behind the Habsburgs and the Hohenzollerns, and the other kings and dukes.

But, how could Francis Joseph have assumed the rôle of a leader of Germany, of the whole of Germany, against Russia in its struggle with the Western Powers? How could he, who, but two years ago, had swept aside the constitution given to his people, lock, stock, and barrel, with perfect sang-froid, now organize a coalition of the whole west and the German center of the continent, against the "hereditary enemy" of the constitutional idea? He, busy at that moment in fastening the modern system of autocracy created for him by Schwarzenberg, Kübeck and Alexander Bach, on to every part of life in his own realm, and repressing, throughout its area, every tendency to modern political thought or modern political freedom, by the use of a military gendarmerie.

Stung by private resentment, Francis Joseph was moved to antagonism toward the Czar as and when he injured and jeopardized vital Austrian political and economic interests. In this frame, he pursued the familiar course of European diplomacy and achieved a momentary success. But to make lasting use of this success, he would have had to do one of two things. He might have thrown the whole of his strength into the scale; played the dominant part in an allied defeat of Russia that the geographical position of his empire would have allowed; and seized the fruits of victory by incorporating the Danubian principalities and the mouth of the Danube in his own dominion. The costs of such action in men and money would not have been relatively much greater than the sacrifices ultimately entailed by the mobilization of his entire army for the mere purpose of an effective armed neutrality. The other alternative was for Francis Joseph to have avoided war and even the threat of armed force. This he could have done had he, realizing, either of his own knowledge or through the advice of some great statesman as counsellor, the facts of conditions in Europe, fundamentally altered his own internal policy both in Austria and in Hungary, and then come forward as a liberal prince to take the leadership of Germany into his own hands. He might then have broken the Russophile policy, widely detested both in Prussia and in Germany generally, of the Manteuffel ministry, and the "Kreuzzeitung" party, which, at the time, dominated more and more completely the unstable mind of the Prussian King.

Any such line of thought is idle. Its premise did not exist—a young Emperor of Austria with a view of his time and of the world that corresponded to that of his liberal contemporaries throughout Europe. Neither was there any Hohenzollern in Prussia capable of or inclined to such views of Prussian and German policy, although the heir to the Prussian throne, Prince William, took a big step to the left of the old Hohenzollern tradition during the Crimean War, and came out strongly against Russian supremacy and his brother's acceptance of it. But the monarchs of the old Europe of the nineteenth century never had these long and clear views of the future.

A hundred years earlier Prussia had possessed, in Frederick II, the single crowned statesman of first-rate mind; but dynastic history shows no heredity of political intelligence. The middle of the nineteenth century had thrown up a Prussian nobleman, already active in politics, who foresaw, very clearly, the possibilities of such action from the center of Europe as would counteract the power of Russia. He, however, had already reached the conclusion that, from the conservative and Prussian point of view, the correct policy was the contrary one, and consisted rather in such a temporary limitation of Russia by the powers of the West as would keep Russian friendship for the Berlin court available to be used at the right moment for a settlement of the German question in an anti-Austrian sense. Prussia, after all, owed its defeat, at Olmütz, to the fact that Francis Joseph, in his struggle against Radowitz's policy of Prussian-German unity, had had the friendship of Nicholas I and the power of Russia at his back.

The course of international politics in nineteenth century Europe resembles a stream which, apparently motionless, nevertheless moves forward in various adjacent channels whose waters, uniting from time to time, raise its level and so provide the necessary force to create mighty changes in the relations of power, the ideas of peoples, and the tendencies of governments. The Crimean War was such a moment of confluence of historic forces; the question was, in which direction their momentarily combined stream was to flow, and what mill it was to drive. One of the hidden but most potent results of the three years of the Crimean War is the fact that Germany never became liberal; liberalism in Germany acquired creative force only in so far as Bismarck was liberal for a time.

One point, at least, is clear. The personal temper of the twenty-three-year old Emperor of Austria, strengthened as it was by the reconstruction he had already carried out in his own realm under the guidance of men like Kübeck, Schwarzenberg, and Bach, made it quite impossible for him to act as the instrument of western liberalism in this crisis of Europe's fate. In so far as he was sincerely determined to wage no war against Russia, he was but following that innate dynastic instinct that had set him in sharpest opposition to the ideas of his age, ever since the day of his accession. Why should Francis Joseph, himself an absolute monarch, holding Hungary and Italy in subjection with his officials, his gendarmes, and his war-tried troops, assist in destroying the power of Russia? In the course of the crises of the war he may well have got over the personal sense of the sin of ingratitude. Helps to that were to be found in the lesson he had learned in Schwarzenberg's school, which provided him with the idea of self-interest as the guiding motive in political action.

It was to the interest of his house and of his realm to refuse to tolerate Russian supremacy over the Balkan peninsula on any conditions. As long ago as 1769, Joseph II had told Frederick II at their meeting at Neisse; "I will never have the Russians in Moldavia and Wallachia, still less in Serbia." This view, rather than the Metternich policy of submission to Russia in the oriental question, conformed to the idea Francis Joseph had conceived of the interest of the unitary realm that Schwarzenberg had formed for him. And he had no need to go beyond it. From the point of view of the interests of an Austrian autocrat, the attempt of the Western Powers to form a real European alliance against the Russian Czar must seem nonsense and contrary to his own interests.

In the critical days during which the opposition of Russian to France and England developed, and Francis Joseph found Count Buol's policy, which he had himself inspired, of open war with Russia attacked by almost all of the Austrian generals, and almost the whole of the aristocracy with Prince Windischgrätz at their head, he had to reflect that he was committed to a certain definite foreign policy, by the brief course of his imperial past, as well as by the absolutist position that Schwarzenberg and Kübeck had built up for him in the interior of his highly centralized, unitary realm. Whether Schwarzenberg would have grasped the position at the right moment, and prevented a breach with Russia at any cost, we do not know. Death spared him the necessity of solving this problem. The uncertain course of Francis Joseph's diplomacy proves that he did not see deep enough into the extraordinarily difficult circumstances with which he had to cope. He did not possess the necessary force of intellect to conceive his domestic and foreign policy as an organic whole, and accept the conditions laid down by the one as governing the other.

Never was he to make his own the fundamental contribution of the nineteenth century to European statesman-ship—the recognition of the fact that in modern society internal and external policy must in the long run be pursued in interdependence. The later course of his rule proves how far he was from recognizing this truth. It made no difference that he was perpetually being reminded of it by parliament and the press, the typical organs of modern state life. In general, the course of Austrian policy during the Crimean War is there to prove that he had, as yet, formed no clear conception either of the roots of his absolutism or of the aim of his realm. In so far as he injured Russia, he weakened his position as absolute ruler of his own lands. In so far as he refused the coöperation France demanded he helped to make inevitable that loss of the Italian possessions of the House of Austria that he secretly dreaded.

In the last analysis, the deepest conviction of the young Habsburg Emperor, dictating all his actions, was that only as an absolute ruler could he hold together the realm he had inherited from his forefathers. But his thought was too faulty to draw the logical conclusion from this premise, that he, absolute ruler over Austria and Hungary, must not now nor for a long time yet help to weaken the might of Russia, even if he had to risk the danger that a revolutionizing of the Christian populations of the Balkans might react on Hungary and Croatia and increase his difficulties there. "The unnaturalness of such ingratitude" as he showed to Nicholas, and the shortsightedness of it, were justly stigmatized by the Czar.

Francis Joseph ought to have seen this himself. He was never to be able to retrieve the terrible mistake he made in becoming the ally, however unwillingly, of the Western Powers against the Czar, when they had got Russia temporarily into a corner. Just because he claimed absolutism for himself as a practical natural necessity, it was bound to be unnatural for him to be on such terms as those of 1855 with the Parisian adventurer, the "almighty knave" as he was, some years later, to describe him in a letter to his then minister of foreign affairs, Count Rechberg. There is something very odd, from a psychological point of view, in the absence of inner disquietude with which he entered into alliance on December 2, 1854, with Napoleon III and Palmerston. True, he knew that there was to be no question of an all-European coalition war against Russia, and the alliance would guarantee his Italian possessions, for the time being. The immediate and tangible determined him, as usual.

In many other tense moments of his life Francis Joseph was to show, preëminently, a sort of nervous concern about the immediate and tangible, and let this decide for him. It was this impatience, often shown in outbursts of anger, that impelled him to acts contrary to his true political instinct. Here we come upon a trait that was to operate again and again throughout his long life as a ruler. It is commonly interpreted as an uncertainty of judgment, a weakness of character. Yet it was not so much insufficient insight as lack of inner discipline and spiritual self-control that caused him, overpowered by the mass of immediate impressions assailing him at any given moment, to choose the wrong way, against his better feeling.

The decisive error committed by Francis Joseph in allowing the breach with the Czar to become inevitable carried in its train all the other mistakes of his alliance policy during the Crimean War. On the one hand his attitude to the Czar necessarily wore the appearance of a breach of faith and was a flat contradiction of the internal policy pursued ever since his accession, on which the confidence of the Czar in and his affection for, Francis Joseph had been based. On the other, Napoleon was bound to see proof of the young Emperor's unreliability in the manner in which, after entering the December bond, he did everything to delay its execution, and to find in that full justification of the distrust with which England and, above all, Palmerston, had from the first regarded the Vienna cabinet.

When, after the death of Nicholas, Francis Joseph refused the proposal, made to him by Napoleon through his minister of foreign affairs, of a firm alliance with France, relations between Austria on the one side, and, on the other, France and England, to whom the Emperor had, after all, rendered important assistance, seemed definitely worse than they had been in 1853. The old difficulties, dating back to Schwarzenberg's time, were still alive, and even increased and heightened by the bitter disappointments caused both in London and Paris by Francis Joseph's policy. They were not lessened by Count Buol's elevating Austria to the position of arbitrator between Russia and the Western Powers; least of all by his coming out against Russia at the decisive moment, with an ultimatum that compelled it to accept the peace conditions formulated in Vienna.

Buol made the peace conditions imposed on Russia more onerous in one by no means negligible point, by insisting on Russia's ceding a large part of Bessarabia to the Danubian principalities. In the upshot, the result attained by the diplomatic skill of Francis Joseph and of his minister was that, while peace was restored to Europe, his bad faith rankled in Russia. The deep humiliation put upon Czar Alexander II and the power of Russia by the Paris Peace was charged to the account of Austria. The actual result was, indeed, one by no means uncommon—the person who, in pursuit of his own interests, offers his good offices to two disputants, and ultimately compels both to accept them, finds, in the end, that the late adversaries are united in their dislike of the peacemonger. The Crimean War account certainly closed with a gigantic debit balance against the obstinate advocate of European peace, to be aggravated by the reaction of all these diplomatic campaigns on internal conditions in Germany and above all the relations between Austria and Prussia.

There is no evidence that Francis Joseph himself passed any such critical verdict on the significance of these events for Austria. One may rather assume that he was well pleased with what he had done. When, however, by agreement between Napoleon and Palmerston, the union of the Danubian principalities, which he had so hotly opposed, was actually consummated; when he realized the degree to which Napoleon's bad feeling for Austria was strengthened after the war and saw the growing intimacy between the French court and cabinet and the Piedmont government—then even the Emperor must have realized that the four years of war between Russia and the Western Powers and Turkey had given him and his realm nothing but the grave disorder of its own finances—the single positive result of Austrian diplomacy. Nor can he have been wholly blind to certain far from exhilarating reactions on the internal politics of the unitary realm Schwarzenberg had created.

Bitter opposition between Russophiles and Russophobes divided society, the court, the army. Even the Emperor's all-powerful aide-de-camp, Count Grünne, fell into temporary disfavor on account of his open pro-Russian sympathies. Prince Windischgrätz, Radetzky, with all his laurels, and nearly all the leading personages of the court, recklessly aired their hostility to Francis Joseph's Russian policy, and even went so far as to inform Petersburg of it through the Russian ambassador, Baron Meyendorff. Here were symptoms of division and of political strife inside that small, very small, circle to which politics were at that time confined in Austria, which the Emperor could not but note with disquiet.

Did not all this constitute a grave warning to him, an admonition of the desirability of thoroughly examining and testing the entire Schwarzenberg system, by which a merely superficial appearance of quiet had been imposed on a realm that was being held together only by police and military force? Did it not indicate that he should employ the services of those loyal liberal statesmen whom Schwarzenberg and, after him, his young pupil, had deprived of any influence and any position in the state?

These questions can best be considered in connection

with the developments in foreign policy resulting from the Crimean War, which produced new complications in their turn, and shook the centralized absolutism at home to its foundations.

CHAPTER VI

IN the midst of the cares and difficulties that grew thicker upon him month by month with the outbreak of the Russo-Turkish War, Francis Joseph experienced the great miracle. He lost his heart to his seventeen-year-old cousin Elizabeth, the daughter of Duke Max of Bavaria and Duchess Ludovika, sister of Archduchess Sophia, whom he met in Ischl in August, 1853. His mother had long planned his marrying her elder niece, Helena, but when the young Emperor met the two girls he had eyes only for the younger. So strong was the impression she made upon him while still little more than a child that his mind was made up, there and then. It was common knowledge at court that he would take no wife save one whom his own heart selected. The very fact that his mother sought to choose for him in this as in other matters may have strengthened his resolve to have none but Elizabeth. As was hardly surprising he won her consent and the agreement both of her parents and of his mother. The betrothal took place in the intimacy of the family circle at Ischl. There was amazement throughout the Empire on the official announcement of the great event by the Viennese press. The marriage did not take place till April 12, 1854.

[183]

The extended period of betrothal and the wedding that followed it opened the one period in Francis Joseph's life of unshadowed felicity. It helped him to support the heavy responsibilities laid on his shoulders by the difficulties of the time. He was not yet four and twenty; his health was admirable; his energy unwearied. He had settled into his rôle of absolute monarch. In the two years that followed Schwarzenberg's death his self-confidence had grown strong, indeed too strong. Nowhere did he encounter any serious resistance. On all sides he heard that the army, from the old Marshal Radetzky to the youngest subaltern, adored their young, energetic, high-spirited, often excessively high-spirited, chief. His ministers did what he told them; the leading mind in his cabinet, Dr. Alexander Bach, enjoyed the respect and admiration of Archduchess Sophia and Cardinal Rauscher, and was busy reorganizing the huge machinery of the state on the lines laid down in the patent of December 31, 1851, and entirely in accordance with Francis Joseph's ideas. Day by day he could feel that he was now and intended to remain, a veritable ruler, as he had planned to be. And now he had taken the most important step in his life as a man, and, perhaps for the first time since his accession, was actually happy.

The biographer must guard against allowing the shadows of later years to fall across the radiance of this period in his life, short enough at the best. Five years of sovereignty, five years of court life and court morals had not ruined the young man. Innocent he may not have been but that is by the way; there can be no doubt that he entered on marriage untainted. The winter of 1850-51 saw a revival of court life in the old Burg in Vienna with the Emperor's mother as its center. The young sovereign who, for all his youth, was an expert in the arts of chivalry, loved dancing. Not to do so would have been unnatural in Vienna where, ever since the days of the congress, dancing had been the life of society. Court correspondence of this period records the pleasure he took in the dances arranged by his mother, how he found delighted partners among the "charming countesses," and how now this charmer and now that was distinguished by his special notice.

Life at court in these winter days resembled that going on in any of the palaces where some young noble had just come of age. The decent "civil" tradition established by Francis Joseph's father, hospitable but never ostentatious, continued; youthful zest was always kept within bounds. Many years ago Bertha von Suttner published a collection of letters written by ladies of the court from which one gets an enchanting picture of adolescent gayety in the carnival time of 1852-53.

In the great Schwarzenberg and Lichtenstein houses, as at the "Chamber" balls given by his mother, the Emperor could taste the pleasures natural to his age. He showed tact in dispensing with real court balls. Even under martial law the old *joie de vivre* reigned in Vienna, and grew stronger year by year both among the middle-class folk and in the population as a whole; and the society surrounding the old palace was positively revivified by the new currents of youth and gayety. The "rejuvenation of Austria," so much talked of at the time, in a political sense, had actually come into being, socially, with the young Emperor, and forms the leading note of the post-revolutionary epoch. The letter of one of the ladies-in-waiting describes a great festivity in the palace, in which all the leading men and their wives took part, including what she calls "the brown-haired cabinet." The old court periwigs of the age of Ferdinand had gone; about the young monarch were young officers and young counsellors; Alexander Bach for example was barely five and thirty.

If Francis Joseph did not give himself up entirely to the pleasures of society in these two or three years of *jeunesse dorée*, the reason was mainly that he had a high sense of duty and a strong desire to rule. He was unwearying in "inspecting" the various parts of his far-flung realm, to see that all was well, and, above all, to take part in military reviews, exercises, and manœuvres, which often took him to the Italian provinces and even as far as Venice and Trieste where the new Austrian fleet was being trained for its distinguished future work by a Danish naval officer, Vice-Admiral Dahlerup. The Emperor was perpetually on the move, he took diplomatic journeys, met Czar Nicholas several times, visited his uncle King Frederick William IV at Pillnitz, paid state visits to Dresden and Berlin, and met the south German princes at Bregenz.

This conscientiousness abstracted him more or less from society, as did his strong sense of personal dignity, which made a certain marked withdrawal habitual to him even towards his court and the aristocracy. After his betrothal he gave up dancing altogether. Thenceforward he was merely the center of court festivities and his demeanor expressed his sense of obligation to represent the ruler almost impersonally.

By way of compensation, another form of relaxation and distraction became almost his solitary personal passion—the chase. At this time moreover the small game on the imperial estates in Moravia, Lower Austria, and Slovakia satisfied him; later he abandoned this and found only delight in mountain sport. Heath-cock shooting still continued to fascinate him, however; it made a special appeal to his early developed genuine hunter's instinct.

Unlike many fellow monarchs he liked to have everything about him quite simple when hunting; any sort of court atmosphere then seemed to him out of place, even odious. He talked dialect with his foresters and beaters; his ordinary German had the specially pleasing accent that belonged to high Viennese society in the old days. On the chase he was happy as at such times he would shake off all troubles and responsibilities, personal and official, and his essential good nature came to the surface as well as his penchant for kindly jokes. He could forget all the lessons taught him by his mother and Prince Schwarzenberg about being severe and on his guard from a sense that everybody was trying to get something out of him, and he therefore must be as unapproachable as possible.

There were, indeed, persons who in general thought very highly of him but who criticized his excessive devotion to this sport, somewhat unjustly since now and later it was his only physical and mental relaxation. It appealed to him the more since he was not fond of talking, and out hunting that is excluded. He was actually very seldom moved to confide and therefore did not care for people who talked a great deal. He early conceived a distrust of good and ready talkers. His natural impatience, anyhow, made him a bad listener. Genuine Austrian and Viennese as he was in many respects, he had none of the Austrian love of chat: he did not even care to hear himself talk, no doubt as the result of the mass of serious and unpleasant things it had been his fate to listen to and speak of even by the time he was nineteen. He had not the least native gift for small talk.

He was well aware that his views and ideas were not those of his day and generation, even less among the middle classes in Germany than at home; nor did he blink the fact that at home no inconsiderable section of the population harbored progressive notions, by him briefly and, he thought, accurately, described as revolutionary. But he felt no necessity for closer acquaintance with a new age that was temperamentally repugnant to him and it never occurred to him to establish contact with its representatives. He read few political books or writings of this school if any; now and later his reading was very sparse. Of course he was compelled from early youth to peruse a mass of reports, correspondence, documents, and memoranda. He did this as a duty; to do so became an inveterate habit. Newspapers he hardly looked at, save in the form of a written summary put before him daily, which certainly saved time.

One definite blank in his practical education is obvious

from all this. Since his social intercourse was confined to the circle of higher dignitaries and officers of the court itself, he had neither opportunity nor desire to know the people of his realm, above all the middle-class people. There were practically insuperable difficulties in the way. How could a young absolute monarch in the twenties, who was at once war lord and his own minister, establish such relationships? From early till late he was pursued by important state papers of all kinds. As one of the first men in Europe, he had to be perpetually receiving kings, archdukes, granddukes, and princes. Every day he had to consult with ministers, ambassadors, and generals about the most complicated and momentous problems, national and international, to ponder over them, discuss and decide. How could he find time even for the most important aspects of the real life of his people, that life which was not comprised in state papers?

It was most unfortunate that a young man on whom so much for Europe depended never did find time to fill up the gaps in his knowledge of life outside the narrow circle of his profession, so to speak, by looking about the world, free of his high office, either at home or in Germany, whose first prince he was; the more so that, for his temperament, knowledge could come only through practical experience. He had no gift for theoretic study. His purely intellectual interests were feeble; he cared nothing for art or literature; he was satisfied to have no one trouble a young ruler with matters of this kind, quite outside his sphere.

The great fact for him was his profession; of that he

was clearly and deeply aware and in that he never wavered. He had to protect and increase the power of the imperial house and rule its territories and peoples to that end. That implied that he must guard them carefully and rigorously against the errors of revolution and care for the welfare of all classes, taking the advice of his ministers in so far as it stood the test of his independent judgment. What paint and marble are to the artist, words and ideas to the poet, resolutions and decrees bearing on the general welfare were for the absolute monarch, who practised the highest of earthly professions. Resolutions and decrees were the implements of statecraft, as he saw it. Therefore, the material power of the monarch, as the indispensable condition for the execution of such resolutions and decrees, must be maintained, likewise the police and the army, and, of course, the economic life of the people on which taxation depended. To this end ministers must work: they were responsible to him and to him alone. This view, in which Francis Joseph grew up, was already out of date from a European point of view. Worse still, he relied in part on an even more out-of-date technique —a paternal method of government that, adequate in the eighteenth century, was entirely out of place in the second half of the nineteenth century.

It should further be added that Francis Joseph suffered markedly from the shyness that is apt to afflict rulers in personal intercourse with those beneath them: a peculiarity the more comprehensible in combination with his highly developed sense of the importance of his own position and authority; and his knowledge that the slightest remark or expression of opinion he let fall would spread not only through the court but all over the country and beyond. He had nothing of the sociability and "kindliness" of his two predecessors. He may have realized the irrelevance of this sort of complaisance to the real work of a ruler, and that in his grandfather's case kindliness was only a mask for an inner coldness. Anyhow it was excluded in his own case by the strongly militarist overlay of his thought and feeling. Accustomed from boyhood up to the stiff formalism of military methods he took naturally to this mode of expressing himself. As it happened, officers and men of all ranks were being trained in the Austrian army at this date in the most rigid obedience and an extreme terseness in expression.

It would, however, be quite wrong to assume that this reserve, this aloof self-consciousness, this disinclination for idle talk and tendency to blunt and brief orders and decisions in matters of government business, gave Francis Joseph any appearance of want of graciousness or prevented his attracting the respect of his elders. Quite the contrary. He speedily won a high reputation among the ruling families of Germany and—which was almost the same thing—of Europe. The Saxon royal house declared him to be the most gifted young ruler in Europe; the Czar's good opinion has been recorded; the confidential letters of Frederick William IV of Prussia to the other German sovereigns show that Berlin was early aware that the young Emperor's will and personality had got to be taken seriously. His manner was naturally freer and less circumspect when dealing with ruling houses than it could be at home, even with the nobles with whom alone he conceived any form of personal intercourse as possible. His personality, therefore, made a stronger impression on princes and on their ambassadors and envoys with whom he dealt in person than on his own ministers and generals, whom at this stage he admitted only to a limited degree of confidence, and with whom he maintained a definite reserve, with emphasis on his imperial supremacy.

The best picture of him at this time is that drawn by Duke Ernest of Saxe-Coburg-Gotha, in a letter to his brother, the Consort of Queen Victoria, who regarded Francis Joseph very unsympathetically. Duke Ernest, a keen and intelligent observer, very different from the Emperor both in character and education, met him for the first time in 1852 and got to know him in the course of an extended visit.

"The young Emperor is a man of great promise and fine physique: his movements are gracious, his bearing measured and uncommonly tactful for one of his youth. His talent for military science and tactics is well known; and for languages. He also undoubtedly has a gift for organization, assisted by a quickness of apprehension and a notably good memory. Were he to enjoy more various intercourse and to see and inform himself by traveling abroad and above all in Germany, his native gifts would then develop into something even more significant.

"I had to-day the opportunity of being much with him and hearing him speak on a great variety of topics, and was astonished by the precision and knowledge with which he handled everything. He spoke little, but to the purpose. He is a master in all knightly exercises and markedly superior to all the Archdukes, even those of his own age.

"The Court is magnificent and one observes order and supervision everywhere. The cabinet comprises many elements but a single idea dominates the whole —to restore the Empire, still in a ruinous condition, to imposing grandeur on a level with the other German states, and to establish institutions, lines, progress—in a word to regenerate it. As to the means to be employed I cannot judge, but the impression I got in Vienna was that the Emperor himself and the men who advise him have the courage and the tenacity that will quail before no obstacles."

The picture may be completed by a note written about the same time by Bismarck to the Prussian prime minister:

"The young men tell me that the Emperor does everything with a balance strange in his years, from his duties as ruler to the chase. He puts an excessive strain on his physical strength by dancing, riding and doing without sleep. He gets up about four and never stops working. . . ."

Thus he made a good impression on sovereigns and ambassadors who knew him as a man. He was less successful in winning a place in the heart of the people of Vienna—partly because it never occurred to him to try.

In Vienna he was never popular: the state of martial law, the identification of the Emperor with the army (which had taken the city in October, 1848, with grape shot and the sword), and the fact that he always appeared in uniform, made it impossible for the masses or even the educated middle classes to care for him. For Vienna, like Austria, except for the Italian provinces, had hitherto never known "militarism." Despite the privileges of its aristocratic "honorary" colonels in the appointments of the lower grades of officers, the old pre-1848 Austrian army had been on the closest and most friendly terms with all classes. The young Emperor seemed to the educated middle classes to represent the new tendency in governing circles which, proclaiming the "faithful" army to be the sole support of the throne, strove to keep it as remote as possible from the life of the civilian population, and the officers' mess as far as possible clear of dangerously liberal middle-class infection. Thinking and feeling thus in Vienna and Prague, in Brünn and Graz, people had no great hopes of a young Emperor whom, since he invariably appeared in a general's uniform, the popular wits of Vienna called, with no great respect, "Lieutenant Red Legs." This soldier's game, new in Austria, displeased the masses. His extreme youth, too, gave much scope for scorn and contemptuous criticism in these early years. Middle and working classes alike were incensed by the sudden appearance of a military atmosphere about the young monarch and convinced that even if he wished to show clemency his advisers would not allow him to do so; the great majority felt nothing better than open indifference for the sovereign.

The harder the young Emperor strove to become a just but severe ruler, the more did public opinion turn against him; above all that of those who believed that an Austrian ruler should necessarily move towards liberalism. At this time there was a revival of feeling for the historic, largely legendary figure of Emperor Joseph II, the "appreciator of mankind"; the reserve and unapproachability of his young successor alienated the sympathy of the very best sections of the society of his capital.

There was no open protest against the suspension of the constitution; gendarmerie and police had habituated the people to hide their political thoughts and feelings deep within their hearts. But an active espionage system could not prevent emigration from going on at a great rate both in the Italian provinces and in Hungary. In 1853, when the prisons in Hungary were full of men suspected of subversive conspiracy, and Mazzini's agents had carried through a series of notably treacherous assaults on Austrian officers and soldiers in Milan, a murderous attack was made on the person of the young Emperor. On February 13, 1853, as he was passing along the escarpment with his aide-de-camp, Janos Libényi, a Hungarian tailor's apprentice of two and twenty, suddenly flung himself upon him with a knife, and only his stiff uniform collar saved Francis Joseph from being mortally wounded. He was seriously but not dangerously wounded; his aide and a citizen who happened to be near succeeded in capturing the would-be assassin. After some anxious days, during which his sight appeared weakened and affected, the Emperor made a complete recovery. The horrible deed influenced opinion in Vienna in his favor. When he reappeared, there were spontaneous expressions of popular goodwill.

Sympathy was excited by the courage shown by the young monarch and by the fact that he said, immediately afterwards, that his pain was mitigated by the sense that he was suffering with his poor soldiers in Milan, who had been attacked in such a cowardly fashion. Nor is it to the Emperor's disfavor that the doubts he had felt some months earlier about the efficiency of the entire police system surrounding him, should have been strengthened by this incident. It is hardly surprising that he did not pardon the assassin but allowed justice to take its course. His kindness of heart was evidenced in the grant of a small pension to Libényi's mother, left destitute by the execution of the son on whom she was dependent; this same kindness appeared wherever political considerations did not stifle it.

From this time on he was unremitting in pressing his ministers and military advisers to raise martial law in Vienna and Prague. Failing in this he suspended it on September 1 on his own authority.

The real evil from which he suffered was the nature of his immediate entourage and closest advisers. This the people of Vienna knew perfectly; they knew and judged Count Grünne, Count Gyulai, and General Baron von Kempen, the minister of police, quite correctly. These men, together with Archduchess Sophia and Archbishop

Rauscher, succeeded in excluding the Emperor from any other influences. He literally never saw or heard a free independent person, not even from among the ranks of the high nobility. He did not even see his ministers often, and then as a rule only on official business. His entire entourage was accustomed to have him set the tone in conversation and reject firmly any attempt to speak at large with him. Above all he never saw any leading Hungarian. Even the "black-yellow" minded magnates he saw only at court festivities; not for any sort of political talk.

Schwarzenberg had instilled into his mind the blackest mistrust of Hungarian society in general and in particular of its political head, the so-called old conservatives. On the occasion of his first official visit to Hungary in 1852, Archduke Albert, his cousin, Governor of Hungary, and the Emperor's Vienna advisers, were at pains to convince him that the masses in Hungary were loyal and contented; the only people who opposed the imperial officials and sowed dissension in the country were the members of the nobles' party and a handful of conspirators who had taken cover and not so far been arrested. He, therefore, gladly took the homage of peasants and army, and of the towns-people, as a genuine expression of popular feeling. In the same way he hoped that Venice had been won over by the establishment of a free port there and the ample contribution made by the government to the trade and shipping of the city of the Doges, and took his good reception there as a sign that the Venetians were reconciled to the new régime.

[197]

His mother continued to exercise the strongest influence upon him and on the conduct of the policy he approved; and from her he got in the main nothing but the ideas of Monsignore Othmar Rauscher, the new Archbishop of Vienna, whom she regarded with the most devout respect. This high ecclesiastic was profoundly convinced of the necessity of boundless centralization and autocracy, in both of which he had a dogmatic belief; finding no difficulty in combining with it an open demand for the restoration of the full supremacy of the Roman church in the Austrian state, which he pressed energetically on the Emperor as a primary desideratum of Austrian policy.

Francis Joseph gave ear to this advice and in 1851 removed by imperial decree one of the structural pillars of church law as set up by Joseph II, while accelerating the preparatory discussions with the Curia for the establishment of a Concordat. In these years his major decisions were arrived at in consultation with Prince Schwarzenberg. After his death everything depended on the young Emperor himself and his predominantly military entourage. Of his brothers, Ferdinand Max, nearest to him in age, began to cause him all kinds of trouble through his restless ambition. It was no secret at the court that this second son was beginning to win first place in his mother's affection. Her wish was to see him, as soon as possible, achieve his own sphere of activity in the state, and the navy then building seemed at first to afford the opportunity for this. He spent a good deal of time on the coast, especially at Trieste. Friction between the brothers seems to have begun early in the fifties. At the time of the Emperor's wound, there was lively anxiety at court on the question of the succession in the event of his death. Count Grünne thought it necessary to ask whether Archduke Max, the heir presumptive, then at Cattaro in the extreme south of the monarchy, should not be summoned to Vienna. Francis Joseph said no; but his brother came on his own initiative. Jealousy of his next of kin then appeared, plainly, in the Emperor.

Ferdinand Max was undoubtedly of a more intellectual bent than his brother, as witness his enthusiasm for literature, notably romantic poetry, and painting, and his devotion to the sea and to the southern landscape. These interests of his had been developed by a teacher for whom he had a deep respect, the Tyrolese Hans von Perthaler, who was both a distinguished jurist and an accomplished writer with a marked taste for poetry and literature generally. Good-natured enough, Ferdinand Max's was a much weaker character than his brother's. He lacked inner balance and from boyhood up had been subject both to a heady ambition and to gusts of envy of his brother. Even in his young days he struck leading men as a man of fantastic imagination. An ambition undirected by steadiness of will foreshadowed in these early years of his brother's reign the tragic destiny that was to overtake him later.

Archduke Charles Ludwig, the second of Francis Joseph's brothers, was from early youth to the end of his days a docile pupil and tool of his religious teachers. The time had come when the Society of Jesus thought that it

[199]

might make its way back into Austria. In 1773, Maria Theresa had suspended the Order and banned it from her states. In 1856, this decree was rescinded to allow the Jesuits full scope at the court and in society in Vienna. The result was an extended conflict: the old conflict that had gone on for years between the "Josephinism" of the secular clergy and the old Austrian Benedictine Orders on one side and the new tendencies within the Church of Rome more or less incorporated in the Jesuits on the other side.

Among the numerous other archdukes three only were important to the Emperor: his cousin Albert, senior to him by some ten years, son of that Archduke Charles who had defeated Napoleon at Aspern; his brother, Archduke William, and Archduke Rainer, a second cousin of the Emperor belonging to the former viceregal Italian line. Between Albert and the Emperor there was a relation of warm friendship; he was his young cousin's oracle in military matters. Albert, in fact, had an intelligence that had been variously and well trained and developed and, as a strategist, he was deservedly esteemed. An authoritarian by disposition, he had no small political influence on the young Emperor, mainly in the direction of strengthening him in his autocratic ideas; while his firm character made him something of a support to Francis Joseph.

The plans for the young Emperor's marriage, which his mother had been busy weaving, were doubtless encouraged in his own mind in the troubled weeks after his attempted assassination. Men who occupy earthly thrones invariably feel a strong desire to secure the succession in their own blood and keep other lines excluded from it. This is the source, as a rule, of the peculiar rancor, seldom successfully concealed, with which the dynast regards his nearest relatives and which they feel for him—such, for example, as existed between Francis Joseph and his brother Ferdinand Max. The most important clause, both under the old princely law and in the statute of the House of Habsburg-Lorraine finally drafted in 1839, is that which declares the Emperor to be the unlimited head of the house, to whom all archdukes and archduchesses are subordinate. This principle of primogeniture, whose effect in practice is to deprive other members of the dynastic house of any rights, was no mere rhetorical flourish but bitter earnest, right down into the nineteenth century,—as the tragic conflicts and incidents that marked the history of the Habsburg house from 1848 to the downfall of the realm are there to prove.

Francis Joseph gave his mother to understand that he intended to marry to please himself. Clever woman as she was and long accustomed to rule, she understood that she must be very careful to direct his choice herself. She had made up her mind to find Austria's future Empress in the circle of her own immediate kin and had in fact selected the eldest daughter of her sister Ludovika, Princess Helen of Bavaria. To this end she invited her sister and her husband to spend part of the summer of 1853 at the imperial family's simple country seat at Ischl.

Traditional accounts throw no very clear light on the details of what followed. But so much at least is clear:

Francis Joseph, in a manner quite surprising, happened first to see Elizabeth. She was but sixteen years old, and neither her parents nor Sophia had thought of her in this connection. Francis Joseph saw her, however, and the impression made on him by the charming apparition was such that he, for the first time, felt the authentic flame of love. Opposition from his mother was met by the declaration that he would marry Elizabeth or nobody. The struggle seems to have been brief. The young sovereign approached the girl, who, at first surprised and almost terrified, at last said yes. On August 18, the Emperor's birthday, the news of the great event was communicated to the Empire by the *Wiener Zeitung*.

All the unspoiled freshness of the young man's nature came out in the frankness with which he permitted those about him to see the depths of his happiness and his pride in the bride he had won. Kempen, the grim minister of police, records in his diary how the Emperor, glowing with joy, showed his ministers and generals the lovely portrait of his bride that an artist had done for him. In those days of young love, clear and friendly traits in his character were continually coming to the surface. Shortly before his betrothal he had a visit from clever King Leopold of Belgium who wrote an interesting letter afterwards to his niece, Queen Victoria:

"I must confess that I like the young Emperor. There is both kindliness and keenness in those warm blue eyes of his and he has a certain attractive merriment, on occasion. He is slight and graceful and

PRINCESS ELISABETH OF BAVARIA
AT SEVENTEEN

even in the midst of a confusion of dancers and archdukes, all in uniform, you can always pick him out as the dominating man. . . . His manners are excellent, free from any arrogance or awkwardness. They are simple, and when he is friendlily disposed as he was to me, very genuine and natural. He keeps everyone in order without giving himself any airs of authority; but he is the master and there is a certain something about him that gives authority although those who have authority often fail to achieve or exert it. I fancy he can be stern, when necessary: there is something very spirited about him."

Reading such descriptions and looking at contemporary portraits one cannot wonder that the royal wooer made such quick work of his royal cousin's heart. This gay, grave young officer of three and twenty, who was at the same time one of the most powerful monarchs in Europe, may well have seemed to the sixteen-year-old princess— hardly more than a child—the embodiment of her dreams. His character—determined, self-conscious, but, at bottom, friendly and winning—must have made an impression on her heart.

A few years before Schwarzenberg had said of the Emperor, "He is a fearless fellow," and since then his character had gained in firmness and sureness. This must have been the real springtime in his life. He made frequent journeys all through the autumn and winter of 1853 to Munich and Possenhofen where the bride's parents had their country seat, and where they spent the greater part of the year with their children, living like comfortable landowners. Duke Max, Elizabeth's father, loved this life, especially all the part of it that had to do with horses. He was an original creature, with many intellectual interests and a passion for music, especially in such popular forms as Bavarian zither playing and folk songs. From him his daughter got the pleasure she always found in contact with simple folk, like the Bavarian peasants, as well as her deep love of nature, especially of mountains, and her passion for physical exercise whether in the form of riding or walking. But what captivated Francis Joseph was a freshness and spontaneity native to her essential self rather than belonging to her age. This, harmonizing at the moment with his own simplicity and youthful bravery, worked a mutual enchantment. Neither had any suspicion at this time of the deep differences of character and mental and spiritual type that were to develop so tragically later.

The process of mutual discovery, the common experience of most of us, was to reveal to Francis Joseph and Elizabeth the deep separation of their souls. But for the moment Elizabeth seemed to all the world a real fairy-tale bride, while the fire of youthful love lit even Francis Joseph's essentially dry and matter-of-fact nature with ardor and released him for the time from the fetters laid upon his soul by his imperial ambition and dominant sense of sovereignty.

Like a veritable fairy princess Elizabeth sailed in the spring of 1854 on the new steamer *Francis Joseph* down the Danube from the valley. Decades later old Viennese

EMPEROR FRANCIS JOSEPH
IN 1853

men and women would tell of the marvellous reception of the Emperor's lovely bride as she went, under garlands of roses, to Nussdorf at the foot of the Kahlenberg, amid the hearty greetings of the Emperor, and of a brilliant gathering not of the court only but of the entire people.

Truly these were new and pleasant experiences for Francis Joseph. He now found there were agreeable prerogatives in his profession of ruler which he had hardly suspected. The wedding on April 12, 1854, was followed by a general amnesty. The number of Hungarians who now came forth from their prisons made a deep impression. In the following years mercy was extended to the many thousands condemned for political offenses since 1849. A large number of Hungarians now returned to beg permission of the Emperor to go free of punishment. Natural in such circumstances that the whole realm should regard the lovely young Empress as bringing happiness with her and heralding a better future. For the first time Francis Joseph enjoyed a certain popularity in his realm, even in Vienna.

The first years of the marriage were thoroughly happy. The birth of two little girls followed in quick succession, the elder of whom died, after but two years of life, of an infantile complaint. The birth of an heir to the throne in 1858, who was baptized by the name of the founder of the dynasty, Rudolf, not only gave supreme joy to the Emperor but gave the great masses of the people, who were still absolutely loyal, opportunity of showing their friendly feeling. The young Emperor seemed to have been granted the most perfect family happiness.

It was, however, soon pretty generally known that this happiness was at times rudely disturbed by the domineering personality of his mother. She seems never quite to have reconciled herself to her son's independent choice of a wife. The young Empress was absolutely a child of nature, unprepared for her position by training or education. Resistance to the perpetual interference of Archduchess Sophia in her personal life compelled latent traits, still dormant in her character and disposition, to develop more rapidly and more sharply than was at all happy for herself. Soon there was bitter strife within the bosom of the reigning family.

The traditional account of the young Empress refusing to accommodate herself to "Spanish ceremonial" does not really at all fit the actual situation of the young imperial couple. Current talk about the court exaggerated this ceremonial at any time, and at any rate at this time it by no means acted so restrictively on the personal life of the Emperor and Empress as the ordinary story would have one believe. The same applies to the talk about Archduchess Sophia's depriving the young Empress of the education of her children, and of their being handed over to their educators and their special household courts instead of being looked after by their mother, which reveals a rather childish transference of lower middle-class ideas and conditions to emergencies more or less present at any court or in any greater aristocratic family. The young Empress was addicted to the pleasures and enjoyments natural to her age; above all she had in her blood a passion for horses and riding. Immature as she was, she was neither so ideally designed for an educator, nor so exclusively filled by a sense of duty in this regard, as to feel that any great wrong was done her by this aspect of court etiquette. It was further said at court that the young Emperor was tied to her apron strings. That, as so often happens, annoyed her mother-in-law but not to the extent that she can justly be regarded as the evil spirit of the house. Much of the imperial couple's time was spent either at Laxenburg or Ischl or elsewhere in the country. Obviously the young Empress for whom life, from childhood, had been dominated by fantasy, could not fit very readily into the regulated forms of a court. Equally true is it that in these early years the young Emperor (much as it may have annoyed his mother) consulted his wife's fancies as far as he could, and did so gladly.

In a great court such frictions as these differences gave rise to were of course more dangerous than in ordinary life, since every step of a monarch is watched every hour by the Argus eyes of his or her suite, and parties at court and intrigues of all sorts are bound to develop out of any family conflict. This reacted, in the given case, in difficulties for Francis Joseph and Elizabeth, whose essential consequence was the premature straining of their own most personal relations. The development of different characters will, in any marriage, bring the possibilities of conflict, but as a rule it brings them slowly, as the years go by, and brings with them always the reconciling power of shared common experience.

So the full happiness of these two was but short-lived. By 1860 there were real and serious misunderstandings of whose true reason no one knows or for long has known anything first-hand. In 1862 a temporary break took place. As a result the Empress, at first in view of her health, for whose failure she was perhaps partly to blame—she refused to see physicians, and there are complaints of her inattention to their advice—retired abroad for months at a time. But all this came later. For the moment Francis Joseph's family life was happy, and the "rejuvenated court" showed its old brilliance and all the splendour that great wealth, assured taste, and the joy of life can lend to a court and an aristocratic society based on highly respected traditions.

A word may here be said about the society of Vienna into which the fairy princess from the Starnberger See came to rule over it as its natural queen. Such a background is necessary too if the young Emperor is to be seen in his true proportions as man and ruler. Viennese court society was in 1850 in almost all essentials what it had been under Charles VI and Maria Theresa, or even, with but small alteration, under Joseph II and Emperor Francis II. It was purely aristocratic. The court was its natural center. Unlike Berlin and other German courts, Austria counted as noble only the historic nobility, the families of counts and princes who to some extent had maintained their position in the hereditary provinces and in Hungary, from feudal times—and those who had been raised by the "Holy Roman Empire" to the ranks of nobility in return for distinguished service in council, army, or diplomacy. The real core of this noble group, traditionally of feudal, but historically of court, origin, was composed of those stocks whom counter-reformation and the consequent expropriation of the old German and Czech knights and landowners in Bohemia, Moravia, and Silesia had raised to be owners of *latifundia* and to positions of power and consideration. First among these were families like Schwarzenberg, Thun, Auersperg, Nostitz, Waldstein, Clary, Czernin, Sternberg, Lobkowitz and Kinsky, together with some two dozen other families, most of them descendants of Catholic statesmen and generals of the Thirty Years War, like Clam-Martinic, Clam-Gallas Taaffe or Boucquoi.

Many of these families had at that time left the hereditary provinces, i.e., Austria, Styria, Carinthia, and the Tyrol for Bohemia where they rose to great wealth and "blood." Associated with them was a small number of old German noble families in the hereditary lands "of the dynasty, at their head the house of the Princess of Liechtenstein," the counts of Starhemberg, Wolkenstein, Attems, and many others, of whom a certain proportion had remained in their old seats.

In Maria Theresa's day the small number of Polish families that counted as belonging to the great nobles were further brought in. The princes and counts Potocki, Sapieha, Lanckoronski, Wodzicki, and others. Only in so far as they could claim relationship with the Bohemian or German Austrian stocks did they count as really belonging to the great Austrian houses, which Francis Joseph was himself later to describe as the nearest class in society to the throne. The Italian nobility from Lombardy and Venetia, who had taken an active part in court life under

Maria Theresa and entered into many family alliances with the Viennese nobles, had since 1815 stood aloof on principle and almost without exception. The reason for this was the national movement stirring in Italy.

On the other hand the Hungarian nobility, which Maria Theresa was the first to attract, skilfully and systematically, to the court, had become from that time on one of the richest and most brilliant sections of Viennese society. Here again these were mainly the historically "junior" families—those which had remained faithful to Catholicism and, having proved reliable partisans of the Habsburg régime in Hungary, had been rewarded by the free gift from the Emperor of land and serfs in the depopulated areas of Hungary and Croatia after the Turk had been driven out, and so grown rich. The leading names among these magnates are Andrássy, Degenfeld, Apponyi, Károlyi, Batthányi, Palffy, and, above all, Esterházy, the richest of them all.

The great change in the court after 1850 was that the Hungarian nobles were rarely to be found there. The revolution and the horrors of the counter-revolution were far from being obliterated, even in this circle. Here the Emperor's marriage seems to have had a happy effect. Elizabeth seems at once to have been attracted by the hitherto unfamiliar character of these Hungarian nobles, whose wealth was often allied to a cosmopolitan culture and spent with notorious extravagance, and who had no traits of "German pedantry" about them. Further, she was pleased by connections with the aristocracy of France and the English peerage which gave these Magyar nobles a European position, assiduously cultivated by them.

The importance of this noble group as a whole for the Habsburg monarchy was incalculable. Napoleon characterized it with perfect clarity. A solid combination of some hundreds of families whose existence was based on great and long-standing wealth now formed the actual milieu of the life of the young imperial couple. In addition, the group took in the younger sons and the more or less impoverished descendants of the collateral branches of these "ruling" houses. The so-called "court service" surrounding the Emperor, the Empress and the entire Habsburg family was almost exclusively drawn from these younger sons and daughters. It comprised the court chamberlains and stewards of the archdukes and archduchesses, the tutors of their children, the officers of the imperial bodyguard, the officials of the great court offices, and most of the aides-de-camp of the Emperor and the archdukes.

This great chain of nobles, of imposing number and comprising all persons who on every important political and ceremonial occasion represented the splendor of the court and of the inner circle surrounding the imperial family, completely closed that family and the sovereign off from every other society or group in Vienna or the kingdom as a whole. It rested on strict notions of court rank, definitely formulated and constituting a special mark of quality, strictly watched by the chief chamberlain. Small was the number of persons lacking it—the middle-class ministers who had come up since 1848 and a few higher state officials of equivalent rank as privy coun-

cillors and highly-placed generals from the lesser nobility
—who possessed the "entrée"; the entrée being the individual sign of court equality.

Apart from this court society was the so-called "second
society," gradually formed in the time since Maria Theresa, and consisting, in Francis Joseph's earlier years, as
then, of old but newly ennobled families of officials and
generals together with a certain circle of long-settled,
well-to-do families of great merchants or industrialists,
as they began to be called. It was perpetually being re-
freshed by new blood, in the shape of gifted young men,
largely from Germany but particularly from Bavaria,
Württemberg, and Baden, who sought to advance their
fortunes in Austria either in the administration or in the
army and allied themselves by marriage with the old
families there.

A number of now old military and official families, well
known to-day, owed their origin to alliances with men
who came from the north or south of Germany in this
way. The distinguishing mark of this "second society"
was that while the representatives of culture, the scholars,
doctors, artists, and writers who, irrespective of means or
social position, composed it, had, at first, been exclusively
conservative, ever since Congress days room and scope
had been found within it for men of "liberal" outlook.
Needless to say, music and the theater, historic inherit-
ances of Viennese life were always understood best and
promoted most zealously by this circle. To it there belonged men like Anton von Schmerling, an offshoot of the
old bureaucracy; liberals like Baron von Sommaruga,

[212]

Baron Andrian, Charles von Kübeck, and Alexander Bach, whose great gifts were to cause him to rise so rapidly. Here Franz Schubert early won a fame that extended beyond the circle of his youthful friends and admirers. Vienna's great painters, Daffinger, Danhauser, and Füger, were in touch with this group. Young Grillparzer, in the period when he still cared for social life, was admired and honored here, where indeed he belonged through his mother's family.

Moreover, this second society had, since the opening of the century, been in close touch with the new middle class growing up in Vienna and described, for example, by Adalbert Stifter in his incomparable sketches and stories and his great novel *Indian Summer*. There was no exclusion of this "productive middle class" as it is called, but it was kept in its place. Strange as it may seem, the middle classes had, from the court standpoint, no social existence before 1848, nor during the first decade after Francis Joseph's accession. Developing rapidly with the great advances in industry and manufacture in Vienna after the Napoleonic wars, this middle class established a peculiar kind of contact with both the great social circles described above through a phenomenon that, while small in range, nevertheless was very important in the development of Vienna. This was the partly Jewish "aristocracy of finance" that began to rise after 1815. These families, most of whom came to Vienna from the trade and industrial centers of southern Germany, e.g., Frankfort on Main, as well as from other towns, had begun to play a part in its life during the Napoleonic wars. In the forties, the salons

[213]

of their great ladies became centers of musical and artistic life.

Of all this the court knew nothing, although many of the great aristocrats were on friendly terms with these circles. By the forties, the society of the officials and the middle classes had begun to constitute an educated public opinion, even in politics. The events of 1848 made the court more suspicious than ever of the middle class and strengthened the isolation, first, of the Emperor and Empress, and even of the archdukes, from the whole of this progressive intellectual and economic activity.

Vienna's best physicians and lawyers and writers, and the leaders in technical and industrial advance, were thus cut off from any contact with the court. The Emperor knew neither the men who were carrying on the intellectual life of the country, its great scientists, geologists, and historians, nor such men as Grillparzer, Bauernfeld, or Adalbert Stifter. Painters and sculptors brought the art of portraiture to the court in some degree, but it was really only the theatre, rising to new splendor in the fifties, thanks to the work of the director of the Burg Theatre, Heinrich Laube, who had come there from Prussia, that constituted a real common and warmly felt interest for all social circles and even for the court.

Although, up to the Emperor's marriage, society in Vienna, in its tripartite division, remained unaltered, his own relations to it were somewhat different from those of his immediate predecessors. His social desires were very limited. Both he and the archdukes regarded the middle classes in general and many of the ennobled official group as concealed democrats and "unreliable" elements in the state. Hence there was a practical cessation even of the harmless intercourse which Francis Charles, the Emperor's father, had been almost alone in trying to promote between the court and the "second society" and middle-class circles.

Francis Joseph had absolutely no interest in seeing any but the people of whose devotion not merely to his person but to his government he was fully convinced—the high aristocracy and the generals and officers, mostly of high rank. It never entered his head that it might be interesting to talk with men and women of the middle classes and, as might seem natural in a young man, discover what they were like and what they thought. In intimate court circles there was nothing but contemptuous mirth for the court of his uncle, the King of Prussia, where every kind of scientific and literary question and even the new problems of industry were discussed with their leaders, and encouragement was given to the great artists and architects of the day. Frederick William IV's personal intimates were men like Alexander von Humboldt, Leopold von Ranke, Bunsen and many another of this highest type. This, for Vienna, was an "abnormality." Even after his marriage, Francis Joseph limited his social intercourse and that of his court exclusively to the "cousinage" of the historic nobles—a fact which influenced, profoundly, both his political views and his methods of government.

Entirely surrounded by people confined within the class

traditions of a period of European society long gone by, to whom any deviation from tradition in any department of life was bound to be alien, he was inevitably strengthened in an antagonism, implanted in him by his education, to everything new and modern, to everything damned in advance as "anti-religious" and liberal; to everything that, in Europe in general, and in Austria, in particular, almost exclusively, came out of the middle classes— those middle classes that were growing stronger economically year by year and consciously keeping step with the west of Europe.

Of these early years, however, the statement so frequently made later that the young Empress found the rigid limitations of the Vienna court disagreeable and disliked the etiquette that cut her off from the living world outside, is certainly not very accurate. Elizabeth had grown up in the simple and natural life of a country nobleman and the stiffness of court forms may have irked her. But though reliable information of these early years is scarce, what there is goes to show that Francis Joseph and Elizabeth, in the early days of married life, carried on an untrammeled existence, both in the Hofburg and the various imperial castles in the country, and that in this as in many other things Francis Joseph was always ready to meet Elizabeth's wishes. Riding, driving, and hunting of all sorts occupied much of his free time; so much indeed that there were loud complaints, for example from his aides-de-camp, that "pleasure" was playing too large a part in his life.

It would be a complete error to assume that the young

Empress was, at this period, animated by the independent or critical spirit that, in later years, after bitter disappointments and conflicts, filled the heart of the woman and caused her to prefer long journeys abroad to the intellectual isolation of the court. In her nature, finely gifted as she was, there was something that incapacitated her for real life. Finding happiness neither in marriage nor in any other intimate relation, she sought to create it through intellectual and artistic interests, into which she threw herself with a passionate and highly-colored imagination, remote not only from the ideas of the court but from those of the average man. But the time for this had not yet come.

She became an Empress when but a girl, as her husband had become Emperor while but a boy. From the beginning her lofty and inevitably isolated position made no appeal to her. All too soon her crown became a source of lasting unhappiness; her diadem brought her no joy. In these early years, however, she was full of youth and the enjoyment native both to her years and to a temperament impatient of any kind of restraint. "The latest news," says Count Grünne to the friend who records his remark in his diary, fourteen days after the imperial wedding, "is that the Emperor goes about everywhere with the Empress, without saying a word to anyone or even taking an aide with him." This freedom was not permitted him for long. All too soon the court began to remark "that there is no sympathy between Archduchess Sophia and her daughter-in-law, but the former makes criticisms and gives orders that displease the young Empress to the last degree."

A creature reared in complete freedom, noble, but not a little spoiled by reason of her beauty, may well have found it hard to maintain her position as Empress in a realm remote from her in spirit, owing to the social exclusiveness of the court, to which she was not prepared to sacrifice her own personality.

Gradually her fantasy broke loose from the bonds that tied it to a throne and to the duty of playing the part of an Empress among people she did not understand, and in a court comprising imperial satellites and no free human spirits. Early must her soul have felt the longing for the far and wide: above all the desire to wander over the great spaces of the earth and sea, to live free of compulsion, rushing over the fields mounted on some glorious steed, to belong to sun and wind and the great liberating forces of nature. Her spirit was not built either for a throne or for the daily round of family life as presented to her, all "Spanish ceremonial" notwithstanding. The irreconcilable antagonism that she must have known within her soul very early may for a time have been held in abeyance by the affectionate tenderness of her young husband. But when the young inexperienced woman believed that this too was gone from her—no one now living knows just how this happened—she fled from her life as Empress to the far south, there to try to build an existence for herself that corresponded to the dreams of her own soul. Francis Joseph, thus bereft of the only happiness he possessed, was sustained by the stern sense of duty to his empire and his house, whose service was for him the primordial law.

The strange de-personalization of Francis Joseph,

which enabled him later to bear with tranquilllity what he could not prevent, dates back to those dark days. To Elizabeth he owed all he knew of personal happiness; to her, too, some of the darkest hours of his life.

CHAPTER VII

THE AUTOCRAT

EASILY had Francis Joseph entered in 1852 on the autocracy established for him by statute. Unperturbed by contradiction he proceeded, from this time on, to rule as a "genuine Emperor," whose will was the supreme law throughout his realm. The unitary empire which Schwarzenberg had planned was a reality; the historic kingdoms and hereditary lands, out of which his forefathers had erected their imperium in the course of close upon six hundred years, were now mere political provinces, with no separate public life of their own; mere subdivisions of the machine of government centralized in Vienna and piloted by the Emperor himself. The departmental ministries continued in the form established in 1848. They only formed an effective unity, a real "government," in so far as they met for consultation under the chairmanship of the Emperor or his representative, and so arrived at draft resolutions finally made effective by imperial signature.

In 1853 the ministry of war disappeared, becoming a department—supreme military administration—under the High Command, alongside of the general staff and the imperial military chancellery and adjutants department. The head of one or other of these departments appeared at ministerial conferences when the army estimates were under discussion.

Kübeck's plan comprised a council of the empire, with himself at the head, side by side with the departments. It considered draft bills submitted to it by the departments and thoroughly examined administrative decrees, reporting direct to the Emperor. The great program of administrative and judicial reforms which had to be put through as the groundwork of autocracy kept both departments and council hard at work. The soul of this grand reorganization was Alexander Bach, Minister for the Interior. Despite remarkable energy shown by him and his colleagues its progress was slower than Francis Joseph perhaps had hoped. A vast "system" had to be created, a mighty structure of offices and officials in the capital, provinces, districts, and areas. In particular, an immense amount of work and a vast horde of officials were required for the subjection of Hungary, Siebenbürgen, and Croatia to this new administrative "strait waistcoat." In addition, there was all the work involved in the establishment of the necessary institutions for carrying out the emancipation of the peasantry throughout the Empire.

The realization of the new administrative, judicial, and financial principles involved a multiplicity of laws, planned and executed with truly German thoroughness and system, and put into effect by subordinate officers. Such was Alexander Bach's task, accomplished single-handed in the face of constant struggles with the heads of other departments, but sustained throughout by the confidence of the Emperor. Francis Joseph now learned every detail of government first-hand: his natural fondness for detail and his astonishing "cabinet diligence" now had full scope. He was specially zealous in all "personal questions," retaining for the most part in his own hands the filling of all posts of the first and second grade. He thus became familiar with innumerable men in important posts in various branches of state service, taking in not only their names but their efficiency and professional careers and remembering them all. He was unwearied in receiving officials when appointed or promoted, in order that he might get some sort of personal impression of them. Thus he trained that extraordinarily retentive memory of his, which caused astonishment in his middle and, above all, in his old age; moreover he thus acquired a certain knowledge of real life.

It has been said of the Habsburgs that many of them had traits of the genuine artist in their make-up in so far as they had a powerful impulse to mold the inchoate in accordance with their will. Certainly an almost esthetic conception of politics as a means to the realization of the idea of domination for its own sake, with Catholicism as its support was, in the old imperial race of Germany, Spain, Italy, Hungary and Austria, the key at once to an obstinate tenacity of purpose and an immovable calm in disaster or any crisis of human fate. This mystic inheritance of his ancestral house does not readily fit in with the dry matter-of-factness of Francis Joseph. And yet in the rigid calm, the almost somnambulistic assurance, with which the young man of twenty conceived the idea of a modern, technically efficient autocracy as the only possible reply to revolution in almost every part of his inherited realm, and carried it through, simply and solely by the force of his own resolutions—in this there is something analogous to the relation of the artist to the material through which he seeks to convey his thoughts and visions to the outer world.

The material here was the men and nations, the subjects and territories with all their historic rights and ethnic peculiarities, which Francis Joseph had inherited with his many crowns; the esthetic idea, that of an unlimited dominion conditioned by no obsolescent or new created rights on the parts of others but as free from any influence of the Estates as it was from "public opinion," from feudal rights in the aristocracy or any dependence on the popular will. Neither Shwarzenberg nor Grünne can have first implanted in his mind the notion of such unlimited power inhering in a single man by divine right; it was already part and parcel of the consciousness of the young man Windischgrätz and Schwarzenberg raised to the throne, strengthened and encouraged there by the ambitious and domineering spirit of the boy's mother. In origin, however, it was an inheritance there in him at birth—an inheritance only strengthened by the experience the quiet, amiable, self-contained boy had encountered at the court of his uncle, that far from royal good-natured being, whose personality made nonsense of the notion of representative imperial power. Francis Joseph learned too little history to have acquired any clear picture of his ancestor Charles V or of Ferdinand the Styrian; probably the only image at all vivid to him, as to

[223]

the rest of his court, was that of Joseph II, honored as
liberator by the peasants, as protector of the new age of
enlightenment by the cities, but really animated by the
proudest sense of being the greatest ruler in Christendom and called, as such, to free his realm and peoples
by admonishment and advice or, if needful, by force, of
their out-of-date notions, and to transform them as their
educator in accordance with his own ideas.

Francis Joseph must have had that "unconscious," sci-
entifically indefinable, understanding of all his forbears
that constitutes spiritual inheritance. This young man,
whose dignified bearing impressed all who visited him;
who in his twenties proceeded to clear away as so much
worthless trash the constitution he had himself promulgated, and that without a tremor or a hesitation; who,
sans phrase, with no more than a bare reference to "the
welfare of his people," declared himself autocrat and
at the same time systematically laid the bases of his autocracy with that affectionate attention to detail characteristic
of him; who could, later, be induced by only extreme
pressure from his ministers to grant the provinces "ad-
visory assemblies"—this young man can only be understood in the light of his historic heritage and the traditional experience of his ancestors.

It is with the heads of other ruling houses whose sovereignty had suffered more or less under the impact of
the revolution that his actions and attitude must be compared. All of them, so soon as they found breath again,
were ready to compromise with the people and bend before the ideas of their age. A clear case is that of his

uncle Frederick William IV of Prussia. He suffered unspeakably from the shame of the March days of 1848,
always called the paper constitution a slur on his royal
dignity, contemptuously rejected the imperial crown
when offered him by the "nebulous" Frankfort parliament—and yet never had the nerve simply to disregard
the constitution he had given to Prussia. As far as possible he got round its too democratic charter, by the
practiced skill of his Junker advisers and ministers. Twice
it was thus modified by royal decrees in favor of the
bureaucracy and the nobles. But the constitutional idea
remained intact, although for more than one decade the
power of the bureaucracy and the weakness of the chamber, aggravated by the three-class franchise and the
existence of a second chamber, kept power in the hands
of the king. Francis Joseph would have none of this.
For him there could be no compromise with ideas and
forces which—fresh as he was from Metternich's teaching—he simply summed up as revolutionary and which
Schwarzenberg had regarded as his deadliest foe.

Here we come upon a basic trait in Francis Joseph's
character: in great things as in small he had a black and
white mind; a thing, a man, an idea, a law was simply
good or bad. Intermediate stages did not exist for him at
this time and all his life long he lacked any subtlety of
thought. Nothing was more difficult for him than to
emancipate his mind to any degree from this over-simple
conception of life and the world. At bottom it was the
natural expression of a mind limited in range and
entirely concentrated on the immediate and obvious.

[225]

From his accession he saw one fact and only one—that his throne had been set up by the army. At the moment indeed his army made him perhaps the strongest prince in Europe, just because it was possible for him to hold on firmly, amid all the confusion of the times, to the single goal he saw before him—he ought to be a genuine ruler and had no doubts that he could be one. This gave him an element of strength of the soul denied to others who could not, as he did, wholly close their minds to the tendencies of the time. He remained aloof, unaffected, conscious of an inherited sense of power that, for the moment, at all events, circumstances appeared to justify.

The improbability, in an epoch still conditioned by revolution, of erecting an autocracy outside all its historic conditions, did not make it any less, for him, the entirely natural and only right thing to do: it expressed his own perfectly honest conviction, unaffected as it was by any profound study of the nature of the state or by any kind of literary influence. He was strong *because* he knew nothing of the ideas of his age, nothing of their historic application, nothing of the power inevitably lent them by the social and economic development of the whole period. For that very reason he was called upon to perform an action which the routine holders of historic power might desire to take but were impotent to accomplish. He was able to do it because he did not belong mentally and spiritually in the least to his own epoch. As supreme War Lord indeed he felt an absolute obligation to gather civil power too into his own hands. When it was done, the old statesmen and generals were astounded to see that it could

be done, quite quietly. There was no tangible resistance
on the part of the peoples. This increased the young monarch's bravery and self-confidence; indeed a shrewd observer noted at the time that there was a hint of bravado
in his bright blue eyes: a victor looked at the world. Not
that he was changed in himself. All who knew him in
these days praise his bearing to those about him as full of
friendly graciousness, always governed by a strong sense
of form. The capital of self-confidence then amassed he
was to need badly enough from 1853 on, in the long conflict with Russia. The happiness of his marriage strengthened it, and helped him to bear the heavy strain of the
years of the Crimean War.

This inner certainty, together with his great diligence
had, meantime, made him feel himself a safe pilot of
the vast engine he had set up for carrying through his
autocracy. He believed that all the threads were in his
hands, although visited from time to time by doubts as
to the reliability of his officials. His confidence in the
army was perfect. Old Marshal Radetzky still held the
most important command, that over Italy. Meantime the
Emperor had grown accustomed to the old Chief of the
General Staff, General Hess, and was not disappointed
with him when, war with Russia seeming to be imminent,
he had to mobilize the entire army.

The error which was to have disastrous consequences
later was Francis Joseph's nomination of Count Gyulai
to succeed Radetzky. The face of this absolutely insignificant and ineffective individual ought to have warned
the Emperor against him. Since 1848 a great reputation

had been enjoyed by General Benedek, a young Protestant Magyar, the perfect type of fighting loyalist. Francis Joseph did not care for him but allowed his promotion. The Austrian army at this date was notable for the number of generals of high nobility it possessed. It did not profit either by their presence or by the "brutal colonels" who regarded roughness and even brutality as the marks of a good soldier. But the worst evil was that the Italian campaigns and their experience failed to keep the passion for mechanical drilling and the whole parade idea within bounds. It grew, indeed, accompanied by resistance to any kind of "progress," any innovation either in technical equipment or the training of the men. They were still taught the old "shock tactics" and schooled in the "moral force" of the bayonet. Moreover, the old "mercenary" notions of the necessity of the most severe disciplinary methods and a terrorizing procedure of courts-martial persisted far too long. Corporal punishment and flogging through the line remained in force long after they had been abolished in Prussia and in France.

Among evils which Francis Joseph did not see was the unlimited scope which the system of control by "honorary" colonels of regiments gave to the reckless treatment and passing over of wretchedly payed subalterns. In all such matters, covering both technique and morale, he relied upon the judgment of men like Gyulai and Grünne, or on the mindless military bureaucracy that grew up in his army administration department. They were distinguished mainly by the unsystematic zeal with which they were forever, but never thoroughly, reforming the organization and uniforms of the army. The result was the creation in it of a most deleterious unrest. The veterans of the army stood fast; the valor and military spirit of the average, poor, utterly loyal subaltern, son as a rule of an officer or of an official family, stood, though not without difficulty; the morale of the army as a whole remained good and reliable. But as early as the mobilization of 1854-55 it was plain that the old defects in the sanitary and health arrangements, of which Archduke Charles had complained fifty years earlier, were still there, indeed were aggravated. This did not reach the young Emperor's ears. A well established system of secrecy and concealment existed within the machinery by which the whole organization and command of the army were concentrated in the person of the Emperor. One has only to read in the diaries of the Commandant of the Gendarmerie, Baron von Kempen, to realize how early Count Grünne and the men who followed him in positions of responsibility had established a tactic of hiding everything unpleasant as long as possible from the young Emperor.

Unwillingness to hear disagreeable things was a basic trait in Francis Joseph. It made him impatient and, contrary to his general habit, brusque to the point of positive discourtesy. This was a by-product of absolutism, as natural as it was disastrous. How were men to grow up in the country capable of maintaining, vis-a-vis the throne, the candor due to their profession and the courage of their convictions? Everything for the officer or civil servant depended on his effect with the "all-highest" lord, on whether his reports pleased or displeased him. General Count Grünne was past master in the art of "sparing" his young master. It seems never to have occurred to him that he was thus doing him the greatest disservice.

There was an army of 800,000 men when fully mobilized, about half of that on the active list in peace time: the strongest army in Europe at the moment. The entire direction, inspection, and administration was immediately in the Emperor's hands. Obvious that the result of such a state of things must be seriously damaging to the army itself. The preference given to men of rank in promotions; faulty selection for posts in the higher commands; and, worst of all, the demoralizing influence of Grünne and his favorites, deleterious as it was to military progress generally, had an adverse influence in the first instance on the spirit of the officers' corps and then on the training of the troops and the entire army establishment. It is really astonishing that in spite of all this the army remained the effective instrument of sovereignty that it proved in all the campaigns of Francis Joseph's youth, and this although on most occasions its generalship was very unfortunate.

The favorite arm both of the Emperor and of the aristocracy was the cavalry. There the young men of "family" collected. The fashion for riding, imported from England, and practiced by the young Emperor and Empress, made service in the cavalry the authentic "knightly profession" for the young blood of society, first and second. The sons of the Hungarian *"Puszta,"* like the Poles and Ruthenians, had special qualification for this, now the smartest branch of the service, while artillery and the engineers were regarded as "middle class," since officers in these branches had to have a certain amount of technical training. Further, the line regiments, the real backbone of the army, began to be looked down upon, as lowest in the social scale.

A sharp distinction, accentuated from decade to decade, grew up between the quiet, simple, unpretentious Austrian officer of the line and the Prussian-German officer of the type so prominent in Europe after 1870. The overwhelming preponderance of aristocratic officers after 1849 gave the Austrian army a distinctively old-fashioned character, inasmuch as it was dominated, through them, by a purely personal conception of loyalty to the Emperor as incorporating the unity of the Empire. The reason why the era of autocracy lasted as long as it did in Austria, despite the low estimation in which its power began to be held abroad, is the success with which this unity was expressed in the system of subordination of the ten different races in the Empire, with as many regimental languages, to the single German language in all army commands: and not merely endured but was strengthened there.

The great silent mass composing the army consisted of peasants of the various nationalities, with an admixture of the lower middle class among the N.C.O.'s. Nothing in imperial absolutism went against their primitive notions of the state. The rank and file were men from the land who, ever since the time of Maria Theresa, had looked to the officials of the Empire to protect and help them against their landlords, and were full of a naïve but very effective sense of gratitude to the imperial house. Further, since the abolition of the excessively long term of compulsory service, the peasant and even the lower middle-class man regarded military service as a rough but useful school of youth. To the town bred and more or less educated, the chance of becoming an N.C.O. promised a certain rise in the world, and the possibility of passing, with the assistance of the laws providing for ex-soldiers in the civil service, from there to the lower grades of officialdom. The sons of such militarized clerks and custom officers might even easily climb through the cadet school to officer's rank.

All these circumstances were familiar to Francis Joseph from childhood up. His fresh intelligence perceived how important they were in an army which was to serve as his instrument of autocracy. He was always readily persuaded to make improvements in the conditions of the men, although he was a stern upholder of rigid discipline and made the utmost physical demands upon them. Pursuing a far-sighted policy, he was no reformer, but always inclined to maintain anything of proved utility. For general principles and large ideas he had no more use in this department than in any other. Though he did not see himself as the Father of his soldiers, he left undisturbed traditions, established by Radetzky and his school, which implied that point of view.

There was nothing contrary to the ideas of his age in his position as supreme War Lord. The fifties saw a strengthening of militarism in all the monarchies of Europe. In France, Napoleon III relied almost exclusively on the army; in Prussia, the heir to the throne and, later, King William, relied on the army and in particular set hopes for the future on the strengthening of the Junker officers' corps; in Russia, the imperialistic policy of Nicholas gave the army pride of place in the state. In relation to the army all the monarchs of Europe had for centuries been autocrats. The peculiarity of Francis Joseph's position in European history in the second half of the nineteenth century consists in his having the courage, nay the perversity, to extend his military omnipotence over the entire area of state life. Civil servants, however, and higher officials, like governors and ministers, corresponded to officers and generals, under this assimilation of the civil to the military government. The Council of Empire (Reichsrat) constituted a sort of "Civil Annex" to the general staff.

Kübeck's great idea was, as we have seen, to get rid of the absolutism of "liberal" ministers and their "constitutional responsibility" and so give full scope to the personal will of the Emperor of one and twenty. For the conduct of government he had his so-called "Council of Empire"—an Austrian imitation of the Napoleonic *conseil d'état* which old Metternich had earlier attempted to introduce without success. This plan was carried out in the decrees of August and in the imperial patent of December 31, 1851; but very soon a great disappointment followed for Kübeck.

The Council of Empire, of which he had been nominated president, consisted of some twelve Austrian bureaucrats and two or three high Hungarian jurists; its task was to study the draft bills and decrees submitted to it by the ministries, and make reports on them to the Emperor, who read them or let them lie. Initiative remained entirely with the ministers, who often enough disliked the subsequent criticisms of the Council, since the result was alterations of their plans and bills. The whole thing did not work out in the least as Kübeck had intended. The Minister of the Interior, Dr. Alexander Bach, whom it was one of his prime objects to jockey out of the saddle, remained; indeed dominated the government. Old Kübeck's talk with his intimates, like his diary, was full of bitter complaints of Bach's unassailable position with the Emperor. The latter rejected a proposal of Kübeck's giving the Council a sort of control over the departmental activities of ministers. Francis Joseph had learned enough to know that anything of the kind was incompatible with an energetic conduct of government. Possibly he thought his personal control sufficient.

It was soon realized in the highest circles that the venerable president of the Council no longer had the decisive voice with the Emperor, although he continued to be treated with great personal kindness. Kübeck, deeply pained by the supersession evidenced in the disregard of his proposals and the overpowering influence of Dr. Bach, turned his criticisms on the foreign and church policy of the ministry as well as on its finance. When he died of cholera on September 11, 1855, the Council lost all political significance, as was almost officially indicated by the nomination of Archduke Rainer as its president.

Thus from the start the absolutism of the young Emperor rested, as it was bound to do, on the absolutism of his ministers. The principal cause for the total failure of Kübeck's grandiose plan was the unique personality of Alexander Bach, a combination of often unscrupulous cunning and eel-like cleverness with unparalleled powers of work, inexhaustible energy, and a wide knowledge of Austrian legislation. He functioned as a sort of vice-autocrat. His enemies, above all Prince Windischgrätz, were never tired of complaining of the way in which he interfered in every department of state and, as a rule, got his way.

The Emperor's idea of autocracy was that he should be informed about everything so as to decide everything himself. Bach in every important matter was ahead of him and succeeded, either directly or by clever manipulation, in directing his young Emperor's will along the lines of his own proposals. His decisive coöperation in the final consummation of church policy through the Concordat with the Holy See in 1855, which went against the consciences even of good Catholics like Kübeck and von Kempen, ensured him the firm support of Archduchess Sophia and consequently of her son. Bach had, of course, early studied the young Emperor's character and showed endless resource in avoiding any collision with him, with his mother, or their spiritual adviser, Archbishop Rauscher. He was helped by the fact that nothing so attached the Emperor to his ministers as attacks on them from outside. From the first he was abnormally sensitive on this point. Any suggestion that men whom he regarded as capable and trustworthy were not suited for their offices he took as an insolent criticism of himself, to be resented by keeping the minister in question in office at all costs.

Dr. Bach was undoubtedly superior to the host of his envious critics, whether bureaucratic or aristocratic; he was retained in office because the Emperor, not unjustly, was convinced of his complete devotion to the system of autocracy. That for Francis Joseph was the deciding point. In addition, Bach was the father and supporter of the system by which Hungary, with its nobles at its head, had been subjugated to the absolute supremacy of the Emperor: his hand grasped all the threads which kept the system working effectually despite the dangerous tendencies of Hungarian society.

This alone made Alexander Bach indispensable, for this was the weak spot in the autocratic system. The pivot of absolutism in the unitary realm was the subjection of the Magyars. Long after anything in the nature of a revolutionary movement in Hungary had been overthrown and the repeated attempts of the emigrés at conspiracies and risings between 1850-53 had either been discovered by the police or proved abortive, bitter discontent lived on in the sections of society there which had for centuries led the country both politically and economically, i.e., the Magyar aristocracy, magnates and gentry. Schwarzenberg's greatest mistake was that he had failed to attract, had even gone out of his way to repulse, that section which had stood aloof from and even opposed radical and liberal movements in 1848 and also the great body of Magyar magnates who had formed the old conservative

party in 1848 and after Hungary had been won back by
the crown aimed only at the restoration of the old constitutional position of 1847.

The cause of the conflict that broke out in 1848
was that the new Hungarian constitution, promulgated
by Ferdinand in April of that year, did not guarantee the
indispensable minimum of internal connection between
the two halves of the realm, but actually made Hungary
absolutely independent of the government and court of
Vienna. This was incompatible with the continued existence of the old monarchy, which besides being a Habsburg
interest, was regarded by the cabinets of the great
powers as necessary for the balance of power in Europe.
But, in 1850, instead of seeking a middle way such as
could readily have been found, Schwarzenberg determined on the creation of a unitary realm which was to
solve all these problems at a stroke by serving as the
basis of a primarily militarist autocracy. The real obstacles to this purely "ideal" construction were the old
historic rights of Hungary, in relation to its king, and
those of Croatia and Siebenbürgen: they must therefore
be destroyed, once and for all, when the Hungarian rebellion had been defeated in the field.

It was Alexander Bach who deduced the necessary legal
formula declaring these rights had been forfeited by
Kossuth and his party's declaration deposing the dynasty in the rump Parliament of 1849 at Debreczén. He
consequently proceeded to provincialize Hungary with a
view to fitting it into the centralized bureaucratic system.
Francis Joseph backed this up, heart and soul, since

the Hungarian rising was in his view the very forefront of the revolution. This rebellion had alarmed him, little as it had to do with the modern phenomenon of democracy which he detested, because it left in his mind a very strong impression of the boundless "disobedience" of his subjects. Moreover since Schwarzenberg had taught him that in Hungary the people were to-day, as they had been for centuries, merely the passive instrument of the nobles, he saw the latter, the old conservative party of Hungary, as the real danger to his throne and his autocracy.

The secret memorandum on Hungary written in 1844 by Prince Metternich was retrieved and shown to him: but neither this nor the aristocratic view of Prince Windischgrätz had the slightest influence upon him. After Schwarzenberg's death, Bach was the main supporter of this policy of holding down the Hungarian nobles and their constitutional claims, with the result that both the policy and Bach were, so to speak, sacrosanct for Francis Joseph. He made Archduke Albert governor and chief commandant in Budapest and Bach sent his most trusty officials with him. The thousands of German and Czech police officers and officials whom Bach substituted for the aristocratic Magyar *vicegespan* (viscounts) and other municipal officers in the counties (*comitati*) and towns of Hungary, served to hold down, and act as spies (often in the most despicable fashion) on, the aristocrats, who had been welded into a homogeneous party by resistance to Vienna and its autocracy.

Although the leadership of the Magyar nobles had not been popular with the mass of Magyars since the revolution of 1848, still less with the non-Magyar nationalities in Hungary, the effort to win the adhesion of the rest of the population of the country to the new system or attach them to Vienna and its system, failed. The result, though Francis Joseph was unable to comprehend it at the time, was to prove that while unlimited autocracy and brute force may to all appearances reduce men to impotence, they will nevertheless irresistibly gain ground if the world can see in them the defenders of ancient rights, and the champions of the idea of freedom, national or civil.

To maintain the system in Hungary required not only thousands of imported officials, and the maintenance of several army corps on a war footing, but, above all, the mighty organization of the gendarmerie created by General von Kempen and developed by him into a masterpiece of higher police. Count Orlow, Minister of Police to Nicholas I, thought the twelve to fourteen regiments of this gendarmerie excessive, when General von Kempen set out all the details of his great work of pacification in Hungary, on the occasion of a visit of the Czar to Vienna.

Between Bach and von Kempen, the two pillars of the new autocracy, there was frequent friction and secret conflict, from the moment when General von Kempen, who for all his roughness was a man of no mean character and personally of faultless integrity, was made police minister, because Bach was continually claiming control over the police supervision of the press, which had formerly come under his department. Nevertheless they managed to work fairly well together, thanks to the strong belief they shared in the necessity of a rigorous police system and their common interest in retaining their personal positions of power. The fact that Francis Joseph was able to keep men so different in temperament, but equally indispensable to him by reason of their remarkable efficiency, in his service for ten years, proves that he must, even in early youth, have possessed some of the elements of a strong ruler.

Access to the hitherto unprinted diaries of the ubiquitous head of the gendarmerie gives a first-hand picture of the working of autocracy at this period. Regularly at least once a week, or oftener, General von Kempen appears in the Hofburg and reports to the Emperor personally on all the more important departments of his activities at home and abroad, on the state of opinion in Vienna and other parts of the realm, and complaints and observations on the press. The diaries further contain interesting remarks about the Emperor and frequent complaints on his reserve, and note every instance of imperial graciousness and all the personal questions taken up by the Emperor with him.

Kempen was further in close touch with Count Grünne and sent political news and hints directly to the Emperor through him. For the military chancellery of the Emperor had, of course, a special police department of its own. As years went by Kempen became one of the few men in whom the Emperor had complete confidence. He is thus in a position to record characteristic judgments of Francis Joseph's on the political situation and brief but expressive hints of his political views. This was one of the rare cases in which the young Emperor departed from his firm rule of merely getting answers to his own questions from statesmen, ministers, or generals, keeping the conversational lead strictly in his own hands. But old General von Kempen, well aware of his value to the Emperor, knew how, while keeping well within the prescribed forms, to lead Francis Joseph on in conversation and get expressions of his own views from him.

In general, Francis Joseph now, as throughout his life, maintained "autocracy" even in talk. He believed that it made it easier for him to gain a view of affairs and protected him from any attempt to infringe on the powers of his ministers and officials, as from any interposition, such as he detested, of unauthorized critics into his relations to his ministers and other officials. He was simply not going to listen to such "chatter" or what he called "useless logic chopping" and permitted no one, except on his own demand, to speak of matters that did not "concern" him.

Since the purpose of the entire state was the fulfillment of his own will, and the laws and decrees issued through his ministers exclusively embodied that will, he regarded it as his supreme duty to see that these laws were really executed. He heard often enough from Kübeck and other statesmen that they were not. For that one reason he increased his own efforts at personal control. There is something naïve in the way in which, possessing neither adequate technical knowledge nor practical experience, his sense of duty now caused him to strengthen the police machine created for him by Schwarzenberg and Bach, and to strive to tighten the meshes of its net over the population: as though control could compensate for the organic intellectual and ethical defects of the system! The upshot was that the vigilant Kempen extended his detective and spy system over all the departments and offices of state, administrative and judicial; had even bishops and high dignitaries secretly watched, and the correspondence, not of suspected persons only but of many statesmen as of foreign diplomats in Vienna intercepted by his Black Cabinet: circumspectly, since Francis Joseph thought this practice wrong, but permitted it to go on.

The times of "good" Emperor Francis seemed to have come again, without the note of apprehension that marked them. For himself Francis Joseph was not anxious. "He is a fearless fellow" had been Schwarzenberg's word for him at nineteen; and he remained the fearless officer, despite all the assassination plots aimed at him. He was continually complaining to von Kempen about his surrounding him with his secret police whenever he went out walking. When the general said he could not bear his responsibility otherwise, he replied, characteristically: "I clear you in advance of all responsibility for my personal safety!" To which Count Grünne observed with a laugh that he was now the sole person with responsibility.

Certainly the new police system was more efficient than that of a generation earlier. It had behind it all the modern improvements advanced year by year (railways and telegraphs) which gave it hitherto unknown possibilities and powers. In general, of course, the new centralized absolutism of the rejuvenated realm had the advantage of the rapid development of modern economic life in Austria, as elsewhere, behind it, to put resources hitherto unsuspected at its disposal. Dr. Bach's reforms instituted the administrative technique of modern bureaucracy, originated by Napoleon, throughout the realm, substituting the will of a responsible chief of department for direction by a corporate group of counsellors.

Despite the indubitable success of the new régime of Bach and von Kempen, Francis Joseph seems soon to have become dubious about the efficiency and reliability of the thousands of state officials. His military advisers in particular assured him that there were far too many officials. The characteristic evils of the older Austria—the excessive number of ill-paid civil servants, their slackness, delays, and loss of power resulting from red tape—had not been cleared out of the new. Now, as then, generals were jealous of the superior pay and position enjoyed by the higher officials and their views began to influence the Emperor. Further there was a widespread mistrust of the court officials. The Emperor often complained of "bad spirit" in the population and the want of influence over it of the officials. Again and again he attributed this bad spirit to the press—and this when the police, under the terms of martial law, had a complete stranglehold on it and could silence it at will, Vienna journalists being forced to write in such a way that one had to read between the lines to get at the truth or take the point of criticism.

Francis Joseph was always pondering how the press could be still further restricted, thus proving himself an apt pupil both of his mother and of Baron Kübeck, who in this respect belonged entirely to the "pre-March" régime. The one political journal in Vienna in these days, the *Press*, belonged to August Zang, a man who had assimilated the dubious characteristics of the new school of journalism in Paris under the Napoleonic régime, and in Austria was the father of press corruption in the modern sense. From this time, too, dates the evil connection between this malleable semi-official press and the rapidly developing interests of international finance and its representatives in Vienna. It is hardly to be wondered at if Francis Joseph had, all his life long, the worst opinion possible both of the "big" and "little" press in his capital and elsewhere. Of course he could not see, either then or later, how powerfully his police supervision contributed, as though of set purpose, to promote the development of the worst traits in modern journalism.

For the rest, his instruction had been such as to cause him to regard anything in the nature of "public opinion" as utterly irrelevant. He was later to realize that while the newspapers could not be simply wiped out they could be used. This was a lesson he was quick to grasp. If he continued to inveigh against the "institution," the agenda and minutes of ministerial conferences show he always insisted on "reforms" of the press laws and repeatedly speaks to his ministers about the necessity of keeping an eye on the press and at the same time increasing influence over it. He never found a solution for the ticklish problem of distinguishing between the decent and the indecent press. For him political newspapers were simply a combination of self-seeking publishers, journalists who could be more or less "influenced," and sheer money-makers. To the last he never achieved the modern point of view which "notoriously" takes the high moral function of the press as a basis of modern liberty and progress. Here as elsewhere he was no child of his age: nothing "modern" about him.

Fundamental, here, as in the rest of his outlook, was his conviction that, at bottom, his subjects had nothing to do with government policy, which belonged solely to him, his ministers, and officials, while their business was to attend to their own affairs. In this he was but following the tradition of his grandfather. At the same time he *Francis II.* maintained the institution of Joseph II which gave every subject free access to the Emperor with petitions or complaints. The habit of imperial audience, recently established by Emperor Francis, was carried on. From the first days of his reign, he received thousands on thousands of his subjects in his audience chamber. In this way he adhered to the basic idea of European monarchy, as strengthened in the eighteenth century. Above all imperial courts and offices stood the Emperor himself, as final extraordinary resort, to exercise his prerogative of mercy as against the harshness of the law and any injustice committed by his officers. Emperor Francis' popularity had rested largely on the fact that he received everyone who made application in the prescribed form and was not suspected by the police. He would listen tranquilly to the sometimes extraordinary wishes of his subjects and their complaints against authority, often discussing their affairs with his petitioners and ending, as a rule, with the words: "We will see into it; we will help you." It is further reported that Emperor Francis once said to one of these visitors: "Did you see that man who has just gone out? I have turned him down twice, but you'll see he'll get what he desires in the end."

Francis Joseph, in audience, was of course not the "easy-going monarch", like his grandfather. His bearing was always dignified, and the time given to each petitioner usually very brief. One of his high generals complained of the coldness of the young Emperor, who "demands devotion and its visible marks from others and is annoyed if it is lacking, but does nothing to win the love of his people or attract affection. Francis Joseph is hard and unapproachable. When (in 1858) he visited the Bohemian Theatre in Prague he barely acknowledged his reception. Emperor Ferdinand, weak in the head but kindly, roused far more feeling in Prague than the young Emperor did."

This complaint was only too just. Among the nobles who surrounded him a deep-rooted belief grew up that he was proud and cold, and nothing affected him. Even Count Grünne, most intimate of his lieutenants, once expressed the view: "Their Majesties change their best servants as readily as their gloves."

Autocracy accustomed the Emperor to regard his peoples solely as objects of government. Nothing is so hard to understand here as his lack of interest in the special characteristics of the various peoples composing his realm, most of whose languages he knew. At this period of his life he thought and spoke about the nationalities like the

young German officers in his army, who habitually characterized the various people in more or less contemptuous
slang phrases. Once, speaking confidentially, young Francis Joseph said—"The Bohemians are numbskulls." He
called the Italians calculating and cheats, the Magyars
obstinate. None taught him in these formative years to
take a deeper view of the historic character of these races,
above all the non-German ones, or their special outlook.
He only knew that all got on together well enough in the
ranks since "no one was stirring them up" and everybody
had got to "fall in." This was pretty much the point of
view, after all, of Grillparzer's famous poem on Radetzky's army: "Thy camp, that is Austria."

The revolution in Italy, Prague, and Hungary had literally shocked and shaken the very best minds in German
Austria, since, for the first time, they saw their country,
to them essentially the embodiment of German power
and culture, suddenly threatened with utter destruction.
The army saved the Emperor and the Austrian Germans
from this dread peril. In 1848 the problem of the Austrian state was revealed to all the world; the rejuvenated
unitary realm was a wholehearted attempt to solve this
problem by simply translating the example given by the
army into the "civil sphere" in the form of imperial
autocracy.

In the latter part of his first decade of absolutism Francis Joseph believed that effort was, on the whole, successful; except, as he knew from observation, in Hungary
and Italy. There things were very bad. Neither the hopeful reports of Archduke Albert from Budapest, nor of

his brother Ferdinand Max from Milan could convince him of the contrary. In both countries the effort to assimilate them in a "rejuvenated Austria" was being resisted ceaselessly, by every available means, by the aristocracy and the educated classes. The masses, so Francis Joseph was convinced, were, whether in Upper Italy or in Hungary, quite satisfied with Austria and its government, but the incessant agitation of aristocratic conspirators and emigrés working in Piedmont and in England left them no peace. This was the source of the disaffection towards army and civil authorities plentifully reported by the police organizations in these two areas.

In both, in Francis Joseph's opinion, there had been administrative failure; a lack of the needful foresight and energy on the part both of military commands and political offices. He came, therefore, to the view that he ought, personally, to see that the right thing was done in these most difficult and perilous departments of his realm. Thus he resolved to go with the Empress and an imposing suite first to the Italian provinces and then to Hungary. A stay of some time was planned in both countries, to afford opportunity for the Emperor to examine conditions for himself, and allow the personalities of himself and the Empress to exert an influence on society. In November of 1856 they journeyed to Italy where they spent three months. Their first visit was paid to Venice, where the beauty of the Empress and the friendly bearing of Francis Joseph not only called forth something like friendliness among the Venetian *nobili* but roused the masses to enthusiastic demonstrations. The government sought to give proofs of its desire to promote the economic welfare of the city. In Milan, where all ranks in society had long been seething with hatred of the alien rule, a partial change was not perceptible till after the proclamation of an amnesty on a grand scale and a program of reforms. The nomination of Archduke Ferdinand Max as governor-general was announced contemporaneously with the retirement of Radetzky, now in his nineties. In addition to the general amnesty, other acts of grace took place; for example the rescinding of the confiscation of estates, decreed as punishment for high treason against the landowners and citizens who had fled to Piedmont, produced a temporary improvement in general opinion. Grievances in relation to recruitment for the army were also met in a series of decrees.

Those measures, however, amounted to no more than an attempt to stem the tide of nationalism gaining power year by year under the influence of liberal and nationalist agitation in Piedmont, powerfully supported by the government of Victor Emmanuel. Ever since Cavour had reconstructed the Piedmontese constitution along definitely liberal lines and his government had become the focus of all the forces in the country striving for Italian unity, a hostility had grown up between Austria and Piedmont out of which serious consequences were bound to develop sooner or later. During the Emperor's visit, a series of sharp notes were exchanged between Vienna and Turin; the chargés d'affaires on both sides were recalled, as the ambassadors had been four years earlier.

In those circumstances, the Emperor's brother was from

the start foredoomed to failure in the rôle assigned to him. His part was, with the young bride, daughter of the Belgian king, whom he had brought home in 1857, to carry on the work of reconciliation begun by the Emperor and Empress; to win the aristocracy and society of Milan for Austria by the splendor of his court and ample proofs of royal favor. Indeed, the great sums expended for this purpose were a source of grave anxiety to the finance minister in Vienna. Bitter comments further were occasioned at court there by the fact that the Milan establishment was much more French than Austrian.

None of these efforts changed the political atmosphere of Upper Italy; it continued to be exceedingly menacing to Austrian suzerainty. On his return home, Francis Joseph, speaking confidentially, said: "Italy has been allowed to go on too long feeling the conditions of 1848-49." He must have felt that the protracted military régime had had a very bad effect. His letters to Archduke Ferdinand Max show, too, that he had not been favorably impressed by Austrian officialdom in Milan and Venice. But he must not have realized the real difficulty—that of permanently holding this great rich region as a province of a German realm, a mere passive object of foreign dominion, against the gathering strength of the movement for Italian unity among the educated classes. His mind at this time did not perceive a nationalist problem, as such. For him it was merely the revolutionary spirit in another of its forms.

The imperial visit to Hungary in the spring of 1857 was even less satisfactory than the Italian journey. An

address on behalf of the Hungarian nobles was presented
to the Emperor by the Cardinal of Gran, containing quite
moderate demands, such as the use of the Magyar language in local offices and the abolition of the fivefold division of the country. Francis Joseph, however, surprised
by being presented with such a petition, rejected, with
deep resentment, what he took as a fresh proof of the
malignity of the detested old conservative party. The
sudden death of their eldest child broke up the visit of
the imperial pair, but in the autumn Francis Joseph came
again and saw more of the country. His views had not
altered meantime, as the holograph letter he wrote to the
governor-general on September 9 proves. It states that
the Emperor is convinced that the institutions now in
force in Hungary had done much to promote the unmistakable advance of the country. "Resolved to adhere un-
waveringly to the basic principles that have guided me
so far in ruling my realm, I desire to have this generally
known and in particular accepted by all the organs of my
government as their definite rule of conduct." So the
"Bach system" was reëstablished in the eyes of all the
world and the plans of the Hungarian nobles rejected
as dreams, and forbidden dreams at that.

The main permanent lines of Francis Joseph's character as a sovereign are there in the picture of the young
autocrat sketched above. Years only served to deepen
them. New influences were to play upon him, in the periods that followed hard on that here described, and a complete change in circumstances to add fresh lines to it. But
this autocratic period fixed his views and his technique

and method of rule and created the man whom successive generations saw at work amid the flux of altering events. The main elements in his nature stand clearly revealed at the close of this period ending with his twenty-ninth year—a dry, matter-of-fact conception of his duty as ruler; a rejection of all empty shows; a tendency to reduce both the problems of statecraft confronting him and the men with whom he has to deal to rigid formulæ: above all an attempt to simplify as far as possible the conditions with which he is faced while endeavoring always to find a middle way between sharply opposed views or solutions, by bringing to dawn on the immediate situation an often sadly unimaginative common sense. Nothing was more repugnant to him than forms of thinking or speaking that touched the abstract, the exalté, or the original. He rejected anything of the sort in his manifestoes, as later in speeches from the throne and other general pronouncements, and demanded of his ministers the same dryness in their official documents.

General von Kempen's diary, already frequently referred to, contains an illuminating anecdote. He records with great glee that when the huge arsenal building in Vienna was completed, the learned Dr. Arneth, director of the archives of house, court, and state, employed great ingenuity in devising a series of classical inscriptions in Latin for the different buildings. They were submitted to the Emperor, who decided simply to have "Imperial Royal Arsenal" or "Imperial Royal Artillery Works" put over the gates. His attitude to business was not intellectual at all: he detested any appearance of learning or anything more or less recondite. Everything should be simple, practical, useful.

An excellent picture of him in this respect is given by Peter von Meyendorff, who, from 1850, had the difficult task of representing Czar Nicholas in Vienna. A brother-in-law of Count Buol, he had opportunities of knowing the Emperor intimately, and did know him well. Shortly before the breach between the Czar and the Emperor, Meyendorff wrote, on June 1, 1854, to his Chancellor Nesselrode, from the depths of a heart almost broken by the failure of his mission: "The only possible explanation of the young Emperor's behavior is that he has made it a rule to take nobody's advice and listen to nobody. If Buol brings him a diplomatic note all he says is: 'Is what you have written exactly in line with what we did before?' Buol says, Yes, and the Emperor signs. The most varying influences simply slide off him, as off marble. The fact that Buol is attacked, as he is, actually strengthens his position. There seems to be a curse from heaven on this Habsburg race. The only one among them who has the stuff in him to make a ruler is blinded by his self-will and the foolish assumption that he can *judge and decide everything entirely by himself*. That is why the prestige he had has vanished."

This last sentence must be attributed to Meyendorff's extreme annoyance with Francis Joseph's opposition to the Czar's policy. The prestige won by the young Emperor was dimmed as the result of European complications of the Crimean War. It was not lost till both his policy and his armies were defeated by France.

CHAPTER VIII

THE WAR AGAINST PIEDMONT-SARDINIA, THE LOSS OF LOMBARDY

CLEAR warning of an approaching struggle with Piedmont-Sardinia was given by the issue of the Crimean War and the course of peace negotiations in Paris. Sardinia's entry into the western alliance and the support it gave to the powers in the Crimea at once markedly raised the status of the House of Savoy in Europe and signalized the alienation of England and France from Austria. Although Sardinia's part in the peace discussions was confined to specific points, its presence gave Cavour the chance of definitely raising the Italian problem at the congress, if in a masked form. It was a diplomatic defeat for Count Buol to have Cavour succeed, with the help of the French foreign minister, in starting a debate there on "the policy of intervention in Italy" and in coming out sharply as the advocate of the whole of Italy against the Vienna cabinet.

Although Austria got Prussia to the conference table before the end of the proceedings, it did not thereby do anything effective to allay the profound dissatisfaction of Berlin with Francis Joseph's policy during the three dark years of the war. The exasperation caused both to the King of Prussia and to all the political groups supporting the Manteuffel government by Francis Joseph's incalculable policy has already been indicated. The peace treaty itself, and the way in which it was carried out in direct opposition to the wishes of the Vienna cabinet, completed Austria's isolation in Europe. Above all, Russia was and remained Francis Joseph's irreconcilable foe. When a great Russophile, like Prince Windischgrätz, met the Czar in Berlin in 1856 and tried to soften the tension between Russia and Francis Joseph, all Alexander replied was: "I am not going to be put upon by Austria."

Decisive, however, were the increasing coolness between Francis Joseph and Napoleon III on the one hand, and the impossible situation in Lombardy on the other. The imperial visit to Milan proved quite useless, in the long run. Cavour's increasingly liberal and nationalist administration was steadily strengthening the influence of Turin and its associated organizations throughout Italy over the minds of leading men and groups in the Austrian provinces in the peninsula, to a degree that caused the greatest anxiety to Francis Joseph and his advisers. A note from Count Buol gave the powers to understand that there was an unbridgable gulf between Austria, standing on the inviolability of the solemn international treaties of 1815, and the political aims and efforts of Cavour. Through diplomatic channels and through the press, Vienna complained incessantly of the disruptive influence of the radical government of Piedmont on opinion in Milan and Venice.

How dangerously things were developing there Francis Joseph was well aware. In April, 1856, he told General von Kempen that he was much alarmed about the maintenance of order in Italy. When Kempen remarked: "If our troops were to be withdrawn to-day, from the duchies and the papal legations, we should have revolution to-morrow," Francis Joseph replied: "It is absolutely impossible to leave these regions without troops." He regarded himself as treaty protector of Modena, Parma, and Tuscany, as of the states of the Church. Since 1849 the immediate object of the Italian revolutionary movement, supported by Piedmont, was to overthrow the ruling dynasties in these states, although, except in Parma, they were popular with the great mass of their people.

How critical the situation was became painfully clear when Orsini, at the time of his murderous attack on Napoleon III, reminded him of his old brotherhood with the Italian revolutionaries and the pledges he had given the Carbonari about the unification of Italy before his election as president of the French Republic. Cavour, that singular embodiment of diplomatic keenness in combination with extraordinary calm and statesmanlike acumen, now embarked resolutely on his task of putting his plan into execution. In the summer of 1858 he met Napoleon at the Chateau of Plombières and succeeded in inducing him to sign a secret treaty for the liberation of Italy "from the sea to the Alps." The marriage very shortly afterwards concluded between Prince Jerome Bonaparte and the daughter of Victor Emmanuel patently strengthened the policy taking root in Napoleon's mind—a policy, that is to say, of reorganizing Europe on the basis of the principle of nationality. This policy was openly proclaimed as part and parcel of the heritage of the ideas of Napoleon III's great uncle. Its first practical success was won when, in the teeth of sharp opposition from Francis Joseph, France proceeded to unite the Danubian principalities in a new national state, Rumania. When at the reception of the diplomatic corps on New Year's day, 1859, Napoleon, in a voice audible to all, expressed to Hübner, the Austrian ambassador, his regret at the deterioration of relations between Austria and France, Europe realized that great events were imminent in that quarter of the globe. It was no longer possible for anyone in Austria to mistake the seriousness of the country's position.

Considerable reinforcements at once began to be sent to the forces in Italy. Strangely enough the Emperor still believed that Piedmont was on the road to ruin, owing to its liberal government! At the same time Vienna proclaimed martial law throughout the Italian provinces. Francis Joseph was informed confidentially by the English government, through his ambassador in London, that Napoleon's plans extended to rousing revolution in Hungary. So eager was the English government to avoid armed conflict between Austria and France, that Lord Cowley was sent to Vienna on an abortive mission.

Count Buol still sat in the Ballplatz, although conviction of his incapacity had long been general in Viennese society. As far back as October, 1858, General Kempen had wanted to inform the young Emperor of the common belief that Count Buol was unfit for his office, and, when Count Grünne opposed any such communication, said:

"Count Buol is busy with diplomatic fire extinguishers but he has no idea of how to remove the combustible materials and explosives that are lying about. He handles these world issues as matters of normal routine, one after another." But Francis Joseph stuck to his habit of turning a blind eye on his ministers. By the end of February it had been decided, after discussions with the Emperor's intimate counsellors, that the army in Italy had to be strengthened and a manifesto to be issued informing the people of Austria of the Emperor's resolve to place his army in the kingdom of Lombardy, and Venetia on the footing necessary for defence: a step forced on him by the provocative action of Piedmont, since he would permit no attack on existing treaties.

The publication of the manifesto was, however, delayed by the efforts of the British government to keep the peace. Yet that war was inevitable was the general feeling in Austria. The government wavered, as was shown by the appearance in Count Buol's semi-official newspapers of articles designed to move public opinion towards a peaceful solution of the Austro-Piedmontese affair. But in Paris the recurrent waywardness of Napoleon had, for the moment, been mastered by a bellicose mood.

On both sides military preparations went ahead at an accelerating speed. In Vienna, the results of bad financial policy now became sensible. The railways traversing the Italian provinces had been sold to a French company, with the result that the railway personnel in the theatre of war was perfectly unreliable. At the beginning of April the government of Milan was suspended and all public powers transferred to the military governor-general. General Kempen heard with horror that Francis Joseph had superseded General Hess, the admirable chief of staff of old Marshal Radetzky, and committed the whole preparation for military operations to General Schlitter, one of the worst of the "underminers of the army" and military bureaucrats.

When the minister reported to the Emperor that rumors were going about of approaching liberal concessions on his part, he listened without saying a word. Similarly he waved aside the suggestion that he should go some little way to meet the desires of the Hungarian nobles with a view to ameliorating the state of opinion in Hungary. On April 19, the Emperor presided at a ministerial council, for whose doings we are dependent on General Kempen's report. The Vienna archives contain no official protocol of this conference, which led directly to war.

Kempen relates:

"Count Buol's arguments were clear and forcible: he urged that a written demand should be sent to Count Cavour to stop armed preparations in Piedmont within three days, failing which the Austrian army would treat these preparations as a hostile act. This evening this demand goes to Milan to be conveyed thence to Turin by a civil official. General Hess proposed the mobilization of the whole army, 600,000 strong; to be followed by the despatch of an army to the Rhine in order to cut France off effectively from Italy. The decision was to take the swift-

[259]

est and strongest steps, the more so that England and Prussia—in Count Buol's belief—are coming out more and more openly on Austria's side."

So, for the first time, Francis Joseph breaks into European history with an ultimatum! Count Buol's hopes of allies, which he may well have shared, were quite unrealized. Neither England nor Prussia was ready to support Austria. The reports of Otto von Bismarck, acting as Prussian ambassador at St. Petersburg at this time, show how completely hatred of Francis Joseph outweighed all other feelings, all other political ideas, in the mind of Czar Alexander II. They show, too, that Bismarck knew how to make his own old dislike of Viennese policy effective both in St. Petersburg and in Berlin with the Prince Regent, later King William.

On April 23, the Austrian ultimatum was delivered in Turin, and rejected with the utmost calm by Count Cavour. Francis Joseph's irate demand had, in fact, removed his one great anxiety lest Austrian delay should prevent the secret alliance entered into by Napoleon in 1858 from coming into operation. The ultimatum was war, the war for which Cavour had been working for years. Archduke Albert was sent to Berlin, where no attempt was made to hide the sharp disapproval felt by the Prussian government and the Prince Regent for the recklessness with which Austria had despatched an ultimatum to Piedmont without consulting Prussia. Characteristically, Kempen reports that the Archduke gave him to understand, in conversation, that he fully shared this disapproval himself. Francis Joseph had thus alienated his outstanding military adviser by his hasty plunge into war.

What use was it, now, for Count Grünne to reproach Count Buol with the feebleness of diplomatic preparation for war on Austria's side? To grumble that "we could forsee nothing, but allowed ourselves to be rushed by external events"? "We are properly isolated," notes General Kempen in his diaries. "I find everyone disgruntled. Even His Majesty was very grave and told me that a military revolution had broken out in Tuscany." The dismissal of Count Buol followed in the kindliest form possible. Francis Joseph, perhaps, hoped that, after this, it might yet be possible to induce a more friendly attitude on the part of the Czar and the Russian government, to whom Count Buol had always acted as a red rag to a bull.

Next, Count Gyulai was promoted to supreme command of the army, despite the fact that, for weeks, he had waived the honor, declaring himself incompetent for such a position and even begging the Emperor through Grünne, not to impose the task upon him. An anecdote that I often heard told in my own young days, and in which there is certainly a basis of truth, may here be cited for the light it throws on the conditions created by Francis Joseph's autocracy. According to this story, Count Grünne finally wrote to the unfortunate General Gyulai, by way of finishing off his scruples: "What is the matter with you? What an old ass like Radetzky could manage at eighty you will surely be able to pull off."

Meantime, most disquieting news reached the government about the effect of the threat of war on opinion in

[261]

Hungary. The Emperor listened calmly, though he did not hide the gravity of his mood. As Count Buol took his farewells of the cabinet he gave one last proof of his lack of diplomatic judgment. According to General von Kempen, he posed the following hypothesis: "Either the Austrian army will be victorious, or it will be defeated. In the first case, the results of the defeat of our enemies are incalculable; in the second the whole of Germany will rally to Austria's defense." He was all too soon to learn how baseless was any such hope.

The Emperor nominated, as his successor, Count Bernhard Rechberg, an honorable, somewhat difficile, but experienced diplomatist of Prince Metternich's school. But it was too late for even the greatest diplomatic genius to retrieve the grave errors committed in the past seven years by Francis Joseph's autocracy and Count Buol's superficial and ambitious diplomacy. The reproaches now levelled at Buol by the court missed their mark. Not any one man but a whole political "system," principles, and methods dominating the country for a decade, were responsible for the catastrophic frame of mind now evident both in ruler and ruled.

Austria's complete isolation in Europe was now revealed. The Russian cabinet refused to make a definite declaration of neutrality; Prussia and the German confederation, on receiving Vienna's suggestions of alliance and participation in the war against Napoleon, would not budge from strict neutrality, unless the French army attacked Austrian provinces belonging to the German confederation. Moreover, evidences of incapacity in the Austrian high command accumulated. Those who knew most drew the worst deductions from the reports of the engagements at Pastrengo and Montebello. At court, excuses were found in a superiority of numbers on the part of the enemy which, in fact, did not exist.

No one could explain why Count Gyulai kept his army immobile week after week, allowing the Piedmontese army to effect a junction with the French undisturbed; public apprehension about the future course of the campaign became acute. On May 28, there was a cabinet meeting, at which Francis Joseph explained that the whole policy of the ultimatum to Piedmont had been based on the assumption that the war against France and Italy could not remain localized, "otherwise the position would be bad."

Actually the Emperor was still hoping to induce Prussia and the German confederation to declare war on Napoleon; an optimism eloquent of the extent to which his foreign policy was rooted in self-deception and inadequate knowledge of conditions and tendencies abroad. If, as he hoped, Germany declared war on Napoleon, a strong Austrian army should be sent to the Rhine. "Lombardy depended on the Rhine"—such was the slogan current for long at court and in the press, taken up zealously in southern Germany, both by governments and by a considerable section both of the Nationalist and Catholic press. But there was a condition—the transference of the supreme command to Prince Regent William of Prussia —which Francis Joseph absolutely would not fulfill. In his open, headstrong way he rejected out of hand the price put by Prussia on its coöperation. To him, personally, this was an intolerable piece of presumption: moreover, it must have implied not merely Prussia's temporary command in the field but its lasting predominance in Germany. And to that he was not in the least ready to consent.

There was nothing in this, for the "Little Germany" politicians of the day, but Habsburg arrogance and an obstinate refusal to recognize Prussia's historic mission to unite Germany, after casting everything Austrian out. After more than two generations, Prussian historians still take the same attitude, although, at the time, there was no conspicuous readiness in any of the other German princes or in the great mass of the people of southern and western Germany and Austria to recognize any such historic mission of Prussia's.

Not on any such grounds can Francis Joseph be reproached to-day, for an alleged shortsightedness in refusing to take an action which must have served to make Prince William military and political overlord of Germany. His fault was, rather, that his autocracy and the whole spirit of Viennese government had annihilated the old sympathy for Austria felt by the great middle class in southern Germany and that, now, he had launched a needlessly aggressive war policy without any preliminary discussion and understanding with Prussia and the central German states.

It was, however, far too late to retrieve such an error. His only hope now was of military success by his great armies massed on the plains of Italy. And of that success he soon began to doubt. When the first unfavorable reports came in to Vienna, the intelligence service of the high command proved extremely inadequate. When General Kempen complained of the unreliability of the information from the theatre of war, the Emperor exclaimed, wrathfully: "Am I any better served?"

His next step was to execute a resolution formed some time before of taking over the command in person. Leaving the capital on May 29, he went to general headquarters at Verona. For the young Emperor to lead his troops in person in the great battles that loomed ahead was a matter of simple duty. The immense responsibility he thus assumed was, for him, overshadowed by his sense of the obligation on the supreme war lord of sharing the dangers of the fray with his officers and men. Such a sense does him honor as an officer, but again reveals a lack of any profounder comprehension of his position as sovereign. To his mind, the supreme war lord, commander-in-chief of the army in peace time, could not possibly act otherwise, once war broke out.

The larger question involved—the risk involved in the assumption of such a responsibility by the absolute ruler of a vast realm, who as an eighteen-year-old lieutenant had shown physical courage in the field, but had neither before nor since proved, either by serious theoretic study or practical experience, military capacity on any grand scale or ability to lead a great army—was simply never faced by the young monarch himself, nor put to him by his military entourage. In the literal sense of the word, he was seriously prepared to "fight" side by side with his troops, as is proved by a last conversation he had with

[265]

Prince Clemens Metternich, then in his eighty-sixth year and very near to death. Francis Joseph asked him specifically how he should make his will and what arrangements ought to be made for a Regency in the event of his being killed. His attitude here lays him open to sharp criticism and certainly proves the immaturity of his general political outlook. Indubitably there was a streak of military romanticism in him in these days, strange enough in a monarch normally so matter-of-fact, but the perfectly genuine expression of his mood at the moment.

Curiously enough, Napoleon III, his opponent, had, in the same way, for years cherished an eager desire to lead the French army to victory in person in the event of a war. At the time of the Crimean War, indeed, it had been decided that he should go to the scene of operations, but nothing had come of it. In the weeks before the outbreak of the Italian War, Napoleon III, too, although he had no military training, was stirred by a military romanticism that gave Paris ample food for more or less cynical *mots*. Thus Francis Joseph's ultimatum to Piedmont gave both monarchs a chance of realizing their dreams of military glory.

When Francis Joseph reached the theatre of war, Milan and Lombardy were already lost. After the battle of Magenta, in itself quite indecisive, the whole Austrian army had retreated across the Mincio. When, on June 23, they again crossed the river, under the Emperor's command, in order to drive back the combined French-Piedmontese armies, there followed, next day, the murderous battle of Solferino. Fighting on a wide front, the Austrian right wing under General von Benedek gained a complete victory over the Piedmontese, but their centre and left wing were driven back by the French. Francis Joseph's assumption of supreme command proved a disastrous mistake. It not only led to great difficulties in the issue of orders but the awful impressions which the actual incidents of battle made on the Emperor's mind, and his lack of strategic judgment, together with his tendency to over-hasty decisions, caused him to order a premature retreat.

As a result, Napoleon and the French command were in a position to send out to the world news of a great victory, although as a matter of fact the gains won by the center and right wing of the French army were by no means decisive. But Francis Joseph had lost his nerve. Instead of bringing up the reserves, which, as Napoleon admitted later, certainly could have won for him the key position of Solferino, he surprisingly ordered an unnecessary retreat. One or two Hungarian and Italian battalions apart, the Austrian troops had fought with the utmost bravery, but everything was ruined by the decisive strategic error of the imperial command and the tactical and strategic incompetence of his generals. "Lions led by asses," was the brief but accurate phrase in which the disaster of Solferino was summed up in Austria and Germany.

There was the less excuse for this display of pusillanimity since French generalship was only moderately good, neither Napoleon himself nor any of his generals showing any great military talent. Actually, on the day after the battle, June 25, the Austrian army still held the ground taken on June 23. It withdrew, unmolested by the enemy, who had likewise sustained very heavy losses, behind the Adige and under the rampart of the famous quadrilateral. Curiously enough, Napoleon, too, was shattered by his first experiences of battle. The horrors he had witnessed lacerated him, so he told Duke Ernest of Saxe-Coburg, who visited him in Paris later. Plainly neither the young Emperor Apostolic nor Cæsar's nephew was intended by nature for leadership in slaughterous struggles!

A year later, Napoleon observed to Duke Ernest that he regarded his victory as a piece of pure luck. He also remarked, on the same occasion, that incredible lies had been spread about the personal danger to which he had been exposed. "Je n'ai jamais entendu siffler une balle." War, nevertheless, struck him as a perfectly horrible affair. "Le hazard joue un trop grand rôle." His men had been in wretched case and his generals had shown no real power of leading a great army. The Austrians had fought better than the French. The Emperor of Austria was, he said, a man of great importance, "mais malheureusement il lui manque l'énergie de la volonté."

The war Francis Joseph had precipitated by his unconsidered ultimatum undoubtedly created a most difficult diplomatic position for him and his realm: remarkable, therefore, that he could, so speedily, recover his habitual equanimity and mental balance. The singular parallelism between the internal reactions of the two Emperors to the war for which they were solely and personally responsible, is one of the strangest historical phenomena of the epoch. A few days after the end of the fighting at Solferino, Francis Joseph had reached the conviction that he must make peace as soon as possible. Napoleon III, victor, though he did not feel like one, was, for his part, no less tired of the war. He had led the French people into the struggle with the Habsburg Empire from purely personal motives, above all, in order to safeguard his life from the threats of the Italian revolutionaries.

To France and the French, Cavour's passionate effort for the union of Italy was a matter of supreme indifference. Actually there was great danger in such a transfiguration of the Apennine peninsula as would be accomplished if Cavour succeeded in achieving his ultimate aim of creating a new state, of great military power, on France's southern frontier. That Napoleon's reward for his share in the defeat of Austria was to be the acquisition for France of the racial home of the Piedmontese dynasty—Savoy, with the strip of Mediterranean coast from Mentone to Nice—was still a dead secret, known only to the allied governments.

Nothing could be less attractive to Napoleon than any idea of letting the war, with Francis Joseph's military power, as yet, hardly shaken, develop to a life-and-death struggle, in which nobody but the Magyar emigrés and Italian radicals had a vital interest. Was he to carry on a war, by no means popular in France, for the sake of Kossuth? Moreover, Napoleon's diplomatic position quickly began to become worse. In view of the mobilization of six army corps by Prussia and the German confederation, to be massed on the Rhine, any energetic pursuance of military operations against Austria must wear a very risky look for him. To Piedmont's advantage, he had based French policy on the principle of nationality; but, if he really meant to carry it through, for instance in relation to Poland, he knew he must reckon on the bitter hostility both of Prussia and of Russia. Could he contemplate, seriously, making himself the head of the nationalist and revolutionary forces throughout Europe and setting out to change its entire map, in opposition to the other great powers? His answer could only be, No, the more definitely since he had no mind to help to realize Cavour's comprehensive plans, as initiated by the expulsion of the Habsburg Grandduke of Tuscany.

The diplomatic reactions of military events, felt in all the cabinets, strengthened Francis Joseph's desire for a speedy peace. He had entered on the war with the erroneous idea that the strength of German national feeling would force Prussia and the Confederation to join him at once. He and Count Buol had hoped that Alexander II would, at worst, show friendly neutrality, inasmuch as Austria in fighting Napoleon and Piedmont was defending the law of Europe, the treaties of 1815, in a word the conservative world against the threat of revolution. He had also expected diplomatic aid from England. None of this occurred.

The deepest blow to the young Emperor was the attitude of Prince William. He seemed simply to be carrying on the union policy initiated by Radowitz in 1848 and overthrown by Schwarzenberg; his view being that he need meet the obligations laid on him, according to Austrian conceptions, by the law of the confederation, only in so far as Austria was prepared to leave Prussia the leadership of the confederation and itself as far as possible withdraw from it. For this reason General Willisen's mission from Berlin to Vienna in April was bound to fail.

But Prince Alfred Windischgrätz, who was sent to Berlin to renew discussions with the Prussian government, found the prince regent in a more favorable mood. The strong dislike of Napoleon animating the German bourgeoisie contributed to this, as did Prince William's recollections of the time when Prussia and Austria crossed the Rhine side by side to defeat the first Napoleon and send him to Elba. Before Windischgrätz was recalled, however, the telegraph gave the world's cabinets the astonishing intelligence that an armistice had actually been concluded between Napoleon and Francis Joseph. Napoleon had taken the first step, in the following letter, written on May 5 at Valeggio to Francis Joseph:

"Monsieur mon frère,
"On me fait savoir de Paris qu'une grande puissance va faire aux belligérants une proposition d'armistice. Si cette proposition était acceptée par V. M. je désirerais le savoir, parcequ'alors je ferais donner l'ordre à la flotte qui va attaquer Venise, de n'en rien faire, car il est de notre devoir d'éviter de repandre du sang inutilement.

"Je renouvelle à V. M. l'assurance de sentiments de haute estime avec lesquels je suis de V. M.

"le bon frère,

"Napoléon."

On July 8, the military plenipotentiaries met and concluded the armistice. On the same day Napoleon proposed a personal interview at Villafranca to his imperial adversary. On the following day, Prince Alexander of Hesse, Austrian general and brother-in-law of Alexander II, transmitted Francis Joseph's acceptance; and on July 10 the meeting of the two Emperors took place. Next day Prince Napoleon, the deadly foe of Austria, brought a résumé of the verbal agreements between the two sovereigns to the Austrian Emperor, who thereupon signed the draft of Napoleon's proposals. He sent Count Rechberg, his foreign minister, to clear up minor points of detail with Napoleon, who, returning to France, on July 24, dispatched another confidential letter, to which Francis Joseph replied on August 2. A holograph letter of Francis Joseph's dated August 18, initiated the final stage in the correspondence between the monarchs. The French Emperor's reply of August 26 and Francis Joseph's answer thereto of September 14, written after the opening of actual peace *pourparlers* at Zurich, concluded this momentous peace transaction, begun by the sovereigns on their own impulse and carried through by them in secret.[1]

[1] The whole of this correspondence, though guesses at its contents are frequent in French literature on the 1859 war, remained entirely unknown until Senator Francesco Salata, the Italian historian, studied the relevant documents in the Vienna archives, after they had, with wise

The considerations envisaged by Francis Joseph, in thus rapidly concluding first an armistice and then peace, were highly characteristic of him. After the retreat from Solferino he at once made up his mind to the loss of Lombardy, but insisted with Napoleon that this portion of Austrian territory should be ceded to him, and not to Piedmont-Sardinia. There spoke his personal rancor against the treachery of Victor Emmanuel and his minister Cavour. Almost a decade later, in a private letter to one of the German princes, he describes the Italians contemptuously as "pickpockets and land thieves." He expected to have a certain portion of the Austrian state debt taken over but said nothing, on this, to Napoleon; to do so did not seem to him consistent with his imperial dignity. When Count Rechberg brought him the proposals of the French plenipotentiaries, he replied in one word: "More."

The continuation of Austrian occupation of Venetia and the quadrilateral was the great concession Napoleon was ready to make from the first, although he had stated in his manifesto, "Italy must be free from the Adriatic to the Alps." He immediately countermanded the attack his fleet was preparing to make on the City of the Lagoons. He went even further. His leading idea had been, from the start, to found an Italian confederation. Francis Joseph took up this idea at Villafranca, since he hoped not merely to be a member of such a league but even to acquire

liberality, been thrown open to the world by the Austrian Republican Government, and published copies of the letters in the *Nuova Antologia* of December, 1923.

predominance in it. For the moment he was concerned to take advantage of the situation for the benefit of the dynasties which had been driven out by the revolution and the threat of annexation by Piedmont. This, for him, was no mere political move; it was an affair of honor. He felt a pressing obligation to help to restore close relatives like the Grandduke of Tuscany and the Regents of Parma and Modena to their legitimist thrones.

At Villafranca, Napoleon appeared quite ready to approve the restoration of these dynasties, though he declared that he could do nothing in that direction himself. If, by other means, the restoration of the Italian dynasties were accomplished, Francis Joseph hoped that with the assistance of the Pope, and his brother-in-law the King of Naples, he, as sovereign over Venice, might once again rule over a federated Italy. A bitter disappointment was in store for him here.

On Cavour's initiative, plebiscites were taken in the central Italian states and used to effect their annexation by Piedmont—an annexation made effective by their permanent occupation by Victor Emmanuel's troops. Napoleon III's letter of July 24 to Francis Joseph shows that, only 14 days after Villafranca, he was faced with the impracticability of a large part of the arrangements then laid down. He reminded Francis Joseph that he had at the time informed him, through his cousin, that he could never offer assistance in the forcible restoration of the dethroned dynasties.

In his answer of August 2, Francis Joseph showed how

near to his heart this restoration was, and that he expected no satisfactory solution of the grave difficulties consequent on the central Italian revolution from a European congress, but only from a direct understanding with Napoleon. Therefore, he told Napoleon that there was an item in his part of the Villafranca pact which he could not carry out, i.e., the guarantee to Venetia of autonomy within the Austrian state. At Villafranca Francis Joseph himself had suggested giving Venetia a status similar to that of Luxemburg in the German confederation. Prince Richard Metternich, whom he sent to discuss the matter by word of mouth with Napoleon, failing to achieve anything, Francis Joseph, on August 18, again addressed a long holograph letter to the Emperor, in which he took the ground that he desired to maintain the relation of mutual confidence developed between him and Napoleon since Villafranca by a further frank exchange of views. The plenipotentiaries at Zurich were at sixes and sevens, above all on this question of Venetia: this is the moment chosen by Francis Joseph to give the Emperor a long lecture on the political nature of his realm:

"Austria is made up of various nationalities and therefore requires, more than any other country, a certain concentration of state power in the hands of the government. As a member of the German Confederation Austria has responsibilities that make it impossible for it to assume a contradictory course of action in another confederation. It is now proposed to me to separate the Kingdom of Venetia completely

[275]

from the monarchy so far as civil administration and the army go.

"But if the provinces of Hungary, Siebenbürgen, etc., which belong to the German Confederation, were all to demand the same privileges, the result would be the dissolution of the army. If I desired to give absolute autonomy to my Italian provinces, the other provinces might endeavor to alter the bonds that mutually unite them and that would spell neither more nor less than the dissolution of the whole monarchy. For these reasons I have, from the beginning, as Your Majesty will remember, rejected any plan of the proposed Confederation, which implies its influencing the internal administration of the Kingdom of Venetia. In the case of Luxemburg, the Netherlands are under obligation to maintain a detachment of Dutch troops there, and the German Act of Confederation in no way binds the King of the Netherlands to establish any special administrative régime in that area."

Finally, Francis Joseph explains that he has always held to the view that any arrangements made between him and Napoleon instead of constituting a part of the Zurich Peace Treaty, should belong to a confederation plan; therefore, he proposes that these matters should only be dealt with personally. His conclusion is characteristic:

"I beg your Majesty to weigh these points well. I beg you to have regard for the inherent difficulties of my position. I beg, finally, Your Majesty to accept the conviction that I extend my hand loyally and shall make every effort so to support you, on my part, as to surmount the obstacles you may encounter in your path."

In the upshot, the Zurich peace could but establish formally the legitimist dynasties of central Italy. Francis Joseph was perfectly aware, in writing his letter, that there was nothing final in the peace settlement. "We shall get Lombardy back in a year or two," he said to von Kempen, on his return from the theatre of war. Nevertheless the events of 1860 must have dimmed any hopes he entertained here. The coup of Garibaldi's Thousand in Sicily and the conquest of the Kingdom of Naples in 1860 made an end of the secret plans, attributed by contemporaries and subsequent historians to Francis Joseph and Count Rechberg, plans presumably aimed at rousing a new Italian war with the aid of Naples, in which France would be prevented from intervening by the interests of the Pope and the state of the church. He was spared making any such trial of strength with the new Italian kingdom.

Prussia had provided the main argument for Francis Joseph's speedy conclusion of peace. Napoleon, very well informed about relations between Berlin and Vienna since the opening of the war, wrote as far back as July 11, when he received Francis Joseph's signature to the peace preliminaries:

"I return Your Majesty our draft agreement. I realize that certain conditions in it have seemed harsh to Your Majesty, but to set Your Majesty's mind at rest I send you confidentially a despatch I have received from Paris. After the first proposals I communicated to Your Majesty, I received not only assurances of readiness to support these proposals energetically from the Cabinets of London and St. Petersburg, but an intimation from the Government of Prussia to the effect that, in the event of Austria's rejecting them, it could count neither on material nor moral support from Prussia. Your Majesty perceives, therefore, that you have gained by dealing with me direct."

Francis Joseph replied next day to this piece of friendship in a letter of thanks expressive of all the proud disdain of the Habsburg for the effort of the Prussian Regent, who had sought to use Austria's hour of need to exact an increase of his own power in Germany: "I should never have yielded to any pressure from the European areopagus, and therefore felicitate myself the more for being entered on direct negotiation with Your Majesty."

Francis Joseph seems to have forgotten that Napoleon himself had offered him armistice and peace because of his own keen anxiety about the attitude of Prussia and Germany, an anxiety that grew in the next few weeks, on his being informed of the mobilization of Prussia and the confederation. Once again, Francis Joseph lost great opportunities through his precipitancy and his excessive resentment of any attempt by the Berlin government to set Prussia even on a level with Austria in the confederation. So deeply did the young Emperor feel what he regarded as the Prince Regent's hostility that the manifesto, in which he informed his peoples of the conclusion of peace, openly expressed bitter reproaches against Prussia. His oldest and natural allies had "left him in the lurch and obstinately refused to recognize the high significance of the great question of the day." The alienation between the two sovereigns was to last some time; it was not bridged until after the meeting at Teplitz on July 26, 1860, between King William and Francis Joseph, arranged by King Max of Bavaria.[2]

Precipitately had Francis Joseph brought about the war which cost him the Kingdom of the Iron Crown, rich Lombardy; precipitately he concluded peace—on terms,

[2] King William's own view of his behavior to Francis Joseph can be seen from a letter written by him on July 17 to King John of Saxony, where he says: "The Emperor of Austria has sent his aide-de-camp to me to propose a meeting. I take the fact that he has thus taken an official step to a rapprochement with Prussia as a silent apology for his Peace Manifesto of last year. As you know he there said that Austria had been left in the lurch by its natural Allies and therefore made peace, although he knew well that the Prussian armies and the German were then on the march to the Rhine, as Prince Windischgrätz kept him hour by hour informed from Berlin. More than that, Emperor Napoleon contradicted the Austrian manifesto by saying that he made peace because he was threatened with war!! Which was the truth. While Austria attacked Piedmont, the war did not concern Germany, under the terms of the Act of Confederation, and all we needed to do was to be ready. When the Austrian army retreated to its own territory, and was defeated at Magenta on June 4, I mobilized two-thirds of my army and caused the march to the Rhine to start on July 1. On July 8, I mobilized the last third and then on July 13 we were surprised by the Peace of Villafranca!! It will be necessary to recall such words, since I noted that Peace Manifesto and the subsequent tension between Austria and Prussia. May God give us reconciliation at Teplitz."

however, that included the proviso that he kept, for his lifetime, the right to give the order of the Iron Crown. The kings of the House of Savoy had to wait nearly sixty years to acquire a right so dear to the hearts of monarchs! Francis Joseph's bitterness against Prussia had been so great that he would not even wait to hear the results of Prince Windischgrätz' mission to Berlin, though he had himself sent him there. His original idea of concluding a firm alliance with Napoleon collapsed owing to the subsequent course of events in Italy. His new foreign minister, Count Rechberg, had from the beginning prescribed freedom for Austria from binding alliances. Rechberg counted on a general improvement in Austria's diplomatic relations to all the great powers. Actually Russia began to incline that way, and the old good relations with England were restored. Isolation seemed to be at an end. To that extent the conclusion of peace produced no small improvement in its foreign position.

CHAPTER IX

THE ERA OF CONSTITUTIONAL EXPERIMENTS

CTUALLY the primary reason for the unexpectedly quick ending of the war was the news from the interior of his realm that reached Francis Joseph before and after Solferino. All classes in Austria were outraged by the course of the Italian campaign: the incapacity of Gyulai and of almost all the army commanders with the exception of Benedek; the unreliability of the Italian and Hungarian regiments; the but too speedily justified reports of corruption in the commissary department; and the grave effects on trade and industry at home, of the sharp depreciation of Austrian paper money—all this, taken together, gave rise to sharp criticism of the men regarded as the real powers in the autocracy and sponsors of what Count Rechberg later described as "a war for which we were neither diplomatically, financially, nor militarily prepared."

Public reprobation singled out Dr. Bach and Count Grünne, seeing the latter all-powerful with the Emperor, for years, in military matters, as mainly responsible for making Gyulai commander-in-chief and filling other high military commands with incompetents. Dissatisfaction in Vienna was so great and so definitely expressed in the liberal press there that care was required in maintaining restrictions and police activities, the more so that the main targets were the Emperor, the court, and above all their policy of the concordat and militarism. There were moments when the whole autocratic system seemed insecure. Even at court and among the archdukes, opinion was unfriendly to the Emperor. As usual the sharpest critics were those who had never before ventured to say one word against the Emperor.

The cabinet took a very grave view of the popular temper. Rechberg, who had presided, went to the Emperor at Verona and put the gravity of the situation at home before him with unvarnished plainness. If nothing were done to prevent the present mood among the people from developing, the very existence of the monarchy was, he declared, in danger. The impression made by such intelligence on the Emperor can be imagined. These were, in fact, the worst hours the young autocrat had yet experienced. Now perhaps for the first time, he realized the peril overhanging the autocrat. For a decade his will had been all-powerful in his great realm; on him, therefore, fell the full weight of the consequences that must follow in the train of the defeat of the army, his own blindly precipitate diplomacy and the hatred of the absolutist system that had been mounting in Hungary ever since his futile visit there.

It says much for his strength of character that, faced with this situation, he not only stood firm but acted swiftly. The peace preliminaries of Villafranca were the first outcome of his personal reading of the position in which he and his realm now stood. The dismissal of Alexander Bach was the next step, followed a little later by that of the police minister, General Kempen (replaced by Count Hübner, hitherto ambassador in Paris) and the appointment of Count Goluchowski, governor of Galicia, to be minister of the interior. These appointments showed anyone familiar with the conditions that the Emperor had quite recovered his equanimity. For he coldly refused to do what the public opinion he despised demanded of him, tantamount in effect to the supersession of autocracy.

He was ready to dismiss Bach, but he had no notion of abandoning Bach's system of unitary monarchy and unlimited imperial absolutism. He was convinced, and without doubt rightly convinced, that means were at his disposal in the German-Slav provinces sufficient to repress any revolutionary movements. In Vienna and the provincial capitals the middle classes had in the year 1848 shown strong anti-absolutist tendencies. But since 1848 there had been no real political life in Austria and therefore the liberal sections were entirely unorganized.

The muzzled press could hardly hold together the numerically tiny group of politically educated persons. The great mass of the lower middle classes was and remained politically passive. The working class was of course still completely excluded from politics. Thus there could be no question either in Vienna or the other cities, of anything like a popular movement, of which the government would have to take account. The appointment of the Polish governor to the most important post in the cabinet was a veritable slap in the face for the small circle of politically educated persons. Who were Francis Joseph's

[283]

advisers in this? Since no one knew, everyone—and not inaccurately—saw it as the expression of his own will, of the scorn with which he rejected any change in his autocratic course.

At the same time, under the influence of his new Prime minister, Count Rechberg, Francis Joseph went so far as to insert in the manifesto of July 15, 1859, announcing the conclusion of peace, a promise to devote himself energetically to the improvement of legislation and administration at home. The program of the new ministry, however, brought fresh disappointment for those who had hoped for thorough reforms of a liberal character. There was a vague reference to the "transference of departments of administrative business to autonomous organs", to a new parish law, and a rather obscure reference to representative assemblies in the provinces. "Grave is the situation, great are the difficulties, deep are the wounds caused to our land by inherited evils, an unhappy conjunction of circumstances and an unfortunate though glorious campaign."

Public opinion endorsed this criticism of the Emperor's but resented the failure to draw its lesson. Everyone knew that it would be difficult to get him to march along the hard way he had now to tread. Actually his own angle to the domestic problems forced forward by the war was the most difficult conceivable; it is only necessary to recall what his new advisers, still almost without exception strong conservatives, were asking of the young autocrat. To his own sense it amounted to no less than the abandonment of the great structure built up by Schwarzenberg and Bach. And he, whose will, but a few weeks back, had been political providence on earth for forty millions of subjects, was now to begin, with his own hands, pulling down the structure of his power?

His fate was the more bitter that Francis Joseph thereby had to admit, of his own motion, that his whole system of government had been an error and a wrong that must now be redeemed by reforms. For this, he felt, was the object of all the demands now publicly made of him. He was told that "they"—the people—were demanding a complete transformation. He read the same desire in the carefully censored columns of the newspapers—for he had long learned, like all his educated subjects, to find "truth" in the newspapers by reading "between the lines." Even in his own immediate entourage he saw that changes were inevitable and a critical eye was cast on his past government. Even the archdukes had been pensive since the army's defeat. He knew that there were people not only in Hungary, but even in Vienna, who regarded his brother Ferdinand Max as a "Liberal" and thought that his government would be better than Francis Joseph's. There are stories of hard words and excited scenes between the two brothers. Of his old advisers, proscribed by public opinion, only Count Grünne was left. He held obstinately to him, did dismiss him as aide-de-camp but appointed him Master of the Horse at the Court. He knew that everyone in Vienna, including the best generals in the army, said harsh things of Grünne and called him the Emperor's evil genius.

For Rechberg, his new premier, he had no personal

feeling. He pressed the need of introducing comprehensive reforms in domestic policy and administration, regarding them as the indispensable condition of an improvement in foreign policy. A few years later, in a letter to his brother, Rechberg wrote: "After the close of this sad campaign, which resulted in the loss of Lombardy, I saw the task before me as that of preventing the monarchy from being involved in another great war before domestic conditions had been so reorganized as to put the whole strength of the monarchy behind the Emperor, before the finances had been restored, the army efficiently equipped and political alliances concluded again with the great powers."

The Emperor now got from Rechberg a picture of conditions at home which certainly was unsparingly critical of the Bach system, since Rechberg represented the views Prince Metternich had dinned into his friend's ears throughout the ten years since '48. He was a conservative in the sense in which that word had become a party label since the overthrow of the revolution. Belonging to very old south German noble stock, Rechberg's own views of the problem of the Habsburg realm were essentially the same as those of the Hungarian old conservatives. These were the men and this was the program that Francis Joseph now found in front of him. Count Rechberg was in close personal contact with the leaders of this party, which had numerous friends and very great influence in the inmost circles of the court.

The leaders of the Hungarian episcopate openly supported the old conservatives; several important members of the Austrian aristocracy shared their political views and approved their aims. Francis Joseph, however, was really profoundly unsympathetic to this aristocratic party: Schwarzenberg and Bach had taught him to dislike them personally and to see them politically as the greatest danger to his power as Emperor. His contemptuous disregard and forcible rejection of the address presented to him by the Hungarian nobles in 1857 is a case in point. Now, however, he had no choice; he must accept the bridge these men offered.

Opinion in Hungary, ever since Solferino, constituted the greatest threat to him and his realm. Archduke Albert, who had long sought release from his post of governor of Buda, now pressed his request in terms that left no room for doubt of the gravity of the situation. The 1851 "system" was untenable in Hungary. Official reports kept coming in of the growing political excitement, primarily in the towns, but also in the country where the middle classes looked to the lesser nobles for leadership. Police and gendarmerie were hard put to it to keep order and restrain the Hungarian press, springing up again in mushroom growth.

The whole of the gentry and a section of the aristocracy were busy reorganizing Magyar national resistance to the Vienna system and its officials. The lower classes, notably the Magyar peasants, gave loyal support to the nobles, as they had done in 1848. No change in the psychology of the peasants had been produced by their emancipation by Vienna from all their feudal burdens. Even in the parts of the country where Magyar landowners lived among Slav, Romaic, and German peasantry, they were able to take the lead politically, and, in part, even more successfully than they had done in 1848.

Hungary, in 1860, still presented, socially and economically, the same picture as it had done late in the eighteenth century, when the upper classes, in their contest with the autocracy of Joseph II, had been able to get the masses to accept them as the embodiments of "freedom"—a rôle in which they had recently been assisted by the persecutions of alien police officials and gendarmes. In the midst of the trouble gathering in Hungary in the summer of 1860, the Vienna government contributed a piece of most combustible fuel to the flames in the shape of an imperial rescript, regulating anew the affairs of the Protestant Church in Hungary, which roused resistance in every non-Catholic.

So serious was the condition of things, indeed, that Francis Joseph now had to take the first steps in the direction of modifying the system of autocracy. They were but dilatory and slow. The decisive impulse came from the state of Austrian finances. There was no chance of raising foreign loans until a firm guarantee of administrative economy was forthcoming in the shape of effective budget control. To this end the existing Reichsrat, the statutory council of state, was to be strengthened by the addition of members, elective by the provincial assemblies promised in the government program of August, 1859, but, for the moment, nominated by the Emperor. The so-called "extraordinary" council thus formed was set up by an imperial rescript of March 5, 1860, and summoned to its first session for May 31 of the same year. It was a sort of "Assembly of Notables" whose first task was to scrutinize and pass the next year's budget.

Of the members summoned from Hungary about half actually presented themselves. The whole body, 59 strong, was to be regarded as the Emperor's confidants. Meantime a great change had taken place in Hungary. Archduke Albert had resigned his governorship and was replaced by General Louis von Benedek, a Protestant Magyar. The letter in which the Emperor announced this change foreshadowed a further momentous step in the new policy:

"It is my intention, as soon as the new organization of the Governorship is in working order, to provide for political administration by the introduction of administrative counties on the plan of the previously existing county assemblies and committees, corresponding in composition and area to the needs of the day.

"In conformity with these arrangements, I command that, after the communal and county organizations are in force, proposals relative to the Diet be prepared."

When the "Extraordinary Council of the Empire" met on June 1, there was a protracted debate on the budget submitted to it, which showed that there was a majority behind the leaders of the Hungarian and Austrian conservatives, while the middle-class liberals were an insignificant numerical minority. The debates on the majority and minority motions on the address, careful as was the language of the aristocratic, ecclesiastical, and middle-class notables, give a sufficiently clear picture of the psychology and structure of Austria, as created by a decade of autocracy and the influences of the lost war.

Two main political views of the nature of the realm and the means to be taken for maintaining and strengthening it revealed themselves. Incomplete as was their form at this stage, these ideas, representative as they were of the two great parties, continued to be the dominant ones over the whole area of domestic policy so far as the western half of the realm went; although, oddly enough, not in its eastern half, namely, Hungary. This is the more remarkable since it was Hungary which had provided the impulse out of which the statement of both basic views arose, and since that impulse was expressly formulated by a Magyar, Count Scèscen, in an address and in a great speech. He, with Count George Apponyi and Count Emil Dessewffy, were the leading minds among the Magyar magnates.

Since the autumn of 1859, Francis Joseph had been in direct touch with these men. All the steps he took along the new way, as described above, were taken under their influence. Hungary was his first and far his greatest trouble. If the realm was to continue a unit and a great power, an effort must be made to induce Hungary to recognize its unity, and to substitute that recognition for the police and military compulsion that had held the nation together since 1850. The old conservatives believed that they had not only the right but the power to get that recognition from Hungary. Their first great aim was to communicate this belief to Francis Joseph; a process that could, in the nature of things, only be gradual. An important stage on the route was reached through the extraordinary session of the council. In the process, the Hungarian nobles had to secure the support of the group in every respect nearest to them, namely the "feudally" minded politicians among the nobles of Bohemia and the other hereditary provinces.

Among these the most notable were Count Henry Clam-Martinic, Prince Charles Schwarzenberg, and Count Nostitz. The political organization of the Austrian nobles as a party culminated in the establishment of a conservative Catholic daily paper in Vienna in 1860 called the *Vaterland*. These aristocratic great landowners, united with their Hungarian compeers by old tradition, family inheritance, and a common hatred of liberalism, constituted, in the eyes of the court, the sole political force in which the Emperor could trust.

Stoutly as Francis Joseph continued to resist any legal limitation of his autocracy, he was prepared to make a concession to an "estate" with historic traditions of political activity, so long as the aristocratic party were able to maintain the unity of the realm and the centralized structure of imperial power. That they would do this was promised in every document, memorandum, and discourse of the Hungarian old conservatives, who, on their part, made but one capital demand: the restoration of the centuries old historic constitution of Hungary.

This implied no less than the summoning of the Hungarian Diet, the suspension of the highly centralized and bureaucratic administration set up in 1850, and the reëstablishment of old Magyar self-government in counties and municipalities. By this means, the magnates hoped to restore the old pre-revolutionary rule of the aristocracy in Hungary and to secure political leadership to themselves.

Francis Joseph's ministers attempted an accommodation to this program by putting the government program, drawn up by Count Rechberg in agreement with the old conservatives, in operation. In Austria, too, a new estates organization was to be set up, which the politically-educated leaders of the Austrian aristocracy sought to make palatable to the people in town and country by labeling it "self-government."

Inside the machine of government there was lively opposition to these plans, for which the new minister of the interior, Count Goluchowski, was responsible: the Vienna bureaucracy disliked him more and more. After the debates in the council and the acceptance of the aristocrats' program, the liberal press, too, mobilized against it. The handful of middle-class members of the council, who openly demanded a modern constitutional government, a piece of "audacity" that incensed both the court and the nobles, were lauded to the skies.

In the midst of a political hubbub most painful to him, Francis Joseph retained his amazing equanimity but could not make up his mind. He could feel no confidence in the Hungarian Magnates. As for their Austrian colleagues, he saw no reason to change the low opinion implanted in

him by Schwarzenberg of their political capacity. He did
not rate either Rechberg or Goluchowski high as statesmen. The plans for replacing the imperial official apparatus, in the western half of the monarchy, by a new-
fangled self-government, caused him grave disgust, and
such of his high officials as came in contact with him,
notably Ignaz von Plener, called in to attend cabinet
meetings and conferences while acting as stopgap finance
minister, markedly increased this disquiet. Moreover,
Archbishop Rauscher was wholly averse to such plans. In
the interest of the Church he desired to see imperial authority maintained intact vis-à-vis the peoples. In August,
Francis Joseph devoted several days to conferences at
Schönbrunn, with the leaders of both the aristocratic
parties. The ground had been most thoroughly prepared.
But he came to no decision.

In the midst of these doubts and struggles, Francis
Joseph acted in home policy just as he had done, a year
earlier, in foreign. He became impatient and cut the knot
by suddenly deciding to accept the old conservatives' program. He thereupon instructed Count Scèscen to prepare
the necessary imperial decrees and letters as well as the
proposed "Diploma." He was impatient because he desired to leave on October 21 for Warsaw, where he was
to have weighty interviews with the Czar and King William of Prussia. Before he went, however, the "problem
of the new settlement in the whole Empire" had got to be
solved swiftly and finally. Count Scèscen had, therefore,
got to perform his immense task within twenty-four
hours.

[293]

A most carefully phrased diploma, to serve from now on as a basic law for the monarchy, and some two dozen additional "Supreme decrees" addressed to a whole range of ministers and simultaneously appointed Hungarian dignitaries, constituted the harvest now garnered by the magnates. The "October Diploma," setting up a new central parliament of 100 members, delegates from the Diets, was a new constitutional law, promulgated by Francis Joseph on his own motion and proceeding from the plenitude of his unlimited authority. The idea underlying it was that the "unitary realm" Schwarzenberg had created could be maintained by accepting the historic basis of the Habsburg monarchy, i.e., the individuality of the component provinces and expressing it through a federal form.

When Scèscen, in the imperial council, expounded the doctrine of the federal nature of the realm, the Hungarian old conservatives accepted it, for the sake of their Bohemian and Austrian associates. Their own concern was merely to recover their own historic Diet, as the most important of all the new provincial assemblies that were being called into being. For its sake they were prepared to have the central parliament, or so-called "larger" imperial council, composed of delegates, and agreed to have the legislative ambit of this council extend to Hungary. The budget of the Empire, its common economic area, and its common army were determined to be imperial concerns. The promulgation of this new basic law was accompanied by the nomination of two leaders of the Hungarian old conservatives as members of the Vienna government: Count Scèscen without portfolio, and Baron Vay as Hungarian chancellor and head of the department for Hungarian affairs.

The constitutional mixture so happily concocted by the aristocratic alchemists in the, politically, somewhat airless chambers of their palaces, was an experiment for them and still more for Francis Joseph. Everything depended on the way in which this wondrous product of aristocratic statecraft stood exposure to the outer world, especially in the non-artistocratic nineteenth century atmosphere which conditioned the lives, ideas, and aspirations of the various nationalities. As it proved, their lordships had to meet one disappointment after another. There were quite a number of old conservatives who never shared the optimism of Count Scèscen, the "true begetter" of the October Diploma. But the storm that broke out in Hungary astounded them all.

Nobody would hear of an empire and an imperial parliament if the old Kingdom of the Sacred Crown of St. Stephen was to be subordinated to them. It was speedily evident that the old conservatives had not a soul in the country behind them. Soon after, when the question of the franchise for the Diet had to be settled, the assembly of notables, selected according to old Hungarian traditional rights, unanimously passed the liberal franchise law drafted by the revolutionary parliament of 1848—whereby the bottom fell out of Scèscen's grandiose plan. Incessant demonstrations in Budapest and the other cities, and riotous proceedings at the establishment of the county and town councils, where Magyar nationalism displayed itself to the full, showed, only too plainly, what the Diet would be like. There was but one opinion throughout the country—the October Diploma, forged by the reactionary aristocrats, constituted a gross breach of the old constitutional law of Hungary and was therefore wholly impossible.

The position of the Hungarian ministers in Vienna was painful in the extreme. What they had promised the Emperor instantly proved unrealizable, and Francis Joseph had light-heartedly carried out his promise to the Hungarian nobles to the letter. He had removed his officials in Hungary and permitted Magyar nationalist self-government to be introduced in counties and municipalities, with the result that, in the space of a few weeks, the land was given over to Magyar intransigence and national and political radicalism, to such an extent that nothing but the existence of strong military forces prevented the outbreak of revolution.

Francis Joseph was deeply perturbed by these events, the more so that a most serious reaction was produced on the war-weakened finances by the systematic refusal of town and country dwellers in Hungary to pay taxes. Nevertheless, the youthful Emperor did not lose his poise, although the conservatives did not get off without some stern words from him. In Vienna and the German cities of western Austria, the middle classes, supported, sub rosa, by the higher bureaucracy, turned against the policy of the nobles. Francis Joseph, however, allowed himself to be persuaded by the conservatives that the extraordinary failure of the October Diploma throughout the realm was mainly due to the unpopularity of the Austrian ministers,

above all of Goluchowski, and that he ought to be replaced by the man for whom public opinion in Vienna and
the German middle classes had long been calling. This
was Anton von Schmerling, member of the German government, appointed by the 1848 Frankfort parliament,
and later minister of justice for a space of time in the
Schwarzenberg ministry.

Schmerling, the embodiment of Vienna's "second society," was known to Francis Joseph, but not much liked by
him; the less that at the Schiller Centenary in 1859 he
had been hailed by the educated middle class of Vienna
as leader of "Progress" and the great statesman of the
future. One characteristic did, however, attract the Emperor, despite this liberalism: he recognized in Anton von
Schmerling the "man of authority" who, in 1848, had
treated the "mob" of Frankfort democrats with a hand
of iron. Once committed to the policy of constitutional
experiment, he was prepared to carry it on through
Schmerling. He perceived with satisfaction, at his first
audience, that Schmerling was entirely of one mind with
him in his view of results in Hungary, of the policy of
the old conservatives, and of the aristocratic exponents of
this policy.

From the first, Francis Joseph had expected little from
the October Diploma and any hopes he had had were now
evaporated. He shared the opinion, now openly expressed
by all his generals who knew Hungary, that the only way
of avoiding revolution and restoring order there was to
restore imperial government and administration. General
Benedek, shortly before he exchanged his Venetian command for the governorship of Budapest, had publicly

stigmatized the "cowardly policy" of the magnates, in words which caused the greatest wrath in Hungarian aristocratic society.

With an equanimity in which there was a touch of humor, Francis Joseph anticipated the new disappointment Schmerling was preparing for the old conservatives. The new minister had made it a condition of his acceptance of the task of "putting through" the October Diploma that the Emperor guarantee that the middle class and German sections in the non-Hungarian territories should have a position corresponding to their great importance in the monarchy, above all in the drafts of provisional constitutions.

Count Goluchowski's feudalistic plans were dropped and substituted by bills associating representation of towns and communes with the electoral corporations of landowners on a system designed, by means of a high electoral qualification and a skilful distribution of electoral districts, to put the Czechs in Bohemia, Moravia, and Silesia, and the South Slavs in Carinthia and along the coast, in an inferior position to the Germans and, in the last case, the Italians. At the same time Schmerling modified the "Diploma" so far as to transform the imperial council (the Reichsrat) into a real bi-cameral parliament, consisting of houses of peers and representatives, with extraordinarily comprehensive legislative scope.

The provincial Diets, from now on, were to be confined to purely provincial business, their principal function being, thanks to franchises designed to favor the Germans, the great landowners, and the *grande bourgeoisie*, to assure the Emperor and his government a safe German and moderate liberal majority in this central parliament.

In Schmerling, Francis Joseph was for the first time in contact with a German party politician of large mold, whose general outlook was progressive. A good judge of men in this case, Francis Joseph never seems to have taken Schmerling's liberalism very seriously. He grasped, in his first conversations with his new minister, that the latter would offer no opposition to his attempt to establish an authoritarian, German, centralization policy in Hungary, nor allow himself to be deflected from it by the fact that by making his own the decidedly liberal and anti-Catholic policy of the Vienna liberal press and a not very considerable section of the Vienna middle classes, he might come into collision with the Emperor.

As a centralist and an unconditional defender of unity against the federalism of the aristocratic factions of both halves of the monarchy, Schmerling soon won the Emperor's confidence. Schmerling's work, carried in the cabinet against the opposition of the Hungarian ministers, and issued by imperial authority on February 26, 1861, signalized a decisive defeat for the Hungarian aristocrats. When the elections for the Hungarian Diet took place, the astounding result was revealed that there was not a single representative of the old conservatives in the Diet.

All the members without exception rejected both the constitutional laws promulgated by Vienna. The Diet divided into two almost equally strong parties. One of these was associated with Francis Deák, honored as the wisest head in the nation, leader of the liberal wing in the revolutionary Diet of 1848, and steady upholder of the most rigid legalism, who, in the recent conflict, had made the inviolable continuity of Hungarian constitutional law the rallying cry for the whole nation in its struggle with Vienna.

Now Francis Déak, for more than twenty years a commanding figure in Magyar public life, revealed himself as the truly providential man. He was one of those rarest statesmen who embody in their individuality, as it were, all the best and most productive forces of soul and mind of a race without its adverse qualities and failings. By his ancestry he belonged to the old Hungarian knighthood, living on their small landed properties and maintaining the old self-government of the nation as duly elected assessors of the county courts and justices of superior courts of law, or as members of the lower house of the Diet. As a leader of the liberal party he had been appointed minister of justice after the success of the March revolution, 1848. When the conflict with the court and government in Vienna began, he strove mightily to stop the boundless radicalism of Louis Kossuth.

After the outbreak of the war of rebellion and his fruitless endeavors at conciliation he retired quietly to his rural home and during all the years of absolutist rule he abstained from any interference with public life. The nation-wide fame of his wisdom and his integrity and his insuperable moral strength made him a tower of confidence with all classes of his people, who all looked up to him as the great sage of the nation. To understand fully Déak's great position in European history of the nineteenth century, an Englishman should remember the great leaders of the Puritans maintaining Common Law against Prerogative, or an American might compare Francis Déak to Abraham Lincoln. Now, in the spring of 1861, Francis Déak stood as the embodiment of liberal ideas and of the old indestructible rights of his nation opposing the governing bureaucracy of Vienna and their policy of centralization and imperial authority.

Déak was prepared to accept Charles VI's Pragmatic Sanction of 1723 laying down the same law of succession in the House of Habsburg for all countries and provinces under Habsburg rule, in favor of the male heirs and, in case such were lacking, of the female descendants of Charles VI, the last Habsburg Emperor, as the lasting basis of a permanent union of all the kingdoms and territories under the hereditary house. The other party, however, dominated by the Kossuth tradition, rejected this, since its real aim was the restoration of the complete independence of Hungary.

From the start the Diet addressed itself to the task of voicing the absolute and determined attitude of the nation to the monarch and his government. By Déak's wish, debates were conducted on the basis of a draft address to the throne of his own composition, in which Hungary's demands for the restoration of legality in the institutions of the country were expressed and argued with masterly force. In the circumstances, Francis Joseph must, almost inevitably, regard such a demand as an absolute condemnation of his accession, his whole government and his theory of autocracy. In this he had the support not only of Schmerling, but of German-liberal public opinion in Vienna and throughout Austria. His rejection of the address and the dissolution of the Diet followed.

The next step was the reintroduction of centralized absolutism in Hungary, under the threat of martial law in the capital. Once again Hungary was back in the condition it had been in the ten years up to 1860—a subject land governed by Austrian police, administrative and financial officials under the protection of an army garrisoned in the country.

Nevertheless, Francis Joseph did not burn his bridges. The fiction was kept up that the basic constitutional laws of 1860 and 1861, though not recognized in Hungary, were in force in the monarchy as a whole. A new Hungarian chancellor was appointed, Count Forgách, as a member of the government, and, in addition, Count Maurice Esterházy as minister without portfolio. They both now did everything in their power to mitigate the new absolutist régime in Hungary, and, in their own persons, represented a link with the aristocratic party of Hungary which, abandoned in the elections by the people as well as by the court, seemed to have vanished from the stage.

Francis Deák, from now on recognized at home and abroad as the unchallenged leader of the whole Magyar nation, retired, as he had done in 1848, when Kossuth drew the majority of Magyar opinion after him, to private life, and Magyar society, following his example, adopted a sort of universal passive resistance which at least preserved external quiet in the country.

Throughout this crisis Schmerling was the Emperor's

EMPRESS ELISABETH OF AUSTRIA
IN THE YEAR 1861

great supporter. He was the more effective in this rôle in that he had induced the German constitutional liberals to support his centralization policy in parliament by votes of confidence. Schmerling hoped to wear down the Magyars by this policy of the iron hand. His idea was to apply to Hungary the motto he had used in other contingencies: "We can wait!"

Since, throughout these events, the Hungarian question, as a problem of empire, had culminated in a personal issue between the Emperor and the country, any further attempt to solve or soften it must come from Francis Joseph himself. Francis Déak, by placing the problem firmly in the sphere of right had prevented the interpolation of any other factor into its solution and confined it to the still discrowned kingdom of Hungary.

But the negative issue of the experiment undertaken by Francis Joseph on the advice of the old conservatives, of effecting an understanding with Hungary by fitting it into a constitution promulgated by his absolute authority, had not weakened his own political position in Hungary as much as one might have supposed. The present unsatisfactory condition of things in that country had been designed by him, in advance, as an experiment, a provisional settlement. Hopes of a resolution of the conflict between him and Hungary therefore depended, by definition, on an alteration in the Emperor's point of view. Nothing was either expected or demanded of Schmerling's present government, his new parliamentarism, or the German constitutional party supporting him.

The anomalous result, then, was that Francis Joseph

once more ruled as autocrat over one half of his realm, namely Hungary, while the unit state formed by Maria Theresa out of the Austro-Bohemian lands was under the sham constitutionalism of 1861. This almost absurd state of things was tolerated the more readily by Francis Joseph because what Anton von Schmerling had given the peoples of Austria in his "February Patent" was but the simulacrum of a constitution, accepted only by Germans, and by German liberals at that, not by conservative Catholics.

The Poles did put in an appearance at the first session of the central parliament, but mostly to protest against the constitution. From 1863 on, the great Polish revolution that broke out in Russia absorbed the energies and interests of Austrian Poles so completely that they did not bother about the parliament in Vienna.

The Czechs, under the gifted leadership of Dr. Rieger, in association with the feudal nobles' faction, also refused to have anything to do with the centralized constitution, demanded the federalistic plan of the October Diploma which Schmerling had arbitrarily waived, and, by 1862, had withdrawn, permanently, from the central parliament in Vienna.

The German liberals alone were sufficiently short-sighted to accept an instrument forged by Schmerling for the political subjection of Slavs and Magyars as realizing their own demand for political freedom and identify themselves, under the title of "Constitutional Party" completely with Francis Joseph's experiment.

It was not long, however, before progressive Germans

in Austria began to see through this empty experiment. Disillusionment with Schmerling was swift; he displayed the most perfect indifference to every attempt to develop the said constitution along genuinely liberal lines. To all this parliamentarism, Francis Joseph paid little or no attention. What concerned him was that Schmerling maintained the existing system of officials and police, that the Council voted new taxes and facilitated the placing of foreign loans by the mere fact of its existence. Further, he was pleased that Schmerling did all he could to muzzle the press, especially the Slav and Magyar press, since his own dread of the destructive influence of a free press grew with the years.

By and large, in fact, Francis Joseph remained the autocrat throughout his realm. At the same time he found the critical attitude of distinguished German parliamentarians hard to tolerate. He did not attempt to hide the annoyance caused him by speeches criticizing Count Rechberg's foreign policy or complaining of failures on the part of administrative officials. The fact that there, in a hastily erected wooden building, wittily described by the Viennese as "Schmerling's Theater," some one hundred and fifty members were sitting, month after month, talking about politics, questioning ministers, actually finding fault with them, even making demands for reductions in the army; behaving, in a word, as though the peoples or "subjects" they represented really had a right to offer advice to the Empire and the government, to alter or even reject their bills—this fact, in itself, disquieted Francis Joseph.

At cabinet meetings, after the restoration of peace in 1859, Francis Joseph would, from time to time, expressly state that, whatever happened, he was firmly resolved never to consent to the grant of a constitution. The Diploma of 1860, traditional in form, expressed throughout in the old language of prerogative, may have satisfied him in this respect. But when Schmerling put his representation bill before the cabinet, it was hard for Francis Joseph to persuade himself that this was still not a real constitution, in view of the fact that the liberal press acclaimed the February patent as one, in the first freshness of its delight. Moreover there was the entire urban German middle class organizing itself into a "constitutional party" under Schmerling's lead. And yet Schmerling seems to have allayed the Emperor's apprehensions of the danger of the degree of constitutionalism he himself had granted.

Yet for Francis Joseph the years between Solferino and his first speech from the throne had brought great changes! He must, in that period, have gone through severe internal struggles. At bottom he still held to his profound conviction that Austria could not be ruled constitutionally, least of all as a unity. Yet under the compulsion of the dangers that surrounded him, he had enough force and elasticity of mind to face the hitherto hated political ideas and aspirations of the age he lived in and to admit them at least to his reception room, to test the political principles of the various parties and take his own counsel upon them. He was still young enough to learn how to attenuate or modify his pre-conceptions

EMPEROR FRANCIS JOSEPH OF AUSTRIA

EMPEROR FRANCIS JOSEPH
IN THE YEAR 1861
(AFTER A PRIVATE PHOTOGRAPH)

of the state and his own position without thereby giving up his basic ideas. And, after all, Schmerling, whatever his deficiencies as a statesman, was a man!

Proud, absolutely self-reliant in bearing, a man whom the Emperor must respect, little as he might love the "*raideur*" of his temper, he early discovered that Schmerling's indolence did not carry with it any of his own hard-working diligence and punctuality. Indeed his own constant preoccupation with problems, conflicts, and difficulties, presented by the work of the central parliament and Diets and cabinet meetings, and sooner or later, somehow or other, to be settled or solved by his personal decision, now gave the Emperor a various and fruitful education in practical politics. Formerly he had only had to do with "administration."

While he might inwardly regard the Schmerling era merely as an experiment, it nevertheless served him as a sort of "constitutional school." The same, in truth, can be said of the peoples of Austria. The middle classes, at any rate, were able to begin to outgrow their political immaturity through actual political coöperation in commune, province, and state. The Emperor, anyhow, soon got such a grip of the new, and, to him, alien, nature of a constitutional state, that he was able to devise a new and strategically well-chosen line of defence for his personal supremacy. At a cabinet meeting in 1861, he uttered a solemn declaration that he was going to make no further concessions to the constitutional principle, and rejected, absolutely, any demand for ministerial responsibility to parliament. He repeated this declaration in the following year, when he was supported, with notable force, by Count Rechberg.

Swift, indeed, was Francis Joseph to grasp the fact that the constitutional experiment confronted him with the necessity of accommodating himself to the new rôle of constitutional monarch. He had soon got hold of the technique, and was not long in realizing that, in the modern political theatre, costumes, scenery, and lighting count for more with the audience than the quality of the play.

A glimpse into this transition period of Schwarzenberg's pupil is given by the narrative of a German publicist, Hermann Orges. Francis Joseph received him in 1861 on Rechberg's recommendation, as a mark of recognition for the fact that both before and after the war he had tirelessly represented Austria's interests in the columns of the Augsburg *Allgemeine Zeitung*. When Orges remarked to the Emperor that while the existence of definite parties made ruling difficult, their formation was no longer preventable, the Emperor replied: "Yes, if only the parties were formed on such lines that one could clearly distinguish them, but that is not the case, and the worst case is when they are silent or pursue aims different from those they profess." There is a good deal of naïveté in this remark of Francis Joseph's, but also an indication of his having begun to concern himself seriously with parties, and to discern what actually underlies the whole of this "phenomenon of progress."

In the course of the long years of his rule, he achieved a practical knowledge of parties and their leaders that was, later, often justifiably to astound his ministers. The beginning of this study can hardly have come easily to him. In general, of course, his attendance at cabinet discussions gave him a mass of information on all departments of state business. In 1863, when he presided over the gathering of kings, granddukes, and princes composing the German confederation at Frankfort, he astonished these high personages and the statesmen who accompanied them by the skill and assurance with which he conducted the business, hour after hour, more or less improvising the agenda, and that in a fashion to promote the ends he had in view.

In all directions the impossibility of the new system became apparent. The secession of almost all the Slav members, and, still more forcibly, the growing opposition of a great part of the German constitutional party, shattered the Emperor's faith in Schmerling's success. Meantime, Count Esterházy had swiftly acquired a great influence over him. Esterházy was certainly one of the most remarkable personalities among all the Emperor's ministers, early or late. A man of unusual culture, his intellectual force was at times sterilized by an excessive faculty for analysis. Melancholic in temperament, he was touched already by the mental derangement that was actually to overtake him later. What made him a calamitous adviser for Francis Joseph was the fact that his influence was felt in a period of uncertainty in domestic and foreign policy that afforded excessive opportunity to his critical bent. Certainly his influence was marked on the young Emperor, the more so since it was he who acted as go-between with the Hungarian old conservatives, whose active partisan he was. He succeeded step by step in modifying the acute antipathy for the magnates that had developed in the Emperor's mind by 1861, while Schmerling who was passionately hostile was trying to communicate his mood to his master.

Esterházy explained to the Emperor that, if the Hungarian question was to be solved, he must return to the "Transaction" policy he had abruptly abandoned, although he should not give up his control over Hungary until a complete understanding with the new Hungarian Diet had been reached. Francis Joseph was already convinced that no internal settlement could be reached along the lines of Schmerling's sham liberal constitution. Esterházy reiterated to him that this constitution must go, otherwise the Emperor was completely in the hands of the German constitutional party.

At the end of 1864, no doubt on the initiative of Archduke Albert, Francis Joseph, in the greatest secrecy, took a highly successful step on the way to peace with the Magyars. One of the most competent among the former high Hungarian officials attached to the governor general, Baron von Auguss, acting on Francis Joseph's instructions, entered into verbal negotiations with Francis Déak on the possibility of an understanding between the Emperor and a new Diet. Auguss communicated Déak's arguments and statements directly to the Emperor: the reports exist in what were his secret archives. A little later Déak published, in Pest, his famous Easter article—in which, after stipulating that the principle of continuity in the basic law of the realm must be observed and the 1848 Hun-

garian constitution must be restored, he went on to say
that, on that basis, the Hungarian Diet might accept definite changes in the constitution, for the vital purposes
of a monarchy, composed of two states, but acting as
one as a European great power. Here was the kernel
out of which the whole program of "dualism" was to
develop.

Déak's propositions produced a profound effect everywhere. Their immediate result was that the Emperor,
most surprisingly, betook himself to Pest, where the temperamental Magyars gave him an extraordinary welcome.
A few days later he dismissed the Hungarian chancellor,
though Schmerling had found him quite serviceable. The
fall of the whole government followed. Next occurred
one of those sudden volte-faces to which Francis Joseph
was addicted. He called on Count Belcredi, governor of
Bohemia and a member of the Bohemian nobles' party,
to form a government, which he did, including in it
Hungarian and Austrian aristocrats and one or two
officials.

Thus the conservatives in both halves of the realm
were back again in power to make a fresh attempt.
Schmerling's 1861 constitution, after putting the basic
law into execution in such a way as to turn it topsy turvy,
and convert a federalistic realm into a highly centralized
one, was now swept out of existence. Once again political
pressure from Hungarian aristocrats had succeeded with
the Emperor. The new Hungarian Diet, which was immediately summoned, was called up for the purpose
of declaring, by its resolutions, how far and in what

form any Empire existed, i.e., under what conditions the Magyars would recognize a central authority equally binding on Hungary and the other kingdoms and territories under Francis Joseph's sway.

Such outcome of the Hungarian Diet's resolutions was thereupon to be submitted to all the Diets of the western half of the realm and, so the government hoped, accepted by them. Through this action of Belcredi's, Francis Joseph accepted one of the decisive points in Francis Déak's program—namely, that a law binding on the Kingdom of Hungary could only be created by negotiation, on the footing of power to power, between the Emperor and the Hungarian Diet and their mutual agreement. This gain—so important from the standpoint of Hungarian independence—had been won for the country by the skilful diplomacy of the old conservatives. The connection between their policy and the Constitution of April, 1848, was not theirs, however; their original ideas were frankly reactionary; it was the work of Francis Déak and the Hungarian liberals, who supported him without reserve.

When the Diet met in December, 1865, it was, of course, completely under Déak's direction. By his side, however, appeared a man destined to play a great part in Francis Joseph's life—Count Julius Andrássy. Actively concerned as a youthful liberal reformer in the 1848 revolution, he had been drawn more and more into Kossuth's circle and been sent as his ambassador to Constantinople. For this he was condemned for high treason by the military courts set up after the defeat of the Hungarian War of Independence, and condemned to death *in contumaciam*. Also his property was confiscated. Not till 1857 did he profit by the imperial amnesty, and return home from France.

Count Andrássy, assured of a leading position in the liberal party by virtue of his remarkable political gifts, now became Déak's most trusted and active lieutenant in the Diet. There were still plenty of difficulties to overcome. Speeches from the throne, addresses by the Diet and imperial rescripts in reply, followed one another, showing that, in consonance with Belcredi's advice, Francis Joseph still held fast to the "idea of the realm"—in other words, demanded Hungary's recognition of the "common concerns" of the realm as set out in the October Diploma—foreign policy, the army, finance—as imperial matters, and its readiness to have their legislative handling committed to a parliamentary body composed of delegates from the Diets of Hungary and all the other kingdoms and territories in the realm. In that sense the 1848 constitution must be altered, likewise.

The decisive moment in the varying contest between the Crown and Hungary came when Déak induced the Diet to appoint a special committee to discuss and settle both the demands made by Hungary and the concessions it was prepared to make to the Emperor and the "idea of the realm" in relation to "common concerns." Déak forced the Diet to take this step because he desired to have Hungary's position made clear to the Emperor and the public opinion of Europe before the war with Prussia, which had been threatening since the early days of 1866, became an accomplished fact. Actually, the draft of a peace treaty between Francis Joseph and the Magyars had been completed by the committee when the struggle for the hegemony of Germany broke into flames early in the summer.

CHAPTER X

BISMARCK later described 1863 as his "heaviest year," and it was no light one for Francis Joseph. Polish revolution, breaking out in Russia, threatened to extend to Galicia. Thus as in the Crimean War period, Austria stood between pro-Polish France and Russia. Worse, Austro-Prussian antagonism on the question of the reform of the German confederation reached a crisis.

In 1862, Francis Joseph had taken the initiative in this perilous diplomatic field, with the result of bringing to a head first, the old antagonism between Great and Little Germans, and second, that between Austria, jealous of primacy in the confederation, and Prussia, who had striven ever since 1850, so to transform it as to create a closer German federal state under Prussian leadership. What had been a struggle of diplomats and pamphleteers became serious, when public opinion, not in Prussia only but in the middling and lesser German states, was roused to demand a settlement of the great question of German political unity. Such a stir had been caused throughout Germany, in all classes, by the events of 1859 that the problem could no longer be burked. The foundation of a liberal association for promoting national union and the growing

[315]

strength of liberal middle-class organization behind the Prussian solution forced every section in Germany to take an interest in the great task of national unification.

Within the next few years Francis Joseph suddenly came forward as leader in the great movement. To the surprise of all Germany, the young Emperor, on his own motion, called a council of all princes to meet at Frankfort on August 18, 1863, and the Emperor went to Gastein on August 2, personally inviting King William of Prussia. Catholic politicians in southern Germany had begun to think that the demand for the unification of German stocks and states, increasingly emphasized by the liberals, might be realized, in the conservative interest, through personal understandings between the German princes. This view was accepted and eagerly promoted by Schmerling, the leader of Austrian liberalism, and by the strict Catholics in the "German Confederation Department" of the foreign office in Vienna.

With a German like Baron von Biegeleben at their head, they soon won Francis Joseph's apparent agreement with their idea. The collapse of this plan, owing to the opposition of the King of Prussia; Bismarck's success in converting his sovereign to his own policy and so surmounting the first great obstacle to his own unyielding determination to establish Prussia's hegemony in Germany, even though it intensified the detestation from the German liberals which he had incurred by his fight with the progressive party in the Prussian Diet on army reform and the budget—all this is too well known to need description here. The same is true of Bismarck's handling of the question of the relations of Schleswig-Holstein to Denmark and the confederation in such wise as to bring humiliation and defeat to the confederation he loathed.

Nor is it any part of the duty of the biographer of Francis Joseph to relate the masterly moves in the game of diplomatic chess played by Bismarck between 1863 and 1866, how he brought about war between Prussia, with Italy and Austria, and so led to Austria's loss of Venetia and its exclusion from Germany. What concerns him is Francis Joseph's personal share in these events which altered the whole balance of power in Europe, creating first the North German confederation and united Italy, and then the Prusso-German empire. Even to-day this, as Friedjung, the admirable historian of the "War for Hegemony in Germany," has stated, is no easy task. Documentary evidence of the Emperor's inner life during this struggle is rather scanty. Yet in the familiar picture there are many lines that can now be drawn more clearly.

In any attempted interpretation of the actors in this great drama, the mind must be freed of the tendency of the average historian to judge after the event. For history is as deeply and fatally tainted as politics and modern life in general by the natural but deeply demoralizing habit of accepting external success as the criterion of moral values in judging historic characters! That Francis Joseph had, for years, perceived the imminence of armed conflict with Prussia for supremacy in Germany, is patent. He had been but two years on the throne when Prince Schwarzenberg, at Olmütz, compelled Prussia to draw back from Radowitz's policy of union.

Francis Joseph, then, cast his weight into the scale in favor of a peaceable understanding with his uncle, Frederick William IV. The mass of diplomatic documents and letters since given to the world show, no less clearly, that he now, again, strove to avoid war with Prussia, notably after his meeting with King William at Teplitz, where the core of their discussions was common action against Napoleon's plan of conquering the left bank of the Rhine.

In this attitude the Emperor was fully supported by his foreign minister, Count Rechberg. In both, the desire to reach a peaceable agreement with Prussia indeed explains the contradictory policy pursued by Austria in the complicated Schleswig-Holstein question, before and after the duchies on the Elbe had been conquered by the armies of the two German powers in their campaign against Denmark.

The great and irretrievable error was committed when Francis Joseph, despite the deep distrust both he and Rechberg felt for Bismarck, fell into the trap he had prepared for Austria in their common war against Denmark. It was recognized as such, at the time, by some of the best brains in the German constitutional party in the House of Deputies of the Parliament, and formed the basis of their opposition to the Schmerling-Rechberg administration and its foreign policy. Yet the main responsibility for this error was certainly Francis Joseph's. He had rightly gauged both Bismarck's personality and his policy from the start. Further, he knew from his contact with the other sovereigns and cabinets of Europe that nothing but Bismarck's demonic force could drive old King William along a line of policy that must lead to war and the dissolution of the German confederation.

These stiff diplomatic struggles showed, even more clearly than 1859 had done, that the young autocrat had not been gifted by nature with the powers of brain and soul adequate for the solution of these great problems of foreign policy. Most of the monarchs of his day were in no better case. What was fatal for Francis Joseph was that, in these crises, he had no statesman to advise him who was mentally the equal of Otto von Bismarck in incomparable clarity and force of thought and in ruthless Machiavellianism of diplomatic and political action.

What made the Austrian cabinet inferior to the Prussian was not, as is so often stated, that Rechberg, Mensdorff, and Esterházy were Catholics. It was far rather the fact that Francis Joseph himself and his ministers lived in another world from Bismarck: in a world which believed that the great currents of the day, mounting to expression in the idea of a national state, and an adversary like Bismarck, consciously directing the force of mass-emotion to serve his own plans, limited as they were by the framework of Prussian royalism, could be met by a cabinet policy with nothing behind it but historic rights and the threadbare ideology of the sanctity of international treaties. Had they not gone to war with Napoleon in 1859 to affirm the inviolability of treaties by arms?

Now the act of confederation of 1814 was held up to Bismarck—after two years of cold-blooded demonstration to the world, in alliance with Bismarck, of the weakness of that same confederation and of national liberalism in Germany, in the question of the Elbe duchies. Francis Joseph was often to lament to his intimates that Austria neither then nor later possessed a man like Bismarck, who might have rendered the Habsburg dynasty the service Bismarck gave the weak posterity of Frederick.

Austria owed the fact that no such man could exist there mainly to "good Emperor Francis," but also to Francis Joseph himself, in whose cabinet there never was any place for a "demonic" statesman. And, in the last analysis, the very nature of a dynastic federation, like Austria, excluded a policy of blood and iron. The actual policy pursued by Francis Joseph as a young autocrat, with the assistance of Schwarzenberg and Haynau, had weakened it profoundly. An Austrian Bismarck would have required the genius of the creator of the new Germany, but he would have to have been, first and foremost, a man of peace and patient reconciliation among the peoples whom Francis Joseph's ancestors had welded together to form a barrier for Europe against the East.

If, in 1863, Francis Joseph wanted to unite Germany, he must have offered himself to the German people as a leader in whom the liberal ideas then animating the middle classes lived with the creative force of youth. He might have met and even beaten Bismarck, who held the Prussian liberals, with a sort of arrogant openness, in leash to the naked idea of power if—a Habsburg could ever have been a liberal. But any such possibility was excluded in advance. How could Francis Joseph be a leader of Germany, when he fought for nothing better than his "Præsidial right," in the Frankfort Diet, admirable as his formal case might be! His own view of his angle to the German problem emerges from a memorandum, recently published, written by Queen Victoria after a conversation with him at her Coburg Castle of Rosenau, on September 3, 1863, on the occasion of a visit paid her there by Francis Joseph on his way home from Frankfort. On the Queen's remarking that the present juncture was very important for Germany and, it was to be hoped, might lead to unity, Francis Joseph replied that he hoped so, too, but Prussia was a great difficulty:

"I rejoined that I trusted there was no disposition to lower Prussia, for that naturally Prussia and Austria must go together, to which the Emperor answered, no one dreamt in Germany of lowering Prussia, which was an impossibility, but that, at Berlin, great pretensions were raised. He believed that it was not the King personally, who made great difficulties, but his Government. I said that I could not conceal from him that the King of Prussia seemed much hurt at the belief that there was an intention to show want of respect to Prussia, and thought that there was a desire to place her under Austria, which I had assured him I believed to be quite unfounded. The Emperor merely repeated the same thing, and said that he thought it was a great mistake that the King of Prussia had not come to Frankfort, in which I agreed. We both agreed that the unity of Germany was of the greatest importance to Europe, as it would keep the Emperor of the French quiet. The Emperor said that it was necessary to be constantly on the watch with regard to the designs of the Emperor Napoleon, and that in England we kept him in very good order. Might I, I said, say to our daughter, the Crown Princess, that there was every disposition on his part to be friendly towards Prussia, and to treat her on a footing of equality? He said, assuredly so, but that he was afraid that there were great pretensions entertained at Berlin. I went on to say that what I believed was expected, and wished, equality between the two Powers; could there not be some arrangement of alternation on the Præsidium and Directorium? He said, this was quite a new pretension of Prussia to have it also, and in Austria they would dislike extremely its being given up."

The struggle for hegemony in Germany could not be settled, however, with the simplicity suggested by Queen Victoria. The report gives an excellent insight into the manner in which great problems of foreign policy were handled by the heads of the great European monarchies, when tête-á-tête. The intellectual level of the above conversation can hardly be called high.

Bismarck, who had, for four years, devoted the force of his unbending will and the whole of his genius as a diplomat to bringing about war, knew perfectly how to put Austria in the position of aggressor. First, he concluded an alliance with Italy, whose martial preparations excited the Austrian general staff and Francis Joseph to such a pitch that there was an abrupt end to the attempt at disarmament on the part of the two great powers, which had just been initiated. Again, precisely as in 1859, Francis Joseph's mind took in nothing but the military point of view. The reason was the profound indignation caused him by what he regarded as the double dealing of the King of Italy and his government.

Once again, moreover, he repeated the error of 1859 in relation to the supreme command. Once again he made a man who regarded himself as unfitted for the task commander of the northern armies. General Benedek, in this case, was no untried aristocratic general, but the most popular officer the Austrian army had possessed since Radetzky: a man who had proved his courage and skill in leadership in many a theatre of war.

In vain did Benedek implore the Emperor not to lay this task upon him, urging his ignorance of the Bohemian theatre, and his want of confidence in his own capacity to handle so great an army. In vain did he implore him to give him the southern army, which he had so long commanded in peace, for the war in northern Italy, where he knew "every tree as far as Milan." So energetic were his appeals that Francis Joseph, after his conversation with Benedek, actually gave up his original plan, only to return to it a few days later, as the result of various influences.

With a heavy heart, Benedek yielded to the pressure brought upon him by the Emperor, who appealed to him to take command as a sacrifice to his Emperor and his country. What was the explanation of Francis Joseph's action? Was he convinced that Benedek was wrong, that despite his pusillanimity, he really was the best man for the historic task of defeating the Prussian army? There is nothing to suggest that such was Francis Joseph's view.

Meantime, the Chief of the General Staff, von Henikstein, a friend of Benedek's, who had been responsible for mobilization in the Italian war, declared, now that war was inevitable, that he did not feel equal to the demands of his position. General Krismanic, who had won renown as professor of strategy in the Military Academy, thereupon, with Benedek's consent, took his place as head of the operations department, i.e., as effective chief of the general staff. This meant that Benedek, whose great gift was his power of taking the offensive, was yoked with an aging theoretician and obstinate devotee of the defensive, with the result that the priceless dash of the commander in chief was lamed, from the start, by the ponderous self-satisfaction of his chief of staff.

The real reason that caused Francis Joseph to put Benedek in command was quite specific and definite. It was connected with his cousin, Archduke Albert, who, knowing the Bohemian theatre as the result of years of study, was nevertheless given the Italian command. What happened was that it was represented to Francis Joseph that a real danger to the dynasty might arise if the northern army were not victorious, and if responsibility for failure could be laid at the Archduke's door. As against the Italians, on the other hand, the victory of the Venetian army was practically certain; further the Archduke had an admirable chief of staff in General von John. Thus, dynastic interest was determinant for Francis Joseph—as it was, granted his outlook, logically bound to be.

In the event, Austria defeated Italy by land and sea. Victor Emmanuel's army was beaten at Custozza, Admiral Persano's fleet, though its ships were much the bigger, was largely destroyed by Admiral Tegethoff, the single great admiral produced by the German race in the nineteenth century. After a three weeks' campaign, however, the battle of Königgrätz was decisive in the north. The army, perhaps the best Austria ever put in the field, fought superbly, but, as a result of Benedek's strategic error in leaving himself exposed to the Crown Prince of Prussia's army, it was defeated, and, by evening, driven back in more or less disordered flight.

Although Benedek was able to get his corps clear away to re-form in Moravia and bring them in fighting trim down the Danube to Hungary, he was relieved of his command. Archduke Albert, called from the south with his army to cover the Danube line, took over the supreme command. In this there was nothing extraordinary. The dismissal of defeated generals has always and everywhere been normal. Did not Napoleon III remark: "La guerre depend trop de la chance"?

But Francis Joseph did not leave it at that. Benedek and many of his subordinates were called before a special military commission, as though after having been given complete independence in the imperial decree of his appointment, he had been guilty of high treason or some

[325]

other crime. Benedek, true to the terms of his appointment, refused to give any information which might have injured his subordinates. He declared that he alone was responsible. The commission found the general and two of his subordinates guilty of errors liable to court-martial.

Thereupon, however, the whole proceeding was stayed by an order from the Emperor. On November 1, Benedek was cashiered. He bore his heavy fate with dignity. The sole desire he expressed, and that repeatedly, was to have an opportunity of speaking personally with the Emperor. This, however, Francis Joseph would not grant him. On the contrary, he made Archduke Albert visit him for the purpose of asking a fresh sacrifice in the shape of his promise on his word of honor not to attempt any public justification of himself. The Archduke asked this promise as a final sacrifice from the unhappy man to his Emperor and his country. Benedek met Francis Joseph's wish; he even committed his promise to writing. The soul of honor, he had already suffered much, but the heaviest blow was still to fall.

A few days after he had given his promise, an official statement appeared in the *Wiener Zeitung,* the organ of the government, condemning Benedek's career as a general in terms of painful harshness, laying upon him the sole responsibility for the disasters that had come upon Austria, and animadverting upon the fact that he had not been punished in the following words: "There is no code which makes deficiency in the higher qualities of the intellect a punishable offense." For a man "high-minded and honorable" as Benedek had always been, no judicial punishment could have been so severe a penalty as the loss of his Imperial Master's confidence and the destruction of his military fame in the eyes both of the contemporary world and of posterity.

His behavior to Benedek shows Francis Joseph at his worst, nor is it any excuse to say that he was certainly acting on the advice of Archduke Albert. His use of "reasons of state," of the flimsiest kind, to destroy the unhappy general, who had been the most loyal of his officers, and his lack of any kind of human consideration, constitute a stain on his character the more striking that the petty and absolutely underhand dirtiness with which Benedek was treated somehow does not fit in with the general traits of his personality. He had accepted Benedek's self-abnegation in taking over supreme command with the knowledge that a man of Benedek's upright and straightforward character could make no greater sacrifice. But when Benedek's presentiment of his own inadequacy was fulfilled, Francis Joseph had eyes only for the humiliation to himself, his power, and his realm involved in defeat, and let the officer, on whose devotion he knew he could count bear the whole burden, and assume a responsibility which was not properly his.

It was common knowledge that the aristocratic generals and archdukes who had served as corps commanders, like Archduke Leopold and Count Clam-Gallas, had simply not obeyed the orders of the commander in chief. Public opinion, which had called for Benedek's appointment, knew many circumstances which greatly lessened his fault. It was known that Francis Joseph himself ought to charge to his own personal account one of the main causes of the defeat in Bohemia, namely the inferiority of the Austrian infantry musket to the Prussian breechloader, since urgent representations on this point made by officers who had served in the Danish campaigns, had been addressed to the Emperor in person and had been ungraciously rejected by him.

Benedek, who lived on for fifteen years after his fall, supported his hard fate with dignified calm. Baron Beust, who came to Vienna on the day after the battle of Königgrätz, with his sovereign, the King of Saxony, relates that the bearing of the Emperor in receiving his ally was quite collected, but his face as white as the uniform he wore. Towards Benedek, Francis Joseph did not preserve his dignity. He showed, there, a complete lack of either human or regal greatness. He and Archduke Albert gave full scope to impulses of personal vindictiveness and petty revenge.

In 1859, Francis Joseph showed undoubted talent for speedy peacemaking. His sword was swift to leave the scabbard, equally swift in returning thither. This time, however, the issues were great and difficult and his mind was perturbed by unmistakable signs of the dangerous state of opinion in Hungary. Those about him noted how careworn he seemed after the terrible evening of July 3, and how this care marked his features throughout all the time that followed. On the adversary's side, however, the will to speedy peace came stronger and sooner to action than Francis Joseph and his advisers could have imagined.

Austria once defeated in the field, Bismarck had only one aim—to give Austria, as quickly as possible, the most favorable terms of peace, on the sole condition that Austria withdraw from the confederation, and Francis Joseph leave the new federal organization of Germany entirely to Prussia and to Bismarck to fashion.

Bismarck, unlike the King and his generals, desired no more victories. He did not desire to occupy Vienna; he did not seek in any way to weaken the Habsburg house, still less to bring it down, although he had himself taken the first step in that direction by his support of the Magyar emigrés and the formation of a Magyar legion.

Bismarck's *Recollections* have made everyone familiar with the poignant scene in the lofty castle of Prince von Dietrichstein at Nikolsburg; the picture of Bismarck forcing the venerable King to make peace, supported only by the Crown Prince, in the teeth of the war-lust of the Prussian generals. Neither Berlin nor Vienna had any conception of the long views of Prussia's foreign minister, of his luminous vision of the final establishment of German unity, or of the dangers from the west threatening Prussia's further steps. Not the Prussian Headquarters, not the Hofburg at Vienna, but Paris held the keys to the complex dangers of the situation.

Francis Joseph was as well aware of this as Bismarck. On the day after the battle of Königgrätz, his ambassador, Prince Metternich, applied to Napoleon for mediation, offering to cede Venetia to him and not to the defeated Italian foe. Bismarck, therefore, need not trouble about Italy. It was not known until later that Francis Joseph had entered into an agreement with Napoleon, before the war, by which he undertook, in the event of an Austrian victory over Germany, to hand Venetia over to France, by way of compensation for Austrian territorial gains in Germany.

This treaty, whose text has only been known in the last few years, casts a very dubious light on the diplomatic acumen of Mensdorff and Esterházy, Francis Joseph's advisers. It shows, further, how little lasting advantage Francis Joseph had taken of Schwarzenberg's teaching. His diplomacy in the weeks before the outbreak of war—his brusque rejection of French and English suggestions of a European conference to prevent hostilities, because he would not have the idea of giving up Venetia mentioned, followed by a last minute promise of this costly possession to Napoleon, in a treaty whose terms were so obscure that the cabinet was unable to make out precisely what they meant—show that, complete autocrat as he still was in the domain of foreign policy, he simply was not adequate to the task laid upon him in a crisis undoubtedly rife with dangers for him.

Once again he was wholly preoccupied with the effort to maintain all the possessions of the hereditary house in Europe, and, if possible, to attain everything at the same time. But it was his destiny, full as he was of an inexpugnable sense of duty to the dynastic interests of his house, never to be ready, never to possess a sufficiently clear grasp of the actual balance of forces, to make a sacrifice at the right moment, but always to have sacrifices forced upon him by defeat in the field.

Venice was dear to him, and he would not give it up to Italy, although it had for long represented a source of weakness rather than a sign of power. He would not share the primacy in the German confederation of his ancient imperial house with Prussia, still less yield it altogether. He wished to hold on to his share in the Elbe duchies, whatever it cost, and it did not occur to him that the great battle in Bohemia would compel him to withdraw from the confederation altogether. After starting a second effort to reach an understanding with the Magyars, instead of putting the discussions through, he let war break out before they were settled. A few days after the disaster in the field he received Francis Déak. Quite quiet, quite unassuming in bearing, he appeared before the Emperor and said, in answer to his question, that he and his nation behind him, asked no more now, after the war, than they had demanded before it. On top of this came the last delay.

Bismarck desired to make peace with Austria, without any annexation or indemnity, on the single condition of Francis Joseph's withdrawing at once from the confederation and giving him a free hand in the transformation of Germany. Dr. Giskra, the President of the Brünn Chamber of Commerce, who came to Vienna with this proposition, as representing the Mayor of Brünn, had difficulty in getting a hearing. For Esterházy scented a trap in Bismarck's offer of so incredibly favorable a peace, with the result that Francis Joseph's acceptance of the invitation to enter on peace discussions on this basis arrived at the Royal Headquarters at Nikolsburg half an hour too late. Meantime, the French ambassador, Count Benedetti, the go-between of the two great German powers, had already arrived there.

Delay after delay, complete self-deception as to his own power, and total incapacity to seize the points favorable to Austria in Bismarck's lucid and audacious policy and strike out a new line of Austrian policy with like swiftness and strength—such was the inevitable outcome of Francis Joseph's policy. He could find no stay in either the well-bred modesty and reticence of Mensdorff or in the unresting scepticism of Esterházy's dark spirit.

The war lasted three weeks; it took as long to get the peace preliminaries started at Nikolsburg. Unspeakably hard weeks these for the Emperor, now thirty-six, and, once again, deeply wounded in his personal position and self-esteem. The peace conditions finally accepted by Prussia struck the world as very mild. "I was generous to Austria because I did not want war with France," said King William, in the following year, to Count Beust. Bismarck had done it single-handed. Yet the consequences of the lost war were of the last severity for Austria.

Least troublesome was the loss of the old position of the hereditary house in Italy. Characteristically, the mind of the Ballplatz, up to the last, was fixed mainly on the Pope and the states of the church. At the same time, the old imperial dynasty, with its hereditary German domains, was shut out of Germany: German unity was to be a Hohenzollern achievement. This, for Francis Joseph and the whole imperial family, spelt the bitterest loss of personal prestige.

There was no compensation to be found in the independence of the south German states accomplished by Napoleon. A few weeks after the signature of peace, Bismarck concluded secret treaties with Bavaria, Württemberg, Baden, and Hesse: Prussia's domination in Germany was thereby secured. Nowhere were the effects of victory so noticeable as in French public opinion. There, apprehension was already stirring of the events, four years later, amid which the French Empire was to vanish forever in a mighty whirlwind.

The diminution in Francis Joseph's personal prestige at first appeared illimitable. It had been his war; he had conducted it as the complete autocrat, although, this time, the aristocrats shared his defeat, or those among them who had driven him along its path, above all Count Belcredi. Francis Joseph was, so far as his own policy went, in much the same position as after Solferino. Again the sheer strength of the man in the face of cruellest disappointment and harsh defeat is astounding. Protocols of ministerial conferences, discussing terms of the armistice and peace, show him weighing the pros and cons of peace conditions with Archduke Albert, and with his generals and ministers, with a steady realism, an absolute self-command, and a complete objectivity in facing the facts and dangers of the situation.

His one great care throughout the peace negotiations was the maintenance of the royal house of Saxony and the integrity of the dynasty. On this even Bismarck had to yield. There was something intolerable to Francis Joseph in the thought that the single German king and country which had been true to its alliance with Austria, and whose army had fought with great bravery for him, might suffer through Austria's military misfortune. The first condition of peace, so far as he was concerned, was the acceptance of his demands for Saxony. His sensitiveness to personal honor determined his action, despite severe political pressure. The next and greatest concern, for him, was, of course, the reactions bound to be produced by the events of the war on the internal problems of his realm.

First and foremost, there were the negotiations with the Hungarian Diet interrupted by the war. In the first week after Königgrätz, Francis Deák was sent for, and gave an answer that must for the time being at any rate have been reassuring. No need, in this interview, whose tone was thoroughly friendly, for either to dwell on the fact that the unhappy result of the war left the Emperor much weakened, both morally and politically, as against Magyar demands.

The impression made on Francis Joseph by Deák, whom he saw for the second time, was profound. Deák refused the Emperor's offer of a place in the ministry, but urged him to lose no time in calling upon Count Julius Andrássy to form an independent Hungarian government. A few days later Andrássy himself appeared before the Emperor and, for the first time, set out quite clearly the plan of a dual monarchy, in the form that had been outlined, before the outbreak of the war, by the sub-committee of the Hungarian Diet.

Francis Joseph's interpretation of his own position had not, however, yet reached the point of making him ready to accept the bridge thus offered him by Andrássy and Deák. On the contrary, it was plain that there were immense difficulties still in the way of his doing so. He was still under the influence of Belcredi and old conservative Hungarian aristocrats in his government. Further, evidence of the existence of a long-standing pact between the leaders of the German constitutional party in Vienna and the provinces and their Hungarian colleagues increased Francis Joseph's disinclination to hurry on the negotiations with Hungary.

The situation may be summed up as follows. On the one hand was the program of Deák and the majority of the Hungarian Diet, the program of "Dualism"—which implied the recognition of Hungary, according to old historic right, as an independent kingdom, and the restoration of its 1848 constitution. This carried with it, further, the rejection, in principle, of the unitary realm, imposed by force by Schwarzenberg, although the idea of the indissoluble cohesion of Hungary with the other historic kingdoms and territories of the imperial house was to be expressly recognized in the existence of a common army and a common foreign policy in the two states, Austria and Hungary, ruled by a common monarch. Matters now legally recognized by Hungary as of common concern were to be handled, constitutionally, by the parliaments of both states, and the nomination of a small number of common ministers responsible to both parliaments. But the execution of this plan implied the setting up of a special parliamentary government in Hungary, to be summoned by Francis Joseph. This program of Déak's had, behind it, the great majority of Hungarian liberals; a minority refused to recognize anything common between the two states but the personal identity of the monarch, and demanded complete independence.

On the other side stood the Belcredi government, ready to meet Déak on most points, but still hoping to be able to maintain the unity of the realm at least in the form of a common representative parliamentary body, to be accepted by Hungary. The real object of Belcredi and his friends was, first and foremost, to get rid, permanently, of Schmerling's constitution in the western half of the monarchy. Behind this lurked the dream which they never succeeded in working out to its logical consequence even in their own minds—the dream of replacing the old German-Slav unitary realm, with its powerful bureaucracy, built up in the seventeenth and eighteenth centuries, by a federalistic constitution based on the "historic-political individualities" of the territories. By this means they hoped to reverse the preponderance given to the German liberals by Schmerling's central Parliament in favor of the Catholic conservative peasants and lower middle classes.

Francis Joseph's dislike, in these days, for the German liberals was shown in the extreme ungraciousness of his reception of the Vienna municipal council when it appeared in audience before him after the battle of König-

grätz, for the purpose of assuring him of its "loyalty"
in an address that was certainly a trifle hypocritical. His
sympathy was still all for men like Belcredi, who promised, by reëstablishing the constitution in the kingdoms
and territories and their Diets, to give real stability and
a new lustre to the imperial status.

But the Magyars repeated, through Andrássy's mouth,
that they could not consent to any federalization of the
western half of the realm. Count Andrássy explained to
the Emperor that the best guarantee of his power as head
of the whole monarchy was the coöperation of the Magyar and German liberal parties.

Historical romantics like Belcredi and the aristocratic
parties in Hungary and Austria were certainly unduly op-
timistic in believing that they could combine federalism
with a strong imperial central power in the form of a
powerful army and a powerful bureaucracy, and, at the
same time, secure a permanent increase of political influence for the Slavs, to say nothing of the fact that all
this was to be brought about in the teeth of the opposition
of liberal Vienna, and the liberal middle class in the great
industrial areas of Lower Austria and Steiermark, in Bohemia, Moravia, and Silesia!

In this complicated dilemma, Francis Joseph could not
make up his mind. His great desire was the power of his
house. Was he, in future, to base this on a political alliance between two nations? Or, more accurately, between
two parties in these two nations, the liberals, here and
there? Such a solution wore, for him, a singular air. He
had never heard of the Magyars being pillars of the

hereditary house. To him there must have been something at first quite incomprehensible in a line of thought which made imperial power dependent on the peoples, wholly dependent on two privileged peoples. Nor was that all. He was, in future, to depend on liberal nobles among the Magyars, and on liberal professors, factory owners, lawyers—Germans both in Vienna and the provinces; in other words, that is to say partly on the Jews, already so powerful in the liberal press! Truly a bad outlook for him.

How much more painful was his position, after the victory of Prussia, than it had been after the lost campaign against France and Piedmont! He looked about for new counsellors but found no one about him to inspire confidence. Count Esterházy retired, Count Mensdorff was asking to be released, and was no statesman anyhow. Schmerling and his friends he refused to contemplate.

The actual way that he found out of this maze caused great astonishment everywhere; and yet no one who understands his personality will find anything inexplicable in it. In the last days of October, 1866, he got his chef-de-cabinet, Councillor Braun, to approach Baron von Beust, ex-premier of Saxony, and ask him whether he was willing to accept the foreign affairs portfolio in Austria, as successor to Mensdorff. Bismarck had made Beust's resignation from the service of the Saxon state a preliminary condition for the peace with the kingdom. Greatly surprised, Beust now joyfully accepted Francis Joseph's proposal, and on November 4 his appointment, hitherto a dead secret, was published in Vienna.

What induced Francis Joseph to take the unusual step of calling on a non-Austrian at such a moment to assume the most important position in his government; a man, too, who had set every method known to diplomacy in motion, for many years, against Prussia and for the Little German unity program; Beust, whose ideal had been the transformation of the confederation into a "Triad," assuring a full share in German leadership to the German kingdoms and middle states, and who had set all his energies to realizing his idea? Why, now, had Francis Joseph chosen as his principal adviser Saxony's leading statesman, who had brought his own little native land to the very verge of destruction?

The determinant reason was, actually, Francis Joseph's refusal, in his heart, to accept the decree of destiny as uttered in the battle of Königgrätz. Just as he refused to regard the decision of Solferino as final, so he now refused to accept Bismarck's settlement of the German question.

From the first, indeed, he was ready to do everything in his power to reverse the judgment of history. There can be no doubt that the desire for revenge on Prussia sprang to life within him on the day of defeat, and he directed his government and policy to that end. For such a policy there could be no better assistant than Baron Beust, who had moreover been for years a true friend to Austria. Beust was recognized, throughout Germany, as a most skilful diplomat; he enjoyed the favor and entire confidence of Napoleon III; and immediately after Königgrätz he went to Paris on a secret mission for Francis Joseph. Moreover, he had had years of practice in governing through a chamber and had, at one time, enjoyed the confidence of the German liberals. His readiness for a policy of revenge on Bismarck, whose press still pursued him with the grossest attacks, was natural. This, to Francis Joseph's sense, made him the right man to meet the present situation. Indeed his appointment was a clearer advertisement of his own feelings and views to the outer world than Francis Joseph's remarkable self-control often permitted. Anyhow, in his view, ministers were only useful tools. At the moment, Beust was the most useful tool for his purpose and he, therefore, summoned him without a further thought.

Archduke Albert, now in enjoyment of his imperial cousin's favor, even respect, approved his resolve. The Empress, who for long had taken no interest in anything political, seems not to have been consulted. Belcredi was not informed till after the Emperor's decision was taken; a fact that alienated him deeply. There could be no sharper contrast than that between the honorable but politically ineffective romantic and the cynically opportunistic Saxon minister. Nevertheless, Francis Joseph had been rightly inspired in his appointment of Beust, in so far as he was concerned to cut the tangled knots of domestic policy.

After taking soundings for a few weeks in Vienna and getting rapidly into touch with the various persons involved, Beust suddenly established close contact with Déak's party, by going to Pest to visit the Hungarian leader. At the same time he succeeded to a large extent in reaching an understanding with the leading men in the German constitutional party in Vienna and Bohemia. Next he conducted conferences between the government and Count Julius Andrássy and other leaders of the liberal party, men who would form the ministry; there the basis of the deliberations, contrary to Belcredi's wish, was not the proposals of the former but the program agreed upon by the Committee of the Fifteen of the Hungarian Diet.

Under pressure from Beust, Belcredi gave way on the points still in dispute, with the result that an astonishing agreement was reached between the Austrian government and the Hungarian party leaders. When Belcredi thought the moment had come for a serious move towards federalism in the west, Beust got him out of the saddle by a piece of delicately skilful handling. Belcredi resigned, and Francis Joseph let him go with a heavy heart. Nevertheless, he at once called on Beust to be premier and form a new government. Beust simply summoned the central parliament, as created by the Schmerling constitution, for which he was greeted with enthusiastic plaudits by the German liberal press and electorate.

In Hungary, things now moved rapidly. The Diet accepted Déak's program with certain minor alterations conceded at the conferences in Vienna. The problem of common concerns of the two kingdoms was met by the provision that the central parliament in Vienna and the Hungarian parliament should elect, each year, delegations of equal strength, to discuss and settle the common budget. In the event of the delegations' failing to agree, a joint session should take place, which could only vote, not discuss. These bodies were to hold annual sessions, alternately in Vienna and Pest. Such was the whole content of the "Imperial idea," all that was left of Schwarzenberg's proud unitary realm!

To Hungary, Francis Joseph had conceded all it had demanded; he had now realized Francis Déak's maximum program. In turn the Hungarian Diet now met Francis Joseph's wishes, one after the other: the necessary changes were made in the Hungarian Constitution of 1848, and the new Army law; and, for the first time, Hungary voluntarily voted its annual share of taxes. Personal relations between Andrássy and the Emperor had rapidly become friendly. The Emperor promised to do nothing in the future except on his request.

When Francis Joseph visited Pest on March 4 he was received not only by the new Hungarian government, but by the whole people with all the enthusiasm native to the Magyar race. The triumph of Hungary and the creation of dualism, i.e., a monarchy composed of two independent states, was naturally a severe blow to Austrians of the old stamp, the men in the bureaucracy, the nobility, the higher army officers, and the old Austrian "bourgeoisie," who believed in centralism, as well as to the middle class of Austrian Germans.

"Empire under notice" was what Vienna called the new system. The common customs area and innumerable other arrangements connected therewith affecting currency and coinage and the whole machinery of indirect taxation were, under Déak's laws, to be settled every ten years by a "compromise" (Ausgleich) arrived at through discussions between the governments and legislative action of the two parliaments. In principle, Hungary had established its right to an independent customs area and complete independence in economic policy.

The remaining problem of getting the compromise law accepted by the Austrian central parliament was solved by Beust with the utmost skill. His first step was to set the wonderful parlor-magic of Schmerling's franchise law in operation and so secure, after the dissolution of the Diets, a German liberal majority in the place of Belcredi's feudalistic Slav one. Thanks to the electoral colleges of the aristocratic landowners, this transformation was accomplished without a hitch. In the central parliament, the constitutional party gave an overwhelming majority for the compromise. The only opposition met by Beust's compromise bill, translating the dualistic constitution from Magyar into German, came in none too earnest a form from a group of old Austrians of strongly centralist views. Beust knew that his majority depended on his reforming Schmerling's constitution in a progressively liberal direction, and therefore gave pretty wide scope to the central parliament.

The new basic laws passed by both houses of the latter went a long way towards the demolition of the old police state; the schools were legally emancipated from church control, and the establishment of a special high court of constitutional law guaranteed a corresponding protection to the citizen's political rights. Beust knew his people and finally ventured to go so far as not merely to lay down legally the principle of ministerial responsibility but to demand the coöperation of the leaders of the German constitutional party in forming a government. In the end Francis Joseph had to see the principle of parliamentary government, existing in Hungary since 1848, recognized in Austria also.

The so-called "Citizen Ministry" was a bitter pill for him to swallow. The head of this ministry was still an aristocrat, Prince Charles Auersperg, and it included two counts. The best heads in the liberal party took over the most important offices, and since they were individuals of extremely definite character, both personally and politically, there was every prospect of the personal rivalry and disunion that is seldom lacking among politicians, even among German democrats.

The secret memoranda submitted by Beust to the Emperor during this period show that this gifted man had no hesitation in strengthening the Emperor's scorn for parliamentary liberalism by pitiless, if to a large extent accurate, characterization of the vanity and consequent harmlessness of the Austrian liberal leaders. At the same time, he explained to Francis Joseph the necessity of all these concessions to modern political ideas. On December 31, the whole of these basic laws and other progressive measures were published, at the same time as the "Compromise Law," and the nominations of the new Austrian government.

Francis Joseph had travelled a long way in the eight years since the battle of Solferino! He was now to show the high degree of external adaptability he possessed as a statesman. He owed this valuable trait to the utilitarian realism that formed the basis of his nature. Internally he adhered immovably to his conviction that Austria could not be governed parliamentarily. But he was prepared to make the attempt, and made it with his usual firm and proud bearing. In the last resort he had as strong a conviction of the impermanence of this apparently complete defeat of his autocracy as of the transitoriness of the losses inflicted on him by the war. His personal outlook on home and foreign policy remained deeply impregnated by the views created for him by the old Chancellor Prince Metternich and the Congress of Vienna. His deep dislike of the political ideas of the day, never demonstrative, known only to his intimates, at once gave him a standing hope of some favorable change in the balance of forces and impelled him to do all he could through the practical work of government so to mold the institutions and principles he had had to accept as to subserve his own purposes as ruler.

1867 was a turning point for the Emperor, and temporarily closes the period of modernization of Austrian political institutions and laws. This year fate also dealt him a heavy personal blow in the bloody termination of an episode which, painful throughout, had lasted over a period of five years. His brother Maximilian and his wife, the Belgian Princess Charlotte, under the drive of a burning ambition to accomplish something grandiose in the world, had, in 1864, accepted the imperial crown of Mexico, offered them, through the influence of Napoleon III, by a small group of Mexican clerical politicians.

They had sailed for that far country, and, two years later, been overthrown by a revolution organized by General Juarez. Maximilian, who might have escaped in safety, fought on to the last gasp and died, like a hero, under the bullets of a "firing squad" of Mexican soldiery.

The whole adventure had been undertaken, altogether against Francis Joseph's will, mainly under the ill-starred influence of his mother, Archduchess Sophia. The frightful end of her favorite son, and the incurable insanity to which his wife succumbed on her way to appeal for aid to Napoleon III, absolutely crushed the hard and aspiring Archduchess. She lived on for seven years, with mind and nature tragically overclouded. Though as late as 1866, Francis Joseph needed all the strength he could gather in moments of quiet to tolerate the cries that met him in the streets, hailing his brother as the hope of the masses, yet his sorrow for that brother was deep. The unhappy Mexican adventure had caused difficulties between them, for Francis Joseph had insisted on his brother's resigning his hereditary rights before he sailed. Otherwise his family life was more cheerful at this time. The disaster of Königgrätz had brought him and his wife close together again. Elizabeth gave up her journeys abroad and supported the new Hungarian policy through her personal influence on the Hungarian nobles and the leading statesmen at Pest, who had long heard from the Empress' own lips that of all the territories and peoples in the realm, Hungary and the Magyars were the only ones she cared for. Count Andrássy would often speak of her as "Our lovely Providence," and praise the assistance she had given to Hungary's cause. In the same way Francis Déak, now old and infinitely honored, let no opportunity pass of showing how grateful he and his nation were to the Empress for her share in the work of reconciling Francis Joseph with Hungary and how they prized it. There is a well authenticated story to the effect that Déak, who, of course, knew that Francis Joseph and Elizabeth had, for years, been living apart, said to the Emperor, in the famous interview in the Hofburg just after Königgrätz, "Let Your Majesty set your own family in order." And so it came to pass; when, on April 22, 1868, the Empress gave birth to a daughter, from now on the center of her care and of her life, the veil was finally drawn over the tragedy that had been in the lives of husband and wife.

CHAPTER XI

KING-EMPEROR: DUALISM IN ACTION

THE transformation of Austria from one imperial state into an Austro-Hungarian monarchy covering two, gave a quite peculiar constitutional status to its forty million inhabitants and nine different nationalities. Learned German jurists at once began exploring every country and period for a "scientific" definition of this new political entity and soon found that the two collateral and combined states ruled over by Francis Joseph constituted a Union, even a so-called "Real Union." For, in view of the vital issues recognized and handled in common as between Austria and Hungary, the association of the two rested not merely on this formal community, nor on the existence of an identical hereditary dynasty, but on a real political and administrative community. This view was sharply challenged by the Magyars and their jurists. They accepted community in fact but not of right. In their view Francis Joseph, in Hungary, was from now on merely the Hungarian King; as Emperor he had no status there. In Hungary he was never called Emperor, only King. In sharp contradiction was the Austrian view, which saw the imperial title as covering the entire realm and serving as symbol of its "real community." This controversy, and the day to day con-

flicts arising out of it, soon led to the development of
something like a "science" of the new Austro-Hungarian
monarchy, as a constitutional special case. There was also
a positive thicket of formal questions about the employment of the two appellations in all the acts of state which
Francis Joseph had to perform as common ruler. And
behind a disputation on fine juristic and ceremonial points
that may well wear for the foreigner a very singular air,
loomed questions of power of great importance for both
sides. For the moment the Magyars accepted the continuation of the traditional form of imperial allocution, the
famous "Imperial-royal" used in all official documents,
titles, etc., in Austria. The substitution for the familiar
initials, *I-R,* of the extended formula "Imperial and
Royal", "I *and* R", was made there only twenty years
later, with the consequent full admission of the equality
of the two states, carried through as a Magyar nationalist achievement.

Francis Joseph now was a dual monarch, Emperor and
King. Since there was no historic precedent, the conception of this dual monarchy held by Magyar jurists and
statesmen was, for the most part, flatly opposed to the
theories and ideas of those of German Austria. Everything turned on the use to be made of a position so hard
to define legally by its actual incumbent, Francis Joseph.
As it was, all these formulæ, legal concepts, and defini-
tions were so many empty legal shells. Until they were
filled by some vital political content there was no determining the real sense or substance of this new species of
realm, discovered for their own advantage by the Mag-

yars, of whom Bismarck said once, "They are all either hussars or lawyers."

Fate thus confronted Francis Joseph anew with a task of immense difficulty. It was a strange destiny. At seven and thirty, after nearly twenty years' autocracy, he had imposed on him the task of bringing into life and effect an entirely new monarchism, which, so far, hardly existed except on paper. He had accepted the Magyars' constitutional structure and had now got to take this dualism—people called it the constitutional Siamese twins,—give it life and make it strong and efficient both for himself as head of the common dynasty and for the peoples of the two states whose Emperor and King he was.

From the beginning it was patent that his own will and personality were to count for far more in creating and conditioning the effectiveness and the future of this new form than anything done by the responsible statesmen in either of the two states. So much was, indeed, implicit in the fundamental propositions of the new Austro-Hungarian constitutional law, which placed a series of most important decisions in the conduct of common concerns exclusively in the monarch's hands. It followed that his personal will and personal view of this new community must have immense influence in the purely political sphere; for it was soon to prove that, despite the independence for which the Hungarians loudly clamored, nothing either fundamental or important could be done, whether in the sphere of legislation or of administration, without "common concerns" being affected and the influence of the Emperor's will being thus brought into play.

In practice, therefore, dualism was bound to be what Francis Joseph chose to make of it. For nearly fifty years this was his task. He and Francis Déak had created dualism: he had to maintain it, preserve it inviolate, use it to meet the needs of the peoples comprised in the whole monarchy, and do this in the atmosphere of incessant friction and conflict inevitably resulting from the existence of two equal and constitutionally independent political authorities in Austria and Hungary.

Francis Joseph was to be the sole dual monarch known to history; his successor, Emperor Charles, was hardly in a position to carry it on. The machinery of dualism broke down under the emergency conditions created throughout the realm by the outbreak of war in 1914 and the fearful pressure of war needs; and so it was till the whole Empire broke up.

Here, therefore, we are in contact with Francis Joseph's own creative work in life. From Schwarzenberg's death down to 1867 he had seen it as his sole task first to maintain and then to defend, through a series of rearguard actions, the unitary realm and the autocracy created for him by Schwarzenberg and Kübeck. Now, however, to maintain the dynasty and its power he had been compelled to assist in building an entirely new substructure for the further development of the two states into which the monarchy was now divided and of their common life.

We are at the turning point of his life—the life of the man predestined by the Sphinx of history to be the last monarch in Europe to incarnate the legitimist ideas of the eighteenth century and carry them over in his own person into the twentieth. His dominant idea—the maintenance of his realm as a dynastic inheritance—had undergone a definite and limited formulation in Francis Déak's victory over the militarist-autocratic centralization of Vienna. From now on, the power of the hereditary house depended on mutual recognition—by the Magyars, of its historic European position as the oldest of the great powers and, by the dynasty, of the complete independence of the Kingdom of St. Stephen and its adjacent territories as ruled by the Magyar race.

One inevitable consequence of the methods by which Francis Joseph had created dualism with the aid of Beust and Andrássy, was that this mutual pact between him and the Magyars involved a third party, which was thereby committed, without being consulted, to the purposes of his policy of supremacy. This third party was the western half of his realm, Austria, far superior to Hungary both in numbers and in culture. In the upshot, the maintenance of his realm—the whole content of his thought as man and ruler—became for Francis Joseph inseparable from the maintenance of the 1867 Compromise.

For the next half century of his life and reign, his "route march" was now fixed for him. From this point of view the main lines of his whole policy, foreign and domestic, are predetermined and inevitable. What was to prove disastrous was that his attitude to all the problems thrown up by the national, political, and economic development of the western half of the realm, of the Germans and Slavs in Austria, was laid down for him rigidly in advance. It had to be such as would, first and foremost, serve the interests of the rulers of independent Hungary.

From 1867 on, Francis Joseph's personal and political life is confined within the narrow framework set to it by the Compromise with the Magyars. At the same time—and this is vital—the confinement of the Emperor within the Hungarian King is not a result simply of external compulsion: Francis Joseph's tenacious will would have resisted anything of the kind, so soon as he felt it personally necessary to do so. But from the beginning he felt a profound inner obligation to the new compromise act, as the logical outcome of his coronation with the crown of St. Stephen and the high solemnity of his coronation oath. Moved therefore at once by his sense of the ecclesiastical sanction of the ceremony, by his own religious feeling, and by the compulsive force of the highest law on earth, he felt himself intimately bound and committed in his conscience to the maintenance of the new Hungarian basis of his entire realm and the supremacy dependent upon it. Therefore, little as his own inclination might speak in this, he grew to feel the idea of Hungarian kingship, containing within itself that exclusive Magyar power, as the real pivot and motor force in his realm. Hungarian kingship in fact became the mystic keystone supporting the mighty arch on which his dominion rested.

At this point Francis Joseph's biographer can survey, at a glance, the fifty years of his hero's life as Emperor and King, and see him throughout their course, from first day to last, toiling to maintain his dual realm, forever devising new expedients for upholding the institutions and the forms of the pro-Hungarian 1867 constitution, while around him there gathers all the time the mounting tide of resistance by all the other nationalities to the intolerable, unjust, and untenable predominance of the Magyar race. In its strangeness, in its tension, in its tragedy, here is a drama unparalleled in contemporary European history.

In retrospect, this long period of fifty years divides itself into two periods, of which the first extends from the year 1867 to about the year 1893, when it closed in Hungary with Koloman Tisza's retirement from leadership of the liberal party and government in Hungary. This event was almost coincident with the termination, in Austria, of the fifteen-years-long administration of Count Taaffe, in whom Francis Joseph found his most powerful support in his effort to make the dual system work and induce Austria to stand it. This first quarter of a century was the most fruitful and, in almost every respect, successful period of Francis Joseph's life. During this time, too, the main traits in his personal character, already known to us in general outline, assumed that fixity and definition that generally occur in the fifties when the powers of mind and body are at their height. At its opening, he was full of the idea of a reconstruction that would give him back complete freedom of action in foreign policy. He showed himself ready to make great sacrifices of conviction and even of conscience to attain this end. For although liberalism, the modern outlook which calls itself "free thought," was profoundly obnoxious to him, and he hated it in his heart, he nevertheless accepted it as the instrument for reform and permitted its leaders comparative freedom of action. It was to the liberal parties of the two "national states," the Magyars in the eastern and the Germans in the western half of the monarchy, that the task of carrying out the compromise was entrusted, and under the same external form in each, i.e., in that of a government of definitely parliamentary type. As far back as 1848 Hungary had initiated a form that in England is the fundamental principle of political liberty; then it was accepted by the Magyar oligarchy and the total nation whose political ideas were deeply imbued with aristocratic traditionalism, as a natural, if belated, outcome of their own old-established feudal constitution.

In Austria the December constitution of 1867 actually represented a complete break with the development of the princely and bureaucratic state that had gone on, in Austria, stage by stage, ever since the battle on the White Mountain (1621). Following the lines of Franco-Belgian constitutionalism, it introduced the principle of ministerial responsibility and seemed, therefore, to be a bridge over which Austria might cross to genuine parliamentary government. Francis Joseph from this time on actually had no fewer than three independent governments, since in addition to the governments of Austria and Hungary there was the common Austro-Hungarian government consisting of the ministers for war and foreign affairs and the so-called imperial finance minister. This last government was nominally responsible to the people, both in Austria and in Hungary, and certainly was so in the sense

[355]

that it was dependent on the voting of the imperial budget. At the same time there was from the first a specially close and well-established relation between the three common ministers and the monarch.

Further, this common ministry was, of course, located in Vienna; and a member of the Hungarian government, the royal Hungarian minister to the imperial court (am allerhöchsten Hoflager) was stationed permanently in the capital, to act as liaison officer between the two other governments, and be directly at the Emperor's disposition. Also, to carry out the equality in principle of the two states, there was, as a section of the Emperor's existing cabinet chancellery, a permanent Hungarian cabinet chancellery to deal with the King of Hungary's written, formal, and current business in Vienna and act as office for the Hungarian Kingdom.

These governments and offices constituted the governmental machine at the disposal of the common monarch, Austrian Emperor and King of Hungary—united in the person of Francis Joseph—for the purpose of information, discussion, and ultimate action as between the realm as a whole and its parts. In one of the great monarchies of Europe, with the fierce light of modern state organization beating upon it, here, was the mystic principle of the Trinity set up as a practical form of government!

It was now a matter of vital concern to Francis Joseph to have reconstruction in Hungary carried through without delay. Count Andrássy's energy left no room for apprehension on this score. The next and most important task before Francis Joseph and his Hungarian government was the creation of his new army on the basis of the new service law. Here there were political difficulties, which Déak and Andrássy surmounted by forcing the independence party, much as they disliked it, to consent to the establishment, with due formalities, of the common army.

The next big task was to get legislative sanction for an understanding between Hungary and the Kingdom of Croatia, which had separated from the Crown of St. Stephen in 1848. Here, too, Francis Joseph showed readiness to accept all the consequences of his position as King of Hungary. He assisted the Hungarian government in solving this extremely difficult problem. He did the same in the transference from Croatia to the central Hungarian government of control over the town and harbor of Fiume, which had been assigned to it by Maria Theresa, and over the whole Croatian seaboard.

Finally, in the teeth of obstinate resistance from military circles, he yielded to the urgent requests by the Hungarian government for the abolition of the so-called "military frontier province" and the incorporation under the civil administration of Hungary and Croatia of the great stretch of territory adjacent to the southern frontier of Hungary—an area that had been administered and governed for two centuries by the Vienna war office as a security zone against Turkey.

Francis Joseph gave his active, loyal, and throughout watchful coöperation in all these great legislative efforts. He also took a marked personal part in the deliberations of the generals and military commissions on the new common army and the new service law. Hardly a technical detail escaped him. His personal effort contributed at least as much as that of the government to the monumental work accomplished, and the settlement of all the questions, great and small, therein involved, from the selection of competent military experts to the final wording of the mass of laws and decrees.

It was, indeed, largely, thanks to his loyalty to his word as given to Hungary, that the entire process of establishing the dual régime within the monarchy, which occupied the years 1868-70, was accomplished, take it all for all, in orderly and rapid fashion, despite animosities, personal and political, hitherto regarded as irreconcilable. Indeed, for the Emperor these early years of dualism and independent government in Hungary were a veritable "high school" in constitutionalism and parliamentary government—in its Magyar form.

After the political "training school" through which he had passed in Vienna under the Schmerling régime, he was now under Andrássy's clever guidance taking something like an advanced course. It certainly gave him a profound insight into the Hungarian party system—ultra "modern" in form, if often "atavistic" and deeply aristocratic in spirit. He certainly did acquire knowledge of permanent value, not only to his personal position in Hungary, but to his greater task of ruling his realm as a whole.

Indeed, it is not too much to say that from his entry on the dualist course Francis Joseph can be seen moving, step by step, and in the purely empiric fashion native to him, towards a new "theory" of the state. He applies its principles in this case and in that; his gathering experience here strengthens, there modifies it. But since he sees it producing an orderly conduct of business and a visible gain in governmental efficiency, his self-confidence and his royal position in Hungary both serve to consolidate his belief in it.

The concept of the state which he had imbibed in the enthusiasm of youth from Schwarzenberg and Kübeck was no longer available for the crowned King of Hungary, but it had not disappeared because of that. In his capacity as common monarch and sovereign over the Austrian unitary state he still cherished it. Even in his attitude to Hungary it constituted a sort of reserve which he could call up, when, for example, after dualism had been in operation for nearly forty years, the Magyar independents had the audacity to attack it. What is truly remarkable in Francis Joseph's post-1867 development as Emperor and King is that he was able permanently to keep intact and distinct in his own mind two theories of the state, built up there by experience of rule; was able, for decades, to apply the orthodox Hungarian theory, proper to a crowned king, in Hungary, while, in Austria, he held fast to his old ideas of sovereignty, and, unperturbed by the parliamentary experiment of 1867, refused to budge from his conviction of the necessity of strong personal government in Austria or to try full constitutionalism in the German and Slav hereditary territories.

So far as Hungary was concerned, the course of events in the decade following the Compromise strengthened his view that parliamentary government there was not only reliable but the only possible régime, and, further, that it left him scope to enforce his will, in Hungary, in all the things that seemed to him personally important, as vital for the maintenance of the monarchy. Andrássy certainly gave him ample opportunity of educating himself thoroughly as a parliamentary monarch.

Not that Francis Joseph always trusted Andrássy. There must have been much that was impenetrable to him in that Hungarian count, with the face of a typical gipsy, a temperament as mobile as quicksilver, a pretty wit and a turn of repartee all his own, and a large share of the bonhomie of the Hungarian *grand seigneur;* it was Andrássy's sureness of purpose and outstanding ability in the conduct of political business that really impressed Francis Joseph most. From him he gained an inside knowledge of Hungarian politics. He began to grasp the authentic structure of the modern party, and to see that the head of a government dependent on a parliamentary majority may look all-powerful but actually, owing to his perpetual struggle to keep his place, leads a very precarious existence. He learned that a king has not the smallest reason either for fear or envy of the head of a modern government and that the parliamentary system, while it frees the "constitutional" ruler of responsibility, tends to give real power back into his hands.

Francis Joseph recognized that the Hungarian prime minister's first requirement for success was the support of the constitutional monarch and the assistance of his prerogative. Time and again he could not, without the King's aid, have maintained himself in power against the vault-

ing ambition and unscrupulous intrigue of other leading
men in his own party and its opponents, as well as of
his own cabinet colleagues. Moreover, Francis Joseph
had, with real skill, instituted a modest practice which
actually gave him more power and imposed stricter
limitations on the Hungarian government than the general public at all realized at any time. He did this by
arranging for the prime minister to submit all important
measures to the King before introducing them in Parliament. This royal "pre-sanction," as it came to be designated, was recognized by Andrássy as a constitutional
right. It is, of course, unknown in the theory and practice
of the British parliament, but since the Hungarian parliamentary system was not based on legal enactments but
on pure convention, it actually developed under the influence of this peculiar practice, devised by the King and his
prime minister. In the event of the King's refusing this
pre-sanction, the minister was, of course, free to proceed
with his bills and pass them with the support of his
parliamentary majority. But the effect of that was apt to
be a crisis both in parliament and public opinion generally.
What minister would light-heartedly risk such a crisis?

Francis Joseph was quick to realize all this. He soon
became so skilful in dealing with parliamentary government, in its Hungarian edition, that after a decade's practice as Hungarian King, he was recognized, both at home
and abroad, as a master in this department. The Deák
party, which had helped him to construct the new Austro-
Hungarian constitution, speedily went the way of all
parliamentary parties. Even during the lifetime of its

stainless founder, it fell deeper year by year into the mire of political and financial corruption, and after Andrássy became minister for foreign affairs this deterioration proceeded with frightful rapidity. Governments followed one another in rapid succession, without producing any remedy for the embarrassment of Hungarian finances.

The independence party gained seats at the elections and attracted the young talent of the country. Francis Joseph, however, had learned to wait; he calmly left things to ripen. Soon the future of the Compromise and, consequently, of the country and the monarchy, was in the hands of the independence party, which rejected any sort of community with Austria. It had been founded in 1861 and since very skilfully led by Koloman Tisza.

But a few years of the new parliamentary régime had convinced Tisza that Hungary had reaped great advantages from Déak's Compromise; that splendid progress was being made in the work of Magyarizing the whole country, covertly or by force, since 1867, and that its backwardness, both cultural and economic, made the financial and economic union with Austria, maintained by Déak, vitally necessary for Hungary.

Finally, Tisza was aware that Francis Joseph put Hungary's interests first and gave its statesmen pride of place in his councils in all matters of foreign policy, and that Count Andrássy's appointment as common foreign minister had immensely enhanced Hungary's prestige in the world, since it was beginning to be regarded as the basis of Habsburg dominion. An Eastern crisis was brought on in 1876. It also brought near the first renewal of the

economic compromise. Quite quietly there was a transference of power from the group of nobles and gentlemen
in Hungary associated with the name of Déak, to the
other group.

Koloman Tisza, in agreement with the dissatisfied
majority of the Déakists, founded a new party which he
designated "liberal," and the overwhelming majority of
his former associates, the "independents," joined with him
in it; all indeed but a small intransigent group. This operation was described as a "fusion," and Hungarian political
writers referred to it as the characteristic native form of
parliamentary rejuvenation and renewal. Actually all that
happened was a fresh demonstration of the fact that, so
soon as any question arose of relations to Austria, the
whole Magyar nation felt, politically, as one. The elections gave Tisza's new party three-quarters of the total
membership of the new house.

Tisza had already served in a transitional ministry; he
now formed a government of his own and proceeded to
rule Hungary for the next fifteen years. Even before his
public declaration that he had abandoned the views of the
independence party, Tisza had given Francis Joseph
pledges on his own behalf and on that of his party
that, as future head of a Hungarian government, he would
uphold the 1867 dualism which Déak had created and
Tisza incessantly opposed; would neither tolerate any
effort to shake it, nor make any such himself. And so it
proved. Was it not natural, at this moment, for Francis
Joseph to feel that he was the real ruler in the country,
when its party government simply meant government by

leaders on whom the King, as guardian of the dualist constitution, laid the obligation to preserve it, consenting to nominate them as ministers on that condition only?

Very different was the Emperor's experience, during this same period, in his capacity of constitutional sovereign of the unit state comprising the old German hereditary lands, the territories of the Crown of Bohemia, the coast-lands and Galicia. In Hungary he had to deal with men of high political gifts, men who certainly were not afraid of responsibility; in Hungary, as he soon realized, the whole body of Magyars, from magnates to peasantry, formed a coherent and politically disciplined mass, for whom the unconditional supremacy of the Magyar spirit and the Magyar race was the first commandment of national politics and obliterated, at any moment of crisis, every other distinction of class, profession or party. But the German-Austrians, on whom for five hundred years social and economic power and the whole state apparatus had depended and still did depend, were anything but a ruling race in the sense in which the Magyars always had been and now were proving themselves to be.

Further, the German element in Austria was politically divided. The peasants, the lower middle class, and the nobles in the Alpine regions were at bottom clerical and conservative. It had required Francis Joseph's intransigent Concordat policy to win adherents from among their middle classes for the liberal party, whose real strength was in Vienna and among the Germans in Bohemia, Moravia, and Silesia. By amending Schmerling's constitutional law, through the basic acts of 1867, Beust had succeeded in inducing the German constitutional party to accept the Emperor's compromise with the Magyars and take over the government.

The central parliament had become a mere Rump. The Czechs refused, as before, to enter it. Soon both the southern Slavs and even strong Catholics like the Tyroleans absented themselves; in the latter case as a protest against the anti-clericalism of the liberals.

The success won by the Magyars in 1867 exasperated the Austrian Slavs, who began to hope that resistance might win them similar advantages. This was notably the case with the Poles, who sought to use their social and economic predominance in Galicia to exact a large measure of political independence there. To that end they also left the Viennese parliament and presented their demands for extensive autonomy in the Galician Diet.

The system of German preference built up by the constitutional party was obviously and rapidly breaking down, but German politicians in Austria showed a total incapacity to forget their personal and sectional feuds in the interest of a common German policy. German-Austrians at this time were not thinking along lines of nationalist policy; the dominating idea among the groups that spoke for them was that the German-Austria stocks, having helped the Habsburgs to build up a mighty unitary state, had got to go on functioning as the "party of state interests." What they meant by this was the rigid maintenance of this unitary state, with its completely centralized administration, with German as the official language, and German ways and German officials in control of the civil service. This state, further, through parliamentary government in the hands of the German constitutional party, based on a majority in the central parliament, guaranteed them by the limited franchise, should be permanently assured of the fullest influence on policy and legislation in Austria and the dual monarchy.

The German liberal leaders had, it is true, laid down complete equality as between all the various languages in Austria, in schools and officially, as a basic principle of the constitution they promulgated in December, 1867, thus giving proof of their liberalism. Unfortunately it stopped at the theoretic enunciation of the principle. Nothing was further from their minds than carrying it out in practice by legal and administrative concessions to the non-German peoples.

This meant that Austria's fate was settled. For it implied a short-sighted misapprehension of the real task before German liberals in Austria, inasmuch as they claimed to represent modern progressive ideas of the state. At the moment when the need of guaranteeing the Compromise with Hungary compelled Francis Joseph to commit the government and extensive political power to the great party which represented the educated German middle class, the liberals had no thought beyond converting the state machine, which eighteenth and nineteenth century absolutism had constructed, into an impregnable stronghold of their own party ascendency.

Adolf Fischhof, a leader in the Vienna revolution of 1848, and both personally and politically one of the noblest and most significant figures ever produced by

Austrian democracy, published about this time his book on *Austria and the Guarantees of Its Existence*, as a warning to the liberals against trying, in an age of democratic progress, to keep Austria a German unit state. With all the force that comes of profound conviction, Fischhof called on German-Austrians to recognize that the Habsburg realm was essentially a state of various nations, a federal state (Völkerstaat), and set forth the consequences of that fact which must be accepted by all who desired at once to maintain Austria as a state and see it develop along genuinely liberal, i.e., democratic, lines.

The policy incumbent on Germans, as the most developed people in Austria, must envisage, not a bureaucratic centralization designed to ensure them for the moment, the support of the old German bureaucracy with its long habit of command, but the extension to all the nationalities of far-reaching national autonomy. The leaders of the constitutional liberals, however, possessed neither the political foresight nor the strong sense of political justice characterizing Fischhof's views and ideas; on the contrary, the exponent of any such plans was, for them, anti-German, and they treated him accordingly.

An opportunity, difficult indeed, but containing within itself the seeds of vast political possibilities was presented, as in 1848, to the German liberals. Had they been able to reach an understanding with the non-German races on a basis of equal recognition, and then to move on to a gradual development of the state from the dynastic form, historically associated with it into an institution, consonant with democratic and progressive ideas, and

[367]

ulimately culminating in a measure of cultural independence and complete self-government for all the
nationalities—then they, the Germans, might truly, and
for the first time, have achieved moral and intellectual
leadership of Austrian policy.

Francis Joseph's reconciliation with the Magyars and
the establishment of the dual monarchy brought the two
great opposing conceptions of the true nature of Austria
and the form of constitution corresponding thereto, as
developed since 1848, into sharp juxtaposition. One of
these, the view represented by the German liberals in
Austria, was, in reality, neither liberal nor progressive,
but "conservative" in the literal sense.

Anton von Schmerling and his 1867 successors really
desired nothing but the maintenance of the old "Compulsion State" in order thereby to guarantee German
ascendancy, although the Germans only amounted to one-
third of the population of Austria, and the liberals constituted a minority within that third. On the other side
was the idea, voiced since 1860 by the aristocratic party
and the Slavs, and first expressed in the October Diploma,
of Austria as a state union of many nations, whose constitution, therefore, ought to be definitely federalist, and
based on the historic kingdoms and territories. Such an
outlook was described by the liberal press as not merely
conservative but "reactionary," although in truth it alone
opened the way to a hopeful transformation of the dynastic unitary state into a monarchical league of peoples on
a footing of national autonomy.

The restoration of the central parliament by the constitution of December 21, 1867, brought the struggle between these two opposing views to the front at once. The German liberal majority behind the government were face to face with a minority in the house representing the vast majority of the population of Austria. The opposition comprised Poles, Czechs, Slovenes, Croats, Italians, and even representatives of the thoroughly German peasants from the Alpine regions, united against the constitutional liberals and their government. The government went ahead with its anti-clerical policy, for the aggressive attitude and actions of Pope Pius IX had raised all kinds of spiritual and political conflicts and problems throughout Europe and especially in Austria and Germany.

But the great political issue already referred to very soon made its appearance within the ranks of the government itself, with results that were positively disastrous to it. A minority within the cabinet, led by Count Taaffe, opposed the policy of high centralization. Such disunity lamed the system of parliamentary government as introduced by Francis Joseph, much against his inclinations, in 1867. Within a decade, the struggles between nations and parties, initiated by the December constitution of that year, had produced the momentous result of destroying German political ascendancy in Austria for good and all. What concerns us here is not the separate phases of this process but the attitude of the Emperor to the problem presented, with increasing urgency, by the western half of his realm.

His deep dislike of liberalism was undoubtedly

strengthened in these years by the experience of personal contact with Austrian liberals and their ministerial leaders, whose faults were many. Above all he perceived that while the support given to these men by their parties was fluctuating, and any kind of real unity between individual ministers and the groups they represented extremely rare, bitter antagonisms, often carried to an extreme, and based as a rule on nothing better than vanity and purely personal rivalry, were exceedingly common.

Austrian liberals and their press never found their ministers sufficiently liberal. They, in their turn, never found their party and its newspapers sufficiently tractable or "statesmanlike." This last expression covered a due regard for the Emperor's concern for the maintenance of his personal position as sovereign and the military force on which that position was based; and, above all, for the conditions created by the dual system and Hungarian policy.

It is hardly surprising that three years of parliamentary government by the artificial liberal majority made Francis Joseph despair of any success to be gained along the route laid down by Schmerling and resumed, six years later, by Beust. He is hardly open to criticism for being dissatisfied with a system of parliamentary government of which the happy and speedy result was that every nationality in Austria, except the Germans, abandoned the central parliament, leaving the constitutional liberals in possession, a party regarded by the Emperor as the inheritor of the 1848 Revolution, a party without a single real statesman among its leaders.

After all, Francis Joseph was Emperor not only of the upper middle class in the cities of Vienna, Prague, Brünn, and Graz, but of the millions of German peasants who knew little and cared less for the "Primadonnas" of Austrian liberalism. He was, moreover, King over the six million Czechs of the Bohemian crown lands, ruler over millions of Poles and Ruthenians, and of the Catholic and anti-liberal peasants and small middle-class folk dwelling in the towns and valleys of the Alps, men whose loyalty to the dynasty had stood the test of centuries. If, for the meantime, he tolerated the liberals' anti-clerical policy, the reason was circumstances abroad and the fact that the men in power in Hungary regarded the liberal government in Austria as a guarantee of the dual system.

Thus, throughout those years, Francis Joseph's public attitude to the two opposing political views described above was undecided. His own mind, however, inclined more and more to the opposition and against the "free-thinking" German "citizens ministry." The opposition leaders belonged from the start to that group among the Austrian nobility which, shipwrecked, and, in his opinion, defeated in 1860, with its creation, the October Diploma, had nevertheless been more or less rehabilitated since through the compromise. And among them a man of statesmanlike determination and experience now arose, a man whom, so it appears, Francis Joseph failed to call to high position in 1860 solely on grounds of personal disfavor. This was Count Henry Clam-Martinic. Leader of the powerful conservative wing of Bohemian landowners, he enjoyed the confidence both of the great old Czech party in the

Diet and of the German Catholics in the Alps. Even in Schmerling's day, Count Clam had achieved the position he still held of effective leader of the entire right in the imperial council, by uniting all the members in it opposed to German liberal rule.

The great events of the Franco-Prussian War impelled Francis Joseph to a complete change in domestic policy. He was now entirely convinced that the time had come for giving the Slavs more political scope in Austrian politics, and for basing imperial government on the non-German races and on those Germans who as Catholics felt the maintenance of Austria a matter of supreme concern, instead of on those, like the liberals in Vienna and northern Bohemia, who were in a state of enthusiasm for Prince Bismarck and his work.

On January 18, 1871, King William of Prussia was proclaimed German Emperor at Versailles. On February 7, 1871, imperial rescripts appeared nominating a government under Count Hohenwart, a conservative. In its first official announcement this government, composed of Germans and Slavs, described itself as "non-party" and its task as being reconciliation among the peoples and the transformation of the constitution along federal lines. For its driving force this government relied on its premier and on Professor Schäffle, a learned economist, who had been called not long before to Austria from Württemberg. Study of Austrian conditions had convinced him that the centralized policy of the Austrian liberal intelligentsia was perfectly sterile; now, with all the energy of a great German scholar, filled with the justice of his own scientific conclusions, he addressed himself to the task of giving them legislative expression as a statesman.

For nearly a year the government struggled against the liberal press, then well-nigh omnipotent, liberal public opinion, and the liberal majority in the Reichsrat. Francis Joseph is known to have had high hopes of this administration, to which he was personally as well as politically attached. He accepted Hohenwart's main plan, a compromise with the Czechs, who sought to secure much the same conditions as the Magyars had won. Francis Joseph, under this, was to sanction laws prepared by the Bohemian Diet, recognizing the domains of the Crown of Wenceslas as a historic unity and giving it an autonomy which though extensive was far less than that granted to Hungary. He was prepared to be crowned King of Bohemia, as his predecessor, still known in Prague as "King Ferdinand," had been.

For Germans in Bohemia this was an absolute crime. Liberals talked as though the battle of the White Mountain, in 1621, were still, in the nineteenth century, the most precious of German national possessions, to be protected as such. Every people in Europe, since modern constitutionalism has put its destiny more or less in its own hands, shows a tendency to transfer the idea of pure force, previously embodied in the monarch, to the party sphere, and to exaggerate it.

The German liberals were no worse, no more "immoral" than the rest. Their great fault, or, if you will, their tragedy, was that, bent on pursuing their own national interests as they saw them, they lacked the lead-

[373]

ership and the intelligence to take a wide view of the vital conditions of the monarchy as a whole. In the same way the Czechs, the strongest Slav nation in central Europe, evinced, in this crisis of their political existence, a zeal to be free of what they felt as the unjust dominance of the liberal Germans, which far outran their capacity for statesmanship.

There was no lack, in these years, of men of outstanding quality capable of acting as spokesmen of the various nations and their political parties, but Francis Joseph did not succeed in selecting any man of strong personality. Certainly he was to blame in this. Apparently it was a temporary concatenation of external circumstances rather than any strong inward conviction that made him come forward as champion of federalism.

Although now a man and a sovereign of ripe experience and in the prime of life, he was unable to free himself of his deep distrust of any and every principle or ideal in statesmanship sufficiently to accept wholeheartedly *one* great political idea and pursue it to its logical conclusions. He had far more in common with aristocratic federalists, Catholic peasants, and even Polish and Czech conservative leaders, than with the squabbling leaders of the "liberal," free-thinking bourgeoisie, who were becoming more and more deeply involved in the ups and down of the "progressive" Vienna stock exchange, while their press had long been in the hands of "unbelievers." But he simply could not see himself as the sovereign of a federal state. For him, as for most Europeans of his day, federalism spelt "small scale business" politically; it spelt weakness.

How was a great army to be maintained if the threads of legislation, administration, police, and taxation were not held in Vienna and, in the last analysis, gathered into his own hands? Moreover, when the bases for the compromise with the Czechs as worked out with the aid of Clam and Schäffle were before him, the Emperor seems to have been influenced by warnings from Andrássy and the Hungarians which chilled his sympathy for federalism.

Hohenwart and his colleagues had been at the greatest pains to avoid infringing on the authority of the Vienna central government and the central parliament in relation to all matters common to Austria and Hungary. In the end, the whole plan collapsed as the result of a combination between Count Beust and Count Andrássy to bring down the Hohenwart administration and the Czech compromise with it. The Emperor had no choice but to recall the German constitutional party and entrust it with government. Its first act was to strengthen its own position by depriving the Diets of the right of sending members to the central parliament and substituting direct election. By this means a piece of the federalist basis established by the 1861 constitution was removed. The liberals hoped, indeed, that they had thereby further checkmated the Czechish policy of abstaining from participation in the central parliament.

Next the radical wing of the constitutional party forced the new government to carry through the reorganization of the relations of state and church necessitated by their termination of the Concordat. Pope Pius IX's papal infallibility decree of 1870 gave Count Beust a welcome excuse for meeting the chief demand of the liberals—the denunciation of the Concordat. Beust took the line that the papacy was so profoundly modified by the new dogma that its promulgation automatically ended the previously existing treaty. The government thereupon proceeded with the consequent legislative changes.

A series of laws reorganized the Austrian Catholic church on the basis of a separation of church and state, restoring at the same time to the state important rights of supervision over the external life of the church, as established by Joseph II but removed by the Concordat.

Throughout the grave conflicts inevitably resulting from the opposition of the Roman Curia and the Austrian bishops, which caused immense excitement for a time in many quarters, notably in German-Austria, Francis Joseph played the part of the strictly "constitutional" monarch, but he made no secret of his strong personal repugnance to this particular liberal success. His radical dislike for liberalism and parliamentary government was strengthened by the outbreak of a great financial and economic crisis in Vienna in 1873. On top of several years of good trade came the inevitable reaction: the artificial overexpansion of the credit system, characteristic of the early stages of capitalism in Austria, caused this to take the form of a complete credit breakdown bringing in its train serious losses, unemployment, and grave distress for great sections of the population in all parts of the realm. The position of the party in power was broken.

A large number of leading liberals, including certain ministers, were at once discredited with the public by their share in speculation and stock exchange gambling. For Francis Joseph there was an indubitable satisfaction in seeing the party thus commit suicide. He regarded liberalism to some extent as a personal enemy as well as the seducer of the popular mind.

The liberal centre of the constitutional party was weakened as the younger generation in the middle-class electorate inclined more and more to the German nationals —a natural result of the foundation of the German Empire and the position of power Bismarck had created for Germany. The constitutionalists further suffered from the old internal feuds and, notably, from the unpopularity of the German liberal leader, Dr. Edward Herbst, a man of vast knowledge as a jurist and economist but inexpert, dogmatic, impatient, and intellectually sterile.

In the upshot, the party machine dissolved into bitterly contending sections—the conservatives, the democrats, and the more and more nationalistically-minded younger men. On top of all this came the disastrous social and economic reactions of the 1873 stock-exchange crash in Vienna. The liberals lost their hold on the urban middle class. Yet, when the difficult renewal of the decennial economic compromise with Hungary had been compassed by the exertions of the constitutional party, though now hopelessly split, and a new Service law increasing the strength of the army had been put through, the German liberals could claim the appellation of "state party": all that was indispensable to the maintenance of the realm had been accomplished. The liberal Moor had done his duty and could now depart!

Thanks to their anti-clerical legislation, however, the constitutionalists still had a certain popular prestige. Francis Joseph, ripened by wide experience into a coolly-considering and long-headed political director, again refrained from introducing one of those complete "changes of system" of which he had once been so fond. For him the time for constitutional experiments was over. He had learned, too, that parties are not rigid or unalterable; "education," i.e., patience and skilful influencing of leaders and press, makes them adaptable. He sought, therefore, to induce the constitutional party to take up a less doctrinaire attitude to the just demands of the Slav nationalities and so secure some sort of compromise with the Czechs that would bring them back into the Reichsrat.

By the spring of 1878 Prince Adolf Auersperg's ministry, after seven years of rule, was breaking up internally. Its most distinguished members, the bright particular stars of Austrian politics, pressed the Emperor to let them resign. Literally, they fled before the petty, small-minded, provincial tyrants and well-meaning but incapable doctrinaires who for the most part led the constitutional party. All the Emperor's personal efforts to form a new government with a constitutionalist majority behind it, prepared to follow a new path in Austrian domestic policy, failed, in the main because of the bitter personal animosities between the various sections and their leaders. What finally determined his action was the opposition led by

Dr. Herbst to Andrássy's foreign policy, and the occupation of Bosnia and Herzegovina.

The Vienna liberals, by the shortsightedness that nullified their undoubted intelligence, now lost the friendship and support of Hungary which they had won in 1871 when they opposed the federalist efforts of the Slavs. Francis Joseph could say, with a clear conscience, that he had done all he could to keep moderate liberalism in power. Liberalism in Austria anyhow owed its rise rather to the faults of his autocracy than to the capability of its own leaders. Playing upon the name of Dr. Herbst (Autumn) Bismarck in a speech in the Reichstag, held up the latter to the scorn of Europe as political "meadow saffrons." They forgot that their temporary ascendancy had nothing better behind it than a quite artificial franchise, invented by Schmerling and the bureaucracy, and really designed to undercut the liberal minority in the urban middle class, which had no permanent roots among the masses in Austria. For some time past even this artificial device had not availed to protect the constitutional party from defeat at the polls both by the Slav and the Catholic parties.

Of all this Francis Joseph was well aware. He had long had a man in readiness in whom he had perfect confidence. Count Edward Taaffe, a youthful comrade of his own, had been the one man he liked and trusted in the otherwise highly unsympathetic "citizens administration" of 1868. He now called on him to form a government, on the understanding that he would induce the Czechs to reënter the Reichsrat and so bring about the inevitable

[379]

shift in Austrian internal policy. The new foreign policy he had inaugurated under Count Andrássy led straight to alliance with Germany, and this, to Francis Joseph's mind, involved a greater concentration of state authority. The main phases in an evolution that, at the close of the first decade of dualism, raised Francis Joseph to the zenith of his career as a ruler, must now be described.

CHAPTER XII

THE DUAL ALLIANCE

FRANCIS JOSEPH'S main preoccupation during the first decade of dualism was to subordinate the King of Hungary and the sovereign of Austria, the western half of the realm, to the Emperor, as common monarch over both. This rôle once imposed on him, he was, to the end of his days, to regard it as his most difficult and most important task. It was to dominate his domestic policy, in Hungary and in Austria. In either state, governments had to remember that beyond their immediate legislative and administrative tasks were other tasks, aims, and political considerations arising out of the fact that Austria and Hungary formed a common empire, and, in consequence, had to meet common obligations, transmitted to them through the instrumentality of common ministers. There was a great area which had to be covered by team work between the three ministries, an area covering the development of the army, the direction of foreign policy, and all the vital economic issues committed to the coöperation of the governments and parliaments of the two states by the decennial customs union, including as it did questions of currency and credit, railways and shipping. Here the common ministry—the imperial chancellor, the war minister, and the common finance minister—naturally had a sort of leadership, since, as imperial cabinet, they constituted the immediate and decisive advisers of the Emperor and King.

To complete the picture of the highly complex governmental machine, it must be noted, further, that, under the terms of the 1867 Act, it was incumbent upon the Hungarian premier to keep himself constantly informed about foreign policy; a proviso which, in course of time, was bound to give a similar function to the Austrian premier. This was the machinery Francis Joseph had to rely upon for the conduct of foreign and domestic policy involving interests represented by two parliaments and their respective delegations, seventeen Austrian Provincial Diets and the Croatian Sabor.

It was the so-called informal crown council, composed of the common ministers, the prime ministers of the two states, and, at times, their finance ministers, and presided over by the Emperor, which actually discussed and settled major questions of foreign policy and the relations between Austria and Hungary. That it could and did intervene, with drastic effect, in Austrian home politics was demonstrated by the fall of the Hohenwart ministry in 1871. It was brought down by Beust and Andrássy, who pressed the Emperor to dismiss the Austrian government.

Striking proof of Francis Joseph's gifts as a ruler, of his skill in handling the men with whom he had to deal, and of his inflexible patience and watchfulness as guardian of his realm, is afforded by the fact that the vast machine of dualism did actually work smoothly from the date of its establishment down to the fall of the monarchy, and that no essential part of the driving gear of constitutional government was ever put out of action, even by the crises, often of years' duration, that developed between Austria and Hungary. His great contribution to the vast work of the two governments and of the common ministers was really his constant care for the maintenance of imperial interests, his constant attention to common concerns in so far as they affected army and navy; that is, in the main, to every point at which the internal policy of the two states affected his policy and vice versa.

From the first Francis Joseph set his will to establishing personal authority over foreign policy and military matters. He knew, from the outset, that, even under dualism, notwithstanding all the ingenuities of Hungarian constitutional law, and the incalculable turns of party strife in Austria, he retained, in these spheres, great monarchical powers. To be, here, an authentic ruler, an absolute ruler such as he had been in the first years of his reign, was the aim of his personal life and of his activity as a monarch, and remained its aim up to extreme old age.

Here he was greatly helped by a singular institution —that of the delegation. The twenty members from the upper house in Vienna, constituting a third of the Austrian delegation, were a sort of reliable political bodyguard for him. In Hungary a similar arrangement was guaranteed him by the prime minister. The foreign minister was, formally, responsible to parliament, but within the first decade of royal and imperial government it had become a matter of common knowledge that so long as the minister enjoyed the confidence of the Emperor his policy had got to be endorsed by the two governments. The constitutional King and Emperor never changed his foreign ministers readily; they were apt to be his most permanent advisers. He had two foreign ministers only during a period extending beyond the first ten years of dualism—Count Beust and Count Andrássy.

Anyone who studies the foreign policy of Austria-Hungary in this decade in the state papers, now open to the world, can see how great Francis Joseph's personal share in it was. From 1867 to 1879, and the same is true of the next decade, he can be described as the decisive and determinant factor in foreign policy. There is no instance in the general policy or diplomacy of the Vienna cabinet of a decision forced upon him against his will. He called Beust to office with a definite object—that of preparing for revenge and adjusting the foreign relations of the realm accordingly. The state papers show that while from 1867 on Napoleon pressed him to meet the aggrandizement of Prussia in Europe by entering into an alliance with France and Italy, Francis Joseph's attitude was, in the main, a passive one of watchful and somewhat suspicious waiting until 1869, when, although there was no treaty, certain understandings were reached between the three monarchs of a purely personal kind.

When Bismarck precipitated war with France, Francis Joseph's first thought was that the chance had come of recovering his lost position in Germany. To his own sense he was still a "German Prince," and as such he felt the union between Prussia and the south German states at the opening of the campaign as a fresh personal defeat. His German feeling, in the modern sense in which that word is used, was not strong enough to prevent his considering whether, if the war went badly at the start, he might not abandon his neutral position and, by taking part in the fighting, regain a position in a reorganized Germanic confederation. On this he was in agreement with his cousin Archduke Albert, and with Beust, who could not be expected to feel any kind of sentimental devotion for Bismarck or his work.

It never came to this, however. Both Beust and Francis Joseph were held back from action by the knowledge that Czar Alexander II had not only promised the aid of his powerful arm to his Prussian uncle in the event of Austria's entry into the war but had definitely made up his mind to act. Count Andrássy, the Hungarian premier, had long viewed Beust with distrust. Moreover, Hungarian fears of Russia made them profoundly antagonistic to any anti-German policy. At the crucial meeting of the crown council, Count Andrássy carried a decision for the observance of absolute, nay, friendly neutrality to Prussia in the war—a service on the part of the Magyar statesman which Bismarck never forgot.

The foundation of the German Empire made a swift and permanent end of Francis Joseph's dreams of revenge. A personal reconciliation with Emperor William, now seventy-three, was arrived at and maintained, despite the mutual want of sympathy of the two men. From this time on hardly a year passed without their meeting during the summer time at Gastein, Salzburg, or Ischl.

In September, 1872, a visit paid by Francis Joseph to Emperor William in Berlin demonstrated the friendship of the two monarchs to the world. Since Czar Alexander was also present on this occasion, at his own desire, the old policy of the alliance of the three emperors reappeared as the basis of world peace. Francis Joseph's more intimate circle was under no illusion as to the difficulty with which he made up his mind to forget. When Czar Alexander visited him in Vienna in 1873 he asked him point blank whether he harbored any trace of ill-will towards Prussia and the Prussian ruling house, and whether he still cherished any idea of *revanche*. Francis Joseph gave a decided no to both questions. His memory of the heavy blows fate had dealt him and the painful experience he had undergone—he replied to the Czar—was still fresh, but he desired to pass a sponge over them and his mind was set to the closest amity.

A decisive factor here was the policy of friendly rapprochement between the monarchs definitely promoted by Bismarck from the time of Beust's fall, a policy which Count Andrássy did everything in his power to promote, both personally and diplomatically. Beust himself had changed front completely, during the Franco-Prussian War, and done nothing to counter Bismarck's diplomatic tactics at that time. But this was only rendered possible by the complete change that took place, in this connection, in Francis Joseph's conception of the European position of his realm and of his own dynastic interest. He finally dropped any idea of winning back what had been lost and restoring the power of the imperial house in Italy and

Germany. This change was made quite plain by his receiving King Victor Emmanuel in Vienna in 1873 and paying a return visit to him in Venice in 1875.

Reconciliation with Prussia paved the way for improved relations to the Czar and his government, after twenty years of severe tension. Once things, here, had been put upon a more or less tolerable footing, Francis Joseph had taken the first step in the direction of withdrawing from an active western policy and turning his attention to Austria's great and long neglected interests in the east. As far back as 1868, Count Beust had expressed the view that the true future of the dual monarchy lay in the southeast, in the Balkan peninsula. Since the foundation of the German Empire, Francis Joseph had begun to share this view. A return to the eastern policy of the days of Prince Eugene began to be talked of in governing circles. Francis Joseph certainly shared this idea, but, with his habitual matter-of-factness, directed it to a definite goal, which became the dominant idea in Vienna's foreign policy. It was a momentous change, a real turn of the wheel of fate. The new goal to which the foreign policy of the dual monarchy was now aligned was to lead Francis Joseph, step by step, into the focus of the great European crisis of the twentieth century and, ultimately, into the World War and the destruction of his empire. Only a very brief outline of this policy and of his attitude to it can find place here.

We have already seen how, in the forties, Czar Nicholas diagnosed the malady of the Turkish Empire as incurable and strove to shorten its presumed death agony by the Crimean War. Hence arose the first great eastern crisis. At that time Francis Joseph informed his friend Czar Nicholas that the Habsburg house had definite interests in the Balkans which Russia must not infringe. Then the key position was the Danubian principalities, but, even then, the real sphere of Habsburg interests was the western Balkans—Serbia and Montenegro, with Turkey's western provinces, Bosnia and Herzegovina.

Before and after the Crimean War, Russo-Austrian rivalry was the axle round which the entire political development of these two states revolved. Both had been built up by Jugoslavs, the fruit of war against the Sultan; both were ruled by the descendants of national dynasties, the house of Obrenovic in Serbia and that of Petrovic in Montenegro; both at the opening of the sixties were still formally under the suzerainty of the Padishah.

From time immemorial, the entire Christian population of the peninsula had seen their political future as tied up with Russia's effort to acquire Constantinople. The fact that no attempt had been made by the Sultan to carry out the solemn promises made to the powers for reform in his European provinces continually stimulated the religious and political agitation carried on by Russia among the rajahs of Bosnia and Herzegovina, as well as among the Bulgarians and Macedonians, and compelled the Vienna cabinet to keep its diplomatic agents, open and secret, constantly busy in the peninsula. Panslavism had progressively gained ground in Russia since Nicholas' day, and it gave steady support to every Balkan movement of an anti-Turkish kind. Serbia and Montenegro were in the

heart of the seething cauldron. There were also close relations between the Serbs in Serbia and their Austrian
brothers north of the Danube and the Sava.

The orthodox patriarchate of Carlowitz in southern
Hungary had, ever since the eighteenth century, stood for
the supreme intellectual and political ideal of the whole
of the orthodox Slavs. The same goal had, curiously, been
set up from a Catholic point of view by the famous Bishop
of Djakovar—Monsignore Strossmayer, the great scholar
and benefactor of Croatia. Obviously everything that happened in the great area between its southern boundaries
on the Dalmatian coast and the Balkans was of direct
concern to the government of Vienna.

Ever since 1848 Francis Joseph had been keenly alive
to all this. Since the days when the Slav Patriarch Rajacic,
and young Stratimirovic supported the imperial armies
against the Magyar revolution, he had been thoroughly
familiar with men and conditions among the South Slavs
on either side of the river boundary. Then, however, he
opposed the idea of extending the Austrian sphere of
influence by incorporating Bosnia and Herzegovina, and
rejected the opportunity, which offered more than once,
of uniting the Serbian state, distracted by dynastic conflicts as well as these regions, to the Empire. He regarded
all these countries as "unprofitable." In the course of time,
however, his attitude to the Balkan problem was cautiously
but thoroughly transformed. There had been no possibility of action except on terms that might hold incalculable dangers for the monarchy, until friendly relations
with Russia had been restored. This was the aim of Count

Andrássy's policy from the first, and one he was set on achieving without any sacrifice of Austrian vital interests in the Balkans.

To this end Czar Alexander II's visit to Vienna was followed, in the next year, 1874, by a return visit to Petersburg by Francis Joseph. Poignant feeling must have stirred in the hearts of both when Francis Joseph stood in silent prayer before the tomb of Nicholas and when Czar Alexander took him into his father's apartments, still kept as they were at the time of his death. But the bitter memories of twenty years were thus at last extinguished. Politically much was gained: a basis of mutual understanding between the rulers had been reached in preparation for the difficulties and potential conflicts already looming ahead of them.

Anyhow, Francis Joseph had acquired certain guarantees against the event of his being forced by circumstances in the Balkans again to face Russia as the champion of Austro-Hungarian interests and expansion. After 1870 the idea of extending the Empire came swiftly and steadily to the front. A contributory cause here was the rising of the Christian populations in Bosnia in 1875 and the Serbian expansionist movement, dating from the accession of young King Milan to the Serbian throne.

Russian Panslav influence had certainly done much to bring about the rising, but the Austro-Hungarian South Slav movement also played its part in it. For years back the Austrian general staff had made a thorough study both of Bosnia and Herzegovina and of Albania. Important posts in Francis Joseph's armies were filled by men of

Croat and orthodox border families. At court indeed the South Slav officers were often described as a special "black-yellow bodyguard" of the imperial house, for ever since Jellacic's day their loyalty and reliability had been a by-word.

One of these high officers, General Rodic, governor of Dalmatia from the end of the sixties on, had been notably active in promoting Austrian influence in the hinterland of his area. He was in close touch with the Bosnian insurgents. He it was who, in 1875, persuaded Francis Joseph to undertake, for the first time, a journey of some weeks through Dalmatia, which was made the occasion for great demonstrations on the part of the inhabitants and for many deputations from the Christians in Bosnia.

The 1875 rising in Bosnia was far more serious than any previous movement of the kind and naturally reacted on the cabinets of both the great eastern empires. At first the idea was that collective action should be taken by each of the great powers to rectify the frightful conditions in its provinces. Count Andrássy's Reforms Note and similar efforts failed. Turkey maintained an attitude of complete passivity. Moreover, Gorcakov, the Russian chancellor, quite obviously intended to exploit the circumstances to revive the old Russian policy of freeing the Christian populations in the Balkans, and obtaining possession of Constantinople.

As things were the question whether or no such a policy was feasible rested with Germany. Prince Bismarck's prime object was to keep both Russia and Austria allied

[391]

to Germany and find a pacific solution of the imminent conflict between them. The danger was great. Serbia had actually launched an offensive against Turkey, with the powerful support of the Russian Panslavists in the shape of money, munitions, and even volunteer contingents. The situation was so critical that a meeting was arranged between Francis Joseph and Alexander II and their respectice chancellors at the castle of Reichstadt, and an agreement entered into which provided that, in the event of a break up of Turkey, Serbia should receive an extension of territory and Austria-Hungary annex Bosnia and Herzegovina.

It is no part of the task of the biographer of Francis Joseph to follow, in detail, either the highly complex diplomatic situation created by the unhappy course of the Serbian War, or the various phases of the Russian War, which, opening in the spring of 1877, brought the armies of the Czar to the gates of Constantinople by the end of the year. The Peace of San Stefano, as dictated to Turkey by Russia, in 1878, violated the Reichstadt agreement at almost every point. The consequent conflict then developed between Austria-Hungary and Russia, and the interposition of the British government led to the summoning of a European Peace Congress in Berlin, presided over by Prince Bismarck.

Throughout the crisis, Count Andrássy's policy had Francis Joseph's whole-hearted support. Endorsement of the annexation of Bosnia and Herzegovina, already accepted by Russia at Reichstadt, was Andrássy's program at Berlin. On this the great powers were already agreed.

Russia raised no open objection. The Sultan's representatives, however, entered strenuous opposition and, in the upshot, Andrássy had to put up with an indeterminate occupation of the two provinces. Nor was this all. At the very last, Turkish pressure compelled him to sign a secret declaration by which Austria-Hungary recognized both the provisional character of the annexation and the formal suzerainty of the Sultan over the provinces.

A year passed before Turkey was induced to sign a convention modifying the content of this declaration. Meantime, Andrássy succeeded in putting into effect the partial military occupation of the Sanjak of Novibazar (separating Serbia from Montenegro), sanctioned by the Berlin treaty. There was plenty of criticism, some of it very bitter, both in Vienna and in Budapest, of the questionable form in which Francis Joseph's realm had been extended into the Balkans by the Berlin Treaty. Notably was this the case among the generals who thoroughly disliked Andrássy's policy of territorial expansion by peaceful means.

The unpopularity that Andrássy's success won him in both parliaments grew as it appeared that Bosnia and Herzegovina could not be occupied peaceably. The Austrian troops of occupation had to face widespread risings. The insurgents, supported by the remnants of the Turkish army, were too strong for the comparatively small Austrian forces. Several army corps had to be mobilized before Austro-Hungarian control over the two provinces was established. That done, a semi-military administration had to be systematically organized. Gradually the provinces were raised, stage by stage, from the condition to which Turkish misgovernment had reduced them, and peace, order, and progress substituted for the miseries of incessant civil war.

Francis Joseph had thus for the first time actually extended his realm, and that without recourse to any but diplomatic means and the credits voted by the two parliaments for mobilization. How much inner satisfaction he felt in this achievement it is not easy to say. At the beginning he certainly felt something unsatisfactory, even unworthy, in Andrássy's having based this territorial aggrandizement by Austria-Hungary purely on international law. For Francis Joseph was wholly the old-time monarch: rule over territories and people grounded on a mandate of the great powers was an idea outside his comprehension. So sensitive was his consciousness of sovereignty, indeed, that though the occupation lasted fully thirty years, he never once set foot in Bosnia or Herzegovina, until after the provinces were annexed in 1908. Then and only then, when the country had been completely freed of the Sultan's suzerainty, could he reconcile it with his dignity to enter it, and, though seventy-nine, did not shrink from the fatigues of such a journey.

The consequences of this expansion of the realm were differently interpreted by the various parties and nationalities within it. The Magyars soon abandoned their Turcophile attitude. Before long, their publicists were busy developing a theory that the occupied provinces belonged, not to the realm as a whole, but exclusively to Hungary,

because, in the fifteenth century, there had been a time
when the national ruler of Bosnia recognized the over-
lordship of the Kings of Hungary!

German liberals in Austria deplored the strengthening
of the Slav element in the Habsburg realm, but a tendency soon gained ground in German Austria which approved Francis Joseph's expansion policy on economic
grounds. The Slav press cautiously voiced a regret over
the submission of Slav peoples to German and Habsburg
supremacy. German public opinion both in Austria and
in Germany agreed in praising a policy which they viewed
as that of Prince Bismarck. Had he not described himself
at the Berlin Conference as the "honest broker" of peace?
Of the few who not only doubted the rightness of this
policy, but saw the dangers it contained for the future, one
may be mentioned—a man who, in 1878, saw clearly what
was realized far too late in 1918 by the Germans in the
Habsburg monarchy. In a private letter, of which the
original is before me, Dr. Adolf Fischhof expressed
his views of the eastern policy of Francis Joseph and
Andrássy in the following terms:

"What do you think of the position Austria owes
to the cleverness of its Andrássy? A sound eastern
policy is possible only on the basis of a rational
domestic policy, non-injurious to the Slav peoples,
since the eastern question is a predominantly Slav
one. Panslavism could have been overcome by the
opposition, to it, of a sound idea: not by mobilizing
a great army. The Panslav bait could have been put

out of action by reasonable encouragement to Slav particularism. But an Austria which repels its own Slavs has no attractive force for Slavs and Turks. That makes a good and successful eastern policy impossible. But there are graduations in evil and, in our good old Austrian way, we have busily promoted the most evil and the most stupid possible result for ourselves.

"Andrássy is our political Benedek. Wrapped in the fog of his own *idée fixe*, like the fog that surrounded his unhappy countryman at Chlum, he was surrounded and taken in the rear, without so much as knowing it. And this diplomatic defeat now is far more momentous in its consequences than military disaster was then, for while the latter reduced our might the former threatens our very existence. In Vienna, as I read, Bismarck's speech was awaited with tense excitement. I confess that it left me quite cold, in advance. In the long run it is not an alliance of princes, nor an entente cordiale of diplomats that is going to help us, but unity at home and the friendly coöperation of all the nationalities that make up our state, for the chasm that divides our nationalities will one day be the grave of the monarchy."

Neither the Emperor nor Andrássy had this prescience; still less the German constitutional party, which could do no better than make long speeches finding fault with the occupation arrangements. As Fischhof said in this same letter:

[396]

"A victorious war against Russia might delay, but could not prevent the downfall of Austria so long as our constitution, instead of being the wax which welds our territories into a whole, is the wedge to drive them apart. Thence and thence only can salvation come. As it is, what is happening at home? What are our monarchy's popular assemblies doing at the moment when Russia presents the hemlock? They are engaged in a desperate feud against a halfpenny tax on their cup of coffee! It is painful, horribly painful!"

Certainly Francis Joseph by no means shut his eyes to the arguments by which Andrássy justified a policy that was apparently only too cautious. The Emperor and his imperial chancellor knew only too well how deeply the Berlin revision of the Treaty of San Stefano had incensed Russian society and Czar Alexander II and how insecure it had made the three emperors' alliance and, in consequence, the peace of Europe. Francis Joseph proved that he really was the "Peace Emperor" he was later to be called. Such wars as he had waged had been for the maintenance of existing treaties on which his own dynastic position was based. If he had secured the expansion of his empire, it had been by diplomatic means alone. He had no mind to involve himself in the risk of war with Russia for the sake of any such gains. He further knew that to avoid conflict with the great power of the north by a foreign policy at once careful and resolute was a vital necessity for Austria-Hungary.

During these troublous years, Germany, in the person of Prince Bismarck, had become the arbiter of Europe. The Berlin Treaty had greatly increased the dislike for Prince Bismarck's policy felt by the Russian government and the Russian Czar ever since 1875, and the first signs of a rapprochement between Russia and France, bent on rehabilitating its own position, began to appear. The result was that, soon after the Berlin Conference, Bismarck, recognizing the vital importance for Germany of covering its eastern frontier by a policy of alliances, had to choose between Russia and Austria. He decided in favor of the Habsburg realm—a decision which brought him more and more into collision with his old Emperor, who, his father having been freed from Napoleon by the Russians, felt himself intimately bound to the Czardom by his sense of filial piety.

In the summer of 1879, Bismarck invited Andrássy to meet him and openly proposed to him the establishment of a binding international alliance between Germany and Austria-Hungary, conceived by the great statesman as a continuation in altered form of the sort of guarantee afforded to both the great German powers by the old confederation. Such a proposal was exactly in line with the views on foreign policy for which Count Andrássy had always stood, views determined in the first instance by Magyar interests. Francis Joseph shared Andrássy's views, and, in consequence, Bismarck's visit to Vienna, of several days' duration, in the second half of September, 1879, sufficed for the agreement, between him and Count

Andrássy, on the brief yet momentous text of the Dual Alliance.

As between Bismarck and Andrássy, the issue narrowed down to a single point. They were both agreed that the Alliance was to be purely defensive, but Bismarck desired it to come into force not only in the event of an attack by Russia, but also in that of one by France. Andrássy prevailed. The fact that the Alliance was directed solely against Russia was a severe blow to the venerable Emperor William, and it required the whole force of the chancellor's powerful personality, and the support of Prussia's most distinguished statesmen, to induce him to sign the Treaty of Alliance on October 7.

Francis Joseph, on his part, was resolved, from the start, to regard the Alliance as permanently binding. To the last day of his life he observed it with absolute loyalty. There is no evidence to suggest that he ever thought of it as other than indissoluble, on his part. Throughout the seven and thirty years of his rule subsequent to the Alliance, it remained the rock on which his whole foreign policy was founded. The Alliance, on whose ratification by both parliaments Bismarck insisted, caused Francis Joseph once again to feel as far as possible an "allied" German prince. Although he had for long now, with the dryness that was a distinguishing trait in his temper as a sovereign, cleared his policy of any emotional tinge, this alliance touched a certain chord of feeling in him which responded still even in the latest years of his reign, when the agreement had stood through decades like a "rocher de bronze."

Germans in Austria and the Magyar ruling caste from the first regarded the Alliance as a natural League of Nations. Among the Germans it, of course, appealed to all that was vital in the sense of German national unity, a sentiment steadily gaining ground among the Germans in Austria. The Slavs on the other hand, though not immediately hostile to the Alliance, regarded it coldly from the first. Hostility only developed with the growth of nationalism among Czechs and South Slavs in the course of the next twenty years. Francis Joseph knew this and took it with his habitual calm. He had created the Alliance; he stood irrevocably by it. For him that was, and remained, decisive.

The attacks launched against it, and against Germany, about the turn of the nineteenth century, by individual Slav politicians in the delegations, affected him only as a mannerless criticism of himself, since to the end he viewed foreign policy as the inviolable prerogative of the ruler. In 1888, Bismarck, after the famous speech in the Reichstag, dealing with unprecedented openness with the threatening hostility of the Czardom to Germany and its ally, published the text of the treaty. It then proved that the ten years that had passed since it was signed had accustomed the whole of Austrian-German and "official" Magyar opinion to regard the Alliance as the cornerstone of their own position in Europe.

On the other hand, at the close of the sixties, Dr. Rieger, the leader of the Old Czechs, had openly established relations with Napoleon III and with Russia; hence, the younger generation of western and southern Slavs grew up in the conviction that the indissoluble alliance between the Dual Monarchy and Germany was unnaturally barring the Slavs off from their natural political friends in the west and from the great brother Slav nation in the east.

Thus, within the western half of the realm, the Alliance acted as a principle of division and separation between Germans and non-Germans and helped to undermine the historic sense of unity and community binding the territories and peoples under Francis Joseph's sway. The point was not made on the platform or in the press. Hardly a single statesman or publicist on the German side either perceived this inevitable outcome of the Alliance or appreciated its significance. The Slavs saw in it an instrument designed to consolidate German and Magyar predominance within the Habsburg monarchy, but even they did not fully recognize its significance from this point of view until German nationalists in Austria began to take up an aggressive anti-Slav attitude, after the fall of Count Taaffe.

True, throughout the fifteen years of the Taaffe era, the whole German nationalist movement in Austria was in constant revolt against the policy of Slav conciliation, and constantly voicing a complaint—intended for Germany to hear—that the Alliance was being used as a cloak for a system of government in the Slav interest. This, however, merely furnished the occasion for a demonstration of the meticulous care with which Prince Bismarck avoided any sort of interference in the internal policy of the partner in the Dual Alliance.

This tradition also was "officially" carried out by William II's imperial chancellors, although considerably modified under the influence of the strong nationalism that developed, from about 1900 on, both in Germany itself and among Austrian Germans. On no other terms could the Alliance have been maintained intact for almost forty years, amid the exasperated nationalist conflicts in both halves of the dual monarchy, and retained its effective force in foreign policy throughout that period. Indeed, it may be said that Francis Joseph's complete identification of himself with the policy of the Dual Alliance at once expresses him most significantly as a ruler and gives him a lasting salience in European history.

CHAPTER XIII

EMPEROR AND CROWN PRINCE

FRANCIS JOSEPH may well have felt the events
of 1878 and 1879 a high water mark in his life.
The inclusion of Bosnia and Herzegovina in the
realm afforded some compensation for the territorial
losses inflicted on it in the Franco-Italian War. He had
emerged from the eastern crisis with enhanced prestige.
Austria now was firmly entrenched in the Balkans, and
this new status gave it a clear line in foreign policy. The
antagonism with Russia seemed to have been more or less
permanently cleared away. From now on Austria-Hungary's relations to its southeastern neighbors must be the
decisive factor in its foreign policy. Rumania, Bulgaria,
and Serbia stood, to all intents and purposes, between
Russia and the Habsburg monarchy and much, if not
everything for the future, depended on the attitude taken
by the Vienna government to these peoples and their
governments. Every year that passed was bound to increase the economic and military strength of these new
states, now fully emancipated from the Turk, and, with
it, a growing nationalism and a desire for territorial expansion, at the expense, in the first instance, of the remaining Turkish possessions in Europe. Here was the great
problem, the so-called eastern question, which Europe

had to face. No power was so directly affected by it as Francis Joseph's. Its unfolding constitutes the real content of the whole of his foreign policy throughout the period of life remaining to him. But before analyzing the task thus set Austria's statesmen and their ruler, his biographer may return for a moment to the Emperor's personal life.

His memory held important anniversaries even before he entered the fifties. At forty-three, with a quarter of a century of sovereignty behind him, his own manhood was at its prime, and his domestic life witnessed a return of tolerable felicity. At this time the Empress was again taking her full share in her husband's personal life and work. A new and absorbing happiness had come to Elizabeth in the healthy adolescence of her youngest child, Archduchess Valerie, whose care and education was her mother's main and happy preoccupation during the twenty years that followed her birth. Her "years of wandering" appeared to be at an end.

After the reconciliation with Hungary, the imperial couple made a habit of spending many weeks, especially in spring and late autumn, in Gödöllö, a castle near Budapest, where Elizabeth devoted herself to the popular Hungarian sport of riding. Her strong predilection for the Magyar country and its people fell in admirably with the political duties imposed on Francis Joseph by the new constitution and the autonomy of Hungary.

In politics, Elizabeth took little or no interest. She had no taste for the rôle of sovereign. Well-authenticated sayings of hers show that her attitude to the phenomena of modern politics was thoroughly ironic. Thus she said that

EMPRESS ELISABETH OF AUSTRIA
IN 1880

at the very moment at which a new minister takes up office full of hope, the death knell of his authority already is sounding. She made no secret of her contempt for the large phrases and loud protestations of party strife and had a keen eye for the real poverty of mind lurking beneath the fine outward show of most statesmen. In Hungary, at any rate, she was on terms of friendship with Count Andrássy and other leading men that gave her an insight into what went on behind the scenes.

The court's periodical sojourn in the eastern half of the realm brought the Emperor likewise into contact with men in the leading circles in Hungarian society. Elizabeth acquired a first-rate knowledge of the language; indeed her mastery of it was such that Maurus Jókai, the Hungarian novelist, declared that she spoke Magyar like a peasant from the interior—indeed the highest praise a Magyar can bestow in such a case. At this time, Magyar was the trump call at the Habsburg court. The Crown Prince and Archduchess Valerie were brought up to speak Magyar and understand Hungarian. A Hungarian bishop acted as tutor to the younger daughter of the imperial family.

In these tranquil years, Elizabeth devoted herself, with amazing energy, to acquiring that knowledge of European literature, especially *belles lettres*, which was later to astound the few who ever knew her intimately. Unhappily there is hitherto very little published, whether in the form of documents or recollections, bearing on the personality of the Empress. Hardly any of her papers or writings have been published so far. Many records must have been preserved, but those who cared for her knew and respected her loathing of public curiosity.

In Vienna, court life proceeded on the old lines. Society maintained its rigorous exclusiveness—the more rigidly that great social changes were going on in Vienna. In the decade following the war with Prussia, the upper middle class in Vienna had rapidly risen to a position both of political and of social dominance; both changing and extending its character in the process. At court, however, there was no change. There, to the end, the principle was maintained—new wealth could never provide access there, right down to the fall of the monarchy. This was the more marked in contrast to the procedure at other great dynastic courts, where, for example, in Berlin after the accession of William II and in England after the death of Queen Victoria, modern views came to prevail more and more.

Visits from foreign princes were more and more frequent in Vienna in the seventies, in response to changed political conditions. They gave opportunity for the display of the court in all its magnificence. Further, the old Habsburg tradition of celebrating the great feast days of the church of course was maintained, such rites as the traditional washing of feet of poor old men and women by Emperor and Empress, on Thursday before Good Friday, in token of Christian humility. Skeptical observers at court failed to find much sign in Francis Joseph of the professed abnegation of spirit symbolized by the act.

In general, the Emperor uniformly insisted on that simplicity of personal life peculiar to him from the earliest days of his reign. All his life long he avoided and even disliked any kind of personal luxury or what nowadays would be regarded even as personal comfort. By this time he had developed an unvarying régime, in every detail of existence, governed entirely by the constantly increasing burden of his work as monarch. He regularly arose at five and got through the greater part of his routine business in these early hours, since most hours of the day were occupied by giving audiences to ministers, generals, and other functionaries and dignitaries.

Although he had a marked preference for bureaucratic methods of business, he liked to keep in constant touch with his responsible ministers and receive reports from them by word of mouth, since only so did he get the full sense of personal sovereign activity which satisfied his monarchical consciousness. It was long since any form of recreation or distraction had played any real part in his life. He took part yet in the sport of deer stalking, introduced by the Empress from England, and frequently practiced in spring and autumn, either on the Hungarian plains at Gödöllö, or on the imperial family estates in Moravia, where stags were preserved.

The "summer holidays" he allowed himself, generally at the beginning of July, were always spent at Ischl. There the imperial couple with their immediate family circle lived in the "villa," which had belonged to the Emperor's parents, after the simple fashion of the country nobleman. Then even Francis Joseph gave himself a partial rest from politics, save for the almost annual visit paid him by old Emperor William, on his way to Gastein.

Nothing could be more erroneous than the legend of

the pomp of imperial existence put about by superficial observers of Austrian life. The Viennese court did deserve the praise often given it by William II of being the most elegant of any. But the personal taste and the excellent upbringing of both the Emperor and Empress excluded anything like display in the arrangement of their private life. There were, of course, a certain number of state festivities; but apart from them, neither Francis Joseph nor Elizabeth cared at all for large social functions.

The Empress had long developed a positive loathing of publicity and had a horror of the curious eyes of a large gathering. This was one reason why her return to public life did not win back for her the popularity she had lost—a fact that troubled her not at all and Francis Joseph little. Experienced statesmen, however, took the view that she thereby lost the opportunity of doing the dynasty what might have been a great service. The fact, anyhow, had one salutary consequence—Viennese society was clear of the sort of snobbishness rampant in other great European centers in those days. Everyone knew that the court was a closed circle, not to be entered by sensation-loving persons of either sex who did not think their own social circles good enough for them. This needs to be said, since the most glaring perversions about the old Austrian court and Vienna in this period are only too common in outside writings about them.

In 1873, Vienna was for the first and last time the scene of an International Exhibition. The occasion made many unaccustomed demands on Francis Joseph and his court. Nearly every reigning monarch in Europe and also oriental and other more or less "exotic" princes gathered in the old capital on the Danube. Francis Joseph made extensive travels through his realm, but the solitary foreign journey that gave him the opportunity of viewing a considerable area of the world outside Austria-Hungary with his own eyes was one in 1869 to Constantinople, Egypt, and Palestine. On this occasion he was present at the ceremonial opening of the Suez Canal and took part in the fabulous festivities arranged by the Khedive. He also met there the Empress Eugénie, whom he had received in 1867 at Salzburg, and met for a second time in the same year on the occasion of his visit to Napoleon III in Paris. England he never visited.

A definite place in his annual program of work and journeys was occupied by the "great army manœuvres" introduced by the new general staff: they took the Emperor into all parts of the realm, even the remotest, in the course of all these years. Up to the nineties, garrison inspection took much of his time. A regular and almost invariable program was followed in his visits to his provincial capitals; military reviews; receptions to nobles, princes of the church, heads of departments, and communal authorities and mayors; and visits to new public buildings, churches, and other important public institutions —all had their scheduled place in it. If visits to Bohemia and Galicia were more or less political events they also fell in with the Emperor's desire, shared by his government, to acquire a first-hand knowledge of persons and conditions on the spot.

After the introduction of constitutionalism, Francis

Joseph's brothers no longer occupied responsible posts, like that of a provincial governor. They were merely private gentlemen. Archduke Albert, the only field marshal in the army, filled the post of chief military adviser to the Emperor. Archduke William acted as master of the ordnance; his position as grand master of the German Order gave him vast wealth which he devoted in the main to social enjoyment and the cultivation of music.

The outstanding figure among the younger members of the Habsburg house was, of course, the Crown Prince. Archduke Rudolf was admirably brought up. After suffering, as his father had done as a boy, the "hardening" normal in the old dynasties, he grew into a slender youth with distinguished and sympathetic features, expressive of unusual intellectual gifts. Like his mother in appearance, he also resembled her in mind and in his high-strung temperament. His education was both thorough and wide; he was well grounded in history, read widely, and was full of liberal ideas. In particular, he was in youth an impassioned student of science, with a really thorough mastery of various branches. Further, he acquired no mean grasp of political economics, under the tuition of Karl Menger, founder of the Austrian School of Economics. He knew the principal European languages and most of the national tongues spoken in the old monarchy. A writer of marked natural gift, he wrote an admirable German prose style. As a matter of course he was also trained as an officer. Thanks to an excellent military teacher, he was well instructed in the art of war, both practical and theoretical.

With his passion for science was connected his delight in the chase. He had all his mother's love of nature, and what attracted him was not the murderous battle, but the opportunity of observing animal life. His real delight, here, was in the most arduous forms of sport—the pursuit of the eagle, the moorhen, the otter, or the bear. The Crown Prince was on terms of friendship with Alfred Brehm, a zoölogist who enjoyed great fame in nineteenth-century Germany. He was also on intimate terms with members of the aristocracy like Count Hans Wilczek, who shared his interest in geographical discovery, the chase, or medieval architecture. He himself wrote an excellent account of his journeys to Egypt and Palestine.

By the time he was twenty he showed an interest in contemporary literature and the press which most certainly was not shared by any other member of the imperial family. His interests and his type were, in fact, entirely modern. His intellectual curiosity ranged over the widest possible fields. At the same time he was a rationalist who regarding the new age to which he belonged with perfectly unprejudiced vision, and, rejecting any kind of dogmatic theorizing, arrived at his conclusions purely by the inductive reasoning of the scientist. His attitude to the church was completely aloof. Already he was described at court as a "free thinker," with little or no religion and a definitely "liberal" turn. He made no secret of views so divergent from his family tradition and was aware that men like Archduke Albert and his own father viewed his development with anxious con-

[411]

cern. The public in general soon came to the conclusion that the Crown Prince was exactly the type of man to command the interests and sympathies of educated circles. It was reported that he desired to pursue his scientific studies seriously at the University, but that the Emperor refused to permit it.

As to Rudolf's relations with his mother, it is not easy to speak. Alienated from her in the years of his childhood, he seems, as he grew up, to have reached a real sympathy both for Elizabeth's independence of soul and for her half romantic, half skeptic philosophy. At the time when her admiration for the poet Heinrich Heine was at its height, Rudolf secured the poet's manuscripts of several poems in the *Buch der Lieder* as a present for her.

Rather uncanny Francis Joseph may well have felt all this, but there is no evidence that he made any serious effort to hamper his son's often rather wild educational ambitions, or bore Rudolf any grudge for judgments often expressed with the extreme harshness of youth, although he could hardly display any satisfaction with his son's peculiar turn of mind. Francis Joseph permitted no deviation from the old rule of the dynastic house, which imposed absolute submission to the Emperor on every member of it. All the Archdukes, even the Emperor's brothers, had to get his permission before going abroad; they could contract no marriage without his consent; they had to adjust every detail of their public appearance to his wishes, as "intimated" to them. Anyone who incurred the Emperor's disapproval could count on meeting a "reprimand" that often lacked nothing in sharpness. But Francis Joseph was no tyrant, and certainly did not treat his only son tyrannically.

The Crown Prince knew that much in his talk and action displeased the Emperor and, from the time when he became independent, lived in a constant state of anxiety and excitement on this account. At the same time there is nothing to suggest that, in his youth, he did not love his father. The older he grew, however, the more clearly did he realize the gap between his outlook and the world of ideas in which he lived and his father's. The inevitable result was that he became critical. Father and son: always and everywhere, two worlds, the old and the new; the one set in what is given, the other living rather in the future than the present. On the one side a realism rooted in bitter experience, deeply distrustful of any kind of idea and acting always in relation to immediates; on the other an avid intellect, incapable of rest, and combined with an almost morbid thirst for action. The Emperor a man in the prime of his age, the Crown Prince, like most intellectuals, prematurely ripe—such a juxtaposition must produce conflict and complication, but need not lead to tragedy. Of tragedy Francis Joseph had no presentiment.

He was concerned to have the heir to the throne married early, despite his youth. After the idea of an alliance with the Saxon royal house had proved impracticable, the Crown Prince went, in 1879, to Brussels, to be betrothed to the younger daughter—she was not yet sixteen—of King Leopold of Belgium and his wife, a scion of the Hungarian line of the house of Habsburg. The marriage took place on May 10, 1881, in Vienna, with all the usual pomp. Empress Elizabeth, who detested King Leopold, had openly opposed this union with the Belgian royal house; but Francis Joseph stood firm, and the Crown Prince agreed. The birth of a daughter in the autumn of 1883 was a bitter disappointment both to the young couple and to the Emperor.

For the next few years the marriage proved a happy one, despite the very different characters of husband and wife. The Crown Prince continued his habits and avocations, occupying himself more or less with politics both domestic and foreign, and gave freer rein to his own taste for quite simple and unceremonious intercourse with statesmen and leaders generally, as well as publicists and scholars, in Vienna and in Budapest. His personal charm, as yet untainted by the febrile nervousness that was later to detract from it, attracted everyone, and won him the friendship of men of high intellectual distinction.

About the middle of the eighties, he formed a great literary plan and carried it through with all the temperamental zest native to him. Under the title of "Austria-Hungary in Pen and Picture," an exhaustive description of the whole realm in all its parts and of all its nationalities was to be produced by the coöperation of distinguished authors and scholars. From the beginning, Crown Prince Rudolf had the whole thing in his own hands. He secured the support of a series of first-rate men and wrote a number of most interesting chapters in the first volumes.

Underlying the whole enterprise was a political idea

that had obviously long been in the Crown Prince's mind. It was to display with the utmost clearness the character of the Habsburg realm as a union of many nations of quite individual stamp, distinct language, and ancient historical culture. He had early perceived the inner meaning of Hungarian independence and realized that unrestrained Magyarism was bound progressively to alienate the other nationalities in the realm from the dynasty and the imperial idea.

More dubious is it whether he saw that equality with Germans and Italians must likewise be guaranteed to the Czechs and the Southern Slavs. In the plan of the great work itself a certain dilettante optimism appears, which, in its later execution, comes fully to the front. There is, in it, a purely literary touch: the rough edges and harsh complications of the actual national life are blurred in a kind of esthetic haze.

The events of these years, which found the heir to the throne occupied with multifarious interests and, in politics, drifting into a position of opposition to his father's government, accentuated by his old distaste for the dominant personalities at court, were, for his father, a stimulus to his sense of personal sovereignty. In 1873, Francis Joseph celebrated his jubilee of the first quarter of a century of his reign; an event which brought him proof, from every quarter, of a loyalty on the part of great sections of the population, especially in Vienna, that was neither forced nor hypocritical.

A sense of the powerful forward impetus given to the economic and general life of the country since 1867 was widespread. Legislative and administrative reform had allowed forces, hitherto suppressed, to expand; Austria at last had become a modern state. The Emperor was given his full and just credit for this welcomed change and its results. The extension of Vienna had begun with the de-fortification of its ancient centre and the creation of the Ringstrasse. Magnificent new buildings were rising in towering pride, art and science were being promoted on generous lines, and great sections of the population began to see the old picture of the autocrat in a new and more favorable light.

The Dual Alliance caused the Germans in Austria, at any rate, to come forward for the first time in support of the Emperor's foreign policy. True, there were many members of the middle class who regarded the collapse of the German liberal government in 1878 as a fresh proof of court intrigues and court hostility to anti-clericalism; but this same period witnessed the rise of powerful movements in the lower middle class which openly aligned themselves behind the anti-liberalism of the court and the majority of the aristocracy.

The new prime minister, Count Edward Taaffe, was from the first in entire sympathy with the Emperor's fundamental view of the task before him. It was to show the German liberals that their dislike to Francis Joseph's urgent desire for more peaceful conditions at home, notably as between Germans and Slavs, could no longer be permitted to bar the way to a policy of conciliation. Count Taaffe induced the Czech members to take their seats in parliament; next he made skilful use of High

Court judgments to effect one or two breaches in the wonder-working electoral machine set up under Schmerling's constitution. By these means he secured a narrow but, for the moment, sufficient majority, which was not inconsiderably increased after the new elections in 1879.

Both in the Alpine regions and here and there in Vienna, there was a marked swing away from the liberals, while court pressure on the nobles produced an increase in the conservative nobles' group at the liberals' expense in most of the provinces. In Bohemia and Moravia, and also in Carniola, a certain measure of support by the imperial administrative officers secured a measure of success at the polls to the rising Slav national party. The German press mocked at the "government above party," as Count Taaffe described his ministry, and at the "era of national reconciliation" which it was to inaugurate.

Since, however, the political parties which supported the new government not only commanded a majority, but were constantly reinforced by the great organic forces of the day, nationalism and social unrest among the masses, Count Taaffe was in a position to pursue his policy undisturbed. The German liberal and German national opposition was powerless to break the "iron ring" formed by the majority in the house, led by Count Clam-Martinic, Count Hohenwart, Dr. Rieger, and Grocholski, the leader of the Poles.

"Reconciliation," however, implied extensive alterations, for the benefit of the Slavs, in the mechanism of German centralization which was felt as a burden by every nationality, even by the Germans outside of Vienna. The obvious line of progress was suggested by the historical individuality of the various kingdoms and territories. In 1880, the language ordinances issued by the Taaffe government considerably extended the language rights of Czechs and Slovenes. The government then proceeded to redress the extremely inequitable ratio of state expenditure on Slav and German higher education, and to restore the ancient Czech University founded in 1348 by Emperor Charles IV, to the status of a national institution.

No injustice to Germans, for whom the existing university was maintained, was involved in any of this; nevertheless, the result was to unleash a conflict in Bohemia and Moravia that lasted from this time on, with only brief and occasional intermission. To keep their seats, German members of Parliament, whether individuals or groups, of moderate views, joined forces with the radical nationalists; but even so, they lost ground, year by year, to the nationalists.

Outside Vienna, nationalism swept everything before it among the Germans in Austria, save where Catholic conservatism stemmed the tide; liberalism foundered altogether beneath it. The lowering of the electoral qualification, introduced by Count Taaffe in 1885, was opposed by the German liberals, because it was bound to help the Slavs.

By 1890 or thereabouts, the political outlook, both among the intelligentsia and the great middle-class body of Germans in Austria, was so completely dominated by nationalism that every other political idea—progress, democratic and social reform—was completely submerged. Count Taaffe did not merely stand out against the storm: he took the offensive himself. His main support, here, was the conservative wing of the nobles' party, which Count Hohenwart had welded into a powerful force by bringing the Catholics from the Alpine regions and from among the southern Slavs into association with it.

Moreover, the younger members of the nobles' party, with Prince Alois Liechtenstein at their head, began establishing contact with every kind of anti-liberal movement in the lower middle classes and even among the working class. At the same time, large-scale industry, notably in Vienna, by reducing the economic status of the artisan, was causing the development, inside the German nationalists, of a strong social reform movement, directed primarily against the Jews, the most obvious and the most unpopular representatives of capitalism.

About 1883, there had appeared in Vienna an agitator of incomparable gifts in the person of Dr. Karl Lueger, who understood perfectly how to gather these various political currents to form a more and more powerful stream. Under his leadership the combined anti-liberal forces in Vienna and the provincial cities were resoundingly successful in the 1885 elections.

The seed of Christian conservative social reform, sown in Austria since 1870 by Baron von Vogelsang and his friends, now began to sprout abundantly. The protection, peculiar to Austria, of the middle classes, of the "small man," was the fruit of this movement, to be plucked by the Taaffe government. Inside the bureaucracy the real exponent of this conservative social reform movement which, with the support of the Church, imposed legal protection for the workman, the legal working day and the system of workers' insurance on industry, was Dr. Emil Steinbach, later to be finance minister.

With all its defects, this legislation, at the time, represented a substantial advance and a genuine achievement on the part of the Austrian civil service which, in more than one department, carried out the grand political ideas of the conservative majority in masterly fashion. True this same government repressed the social democratic movement among the workers with extreme severity, modeling its action in this as in other directions on the domestic policy of Prince Bismarck.

Francis Joseph was in complete agreement with the main points in Count Taaffe's policy—anti-liberalism, friendliness to the Slavs, and a very gradual encouragement to national autonomy. It was something else, however, which won his lasting confidence. Very quietly but most thoroughly, by the use of an unprincipled tactic peculiar to himself, did Count Taaffe transform the infant constitutionalism of Austria. After a brief transition period, the government, under him, passed out of the parliamentary into the predominantly bureaucratic form: the only parliamentary element was provided by the nomination of two members as ministers for Czech and Polish affairs. Governmental policy and the initiative in legislation and administration were once more wholly in the hands of the only persons who, to Francis Joseph's sense, were fitted for such tasks—tried high officials in whom the Emperor could have complete confidence: their attitude to the people was that of instruments of the imperial will. Count Taaffe liked to be called a veritable "emperor's minister." The phrase, indeed, aptly conveyed his own view of his function, his inward sense of responsibility to the Emperor, and to the Emperor alone.

This species of constitutional doctrine was, plainly, an imitation of the specifically German theory of constitutionalism, as developed in Prussia after 1848 and subsequently carried to its logical conclusion by Prince Bismarck. Professors of jurisprudence at the German universities thereupon proceeded to a so-called "scientific" definition of the species and proved to their own satisfaction that by its means, the "true" state, corresponding to the peculiar political genius of the German race, had been happily preserved and distinguished from the less happy "west" which had fallen into democracy.

Nothing could show more clearly how essentially German was the Austrian state and how irrevocably was Francis Joseph a "German prince" than the close correspondence thus revealed between the political ideas of governing circles in Austria and in Germany. During the Taaffe era, however, only a much modified form of this German system of monarchical government, under which the will of the sovereign is the true motive force in the state, was applied in Austria. The Taaffe government depended, throughout, on a firmly compacted coalition majority which really corresponded very closely to the actual nature of the Austrian state in that it combined German and non-German groups.

The liberal opposition tried to split this majority but failed. In fact a very large section of German liberal members shared the desire for an understanding with the Czechs in Bohemia which Count Taaffe was seeking on the Emperor's wish though himself taking a somewhat reluctant initiative. The younger Plener, who represented the Germans in Bohemia in the preliminary discussions, succeeded in reaching agreement on various outstanding points of national conflict with Dr. Rieger, the Czech leader, and legislative effect was actually given to the first part of the understanding thus arrived at.

Unhappily, the great work broke down at this stage. In the elections for the Bohemian Diet the Young Czech radical and nationalist party defeated their conservative opponents so completely at the polls that it was obviously useless to attempt to carry the discussions any further. This unexpected turn gravely weakened the Taaffe system. A section within the cabinet desired to have the German liberals taken into the government; whereupon Dr. von Dunajewski, the Polish finance minister, tendered his resignation. This opened the way for the appointment of a German liberal as minister without portfolio, and so detached the majority of the German liberal members from the opposition.

But the protracted struggle left its traces: there could not possibly be any firm mutual confidence as between the prime minister and his German opponents. All Taaffe's efforts to cement the coalition with the German liberals were bound to break against the radicalism of their nationalist group. Nevertheless, the government, as created by Francis Joseph entirely in accordance with his own will, had grown so strong that, although entering its second decade, it commanded a powerful majority in the House prepared to carry its legislative and financial proposals. The old bureaucratic machine had been immensely extended: it worked reliably and forcefully.

Moreover Count Taaffe had long established an extensive influence over the press both in Vienna and the provinces. He was particularly concerned to have public opinion kept thoroughly informed of the fact that the Emperor's authority was behind him, and that he enjoyed the loyal support of every race in Austria.

In the period of more than twenty years that had elapsed since Königgrätz, a new generation had grown up. The prestige of the imperial government, restored by the liberals, had grown strong. The new army, based on the principle of compulsory service, had proved its efficiency and even acquired the glamour of a national institution, symbolic of the various nationalities. It was indeed this imperial army, with its democratic basis of universal service that made the amplitude of Francis Joseph's personal power a reality to the mind of the masses, and in its turn enhanced his position as ruler with the majority in every race.

The Emperor's own self-confidence—the inner certainty of a man ripened in the harsh school of bitter experience—had long been restored, nay, definitely increased. The constitutional monarch looked out upon the world about him with the old equanimity, but with more of understanding and of gentleness than had been possible for the young autocrat. The celebration of the twenty-fifth anniversary of his marriage was the occasion of quite extraordinary celebrations throughout the realm. In Vienna the great painter, Hans Makart, arranged a pageant which remained imprinted on the memories of all who beheld it. When the great procession paused to salute the imperial couple, even Francis Joseph's old heart, closed as it was to any kind of demonstrativeness, was deeply touched.

He was not using any mere court or official phrases when he said, in the letter written in his own hand to the prime minister, to express his thanks to the people of his realm:

"During a reign of more than thirty years I have, it is true, shared many dark hours but also many joys with my peoples. Purer and deeper joy could hardly be given me than that of the days that have just passed. The love of my peoples gave them to me. We are deeply touched, I and the Empress, by these spontaneous marks of genuine love and faithful devotion."

Undoubtedly the Taaffe régime at once strengthened Francis Joseph's sense of sovereignty and softened its manifestations. In Count Edward Taaffe he had, for the first time since Schwarzenberg's death, a statesman after his own heart. Francis Joseph was shy; he shrank from

new people; but Taaffe had been his playmate in boyhood, and the sympathy between them had lasted ever
since. On this solid basis their common work was
grounded. Francis Joseph had noted Taaffe's skill and
resources as a minister in the painful period of the first
liberal administration; he was the only man among his
statesmen whom he regarded as a personal friend.

Taaffe, though not a mind of anything like the first
order, was superior to the average Austrian bureaucrat
called to "the practice of politics." His views were purely
empiric, the direct outcome of years of practical experience in administrative statecraft. His natural modes of
thinking and acting were akin to Francis Joseph's own.
A man who lived from day to day, always occupied with
the immediate and purely practical, Taaffe had no use
at all for ideas or ideologists in politics. Persons of that
type he tended to keep at arm's length, preferring to
work with intelligent and practical men concerned, like
himself, only with the task immediately before them,
thinking only of the "possible" and, as a result, never
at a loss in devising modes of extricating themselves
from any juncture circumstances might present. Hence
he could with perfect candor tell parliament, in a
famous phrase, that his policy was the art of "rub-
bing along" or "muddling through." He saw no harm
in that.

Few knew Austria as well as he did, and in Austria,
as he knew it, far-reaching political concepts based on
"irrefutable principles" seemed to him unnatural and
futile. He greatly preferred men with a sense of humor,

who did the day's work without too much thought of the morrow, to those given to considering things too deeply, to the anxious or the doctrinaire, concerned with theories and vexed by fears and scruples, however learned the latter might be. Taaffe himself was blessed with a sense of humor that did not desert him even in the darkest hour, and a caustic mother wit which again and again served him, though he was no orator, as a most effective weapon in parliament.

It was, however, in the "nonchalant" but thoroughly good-natured and lazy intercourse his unprejudiced mind affected with men of all kinds, degrees of education, and classes, that this gift appeared to the greatest advantage. His special admiration, in politics, was for men of wide education like his friend, Dr. Emil Steinbach, the finance minister, whose knowledge was always immediately available for practical application. Deep in his thought and action, an ideal Austria lay buried: his ideal—"the ideal being what one can never quite attain," as he once iryly explained to the House—comforted him for the immense gap which seemed to lie between it and actual circumstances.

Nothing jarred on him so much as a devotion to abstract principles; for that reason the doctrinaire liberalism of the Germans in Austria was particularly detestable to him, as to his Emperor. He made many enemies by his trick of using a tone bordering on frivolity to dismiss men of real worth, who while insisting on basing every step in politics on large general ideas and principles simply failed to see real life and its needs. Yet he often enjoyed the keen edge of an opponent's wit, even if it happened to be turned against himself.

When his contemporaries, and especially the highly educated German liberals, denounced him as a cynic, they were largely unjust. He could only take the world as he found it. Personally he knew that he did not deride what was deserving of true respect, but it was impossible for him to play the hypocrite and take politics as seriously as did the professors of the liberal party or a rude curmudgeon like Dr. Herbst.

An ancestor of his own had come from Ireland to serve in Wallenstein's army and there was a notable infusion of Irish wit and a jesting *savoir vivre* in this late descendant of his. The Counts Taaffe still figured in the list of Irish Peers of the Realm as late as October, 1914; they were struck out of the list, together with all other peers domiciled in Austria-Hungary and Germany.

By and large, however, Count Taaffe was a thorough Viennese of the old stamp, and for well nigh fifteen years he kept the Austrian state coach on the safe track for Francis Joseph. In relation to the Emperor he liked to be wholly the faithful servant of his master. When his successors liked to see the press ringing with their praises, the old Count, then near his end, remarked, "That was not my way at all. I often arranged to have myself attacked and sharply criticized in the press, and then begged the Emperor for his support. For the Emperor did not like to have his ministers spreading themselves and their popularity in the press." To his mind, the Emperor's judgment alone decided the work of a minister. Count Taaffe knew his imperial friend and master well.

In Hungary, too, despite many an awkward constellation in the parliamentary heavens, conditions at the end of the eighties were tolerably good. There reigned Koloman Tisza, the embodiment of all that was intelligent and self-reliant in Magyar calvinism, and acted, both in great things and in small, as pleased Francis Joseph.

The year 1887 brought round the second renewal of the decennial compromise. Parliaments and the official bureaucracy in either country had long regarded it as their high duty to make the transaction as difficult as possible, yet it went through pretty smoothly, despite the "heroic" struggles, regularly staged, and carried on with great gusto and a plentiful lack of wit, for the benefit of newspaper readers in Vienna and Budapest. Hungary was, as yet, content with the customs union, and such sacrifice of vanity as had to be made to Magyarism in the common bank question and other similar points did not unduly perturb the men who directed Austrian economic life.

In foreign policy the period was not without its crises and moments of difficulty for Francis Joseph. They were the inevitable outcome of the new Balkan policy initiated by Andrássy in the Bosnian occupation. Here, however, Francis Joseph had one piece of real good fortune. On the death, in 1881, of Andrássy's successor, Baron von Haymerle, he found a foreign minister in Count Kalnoky, who both as man and diplomat had all the qualities he regarded as essential for such an office. Count Andrássy had hoped to be himself reappointed to the post but the Emperor refused, for, as he said, what was now needed for the position was a man who would patiently and carefully unravel any foreign complications rather than cut the knots as Andrássy was inclined to do.

Francis Joseph's judgment of Kalnoky proved quite accurate. He found his extremely aristocratic personality highly sympathetic—though he disliked the monocle the minister always kept fixed in his eye. Another important point was that his new foreign minister was from the start *persona grata* both with Prince Bismarck and at St. Petersburg, where he had been ambassador and had made himself popular at court.

For more than fourteen years, from 1881 to 1895, Francis Joseph's adviser and chief officer in all matters of foreign policy was this well-bred, chilly, reserved being, whose entire attitude to life and political outlook belonged to the old, pre-dualist Austria. Entering diplomacy as a young cavalry officer, Count Kalnoky had acquired a sound political education entirely by his own efforts. His diligence was renowned throughout the diplomatic service. He wrote most of his diplomatic notes and documents with his own hand. He did nearly everything himself; he lived solely for his work: his social relations were confined to the ranks of the aristocracy. He was later to boast that he had never received a newspaper man—a practice he regarded as not only unnecessary but as unworthy and almost dangerous. Though called proud, he was not really so in the least. To the Emperor, or in his dealings with Prince Bismarck, he would express his own views without any alteration in the normal calm of his demeanor.

Russia's wrath over the Berlin settlement in the Balkans and the nomination of a Battenberg prince, of the house of Hesse, to rule over Bulgaria, acted as a standing menace to the peace of Europe. An informal division of the Balkans into Austrian (in the west) and Russian (in the east) spheres of influence had been arrived at. Revolution in eastern Rumelia, supported by Sofia, led to the incorporation of the latter in Bulgaria, whereupon King Milan of Serbia recklessly launched a war against Bulgaria which led, within a few days, to the defeat of Serbia and its invasion by Bulgarian troops. At this juncture it was on Francis Joseph's personal initiative that Count Khevenhüller, Austrian minister in Belgrade, took action which led to the arrest of the Bulgarian advance and compelled them, though victorious, to withdraw and make peace. This action from Vienna weakened the authority in Serbia of King Milan, long known there to be a partisan of Austria and unpopular for that reason.

Shortly after, the Russian government of Alexander III first caused the expulsion of Alexander of Battenberg from Bulgaria by fomenting a military conspiracy in Sofia and then, after Alexander's abdication, was obviously bent on establishing its own direct control of Bulgaria—a conscienceless policy that threatened war with Austria. For, obviously, however well disposed the foreign policy of Austria might be, such a breach of the Berlin Treaty could not be tolerated.

Francis Joseph's policy at this perilous crisis was de-

signed, by a series of firm but careful steps, to induce the
Czar and his advisers to retreat from the stand they had
taken up in relation to Bulgaria. The election of Prince
Ferdinand of Coburg, a Catholic, resident in Vienna, to
succeed the Battenberg prince in Bulgaria seriously aggravated the difficulties of the situation for the moment.

Prince Bismarck devoted the whole of his matchless
skill in the arts of diplomacy to preventing the threatened
clash between Austria-Hungary and Russia, which must
have involved Germany too. In the spring of 1887,
decision between war and peace was balanced on a razor's
edge in Vienna. The voting of military credits by parliament and the commissioning of the Galician fortresses
showed how grave the situation was. A year earlier Count
Andrássy had addressed some very severe criticisms on
Count Kalnoky's policy in secret memoranda to the Emperor; now he openly attacked Kalnoky's cautious and
conciliatory tactics before the delegations and on the floor
of the Hungarian Diet. He declared that Kalnoky was
about to abandon what he, Andrássy, had won in 1878.

A large number of Hungarian politicians were openly
anti-Russian. Crown Prince Rudolf saw nothing but
deadly weakness in his father's policy. In the upshot, it
was mainly due to the personal efforts of Francis Joseph
that, despite all these adverse circumstances, peace was
preserved and fresh agreements actually concluded with
Russia, for he supported Kalnoky's policy of an understanding with St. Petersburg, in the face of all the influence exerted upon him in a contrary direction.

In the course of 1888, the death of the two first Ger-

[431]

man emperors made Francis Joseph "senior partner" in the central European alliance, transformed by the efforts of Bismarck and Crispi into the Triple Alliance. It was a year of high success for Francis Joseph in the sphere of foreign policy. Now it was that the press of Europe began to call him the "Peace Emperor." Actually, Francis Joseph had notably raised both his own European standing and that of his country.

His life, indeed, seemed, both in its personal and in its public aspects, to have reached an eminence commanding fair prospects for the future, when a hideous blow struck at the heart of his family and human feelings. On the morning of January 30, 1889, Vienna learned of the sudden death of Crown Prince Rudolf. It was reported that he had been found dead that morning in his bedroom in his little hunting box at Mayerling. Soon after the further intelligence followed that the corpse of the lovely young Baroness Mary Vetsera was lying in the same room. The most dreadful rumors flew about, causing unprecedented excitement, not only in the capital but throughout the realm. It was necessary for a public intimation to be issued, by the Emperor's orders, to the effect that the Crown Prince had ended his own life and that of the young woman by his side with his own hand.

To this day no full light has been thrown on the events immediately leading up to this awful deed either in the form of written or spoken reports by persons whose evidence could be taken as authentic. They bound themselves to absolute silence, kept their oath inviolable while they lived, and to-day have all passed away. When the state archives were cast open by the revolution, the papers bearing on the Crown Prince's death were not among them. The official statement that the Crown Prince had committed suicide undoubtedly reported the simple truth.

On the human side there was nothing very enigmatic in the terrible deed, unique in dynastic history, when the relations between the Crown Prince and the young woman who shared his death were more fully known. In the years immediately preceding the catastrophe, Rudolf's married life had become very unhappy, partly through his own fault, partly through his wife's tormenting jealousy. In Mary Vetsera, a girl of most unusual beauty, of Greek blood on her mother's side, he evoked a passionate love. He contemplated the dissolution of his marriage and so far forgot himself as to approach the Pope directly, with this in view.

When Francis Joseph was informed of this by communication from the Roman Curia, there were most painful scenes between father and son, and Rudolf finally promised on his word of honor not only to abandon such plans but to break off his relations with Mary altogether. A meeting between them on the following day produced catastrophe. Baroness Vetsera fled from her mother's home with the Crown Prince's connivance and, with his help, betook herself to his hunting box at Mayerling, deep hidden in the woods but a few miles to the south of Vienna. Then, the combined pressure of his deep sense of guilt toward the girl herself and her family, of responsibility to his own family, and the crushing knowledge

[433]

that he had broken his solemn word of honor, given to his father, was too much for the long over-wrought nerves of the unhappy Prince.

Shortly before the catastrophe, he had spent strenuous hours out hunting, in the hope, no doubt, of finding some escape there from the conflict that racked his soul. The result, however, was a physical exhaustion which aggravated its malady. Mary Vetsera, on her side, from the start the active partner in their unhappy relationship, had long been playing with the notion, born of dark, romantic broodings, of a mutual *"Liebestod"* and had confided this idea to the despairing Prince. Two days passed, however, before he found the resolution to carry through the tragic deed, wrote his letters of farewell, and then, at the gray hour of dawn, turned the mortal weapon with unfaltering hand on his companion and himself.

That a man like the Crown Prince could have been driven to murder and suicide by a hopeless love affair was hard to believe. Before long rumors began to get about to the effect that what had really so acted on the Crown Prince's mind as to make him despair of life was deep political disappointment, and a sense, arising therefrom, of personal hopelessness. Other reports implied that circles at court hostile to the Crown Prince had exploited his love affair through "Jesuitical" intrigues designed to get the future liberal ruler out of the way. Yet others suggested that Rudolf had got himself too closely mixed up with the group of aristocratic Hungarian politicians then making violent attacks on the Tisza government and the new military service law, and had possibly compromised himself with them.

Thence a story grew up of conspiracies and plots, in which the Crown Prince was supposed to have been involved, with the support of Archduke John Salvator, a cousin of the Italian line, which, with Hungary as a base, aimed at the Emperor's abdication and Rudolf's elevation to the Hungarian throne. This last story lived on the longer since support for it seemed forthcoming in the fact that Archduke John shortly after applied to the Emperor for his release from his rank, and, that done, sailed off as captain in a sailing vessel on a voyage to South America, and in the Pacific, no doubt overtaken by storms, he, ship and crew disappeared, without a trace from that day to this.

But all this web of legends, sagas, and rumors woven around the head of the hapless Crown Prince are nothing but fantastic exaggerations of indisputable facts. The actual kernel of the whole mythology is obviously the fact that, in the last years of his life, Rudolf took a passionate interest in the political problems of the Habsburg realm, and consequently came more and more into opposition to his father and his government. The collection of letters written by him over a series of years to his closest political friend, Moritz Szeps, editor of the democratic *Neues Wiener Tageblatt*, and now published, enable us, almost forty years after his death, to draw his political portrait.

These letters reveal clearly both his preference and friendship for France and his admiration for Gambetta, its democratic hero, and his dislike for the Germany of the Hohenzollerns and profound antipathy for William II, whose true character Rudolf must have penetrated very early. It is easy to conceive that the young prince, passionate and highly strung, looked forward with nothing but horror and hopelessness to a long future of constant conflict with those immediately about him and, beyond that, sooner or later, with his father's political methods and ideas. Further, the need of keeping secret his "déclassé" intimacy with radical publicists at home and abroad was often oppressive and disgusting to him.

On top of all this came the sudden crisis in his love affair with Mary Vetsera, which had caused him deep shame. This was the last straw. It came upon him with such destroying anguish that he no longer felt he had the strength to carry on a life already disintegrated by secrecy, or face the probability of bitter humiliation.

A young Italian writer, G. A. Borghese, published, a few years ago, what is certainly, so far, the best book on the tragedy of the Crown Prince. He talks of Rudolf's creative spirit, and of the "titanic" struggles to which he succumbed. Gratitude is due to this author for the sympathetic insight and delicacy and thoroughness he has brought to his analysis of the Crown Prince's death and, above all, for his clearing the young man's memory of the lies and perversions which have so generally distorted it.[1]

[1] Just now in the year 1928 a most thorough biography of Crown Prince Rudolf of Austria and a very exhaustive edition of the letters and papers of the unfortunate son of Francis Joseph is to be published by Oskar Baron Mitis, the former head of the Imperial Archives in Vienna. This very valuable book is published by the Insel Verlag in Berlin.

Borghese rightly rejects the traditional view that the gifted Prince had led a dissolute life and fell a victim to its consequences. The primary strains in Rudolf were his thorough intellectualism and passionate interest in politics, on the opposition side. That was why his last weeks and months were so shattering. They direfully increased his sense of hopelessness. In the Europe there forming he saw no future for himself. Mental depression crushed his neurasthenic spirit at the moment when the ring seemed to close round him with the exposure of his futile love story.

At the same time, Signor Borghese overrates the Crown Prince's powers as a statesman. His letters make it difficult to believe that he had worked out any clear plans of reform. He shared the opposition common to his generation to the spirit embodied in Francis Joseph's post-1867 régime—a cautious foreign policy and a domestic policy based on steady protection of Magyar rights.

But it must be asked—How would Rudolf have sought to alter this policy? He was hostile to Count Taaffe's friendly approach to the Slav, since, for him, the "German liberal bourgeoisie" was the backbone of Austria. He had an enthusiastic admiration for the Austrian-German liberals, men whom Bismarck had mocked at as the "meadow-saffrons," that is those flowers which always rise when the summer has passed. They appeared to Bismarck equally hopeless, as belated representatives of a passing epoch. How could the Crown Prince have reconstructed the Habsburg realm with the help of men of this type, honorable enough personally, but polit-

[437]

ically suburban. For the Magyars Prince Rudolf had much sympathy, though he knew their faults, but he was blind to the grave peril involved in the growing political and administrative oppression, by the Magyars, of the Slav and Romaic nationalities.

At the time of his death, he was rather an idealist, drawn into politics by his dissatisfaction with things as they were, than a statesman with clear vision of a goal. At the same time he was a thorough imperialist, and longed for war with Russia which he saw as hampering freedom in Europe. Gifted as he was, his development into a ruler of truly creative stamp in the last decade of the nineteenth century is certainly conceivable, but by no means probable. Above all he lacked the patience, the inner calm, and the nervous energy for such an enterprise. He lived fully but fast, too fast; he bloomed too early. Rarely does fate grant fruitage to such early bloom.

No one but the Empress had the courage and the force to break the fearful news to Francis Joseph. It was her almost superhuman self-command and greatness of soul that prevented him from breaking under it. She was a tower of strength to him throughout the darkest days. To a deputation from the Reichsrat, which came to bring him the sympathy of parliament, he uttered these memorable words: "I can find no words in which to express the gratitude I owe to the Empress, who has been so great a support to me in these days, and humbly do I give thanks to God for granting me such help. The more widely you spread these words, the greater the obligation I am under to you."

Yet the Emperor was the first to be comforted. He was held erect by the "world-without-end-clock" of service to the realm and for the realm, and led to tranquillity along the familiar path of duty done. But the effect of the appalling event on him showed as time went by. From this time on he became still more reserved in his attitude to the outer world, and harsher in his immediate circle, like a man who no longer expects much of good from life and the world.

Towards the Empress, his chivalrous devotion was redoubled; he submitted his will wholly to her wishes. From this time on, he allowed her even greater freedom than before in the ordering of her own life. This noble and unhappy woman, who showed such strength in the worst crisis of her existence, suffered in silence; she was never really to escape from the pain caused her by the death of her only son. The rest of her life was a Calvary. From this time on she was never out of mourning, laying it aside on one occasion only—the marriage, in the following year, of her beloved daughter to a distant cousin, Archduke Francis Salvator. She suffered much, too, in health, and her second cycle of years of wandering now began. In the old Hofburg, silence reigned about the Emperor, who now, with health and strength unimpaired, entered on his seventh decade of life and the last of the century.

CHAPTER XIV

THE WRITING ON THE WALL

THE 1890 election undoubtedly weakened the Taaffe government. Ominous for the system of balancing pursued by that government, which instead of reconciling Slavs and Germans had cleverly played them off against each other, were the success at the polls of the democratic and nationalist Young Czechs and the rise of a Pan-German party under George Schoenerer, who had for years been preaching the union of German Austria with the Hohenzollern realm with all the fervor of a new gospel. The system, indeed, had weakened all the parliamentary parties while strengthening the bureaucracy, making it indeed once more the real master of the state. In the House, the German constitutionalists were still, numerically, the strongest party, although torn by internal feuds. The authority of the old party leaders was menaced by the constant and successful attacks of Dr. Lueger and his Christian socialist party on the one side, and the radical nationalist movement among the Germans in Bohemia on the other.

Taaffe failed, however, in his attempt to make a coalition with the German liberals, although the need of strong government was the greater in view of the rise of the young social-democratic party, as reorganized by Dr. Victor Adler.

In these circumstances Dr. Steinbach won the premier over to a bold plan which he had formed some time back and now carried through. His idea was to stem the tide of nationalism within the various nations and their parties, and give full scope to economic and social tendencies, by franchise reform of a thoroughly democratic character. The idea was grandiose though lamed by the strongly conservative bent of Dr. Steinbach's mind. For what he and Taaffe actually determined to do was to graft manhood suffrage on the dubious remains of the Schmerling electoral law of 1861. Thus, in the future, the representative assembly was to be based on equal and direct universal suffrage in town and country, but the corporate franchise of the great landowners, which elected some hundred members, and of the chambers of commerce, electing about fifteen, was to remain intact.

Unhappily, too, as so often in old Austria, secrecy in the preparation of a reform was assumed to be the best guarantee of success. The parties composing the "iron ring" which had supported the ministry for one and a half decades, were as completely taken by surprise as the German parties, when, on October 13, 1893, Count Taaffe introduced his draft bill. The inevitable result was a literal revolt on the part of the leaders of the Catholics, the Czechs, and the Poles, who had long been his trusty allies. Within a very few days the public learned with astonishment that an understanding had been reached between the "bolting" conservatives and the

[441]

Germans to prevent democratic reform from being carried out.

Taaffe had no alternative but to place his resignation in the hands of the Emperor, who had approved Steinbach's plans. A coalition having been formed, comprising all the great parties, Germans and Slavs, anti-clericals and clericals, a "constitutional" Emperor had, willy nilly, to appoint a coalition ministry. As its head he nominated Prince Windischgrätz, a grandson of the old field marshal who had saved the dynasty in 1848. It was no easy step for the Emperor, this. Everyone knew, from the first day of the new government, that the Emperor disliked, as heartily as did the politically-educated sections among the electorate, this unnatural alliance of opposing parties. The Young Czechs and Christian socialists assumed the rôle of opposition, in the conviction that this course promised them the maximum advantage.

Count Taaffe's star was suddenly extinct. He himself died, barely two years after his fall, of the malady from which he had long been suffering. It pained him deeply that from the outbreak of the crisis the Emperor never asked his advice, not even when he visited him in his own house as he lay sick—a proof of singular friendship such as he had shown no minister of his since Schwarzenberg's death. He did Francis Joseph an injustice. He ought to have known that for decades now it had been one of the Emperor's inflexible principles never to discuss immediate political matters with a minister who had left office.

Francis Joseph, moreover, knew that, much as he disliked his new ministry, whose strongly parliamentary character made it, for him, an unwelcome relapse into a period that he had thought over and done with, it was not destined for long life. The combined leaders failed to accomplish the "task" committed to them by the Emperor of carrying the franchise bill. A conflict of no intrinsic importance between Germans and South Slavs over the erection of a Slovene Intermediate School sufficed to break up the coalition after less than two years.

The failure of the coalition government demonstrated the inapplicability of the principles of party parliamentary government to a state in which the constant growth of nationalism drove all the parties to a mutual hostility that often seemed absolutely senseless. Francis Joseph might see, in this, fresh proof of his old dictum—"Austria cannot be parliamentarily governed." His object, naturally, was to nominate a strong non-parliamentary government in which the assembly he despised would find its master.

The providential man for this work was already there —Count Casimir Badeni, governor of Galicia, regarded by the Emperor as a capable and energetic statesman, had long been marked out by him for this post. Unhappily this Polish count was a mere "local" celebrity, impossible in any wider sphere than that of the "old-fashioned simplicity" of the Polish aristocratic régime in Galicia. Outside of his native land Count Badeni had little knowledge of the political, social, and national forces of Austria. From the first the attitude of the higher bureaucracy of Vienna was sceptical and unsympathetic towards him. These people knew all about administrative conditions in

Galicia and were familiar with the singular political ideals of the Polish nobles, as carried out by them undisturbed in the administration of Galicia, by the Emperor's tacit consent. This had gone on ever since the last years of the sixties, since the Poles had acted as a bodyguard in every one of the Emperor's ministries, a member of the Polish Club always having a place as "national minister" (Landsmann-Minister) for Galicia.

Count Badeni's appointment was the worst mistake made by Francis Joseph since his nomination of Count Gyulai as commander-in-chief in 1859. He was induced to commit this mistake mainly because his generals had for some time back been dinning praise of the governor of Galicia into his ears for having proved a "most patriotic," serviceable and firm administrator in 1887-88 when war with Russia threatened.

No stronger recommendation of a high official could be given to Francis Joseph than that of the high command. He was still inclined to regard the restlessness of a high administrative officer as connoting political force. He still lacked understanding of the special quality of mental energy and strength proper to the statesman. Youthful recollections, dating from the days of autocracy, of the driving force of Felix Schwarzenberg's untamable will, would rise to the surface of his mind whenever a difficult political situation faced him. How short that time had been, though! He had long ago become another man. Schmerling, Beust, Taaffe, had taught him that the constitutional monarch could accomplish more by patience, by unostentatious and often invisible means, by tenacity and cunning, than he could by the exercise of his material might. He had had a long training in giving way. First from the liberals, alien and unsympathetic; then, notably, from Count Taaffe, the ever cautious.

The ruling instincts inborn in him sank gradually more and more as it were into his subconscious mind, and by the end of the first quarter of a century of constitutional government, appeared in a much modified form. He felt this himself: had not his unhappy son to his knowledge passed harsh criticism on him for hesitating to take strong resolutions? Yet this Polish count might be the right man for his purpose. So, he committed the government into his hands, while putting officials at the head of all the great departments of state.

At first all went well. Count Badeni found certain Poles in influential official positions in Vienna, and they gave him quite good advice; it was hoped to win over the press, sooner or later. The electoral reform bill was accepted, without much difficulty, by both houses of the Reichsrat. True, it was not a masterpiece. Upon the existing electoral colleges of privileged voters in town and country, and those of the great landowners and chambers of commerce, an electoral college based on universal suffrage was superimposed, with the result that the vast body of voters, voting on the basis of equal direct and universal suffrage, returned a bare six dozen members,—72 out of a total of 425 representatives of the people! For radicals and social democrats, this was far too few, for the older parties, far too many!

Next came the second great "task" assigned by Francis Joseph to this government—the introduction of the new trade and tariff union, agreed upon with Hungary. To find a parliamentary majority for this was indispensable. Count Badeni sought to create one with the aid of the Czechs, at the price of a new language ordinance for the Sudetic lands. This went much further than its predecessor of 1880, since in these provinces it put Czech on a footing almost of equality with German, except for the purpose of the central offices in Vienna.

Calmly considered, this could hardly be regarded as a flagrant injustice to Germans. At the same time it definitely contravened the German view, a view which certainly had never been given legal sanction, that German was the Austrian "state language." The ordinance certainly did represent a notable encouragement to the rising Czech civil servant and intellectual. For the same reason, it was felt by the German middle class in Bohemia, Moravia, and Silesia as a serious infringement of their interests and their position in the service of the state. The storm that now broke out, in the first instance in the press and innumerable public meetings, gave striking proof, not only of the real and deep excitement among the Germans in those regions, but of the great advance made by party politics there. There was little talk, now, of material interests; far more of the irremediable wounds dealt at the whole "Austrian state idea" by the Polish count.

In autumn, the session opened with the submission to the members of the draft of a Trade and Tariff Union with Hungary. The German parties at once offered the most strenuous parliamentary opposition. After months of turmoil and agitation, through the length and breadth of German Austria, there was no one on the German side with any pretence of calm—a fact soon hideously evidenced in the parliamentary arena. After a few meetings of the House of Deputies, the Parliamentary situation was critical. The Germans now made the fullest use of the weapon of obstruction, on the model employed against the coalition, two years earlier, by the Czechs. But the *furor Teutonicus* went incomparably beyond its Slav prototype.

An unskilful attempt on the part of the Polish vice-president, to break down legal obstruction by the use of his authority as chairman, as Speaker Brand broke the Irish obstruction in the House of Commons in 1881, led to really alarming scenes—physical resistance on the part of the opposition and attacks on the chair. Attempts then made by the Czech vice-president, Dr. Kramarz, and Count Badeni, to clear the obstructive members from the chamber by police force, transformed parliament temporarily into a madhouse. The temper of the German members, raised to boiling point by this procedure, very soon spread to the whole population of the capital and showed itself in the streets of Vienna. Police and then soldiers had to be called out to check first student demonstrations, and then the general populace, roused to action by the social democrats.

By November 27, 1897, conditions in Vienna were almost revolutionary. On the ill-judged advice of Badeni, Francis Joseph had twice, in the preceding year, refused imperial sanction to Dr. Lueger's repeated election as mayor of Vienna by the Christian socialist majority in the town council. Now, not to be outdone by the Pan-German movement, Dr. Lueger pulled out the German stop in his ample political organ. Two days later, on his return journey from a visit to his daughter in Upper Austria, Francis Joseph saw the mass demonstrations in the streets. Within the space of an hour or two he had countersigned the formal request to be released from office which Count Badeni had proffered some months earlier. The "strong man" game was over; the Emperor had simply dropped him. Francis Joseph regarded no minister as irreplaceable! Not that he believed in "revolutionary" Viennese, or any Germans; when his ministers talked so, he merely smiled.

Victorious German obstruction certainly had not saved the "Austrian state idea": the language ordinance remained in force. Equally certain was it that the constitutional principle had been smashed, in parliament, and by the Germans. Obviously, the reaction of this on the Emperor's authority was bound to be bad. Looking back on these days their meaning is clear: no one saw it at the time. *From this moment the Habsburg realm was doomed.*

Francis Joseph himself was miles from being unnerved or even shaken by these events. He nominated two governments in swift succession, naturally purely official in composition, designed to carry on the business of the state and prepare the way for orderly parliamentarism. Neither Baron Gautsch nor his successor, Count Thun, could make an end of German obstruction. Parliament was like a broken-down clock. In Bohemia the Pan-Germans organized the so-called "Free from Rome Movement," whose object was to Protestantize German Austria and so prepare it for incorporation in Germany. These events incensed Francis Joseph deeply. Patently, too, the raging conflict between the nationalities was reducing Austria's prestige abroad.

Particularly displeasing to Francis Joseph was the hostile attitude of public opinion and leading men in Germany, and their expressed concern over the oppression of Germans in Austria. Berlin certainly never troubled much to understand the real composition of its ally monarchy! All this caused the Emperor no small vexation of spirit. Further, as conscientious head of the whole realm, he was distressed that absolutely no progress was being made with the renewal of the trade and tariff union with Hungary, provided by the compromise act and now overdue; that three years had passed without any legal budget in the western half of the realm; and that, throughout this period, the daily work of legislation was at a complete standstill. The day-to-day needs of realm and state had got to be met in Austria.

Fortunately there still was a fragment left of Schmerling's sham parliamentary system, in the shape of the right of issue of "imperial emergency decrees" with which the "Father of the Constitution" had endowed the government in 1861. This instrument of absolutism had not been forgotten in 1867, but all that the liberals had then done was to make its employment more difficult, and that superficially only. Such was Paragraph 14, now to achieve high honor and, soon, a European fame.

These imperial emergency decrees were the means, long

held in reserve by the bureaucracy, by which a non-parliamentary government, apparently defenceless against obstruction, could and did tranquilly carry on legislation. They lent the necessary "constitutional cloak" to the absolutism of departmental bureaucracy. In Prague and in Vienna, learned professors of constitutional law obligingly constructed a theoretic right on the part of the state to defend itself against obstruction; and so devised a fine-drawn proof of the legality of the emergency decrees. Francis Joseph let them be. He never doubted the capacity of jurists to find a way of saving the forms of law whenever necessary. In this case he did not bother an atom over theoretic controversies, so long as orderly administration was maintained, the courts functioned, and the army was kept out of politics.

This is not to say that the Emperor was unaffected by the reactions of the German-Czech conflict, the very unpleasing pressure exercised upon him by the Hungarian government, or the embarrassments caused his foreign minister, Count Goluchowski, by the not invariably tactful advice freely proffered him from Berlin. On the contrary, one of his sudden dangerous changes of mood declared itself. He brusquely dismissed Count Francis Thun and nominated a fresh cabinet to which a single task was assigned—Count Clary had one thing and one thing only to do, to recall the language ordinances. That done he departed. His place was taken by a new high official, Dr. von Koerber, and an openly bureaucratic ministry. Dr. von Koerber had long been known to be the best political brain in the Vienna bureaucracy. Unhappily, the one immediate result was the substitution of Czech for German obstruction in the Reichsrat. Comprehensibly enough, when the Czechs found what they regarded as their rights suddenly taken from them, they were just as indignant as the Germans had been when their "state idea" was violated by the language ordinances.

All that Dr. von Koerber's skill and guile could achieve was a sessional suspension of parliamentary obstruction. He took advantage of this pause to commend with many honeyed phrases a great system of state undertakings, vital both to the Sudetic and to the Alpine lands, a system of internal canals, a net of great new Alpine railways, and an extension of the harbor of Trieste. But the Germans had brought three governments down on the language ordinances: the Czechs must do the like to one, and that the government of Vienna's most distinguished bureaucrat.

Things did not move quite as fast as they at first hoped. Von Koerber stuck in the saddle. He was determined and had promised the Emperor that the government would not yield to obstruction. He had no serious intention of dealing legislatively with the language question as part of a great work of reconciliation of Czechs and Germans. He worked out a very stirring and quite modern draft, but did nothing to realize his notions of organization. In 1900 he produced bills suggesting the establishment of regional governments in Bohemia and presided at discussions thereupon between the leaders of the German and Czech parties. But he never went the length of putting his whole strength into any of this; and, in the upshot, nothing came of it. He did not offer the helping hand of the government to assist the later efforts of the moderate Germans in Bohemia to get into touch with the Czechs. He simply did not believe that any lasting compromise between the two nationalities was possible.

If Francis Joseph had ever had such a belief, he no longer possessed it. It was already being said, in parliamentary circles, that the Emperor feared such a compromise more than he desired it, for, as his daughter Archduchess Marie Valerie was said to have put it, "If Germans and Czechs come to an understanding, it will be like Hungary, and the Emperor will lose his power there too."

The Emperor valued von Koerber especially because he succeeded by a series of juristic devices in getting the trade and tariff union with Hungary fixed for seven years on a basis of effective reciprocity. At the same time he provoked the hostility of the Hungarian statesmen by his open condemnation of the official Magyar interpretations of the Compromise of 1867 strengthening the movement for full independence of the Hungarian kingdom. The necessary legislation von Koerber supplied by means of imperial emergency decrees. The constitution thus remained to all intents and purposes in suspense, the bureaucracy reigned unconditionally in order to "maintain the state."

Koerber's main service was that he infused a more modern spirit into the bureaucracy, notably in economic matters, and accelerated its working tempo. He interfered personally in administration, in great and small concerns, for his was a thoroughly domineering disposition. Hence he tended more and more to transfer every important decision arising in the departments from them to his own office, the so-called cabinet præsidium, which thus developed into a sort of "super-ministry." This could not but undermine many a good old Austrian tradition, including the sense of responsibility of the various departmental heads.

Koerber would have liked to handle all and settle everything that concerned the state himself. But this system automatically involved the interpenetration of the entire administration down to the smallest detail by politics, and nationalist party politics at that, and its being treated by the prime minister as the primary instrument for promoting his political ends, whatever they happened to be at the time. It degraded the other departmental ministers to mere assistants of his, while he became a sort of modern Richelieu, a state "chancellor" of unlimited authority.

The vital point about this system, however, was that it was worked out, invisibly so far as the general public were concerned, by the active coöperation of members of parliament with the result that the legal show of constitutional government with all its institutions was maintained while in point of fact the government was a bureaucratic absolutism, carried on in the name of the Emperor under Koerber's direction. What happened was that each year the Reichsrat met but, owing to obstruction, never got to work. Meantime, members either individually, or as leaders of political clubs and party bodies, were constantly putting before the prime minister the desires and claims

of their constituencies and their "national" and administrative interests, and he, after carefully weighing the
political situation at the moment, made such concessions
as seemed possible to meet them. The lion's share of such
favors of course fell to the ministerial member or club,
but by backstairs work and with the aid of helpful go-
betweens; yet administrative "considerations" were also
extended to complacent opposition members and even the
opposition press. Inside parliament obstruction went on,
as before. On its prorogation, indispensable legislation—
primary provision for the army and finance—was accomplished by the issue of emergency decrees.

Under this system the *quid pro quo* received by the government was that, although inside the chamber members
kept up their theatrical thunder, they did not really attack
the government seriously; on the contrary, their tolera-
tion was actually an effective support to it. One of von
Koerber's strongest aids was the press. It was always his
first concern to win the papers of all parties, including the
opposition, as far as possible to his side. The art of semi-
official press manipulation was one in which he was a real
virtuoso; his favorite officials were those who distinguished themselves in this field; they rose rapidly to the
highest posts in the service, and had distinctions heaped
upon them.

Koerber's own views were entirely modernly liberal.
Proof of this was given by his immediate instruction to
the heads of local authorities and of the police to relax
the out-of-date press law and the highly elastic regulations under the law of meetings and associations in the

direction of greater political freedom. So, great sections of the population and, especially, the working classes, regarded the Koerber era as a period of welcome alleviation of the rigid police régime, dating from the absolutist epoch and vigorously maintained under Taaffe. Koerber's relations with the social democratic leaders were positively friendly; he further proved, in action, that his view of social policy was decidedly modern. This, of course, in no way prevented his promoting the development of Austrian industry with real understanding, along the most varied lines, and consequently winning the confidence and high regard of the great employers. A purely official career had not prevented his maintaining close contact with the great forces of modern life. His was a personality of great capacity and undeniable efficiency.

If he failed to develop into a great statesman, the fault certainly lay to a large extent with the incredibly difficult circumstances of Francis Joseph's realm, more particularly in its western half. But, in the last analysis, what was his whole system of government but a piece of political legerdemain, intelligent in invention, most cunning in execution, and publicly staged by a highly gifted statesman who knew how to exploit the men and circumstances of his day, and not seriously disturbed either from above or below? Needless to point out the grave consequences of such a system on the moral authority of government and the ethics of public life in general. The profound demoralization of Austrian parliamentary representation dates from this time. Members were regarded by their constituents more and more as their agents and advocates, whose practical success depended on the good graces of the government or the dread with which a given personality could inspire it.

The disappearance of what remained of liberal political idealism is as obvious as the fact that this system paved the way for unbridled demagogy in Austria, both nationalistic and socialistic. Koerber did little to resist this during his period of office. He believed that he was doing his best for the Emperor and the state. What the public in general did not realize was that the "system" was breeding, in corruption, a highly effective poison which thoroughly penetrated the entire state and all the peoples in it, with the effective coöperation of the press— journalists understood the game better than the politicians did, but wrote nothing of that. Certainly Francis Joseph realized nothing although he heard, now and then, from his elder statesmen that the methods of the Koerber government were undermining the pillars of the state and encouraging the growth of social and political radicalism.

Constitutionalism, under Francis Joseph, had been, from the beginning, largely show and little content: now everything was show. Parliament was a show, so was the government. It might keep up a pose of force, honor, and purpose, but in fact it simply did what had been arranged at a veritable game of political chess in the ministers' room between the premier and his assistants on the one hand, and on the other, the very members of parliament who kept parliament at a deadlock. The scornful phrase in which a wily Italian member had stigmatized the Taaffe government as a *luogo di traffico* was a far more accurate description of the government which carried on a daily exchange and mart with each party in turn.

It is all too comprehensible that, as parliamentary life sank deeper and deeper into a morass in which anything in the nature of a principle was perishing, and administration was more and more subordinated to the immediate party exigencies of the prime minister of the day, conscientious politicians who could take longer views saw no way out save that of whole-hearted constitutional reform. Primarily, along the lines of a forthright democratization of the franchise.

Throughout Austria, and notably among the younger generation of intellectuals, universal equal and direct suffrage became a popular demand. It came, above all, from the social democratic party, with all the verve and confidence of youth behind it. The decade ending about 1905 had seen a notable economic expansion in Austria; there had been an immense development both of banking and heavy industry, especially in Bohemia and Vienna. Economically and socially, Austria had become a capitalist country. As a result, even conservatives were bound to recognize the increasing political importance of the working class.

The immediate cause of Koerber's fall was that five years had fatigued and exhausted all those who had any part in his government. He himself had gradually gathered no less than three departmental ministries into his own hands, and had become so irritable and nervous as a result of overwork that a story, later, went the rounds at court that the Emperor had remarked: "Koerber has reached the point of shouting at me." Koerber in fact fell at the moment when Dr. Kramarz, the leader of the Czechs, said to his old friend Baron Gautsch that if he formed a government in Koerber's stead, the Czechs would stop their obstruction.

When Koerber, without saying a word to his colleagues, placed his resignation in his sovereign's hands, Francis Joseph desired to keep him in office. He changed his mind on this, however, when he heard of the prospects held out in case of the appointment of Baron Gautsch. The latter had been for long minister of education under Taaffe and later prime minister for a very brief period. Francis Joseph valued him as a "general utility" statesman and regarded him with high favor. Another very important factor in the Emperor's decision was the disquietude he had long felt about political conditions in Hungary, aggravated as they were by the paralysis of the Reichsrat. Further he believed that no Austrian prime minister was so obnoxious to the Magyars as von Koerber.

Generally speaking, Francis Joseph's relations with Hungary had remained more or less on the lines fixed by Francis Deák and Julius Andrássy up to the retirement of old Koloman Tisza in March, 1890. True, since 1886 a certain element of friction had arisen out of the first direct attacks made by the independence party on the core of the dual constitution—the common army and its firm "yellow-black" tradition. In the end Tisza had, though with no particular enthusiasm for the task, succeeded in overcoming these difficulties. The old Deák

party, for some time now known as the "coalition liberals," still functioned more or less as guardians of dualism
and displayed no mean skill in wheedling or compelling
the Emperor to grant "national achievements" to Magyarism.

For thirty years, Francis Joseph, as King of Hungary,
had invariably been complaisant and friendly to the Magyars. Thus the second line army, the so-called Honvéd,
had been permitted, so far as language went, to become a
sort of Magyar army—at the expense of the non-Magyar
majority of the population of Hungary. But the liberal
party was growing old and worried, since they saw the
Kossuthists and the independence party shooting up, faster
and faster. Youth turned to them, while the liberals obviously split into a radical majority and a conservative
minority on the question of obligatory civil marriage,
forced by the larger section on the smaller. This was an
innovation which Francis Joseph opposed with all his
might.

The struggle, after lasting for several years, led to the
fall of the foreign minister, Count Kalnoky, who opposed this piece of anti-clericalism—a fact that increased
the exasperation caused Francis Joseph by his inability to
prevent the introduction of civil marriage in Hungary.
His displeasure was so obvious that the Wekerle government, which was responsible for this liberal victory, had
soon afterwards to retire.

Events immediately followed which markedly accentuated the "independence idea." The death of Louis
Kossuth, the solemn homecoming of his corpse to Buda-

[459]

pest, and the return to Hungary of his son, Francis Kossuth, to assume the leadership of the independence party there, strengthened the dislike of Magyars in every class for dualism in a manner calculated to cause Francis Joseph the gravest concern. The idea of complete independence, and the substitution of a purely personal union for the dualist constitution of the realm, took possession of Magyars of every class with positively revolutionary force. In such circumstances it was hardly surprising to find even the liberals, weakened as they were by the secession of prominent aristocrats like Count Albert Apponyi and his friends, and discouraged by the impotence of parliament in Austria, beginning to toy with the idea of independence.

To this end, their leaders stated publicly that the 1867 compromise gave Austria no immediate rights; that it was not to be regarded as a Treaty; and that Hungary had a right to independence and could at any time make an end of the common institutions so far as it was concerned. Disagreeable enough this, for the single living architect of the 1867 compromise, the King of Hungary!

Francis Joseph, however, still concealed his deep displeasure. His patience lasted until the movement began to lay hands on the institution of the common army and openly aimed at breaking it up. The new service law of 1903, with its demands for an increase in recruitment consonant with the increase in population, produced the clash between the Magyars and the King who wore their crown. The bill was resisted by the independence party with every weapon of aggravated parliamentary obstruction, and the

Széll liberal government fell. Francis Joseph hoped that he had found the "strong man" who could stamp on Kossuthism in Count Khuen, who had for a quarter of a century been Ban (Governor) of Croatia, where he had, by corruption and brute force, held down the great and growing opposition of the Croats to the exploitation, by the Magyars, of the so-called "Compromise" of 1868.

But Khuen fared in Budapest as Badeni had done in Vienna, if for different reasons. Obstruction went on, in the most offensive forms. The "street" was under the control of the radical nationalists, with demonstrations at every corner.

Now, for the first time, Francis Joseph took a serious tone with the Magyars. From the manoeuvres in Galicia he addressed a proclamation to the army, in which he stated:

> "My Army is hereby informed, in view of the one-sided efforts now being made in certain quarters to undermine its healthy and efficient organization, regardless of the high tasks it has to fulfill for the weal of both states of the monarchy, that I shall never yield the rights and duties guaranteed to its supreme commander. Common and unified as it is shall my army remain, the sure shield of defense of the Austro-Hungarian monarchy against every foe."

In Austria these words met with the fullest agreement from all the nationalities, with the possible exception of the Czech radicals, but in Hungary they were the signal for the unleashing of a storm, encouraged by most of the intellectuals and by the press, that raged with the fury which only nationalism, devoid alike of sense and morals, can rouse in our time. The agitation of the Kossuthists impelled the liberal party to draft a military program of its own, which sought to secure fresh concessions from the Emperor in the shape of further Magyarization of the Hungarian regiments.

Francis Joseph, now old and peace-loving, finally accepted this program in the modified form ultimately given to it by the new prime minister, Count Stephen Tisza, son of Koloman Tisza. An armistice was concluded with the opposition in March, 1904, and the service law was passed. Next year, however, Kossuth obstruction was renewed, and parliament had first to be adjourned and then dissolved.

Count Stephen Tisza was a fervent Calvinist and the one genuinely strong man whom Francis Joseph was to find in the years that remained to him. He was singular enough to desire not to conduct the election on the usual Hungarian system of corruption unparalleled in Europe. He desired a clean election. As a result he was utterly defeated in January, 1905. The liberal party now disappeared from the political scene; and Francis Joseph was faced with the alternative of entrusting the formation of a government to the coalition parties, with the Kossuthists at their head. They demanded nothing short of the introduction of Magyar as service and command language in all regiments recruited in Hungary; in other words the creation of a Magyar parliamentary army. If on no other grounds this was made impossible by the census figures; far more than half the soldiers were Slovaks, Rumanians, Ruthenians, Serbs, Croats, and Germans. The real aim of this policy of Magyar "national achievements" in relation to the army is thus patent: the army was to become a powerful instrument for Magyarizing the other races in Hungary.

Francis Joseph's gravest political sin now began to work out its retribution. For six and thirty years he had not taken the slightest interest in the fate of the non-Magyar majority in Hungary. For a generation, he had simply looked on, unconcerned, while Magyar administration and legislation there carried through a process of denationalization of other races that was unique in Europe in so far as it was accomplished insidiously rather than by force: neither the complaints of Saxons in Transylvania nor the heavy terms of imprisonment imposed on the Rumanian students by Hungarian courts in the "Memorandum" case could stir him to intervene. Did he not know that unconditional Magyar dominance in Hungary was the unformulated but most important condition of the dual system created in 1867?

Throughout all these years, Francis Joseph had maintained and protected Déak's compromise law from a strictly Magyar point of view. Now, however, the majority in the Budapest parliament was demanding no less of him than the voluntary surrender of the *other* fundamental condition of the 1867 Compromise, his own condition, i.e., the maintenance of the unity of the army and of unlimited imperial and royal command over it. He was filled with a profound wrath against the faithlessness of the aristocrats and "carpet-bagging" politicians leading this majority that demanded a merely personal union of both states composing the Empire. He knew that he must not yield. He knew that his hitherto endless complaisance towards Hungary had caused disquiet and deep resentment throughout the officers' corps and among his generals.

With the swiftness that characterized his action at decisive moments, he now turned the tables on the Magyar politicians. He called on one of the most faithful of his faithful generals, Géza, Baron Féjérváry, Hungarian General, Grand Cross of the Military Order of Maria Theresa, to take the post of Hungarian prime minister. Even this popular Magyar general, however, could do nothing with the leaders of the coalition parties. Thereupon Francis Joseph summoned the leaders of the party, Counts Julius Andrássy, Albert Apponyi, Aladár Zichy, with Baron Bánffy and Francis Kossuth, to come to him on September 22, 1905.

It deserves note that he received the son of the dynasty's mortal foe calmly and courteously. The audience lasted but a few minutes. Francis Joseph, from a paper in his hand, read out to the assembled Magyar statesmen the conditions he imposed on them in forming a government, and then dismissed them. But even this had no effect on the obstructive parties. They rejected fresh negotiations with Count Goluchowski, the minister of foreign affairs, on the ground that he was not a Hungarian. Even when Francis Joseph entrusted to a Hungarian

EMPEROR FRANCIS JOSEPH OF AUSTRIA

EMPEROR FRANCIS JOSEPH

AT SEVENTY

grandee, Count Cziráky, the task of acting as "royal pleni-potentiary," there was no result.

Francis Joseph's reply was to entrust General Féjérváry once more with the task of forming a government, this time non-parliamentary. The minister for internal affairs in this administration was a man unknown in Hungary, Joseph von Kristóffy, a thorough Magyar, who had long been full of the idea of introducing universal suffrage in Hungary. He seems, further, to have been responsible for winning over the new prime minister to the plan. Magyar politicians, at first taken aback, protested loudly against the alleged breach of the constitution and at once launched a regular crusade against the new government.

A quite unforeseen measure was now taken. Parliament was summoned for February 19, 1906, and simultaneously came the announcement that the Honvéd General, Alexander Nyiry had, under the old Hungarian law, been nominated royal commissioner for the kingdom. The president had just time to close the session when the Honvéd Colonel Fabricius appeared in the chamber with his soldiers and police, to read the decree adjourning parliament and then proceed to clear the building.

Meantime Kristóffy had carried through his task. In July, 1906, a bill introducing universal equal and direct suffrage was laid before the house of representatives in the Hungarian parliament. It anyhow brought the independence party to its senses. They abandoned their military demands of the King for the sake of getting into power.

The agreement concluded to this end with Féjérváry

[465]

comprised the promise of electoral reform. The result was the establishment of a new parliamentary government under Dr. Alexander Wekerle, on whom Francis Joseph had learned years ago that no reliance was to be placed.

Nevertheless, Francis Joseph was victorious. Years of obstruction, directed to securing the introduction of Magyar as service language in the Hungarian regiments of the army, ended in complete failure. During the three years of this government it naturally did not make the smallest effort to carry democratic electoral reform. The dissolution of parliament led to a new election early in the summer of 1910.

Its guiding spirit was that of Stephen Tisza. For more than four years he had been out of active politics and under a cloud of heavy unpopularity, thanks to the fact that he was the one upright man who had had the courage openly and consistently to attack the aims of the Kossuth party and their allies and defend dualism as a vital necessity for Hungary. As far back as January, 1889, he had declared, in a speech:

"The darkest trait in our public life is the systematic agitation that divides the army and the nation into hostile camps. For more than twelve years the danger of a European war has threatened us. We must prepare against this war in time of peace. This war will be no child's play: it may well determine the life or death of the Hungarian nation."

Count Tisza was to live long enough to know that he was a good prophet when he spoke these words. Tisza laid long plans for a complete change in political conditions in Hungary. By the expenditure of large sums placed at his disposal by the banks and great industrialists of Budapest, and by great personal sacrifices he succeeded in building up a new party, on the basis of accepted dualism, which took the name of the "national work party."

At the election it secured a big majority. In 1912, Count Tisza took over the office of president of the house of representatives and so became the real leader of the new government, pledged to the maintenance of the compromise, of which Count Khuen-Hederváry was for some time the nominal head. Before Tisza succeeded him, he had carried through the task of permanently breaking obstruction. In 1912, the independence party made a fresh attempt to limit the Emperor's constitutional supreme command over the army and resumed obstructive tactics for this purpose. On June 4 of that year, Tisza dealt a death blow at the thing he loathed. He forced his bills through the house in the teeth of obstruction, and further introduced a new procedure act regulating the conduct of parliamentary business. From that day to the day in 1917 when Emperor Charles released him from office as prime minister, Tisza was to all intents and purposes regent in Hungary.

The biographer of Francis Joseph may well see the turning point in his struggle, year after year, to maintain the unity of the army as reached when, at the crisis of the conflict, he approached the idea of attacking the Magyar oligarchy at its roots by the introduction of universal suffrage. We have no knowledge as to how far Francis

Joseph took Kristóffy's great plan seriously as the basis of a new imperial policy, or how far he merely regarded it as an instrument of pressure on the independence party and the aristocrats acting in coalition with them. Certain it is, however, that Kristóffy's idea had far-reaching consequences—strangely enough, however, in Austria, rather than in Hungary.

Since the autumn of 1905, social democratic agitation for universal suffrage had gained ground tremendously in Vienna, and was supported by very considerable sections among the educated classes there. The new prime minister, Baron Gautsch, pledged himself to introduce an extension of the suffrage, but made some compromise between the nationalities a preliminary condition. But when the great question came up in the house, 155 members voted for universal suffrage and 114 against it. Exactly a month later, the ministry, to the immense astonishment of the public, declared that it was ready to coöperate in introducing universal suffrage and three months later a bill on these lines was actually introduced. Thus, during the month of October, the government executed a complete volte face, which could only mean that a complete change had taken place in Francis Joseph's attitude to this vital question. This was indeed a fact.

The motives that induced him to take this apparently sudden and apparently unprompted decision cannot yet be fully elucidated, since the confidential papers bearing upon it are not yet available. This much, however, can be stated: this seemingly precipitate turn on his part was not due to any advice from his Austrian prime minister; on the contrary it was the Emperor who showed Austrian bureaucracy along the path of democracy, nay, forced them to tread it.

Further, a second point is no less indubitable: Francis Joseph held to his resolution, unaffected by the resistance he had to meet, since the beginning of this great reform, from most of his elder statesmen, whether they belonged to the higher bureaucracy or to the aristocracy.

It was soon clear that Baron Gautsch was not the man to overcome the difficulties presented by carrying democratic reform through the Reichsrat. Francis Joseph, therefore, called on the governor of Trieste, Prince Conrad Hohenlohe, to succeed him—a man who enjoyed the reputation of being an administrator of advanced outlook, friendly to the workers. When a conflict developed out of economic negotiations with Hungary that compelled Hohenlohe to resign, Francis Joseph called on another high official, Baron Max Beck, a man of high political education and distinguished talents as a diplomat.

He struck out a new course, even in the formation of his cabinet. Although he filled the most important offices with officials, he at the same time included in his ministry the leading men in the great parties, so that it comprised six ministers who were parliamentarians and sat there as representatives of their parties. This peculiar semi-parliamentary government accomplished its task between June 7, 1906, and the end of December—a result greatly furthered by Baron Beck's personality and his tireless efforts at bringing understanding about.

Success was actually secured through the sincere and

united efforts of all parties coöperating in this great piece of democratic reform. Even so it would have been impossible had not Francis Joseph, from first to last throughout this crisis, put the whole of his personal weight behind the government. The opponents of reform, above all the two aristocratic sections combined in the landowning group in the lower house, gave way before the expressed will of the Emperor, as did the anti-democratic majority in the upper house. When the Polish nobles, the bitterest antagonists of reform, refused to follow this example, the Emperor sent for their leader, the minister for Galicia, and ordered them, in threatening terms, to give way. Francis Joseph was the begetter of universal suffrage in Austria; his was, still, the strongest will in the disrupted realm.

If the question be now repeated, what was the driving motive impelling the sovereign, now in his seventy-seventh year, to take this course, the answer must be that Francis Joseph had really been won over to the idea of reform at the time of Count Taaffe's laying his project for it before him. Certainly he had never forgotten Dr. Steinbach's proposals. They were commended to him, at the time, on the basic assumption that nothing but fresh and far-reaching social reforms could assuage and ultimately solve national conflict in Austria. For Francis Joseph's elder statesmen, and even for many liberals, that was tantamount to saying that only "Satan could cast out sin."

As we have seen it was the conservative aristocrats who had first put before him the great historic task of Austrian statesmanship in the nineteenth century—the transformation of the realm on federal lines. At the time, this solution seemed unavailing, after the attempt of the Hohenwart government had been frustrated by the German liberals and the Magyar ministers, with his consent. After that, as he knew, there was no prospect of carrying through any such plans, so far as the western half of the realm was concerned, since they would be immediately answered by Hungary with the proclamation of a merely personal union.

Further, from the very beginning of his reign, Francis Joseph had avoided doing anything to open up the national problem in Hungary itself. He did not do it during his period of autocracy when Hungary was under the heel of Bach's military administration. He had always accepted Magyar ascendancy there. It was, therefore, quite inconceivable to him that he should now, with or without suspending dualism, transform his realm into a federal union of equal national states against the will of the Germans and the Magyars.

Kristóffy's plans, which at last Francis Joseph had dropped, may have encouraged him to believe that the introduction of universal suffrage in Austria would inevitably have such an effect on Hungary that, in time, a democratization of the franchise and of the entire constitution would take place there. What he certainly did think was that this task was rather for his successor on the throne than for him. He thought that he had done enough in making himself responsible for introducing the great experiment of universal suffrage in Austria.

CHAPTER XV

FRANZ JOSEPH AND FRANZ FERDINAND

SILENCE reigned about the old Emperor in the Hofburg after the death of his son and the marriage of his youngest daughter. The Empress had resumed her old habit of travelling abroad and was but rarely and for short periods in Vienna; her health was again precarious, and she went regularly to the baths at Kissingen, Nauheim, and Wiesbaden, as well as doing all sorts of special cures. In the winter she again generally went to the Mediterranean countries, frequently visited various parts of northern Africa and Spain, and sometimes passed her time in the villa she had had built on the Island of Corfu, the Achilleon, though she began to care less for it than once had been the case. In art and literature she had long been specially attracted by Hellenism, both classical and modern. For many years, her small suite had included a Greek reader, a post latterly filled by M. Christomanos, whose subsequent reminiscences have preserved many interesting sayings and characteristic traits of Elizabeth's.

For years now the relations between husband and wife had settled into friendship. Franz Joseph's view of woman was full of genuine chivalry and he had for Elizabeth a deep and reverent admiration; where her wishes were concerned, he was boundlessly generous. Thrifty as he was, and increasingly so, he did not mind what she spent on her journeys: nothing was too much for her. Every year, as a rule in the winter, he would himself travel to join her, usually in the south. Between them, a regular and constant interchange of letters and telegrams was kept up. For the Emperor this was a matter of the first importance.

This strong interest in each other's personal welfare was the basis of the relation between the imperial couple, both now well advanced in years. Elizabeth took no interest in politics, and the Emperor had no understanding of her hyper-intellectual life: though his attitude to it was always respectful, any share in it was for him impossible. Any hopes the Empress may ever have entertained of communion, here, had long been given up. Her life, in the years that remained to her after the Crown Prince's death, was often remote even from the small and carefully selected group that surrounded her, deep as was their devotion to her. Dark shadows lay across her way; she suffered incessant pain over her son's death, self-reproach, and, at times, physical agony. Only with her younger daughter was she on terms of intimate affection. In Vienna, no one missed her. In the cities of the monarchy she had become a complete stranger. In Switzerland, Italy, or elsewhere abroad she lived and travelled incognito under the title of the Countess Hohenembs.

In her correspondence with the Emperor she employed a singular name for him, the Greek word "Megaliotis," the "Great Lord." She well knew that he missed her more, year by year, than he had done in their earlier epochs; she knew that her constant absence deprived him of the solitary being with whom he could and would speak confidentially, and as one human being to another. Indeed, so far as the Emperor was concerned, anything like a private life and a purely human interchange of mind was possible only when he had the Empress with him. Friendship, as we know, he never had cultivated, and never could.

Shy and silent as he was, he, like any other man, had need of what we call "small talk": the relief and distraction given by the day-to-day conversation of intimates and the free interchange of opinions. Knowing this, the Empress sought to make good for the Emperor what he must lack altogether through her absence. Chance and the extraordinary tact of her woman's heart enabled her to do it.

Towards the end of the eighties, Franz Joseph had, at an audience, made the acquaintance of a court actress recently called to the imperial Burg Theatre—Frau Katharina Schratt. The charming and sympathetic appearance of this young woman—she was married to a certain Herr von Kiss and the mother of a son—immediately attracted the Emperor. She struck him at once as being, what she really was, the attractive embodiment of all that is best in the genuine Austrian woman, both in natural gayety, genuine simplicity, and a warmth of heart that was all her own. Grillparzer, in his finest dramas, presents such women, with all the creative insight of a great poet, as the fairest exponents of all that the culture of Old Austria meant both in the individual and in social life.

Born of good burgher parents in the old town of Baden near Vienna, an inner vocation took her to the stage. An artist of genuinely natural stamp, she was a great favorite with the public of Vienna and highly esteemed. If I am rightly informed, Empress Elizabeth knew her before the Emperor did, and was much attracted by her. There grew up in her mind an idea which developed into an eager desire to have this charming woman bring a little light and color into the Emperor's lonely, care-worn, and dreary life, darkened as it was by her own long and frequent absence. Soon, a visit to Frau Schratt became a precious habit with Franz Joseph, thanks in part to the charm of her conversation, which never touched on politics, and still more to her real tact, the tact which comes from the heart.

Elizabeth, in creating for Franz Joseph this friendship with Frau Schratt—she and her daughter both visited and received her regularly, especially at Ischl, near which she always spent the summer—once again gave him the best she had to give. How, otherwise, could Franz Joseph have endured his last quarter of a century of existence? Apart from his youngest daughter, who with her numerous children gave him something of the warmth of family life, he would not have had a single creature about him who treated him as a human being.

Those about the Emperor learned to understand something of this when his worst though not his last tragedy overtook him. On September 10, 1898, the Italian anarchist, Luccheni, killed the noble Empress with a single stroke of his murderous weapon as she was in the act of stepping on board a steamer at Geneva. This frightful event smote Franz Joseph with all that his soul could still suffer in personal anguish. When, in a voice strangled with sobs, he said to one of his faithful generals, Count Paar, a man almost his own age, "The world does not know how much we loved each other," the words expressed not only bitter woe but an unspoken accusation of himself and fate.

From now on Franz Joseph was thrown back wholly on himself. Two of his brothers were still alive. The younger, Ludwig Victor, had lived, since about the middle of the nineties, in exile in his castle of Klesheim near Salzburg. The Emperor had regarded his brother, since his early youth, as an idle good-for-nothing, damning him for what he judged as moral failings, though from a modern outlook they were rather mental aberrations than wilful depravities; and refused ever to see him again. With the older of the two, Archduke Charles Ludwig, Franz Joseph had less and less contact. He died in 1896. His two elder sons, the Archdukes Franz Ferdinand and Otto, were, after the death of the Crown Prince, the nearest agnates to the throne.

In the autumn of 1894, Archduke Albert and his brother, Archduke William, who had been the nearest to the Emperor of all of the princes of the imperial house, died within a short space of one another. Mere difference of age set a certain remoteness between the Emperor and the young Archdukes. He was in fact a resolutely isolated

[476]

figure amid the crowd of younger members of the imperial house that had grown up around him.

The Habsburgs of the younger generation gave him little satisfaction, much anxiety and care, and even poignant humiliation. His two young nephews in particular had been guilty of various youthful pranks both in garrison in the provinces, and in the capital, that had earned them a bad name with the public. Archduke Otto, indeed, had made himself positively notorious—not for his remarkable good looks only. The markedly clerical atmosphere of Archduke Charles Ludwig's house had not borne good fruit. While still very young, both his sons had made themselves unpopular by acts of undisciplined arrogance.

In Parliament, Engelbert Pernerstorfer, a highly-educated and most distinguished member, with a wide circle of friends and admirers, both among German nationalist and social democratic circles at the University, described some of the more culpable gasconnades of the two young Archdukes; whereupon they or their friends had the member attacked and insulted in his own house by a gang of subalterns in mufti.

This affair caused deep indignation throughout Austria and gravely compromised the prestige of the dynasty. But no adequate punishment was exacted by the Emperor. Anything of the sort seemed impossible to Franz Joseph, with his deep sense of the solidarity of the dynasty, of which he was the head, as against the people. This failing of his, this refusal to be responsible, could not but extend in a measure to the rest of the imperial house.

Here was another evil consequence of his inbred sense

[477]

of the unassailable heights on which he, as Emperor, stood exalted above other mortals. In his case, this sense had always been combined with the maintenance of a supreme self-control and dignity in all his public appearances. His nephews and cousins did nothing of the kind; nevertheless, he had no hesitation in upholding the exclusive position of the dynasty in society. This began to be felt as a species of pride out of place in contemporary life, and, in the long run, served to alienate public opinion from the Emperor.

Specially troublesome to him was the Italian branch of the family, particularly the sons of the friend of his youth, the last Grandduke of Tuscany. The behavior of his children, Archduke Leopold and Princess Louise, wife of the Crown Prince of Saxony, whose want of self-control was no doubt in part due to mental instability, caused a European scandal, and undoubtedly injured the credit of the imperial house—to an extent hardly lessened by the fact that Franz Joseph cast them both out of the family. In the case of the Princess of Saxony, the Emperor attributed a major share of blame to the incapable old King, George, and his son, who ought, in his view, to have avoided a public scandal at all costs.

Yet, much as the Emperor despised most of the members of the dynasty and kept them as far as possible at arms' length, in the end he invariably shielded them. The Archdukes feared him as a stern head of the family. Actually he was all mildness towards them, generous with money and always benevolent, unless he had to deal with a really serious sin. Indubitably, however, he never showed a happy art in guiding and directing his mighty house. The necessary qualities of temper were lacking. He was too reserved, too much wrapped up in himself and his task as sovereign; above all he had too little feeling, too little warmth, even in intercourse with those whom, as members of the dynasty, he desired to maintain at his own elevated level.

Court life had been reduced to a minimum even before the Empress's death; after it, it remained so. The Emperor did not really take much notice of the Archdukes and was at no pains to establish contact even with the heirs to the throne. At the same time they all held high, and some the highest, commands in the army, irrespective of capacity and of whether or no they took the service seriously. The Emperor lived in the Hofburg. Since the middle of the nineties he had spent spring and autumn, and often later even the rigors of winter, in the charming old Palace of Schönbrunn. Even in his old age, he proceeded every day to the portion of the Hofburg he occupied to give audience and tirelessly receive the endless stream of ministers and diplomats, foreign ambassadors and envoys, and all the statesmen and officials whom he found it necessary to summon to deal with business.

His way of life and methods of work remained unaltered, in the form already described: both the general plan and all its details were meticulously regulated and conformed to. Now as then he strove to follow, to test, and to direct the working of the gigantic administrative machine of two great states and all that was comprised under their army—on the military and administrative sides and on that of technical progress, going as far as possible into details, especially in the case of the army. The task was vast and continually extending, but his love of detail and fondness for questions of personnel remained, with the result that, lost in details, he had often no power of fully grasping the real decisive points or fundamental problems involved.

To one of his aides-de-camp in this late period of his life, Naval Commander Ludwig von Hoehnel, who also enjoyed a high reputation as a geographer and African explorer, we owe a picture of Franz Joseph and the court of Vienna at the turn of the century, whose unassuming character makes it the more valuable as a candid reflection of first-hand impressions.

From this source and other personal information received from members of the former imperial household a comprehensive view of Franz Joseph's daily life in his old age can be obtained. This evidence shows the Emperor's whole time, from very early in the morning to the evening, burdened by the official work extending round him in a complicated and evergrowing network; it shows the immense burden of representative duty he carried on right into his extreme old age; the rigor with which he maintained a fixed order in every part of his work; his refusal to have any change whatever made in his rooms in the Hofburg; and his insistence, when the superb royal palace in Budapest was completed, on avoiding the magnificent new apartments, and living, as he had done in the first years of his reign, in his rooms in an older part of the castle. They show the private life of the

FRANCIS JOSEPH
IN THE DRESS OF A TYROLESE MOUNTAINEER
AND HUNTSMAN
(ABOUT 70 YEARS OLD)

Emperor, at Ischl, with his daughters and grandchildren, and in the little old-fashioned castle at Gödöllö where, after the Empress' death, he always stayed, alone, with none but his household with him; also his hunting, after the old Alpine fashion, at Ischl and at Mürzteg. They show him observing to the last the simplicity and plainness in personal habits that had belonged to him in his boyhood days. They show him invariably hospitable, polite, and yet always dignified not only to guests but to his suite and servants: every inch an Emperor to the last.

The picture that emerges from the recollections and observations of civil and military officers, who served in his household, can be summed up by saying: Francis Joseph in his age was the embodiment of the perfect gentleman on the throne of the last imperial German dynasty. This trait in him was unaffected by his harshest experiences and even the shrewdest blows dealt him by fate. The tragic case of General Benedek apart, hardly another instance can be cited in which he failed either in human understanding, or, in these latter days, in the gentleness of a nobleman ripened by much experience to any who served him or came in any way close to him.

Here is part of the explanation of the fact that every statesman and high official, every general and aide-de-camp,—all the people, in a word, who served as his assistants or advisers in his lofty task of sovereignty—fell under his spell, and stayed so, long after they had left his service.

This, too, was true even of men who came near him in other ways than through service at court or by virtue of their rank; numerous men of strong and independent individuality whom ability raised from the parliamentary ranks to ministerial positions and so brought into immediate contact with the Emperor at work; men like Koloman and Stephen Tisza, Julius Andrássy the elder, Maurus Jókai, and Dr. Max Falk in Hungary; statesmen like Anton von Schmerling; like Joseph Unger, the greatest of Austrian jurists, president of the imperial court of constitutional law; like Ernst von Plener, the old leader of the moderate German liberals; a woman of brains like Princess Pauline Metternich—all of these and many more were unable to resist the charm of Franz Joseph's personality.

Many as were the criticisms made of him as a politician, a diplomat, or commander-in-chief, by his ministers and generals, all were won over, in the end, by his simple and yet impressive human individuality; and it was rarely that any harsher word was said of him than that he lacked firm personal judgment.

"With the Emperor the last speaker is nearly always right"—these words cover the sharpest reproof of him passed by those who worked with him and knew and admired his immense conscientiousness as a ruler. Well as they might know the Emperor's weaknesses and the defeats he had brought upon himself as autocrat in the council chambers of the Hofburg and in his workroom, actual contact with him brought them afresh under the spell of this great European gentleman who survived from an older world into a new age which he overtopped.

There could be no more interesting instance, in this connection, than the extraordinary impression made by Franz Joseph in his eighties on ex-President Roosevelt. Franz Joseph, who received him almost with the honor of a sovereign, said with a smile at the beginning of their interview: "You see in me the last European monarch of the old school." The description could hardly be bettered.

When in the last years of his life, Edward VII paid him frequent visits at Ischl, Franz Joseph made a deep impression both on a monarch of a type utterly opposed to his own and on the keen men of the world who accompanied him. Nor can any Austrian who lived through the period of his latter age deny that, with the years, the aged Emperor enjoyed great personal popularity and genuine respect among the mass of the population. For the younger generation, born twenty years or more after Solferino and Königgrätz, the Emperor's rule—already many decades long—seemed to express the strength of life and will embodied in him. At the turn of the century, respect for the weight of years he bore with such elasticity was added to this. Up to 1912 he still took part in the grand army manœuvres, riding on horseback at the head of his suite, for right on to the early eighties his horsemanship was wonderful.

If, however, we turn to consider him as statesman, as constitutional monarch, we find the basic traits in his character only the more pronounced with the years—his dislike of being contradicted by or hearing anything disagreeable from his ministers leading, inevitably, to a progressive limitation of his awareness of the real condition of things in parliament and the government. Consultations

[483]

between him and members of either house and privy councilors, whether they took place on the prime minister's initiative or spontaneously by these personages presenting themselves in audience, were apt to be fruitless, because the Emperor tended, in such case, only too generally, merely to take the standpoint of his prime minister. Thus everything depended on the character, insight, and gifts of this one man. When the prime minister was an aristocrat, like Count Franz Thun, lacking the real political education, intellectual independence, and even, at times, the moral earnestness so great an office demands; or when he was a man disposed to seek safety in a Byzantine attitude and, as the phrase went, "spare" the Emperor from "worry"; or, instead of resigning, to talk about his unwillingness to leave the old Emperor in the lurch—then it would happen that great opportunities, such as could not be expected to recur, were missed, and errors committed which could only be retrieved with time and at a heavy cost to the authority of the government and of the crown.

Nor, with a monarchical government of this type, was it of much avail that the old Emperor was often far superior to his prime minister both in political experience and knowledge of men and things. What the recurrent crises really called for was the quality of moral force in the brain responsible for decision, and the power to use given facts and conditions in a constructive fashion. And here age had not given the Emperor capacity denied him in his youth.

Although, as has been noted, Franz Joseph continued to regard the group of young archdukes with increasing indifference, he was bound to make one exception, in the case of the heir to the throne. Since 1894 this position had been occupied by Archduke Charles Ludwig's eldest son —Archduke Franz Ferdinand. At first this young man, then barely thirty, was treated by the Emperor little differently from the other archdukes. He could hardly have been said to enjoy his uncle's favor; the less that it was still uncertain whether he really could hope for the succession. For in 1895 Franz Ferdinand, very soon after his return from a year's journey round the world—he had already accomplished the normal period of service as a cavalry officer in Bohemian and Hungarian garrisons— was suddenly affected by lung trouble, and sent south to spend some considerable time in Egypt. Actually he recovered completely, thanks in the main to the iron determination with which he set himself to do so, and by 1897 was able to return to the army.

But his malady was taken seriously enough to cause the Emperor to contemplate for some time Franz Ferdinand's brother Otto as his successor. This experience, aggravated by the fact that, during these years, he felt himself left in the lurch by all his friends and relations, exercised a profound and lasting effect on Franz Ferdinand's character. From it date the contempt for humanity and darkness of mood that were henceforth to mark him. Gay and cheerful in his youth, there now unfolded as it were from the deeper recesses of his being, a sombre and singular character that presented great difficulties to those about him. His education, like that of most of the archdukes, had been extremely deficient. During his years of illness, in which the thought of the succession occupied his mind exclusively, he worked assiduously at filling up its gaps. Councillor Baron Max Beck, later to be prime minister, was not only his teacher but his most friendly adviser; he helped him to acquire a comprehensive knowledge above all of the history and politics of Austria. This made him resent all the more keenly the fact that Franz Joseph made no sort of attempt to give his future successor any practical insight into affairs of state or in any way to associate him with himself. The result was that, in his old age, Franz Joseph was threatened with a repetition of the tragedy that had come between him and his only son, the Crown Prince.

Here again, it was a woman who precipitated a crisis in the relations between the two. Despite the recovery of his health, Franz Ferdinand had taken no interest in the marriage plans put before him by the ladies of his own family and, possibly, by the Emperor himself. In 1898 the public was suddenly made aware of something unknown, until a very short time earlier, to the imperial family and even to Franz Joseph. Franz Ferdinand had lost his heart to the Countess Sophie Chotek, whom he knew in her first youth and met again as lady-in-waiting at the court of Archduke Frederick at Pressburg, and had affianced himself to her. When he now approached the Emperor for his approval of this marriage, the request, which threw Franz Joseph into a state of painful excitement, was refused point blank.

After a painful dispute between uncle and nephew, a delay of a year was imposed on the latter, whose firm determination was not in the least shaken thereby. Fresh conflict, therefore, arose. Franz Joseph's objection to the marriage was based on the fact that the Choteks, though a very ancient Bohemian noble family, did not belong to those recognized by the German Confederation Act of 1814, either in virtue of their status in the Holy Roman Empire or as mediatized princes, as within the degrees of marriage for princes of the reigning house.

Even in the twentieth century, this fundamental principle of the private law of the German princes was for Franz Joseph sacrosanct and not to be infringed. This conception of his, of absolute legitimism as the basis of imperial and dynastic status—a conception not only in sharp contrast with the views of his day but regarded as overstrained by many reigning families—brought about a profound division between him and Franz Ferdinand. Ultimately Koerber, then prime minister, devised a working compromise, satisfactory to neither party. The Emperor gave his consent to the marriage on condition that it was morganatic.

On June 28, 1900, the Archduke, in presence of a solemn assembly of the court and the privy council, had to take an oath to the Emperor that, while his personal rights and claims remained intact, he deprived the children of his marriage of all the prerogatives of rank, above all the right of succession. Since morganatic marriage was unknown to Hungarian law, the Hungarian government had to undertake to incorporate the Archduke's promise into the Hungarian code by means of a specific enactment. This was done in the course of 1900; nevertheless it did not invalidate the point made from the beginning by Magyar jurists and statesmen, that, if Archduke Franz Ferdinand ascended the throne, his wife must, by Hungarian law, be at once recognized as queen. Meantime, Franz Joseph raised the heir apparent's wife to the rank of Princess of Hohenberg.

The marriage that took place at Reichstadt on July 1, 1900, was, for the Archduke, the foundation of a deep and lasting personal happiness; for Franz Joseph, the source of endless trouble and disquiet. The position at court assigned by the chamberlain, with the Emperor's agreement, to the wife of the Heir Apparent proved intolerable both to her and her husband. Ever recurring tension and conflict of the most painful character between the heir apparent and the monarch were caused by this family arrangement, in a sphere where rank and precedence were maintained with all the rigidity of long-past epochs.

True, the passage of time did something to help. The German Emperor did more than anyone else to break down the ban imposed by Vienna on the consort of the heir. William II had, previously, shown little attention to Franz Ferdinand. Now, however, he saw the importance, on political grounds, of winning him over. In Berlin he received his wife with all the honors of an archduchess and thereby raised her position at home. In 1906 she was raised to the rank of Duchess of Hohenberg, a decidedly higher rank in the imperial family than before, and subsequently appeared at court. A stumbling block seemed hereby to have been cleared from the path.

Other reasons of a kind that appeared far more serious to mortals outside the court, made Franz Joseph's relations to his successor very bad. The Archduke, on reëntering the army, had been given no special command, the Emperor having merely placed him "at the disposition of the supreme command." At last, after endless conflicts with the Emperor and his military cabinet, the Archduke's pressure for an adequate military position and influence led to a considerable increase in his power there, long before he was, in 1913, nominated inspector general of the entire "forces."

Here, within certain limits, he was in effect commander-in-chief in the department of sovereignty that was from the dynastic standpoint and in practice the vital one, although Franz Joseph continued to control things by his own military chancellery and naturally retained all the constitutional prerogatives of the "all highest" commander.

Thus what Franz Ferdinand acquired in these years was not so much formal as actual power. Further, again at the cost of severe struggles, he succeeded in getting men in whom he had full confidence appointed to key positions in the army. First and foremost, the chief of the general staff, Baron Frederick von Beck, an intimate friend of the Emperor and of his own age, was compelled to retire from a position he had held for a quarter of a century. He was replaced by General Conrad von Hötzendorf, long recognized as the brains of the general staff, and now appointed by Franz Ferdinand to carry out the reforms he had long had in mind.

As regards the navy, the appointment of Admiral Haus to command had a similar significance. The Emperor, however, retained Baron von Schönaich, a man of marked personality, whom the Archduke did not at all like, at the war office. Under the driving force of Conrad von Hötzendorf, the alarms and excursions of the foreign policy of the period were reflected in a series of drastic and in part over-hasty reforms throughout the Austro-Hungarian army.

It is impossible to describe here, in any detail, the curious system of co-regency on the part of the heir to the throne thus introduced. It meant that Franz Ferdinand, although still, as it were, behind the curtain, came into direct contact with parliament, public opinion, and the political parties. Certain leading traits in his political mentality soon became widely recognized: the tenacity of his will, his markedly authoritarian temper, his deep dissatisfaction with the harvest of his uncle's sixty years of rule, above all his passionate dislike of the Magyars and of the 1867 Compromise, as well as the fearlessness of his utterance of his own views everywhere, even to the Emperor, the brusque and inconsiderate sharpness with which he frequently treated his inferiors, and his complete disregard of anything like popularity with the masses.

The consequences were inevitable. Rumor busily spread reports of his faults, in grossly exaggerated form, throughout the realm, while his merits were overlooked— the way, so unlike Franz Joseph's, in which he went about quite unceremoniously gathering information for himself on every topic, while leaving state papers alone as much as possible; and, above all, an outspoken sense of justice, which certainly included an unsparing severity of judgment on any who seemed to him neglectful of their duty or unreliable in its performance. On the other hand, his neglect in treating affairs touching public interest, his curious lack of observance of the strict legal limits of the powers of public officers, when they curbed his private interests—for example in the case of his shooting box in Blühnbach in the Duchy of Salzburg—tended to rouse public sentiment against him and to make him more feared than respected.

Franz Ferdinand's hot temper made difficulties for him during this period of co-regency in the military sphere; it would certainly have been a danger had he come to the throne. The head of his military chancery, who knew him better than any one else, said, very aptly, that he was "explosive rather than impulsive." His political aims and plans were thoroughly and repeatedly discussed with a large group of confidants whom he gathered about him; they were by no means to be regarded as inalterably settled.

Fixed points in his political outlook were his hatred of dualism and the Magyar politicians and nobles, and further the definitely clerical standpoint given to him by his education and fortified by the influence of his wife. Putting together all that is known of his views, one finds him nearer to the princely ideas of the seventeenth than of the twentieth century. Undoubtedly he acquired, as years went by, a much deeper understanding of the nature of the Habsburg monarchy than Franz Joseph ever possessed. He realized that if the realm was to continue not only must equality be granted to all its nationalities but guarantees must be provided for the free development, both cultural and political, of them all.

From this point of view he criticized the denationalization of all the races in Hungary carried through by the Magyar oligarchy under the protection of the 1867 Compromise. That this deeper insight would have made Franz Ferdinand an emperor of constructive force can neither be affirmed nor denied. Fate denied him the opportunity of testing his powers of solving the great questions that were now insistently pressing on the peoples and governors of Austria-Hungary.

Naturally enough, Franz Ferdinand was not satisfied with military authority but, from 1906 on, obviously strove to exert his influence in domestic and foreign policy; strove for a real co-regency, such as that to which Maria Theresa admitted her son, Joseph II, when he wore the German imperial crown.

Here, however, there was no moving Franz Joseph. In 1905, Franz Ferdinand was complaining that he had to learn everything from the newspapers, that the Emperor never listened to him, and that he was told less than "the under footman in Schönbrunn"; after that, however, there was a change in his position, in practice, if not officially, for the Emperor refused him any formal status outside his military one.

Thanks to the remarkable political gifts and dominating personality of Major von Brosch, whom the heir apparent made head of his military chancery, he soon became one of the best informed men in the Empire in every department of political and social life. Within a short time the Archduke's military chancery had grown into a new centre—with no statutory existence, of course—which, apart from its official military business, was in constant touch, both by interview and correspondence, with most of the ministries in Vienna (though not in Hungary), and was not only *au courant* with everything but sought to interfere in many governmental matters.

Of course its success in this depended entirely on the goodwill of the departmental minister and his officials. In addition, the military chancery, under Brosch's direction, began to make extensive preparations for the event of a change on the throne—an event awaited with a less than tactful impatience in the superb Belvedere Palace in Vienna, where Franz Ferdinand and his family likewise had their residence.

Franz Joseph knew all; there were plenty of busybodies, buzzing between him and his nephew. The old Emperor was jealous of his authority; found constant source of irritation in the growing activities of his nephew's chancery and in the influence exercised by Franz Ferdinand on home and foreign policy through his friends —for the most part Bohemian aristocrats—in both houses of parliament in Vienna, and in the delegations.

Some years earlier he had transferred to his heir the so-called "Court of Mercy," i.e., the exercise of the imperial prerogative of pardon. After a time, however, on representations from the prime minister, Koerber, he had to resume this privilege of majesty, since, so Koerber reported, the Archduke paid little attention to this sphere of activity and let appeals for mercy lie unheeded. The prime minister not unnaturally regarded this as injurious to the interest of the dynasty. Franz Ferdinand was not specially compassionate—that was not in his character—not the right man to exercise this royal prerogative.

After a conversation which must have been an awkward one for Koerber, the Emperor said that he would resume the Court of Mercy, adding, half jestingly, "It is about all that is left me." Such was the view of his constitutional position taken by the venerable man who had been a real autocrat in the fifties!

It must not be assumed that the endless guerilla warfare waged by the Archduke against those who were loyal to the aged Emperor often led to anything like a personal conflict between uncle and nephew. In his personal relations with his uncle Franz Ferdinand invariably observed the respect and obedience due to the Emperor. This, however, only made him speak all the more sharply, in his own circle, against the Emperor's servants, above all against Baron Aehrenthal, who succeeded Count Goluchowski as foreign minister; against General Bolfras, head of the imperial military chancery; and, above all, against the court chamberlain, Prince Montenuovo, grandson of the French Empress Marie Louise (the great Napoleon's wife) by her second marriage with Count Neipperg.

All those who knew the court of Vienna in these years were aware that the personality and activity of his heir constituted a heavy burden on the aged Emperor. Francis Joseph was possibly the more sensitive on this score because he had no sort of family affection for his nephew, and because the eagerness of an heir in the fifties for position in the state seemed somehow rather sinister to a man whom his own uncle's abdication had brought to the throne at eighteen.

By 1910 things had reached such a point that "Schönbrunn" and "Belvedere" sat on their respective hills like the residences of rival monarchs. It would often happen, too, that when the Emperor, apropos of some important decision to be taken, had to hear the views and opinions of the Archduke, he would exclaim, with astonishment and disdain, "Really! He is troubling about that, too, already!" and then do—whatever was the opposite of the heir's opinion.

This was a state of things that, naturally, grew more and more intolerable to the Emperor. Everything in the Archduke's way of handling men and things went against the routine he had himself observed for decades. He yielded more and more to Franz Ferdinand's demand for new men; but when he had done so, he would say that this or that new minister was not "his man" but the heir apparent's. Worst of all, he never could feel confidence in Franz Ferdinand's favorites, least of all in the new chief of the general staff, Conrad von Hötzendorf, whom he found too "theoretical," too sudden, and above all much too fond of new-fangled ways. "He is clever," the old Emperor said, "but not prudent." Yet it caused him great perturbation when the Archduke suddenly dropped his leading military adviser, only to call him back to the head of the general staff after less than a year.

In Berlin the changes in personnel, especially when introduced out of the blue as was usual with Franz Ferdinand, caused considerable astonishment. But so far as possible, William II and his general staff supported him in his zeal for army reform, particularly in the case of Conrad von Hötzendorf and his work. Despite endless conflicts between the Emperor and his nephew's men, Conrad von Hötzendorf, General Krobatin (war minister), and Admiral Haus strengthened the army and navy and carried out great work of technical improvement in all branches of the forces.

Court and government circles were increasingly dominated by the sense that events decisive of the fate of empire and dynasty were preparing in all quarters of Europe. After the first Balkan War in 1912, the atmosphere was charged with electricity, tense with excitement. No one was more astutely conscious of this than the heir to the throne. Franz Joseph himself, since his eightieth birthday, suffered from a periodic lassitude, that perhaps made it easier for him to close his eyes to the grave anxieties caused not only by conditions within the Austro-Hungarian monarchy but by the dangers to the peace of the world, involved in the system of European alliances, —dangers that rose clearer every day before the nations and their rulers.

CHAPTER XVI

SERAJEVO

AS we have seen, Francis Joseph's foreign policy was inalterably determined by the occupation of Bosnia and Herzegovina and by the Dual Alliance. As years went by the Emperor grew into the Alliance; it became part of his being: consequently there was only one direction in which an active policy was possible for Austria—the East. This meant, however, that Russia must become inevitably the polar opposite for Austro-Hungarian policy. In Italy, although there were difficulties—an irredentist movement grew up after the death of King Humbert, for whom Franz Joseph had a marked personal esteem—official relations seemed to have been stabilized by the Triple Alliance.

Between the two eastern empires, as has been briefly shown, despite the continuance of subterranean rivalry which gave rise from time to time to tension, peace was maintained from 1878 on, thanks mainly to Franz Joseph's own efforts. Count Kálnoky and Count Goluchowski, both of whom held office as foreign minister for long periods, were but advisers and executive instruments of the imperial will to peace. He believed that Austria-Hungary had reached the position of a satisfied and therefore peaceful power, interested only in maintaining what

[497]

it had. Clear proof of this was given when the assassination of King Alexander of Serbia on the 11th of June, 1903, threatened to upset the balance of power in the Balkans. Francis Joseph energetically rejected any proposals for intervention, although the Russian government, with the horrors that had just taken place in Belgrade in mind, informed Vienna that it recognized its complete liberty of action in Serbia. From this time, however, dates a sensible deterioration in the position of the Habsburg monarchy in the Balkans, foreseen at the time by those who knew conditions there best both in Vienna and in Budapest.

The accession of the new Karageorgievich dynasty to the throne in the person of King Petar, and the advent to power of Nicola Pasitch, leader of the Radical party meant that the Russian government was all powerful in Serbia. From now on, the acquisition of Macedonia became the real object of Serbian policy and the propaganda now initiated there. For the moment, indeed, Russia, in view of its war with Japan and the liquidation of its eastern expansion policy, showed a pacific face. When Nicholas II visited Emperor Francis Joseph in his hunting lodge at Mürzteg, he abounded in expressions of friendship. The policy of maintaining the status quo in the Balkans, which Francis Joseph had already laid down at the time of his own visit to Petrograd in 1897, was expressly confirmed. But this plan of friendly coöperation with Russia, based on a species of division of the Balkan States, eastern and western, into spheres of influence, almost immediately received a severe shock, through the Turkish

THE IMPERIAL PALACE OF SCHÖNBRUNN

revolution and its results. Shortly after Count Goluchowski was replaced in the Ballplatz by Baron Aehrenthal, previously Austrian ambassador in Petrograd,
the momentous proclamation of a constitution for
Turkey took place. Baron Aehrenthal and Baron
Burián, Austro-Hungarian minister for Bosnia and Herzegovina, agreed in holding that the international guarantee of the occupation of this part of the realm was no
longer adequate: the government accordingly determined
to proceed to annex these two territories, still formally
under the Sultan's suzerainty. Russia had agreed to annexation as far back as 1876: that it had not been carried out
then nor later was now to entail bitter consequences. Its
execution now led indeed to grave complications, for not
only Russia but England chose to regard it as a one-sided
alteration in the Berlin Treaty and supported Serbia's
immediate diplomatic protest. Isvolsky, the new Russian
foreign minister, in his earnest concern to win the freedom
of the Dardanelles for Russia, on July 2, 1908, renewed
the offer of Russia's agreement to annexation; and at a
meeting between Isvolsky and Count Berchtold at the
latter's castle of Buchlau an agreement was arrived at,
Austria-Hungary on its part stating its readiness to meet
Isvolsky's wishes. They came to naught, however, in view
of the attitude of England. When the annexation of
Bosnia and Herzegovina was actually announced on October 5, 1908, very shortly after Czar Ferdinand of Bulgaria's declaration of his country's complete independence
of Turkey, passionate opposition was expressed both by
Serbia and by the Turkish government.

Europe was in a highly tense condition, owing to the formation of the Entente between Great Britain on the one hand, and France and Russia on the other, which was actively preparing under the leadership of King Edward VII: the annexation crisis heightened this tension to a notable degree. Nevertheless, Baron Aehrenthal succeeded first in reaching an understanding with the Turkish government, and second, thanks to the active coöperation of Emperor William II and the German government, in avoiding the menace of war with Serbia. Finally, all the great powers, even including Russia, agreed to the unilateral alteration of the Berlin Treaty. But from this point on the antagonism of the two great eastern European empires in the Balkans developed irresistibly. Isvolsky, unjustly, described himself as having played the part of the deceived partner at Buchlau. He went as ambassador to Paris. From now on he and his successor in office, Sazonov, set the whole apparatus of Russian agitation, official and subterranean, at work throughout the Balkans, against the Habsburg monarchy. Isvolsky's grand design, in all this, was neither more nor less than the resumption of the old policy of Nicholas I, Russia's possession of Constantinople and hegemony over the Orthodox Balkan States. This was now to be achieved through a European war in which Russia, with France, England and Italy as allies, would finally clear from its path Germany and its Austrian ally, hitherto impregnable obstacles to Russian imperialism in Europe. It was to be promoted by the Quadruple Entente, of which Edward VII was the real begetter. Isvolsky's published correspondence

shows that the realization of this aim was the single purpose dominating him and Poincaré between 1911 and
1914. Two factors served effectively to promote their
plans—Italy, though formally a partner in the Triplice,
really acted in the Entente from the time of the Raccon-
igi agreement; and the imperialist wing of the English
Liberal party was increasingly alarmed by the growth of
the German navy. Documentary evidence on German policy and such of the Austrian state papers as have been
published show, equally clearly, that the leading men in
both the Central Empires, although perfectly aware of
the real aim of Isvolsky and his French colleagues, were
entirely at a loss when it came to action designed to relax
the steadily growing tension between the two armed camps
and so prevent the danger of war.

Italy's Tripoli war gave Russia a fresh impulse to
action. Petrograd now addressed itself along a new line
to the old goal of the destruction of the Turkish Empire
and the Russian occupation of Constantinople. Under
Russia's ægis, the Balkan League was formed, primarily
against the Habsburg Empire, though its first action
was war on Turkey. The whole of Macedonia was occupied by the enemy, and the Serbs advanced to the Adriatic
coast. Profound disagreement between the Balkan allies
over the division of their gigantic spoils then led to the
Serbo-Bulgarian War and Rumania finally joined in the
military campaign against Bulgaria to secure its share of
the profits. The sole result of the wearisome negotiations
of the London Conference was Austria's successful demand
for Serbian withdrawal from the coast and the establish-

ment of Albania as a sovereign principality. The Treaty of Bucharest, however, which followed the Second Balkan War in the summer of 1913, not only deprived Bulgaria of its share of Macedonia and Thrace but compelled it to cede the Dobrudja to Rumania.

We are only concerned here with the part played by Francis Joseph in these great and revolutionary events. It is not open to doubt that the whole solution of the eastern question constituted a blank humiliation and sensible weakening of Austria-Hungary. Count Leopold Berchtold, who had succeeded Count Aehrenthal as foreign minister on his death in 1912, had posited the principle of unconditional maintenance of the status quo in the Balkans at the beginning of the first war, but had entirely failed in his efforts to impose this policy on the victorious Balkan States. The failure of his protest against the Peace of Bucharest and the consequent weakening of Bulgaria was the more painful in view of the strong support given to Rumanian policy throughout by Emperor William II and his imperial chancellor. Nor is it open to doubt that the determining factor in Austria's attitude throughout these fearful crises was Francis Joseph's profound aversion to any sort of military action on the part of his realm. But the decisive result was the aggrandisement of Serbia which, together with Greece, actually entered into Turkey's inheritance, and a marked increase in its hostility to Austria owing to the establishment of an independent Albania. Since the annexation of Bosnia, a conviction had taken hold of every section in the population of Serbia that destiny assigned the same rôle to their nation in the

Balkans that Piedmont had successfully filled in Italy against Austria. The acquisition of Macedonia, where the Serb element in the population had been far the weakest hitherto, the military glory won by the Serbian troops, and the steady friendship and aid of Russia made it the common opinion of the entire population, from 1912 on, that Serbian policy must be directed unconditionally to the grandiose end not only of winning Bosnia and Herzegovina but of uniting the southern Slav territories of the Habsburg monarchy into a greater Serbian kingdom. Hartwig, the Russian minister in Belgrade, was like Isvolsky a pupil of Count Ignatieff, Russia's earlier champion in the peninsula, and did everything in his power to promote these views. They soon dominated not only the educated classes but the rank and file of the people in Serbia.

A brief retrospect over conditions in the two states of the monarchy is necessary for a true appreciation of what this Greater Serbian agitation, grown to such gigantic proportions after 1912, meant for Francis Joseph and his realm.

Hungarian policy, both in relation to the Croats and to Serbia, had long constituted the root evil from which the whole body of the realm was sickening. The methods employed by the Hungarian government to maintain its ascendency over Croatia had for long been the cause of a progressive political alienation of the millions of southern Slavs comprised in the Empire. The Hungarian government had to all intents and purposes eradicated the old Croat feeling of loyalty to the Habsburg house. Even a section of the Magyarized Croatian nobility began now making common cause with the intelligentsia and peasantry in resistance to Budapest. The struggles between the Magyar independence parties and the Throne had definitely weakened the status of Austria-Hungary in Europe. Neither Berlin, nor, still less, Paris or London, fully grasped the more serious source of weakness represented by the deterioration of relations between Hungary and the Kingdom of Croatia, incorporated within it. This was a "domestic" issue, but it was inextricably bound up with the relations between the Danubian monarchy and its South Slav neighbors, Serbia and Montenegro. Differences between Magyars were submerged in a hatred, often rising to a positive passion, of their South Slav fellow citizens. Indeed, the opening of the twentieth century saw a coalition formed in Croatia between the young Croat intellectuals and the Serbs there, which while bitterly opposing the Magyars, openly revived the old Illyrian dream of the re-union of Catholic and Orthodox Slavs in all parts of the Habsburg monarchy. Croats and Slavs in Dalmatia, and also in Bosnia and Herzegovina, began coöperating with their brothers in Agram, though the strict Catholic sections in all these regions still stood out against such far-reaching change in the position of the southern Slavs under Francis Joseph's sway. By force and by corruption the governors sent by the Hungarian central government to Croatia to carry its steadily repressive policy there certainly succeeded in maintaining external order, but at the price of embittering the South Slavs both within and without the monarchy.

This had its reactions on Austrian policy, too. The first parliament elected under universal suffrage met in Vienna in the summer of 1907, and the semi-Parliamentary Beck government scored a big initial success: the periodic renewal of the compromise with Hungary, which had been in suspense for the last ten years, was put through. That done, however, the old antagonisms between Germans and Czechs in Bohemia and Moravia and between Germans and South Slavs in Styria, Carinthia, and Carniola broke out anew, and the existing government was plainly no more willing or capable than its predecessors to undertake any plan of reform such as might, at worst, have produced a truce in the conflict that was gnawing at the vitals of the state. Universal suffrage had changed the form of the conflict itself, in a manner no one had foreseen. Now, on the floor of the Chamber in Vienna, there stood, in mutual opposition, organized parties comprising every political grouping within the several nationalities, fused in one common national purpose. Even the Social Democrats, with their internationalist basis, were divided into a series of national parties, combined on Socialist issues when they arose, but in general ready to support their national party organizations on any nationalist question. Further, the increased "nationalization" of party life resulting from universal suffrage meant that fundamental questions of foreign policy began to play a much larger part in parliament than ever before. The deep dislike of the Czechs for the German Alliance, and, above all, the provocatively aggressive attitude taken up by Serbia since the annexation of Bosnia, called forth loud echoes from all the

[505]

Slav parties in parliament, with the exception of the Poles; and the Poles had for years been alienated from the Alliance by the anti-Polish policy pursued by Prussia in its eastern provinces. Anyone who lived through these years either as a member or a minister knows that, from this time on, the atmosphere of the central parliament of Vienna was heavily charged with the electricity generated by the interaction of events at home and abroad; and that every Balkan event, and every resultant of the fact that the great groups of powers now stood facing each other, sword in hand, was directly reflected in the struggle of Germans against non-Germans on the floor of the Chamber. Naturally, obstruction once again became the main instrument of parliamentary strife. The distribution of seats gave the government a bare majority, but that majority sufficed only to put through election to the delegations and certain bills covering matters of imperial defence. Measured by any test of sound constitutional life, this universal suffrage parliament was practically impotent for productive or legislative work: nor was it assisted by the fact that the personalities composing the series of governments of officials were more and more insignificant. When Baron Beck, who had openly opposed Aehrenthal's annexation policy, and fallen out of favor with his old friend, Franz Ferdinand, resigned, he was succeeded by Baron Bienerth, an official quite incompetent for the post. He regarded himself as the mouthpiece of the policy of the heir to the throne, but possessed neither the mind nor the will to bring about any real improvement in conditions at home. His government really took its lead from the Christian Socialist party, which claimed to be the main representative of dynastic policy. In 1911 the deep discontent of the masses caused a big increase in the strength of the Social Democrats in the Reichsrat: Baron Bienerth's cabinet of officials vanished and his place was taken by Count Stürgkh, an old pupil of Dr. Koerber's, who barely troubled to conceal his intention of allowing parliament to discredit itself, while he met the so-called necessities of state by means of the emergency or dictatorship "paragraph fourteen" of the constitution.

Easy to comprehend the disappointment caused to Francis Joseph by the working of universal suffrage. Yet, although it was he who had actually brought this great democratic reform into existence, he now refrained altogether from grappling with the causes of the failure of his new parliament. He let it be. Here we touch the reason for the breakdown of the last chance of any cure of the ills from which Austria suffered, the last hope for the monarchy as a whole. He was now almost eighty. He could hardly be expected to show the mental and moral force necessary to steer the Habsburg realm safely through the immediate perils with which it and the dynasty were menaced by the nationalist megalomania of the Magyars on the one hand, and, on the other, the incapacity of the Austrian bureaucracy to transform the centralized unit state into a union of national democracies in which Germans and Slavs were equal partners. The existence of the realm depended on the solution of these two great and complex questions. But any such solution was rendered almost impossible by the unremitting and cumulative pressure upon it, even since 1908, of acute problems of foreign policy. How could Francis Joseph, at this date, have done what one or two longsighted German politicians of old Austria were then urging, namely, in the interest of the monarchy as a whole, disregard Magyar opposition and proceed to unify the southern Slavs, by substituting so-called Trialism for Dualism, and so avert the perils with which the idea of Jugoslav national unity was fraught in the form in which it threatened from Belgrade, a form fatal to the monarchy because Russia was behind it? Who was, at this date, to teach the Austrian Germans that their conflict with the Czechs in the Sudetic lands, or against the Slovenes in Steiermark and Carinthia, was a merely "provincial" question: that the authentic task of Germanism in Austria could not be accomplished at Pan German meetings in Germany: that Germanism, as the greatest national force in Europe, required something beyond the simple formulæ of French nationalism as its model: and that, in the future as in the past, the major European interests of the German nation as a whole were tied up with the maintenance of the great Danubian monarchy? It could hardly have been done, even had there been men among them capable of rising above the ideas of force in politics, omnipotent in Berlin since Bismarck's fall and strongly felt among Austrian Germans, substituting for them newer ideas of the coöperative community of nations and spreading those new ideas among the Germans of the Empire.

What is clear to the retrospective historian was plain to a very small number of contemporary observers of the political welter of their days. Men of modern outlook upon statesmanship knew and understood well enough that it must come to a life and death struggle, before the fundamental ideas of dynastic power, incorporated in Francis Joseph and in the forces—national, economic, and political—vitally interested in their maintenance, could yield to the new nationalist tendencies, promoted from without, which demanded nothing less than a total revolution of the existing European order. Even had it been possible to inspire the circles immediately surrounding the Emperor with a deeper insight into contemporary facts and forces, there could have been small hope of practical results. Peoples as well as monarchs are unteachable save by experience—and experience in this case meant the actual collision of conflicting ideas and forces.

For those who could see and would understand, the annexation crisis opened a window on to the mighty crisis preparing. At the moment, however, the peaceful solution Count Aehrenthal had succeeded in securing, was taken as a feather in the cap of Austria-Hungary, even by those, deeply concerned for the maintenance of the Empire, who had long been harboring grave doubts in this connection. To Francis Joseph himself, 1908 and the period immediately following brought much satisfaction and re-assurance. In June, 1908, the celebration of his jubilee of the completed sixtieth year of his reign was made the occasion for great demonstrations on the part of all the peoples of Austria. Vienna was the scene of a historic and ethnographic pageant; deputations from every region in the realm once more presented to the Emperor's sight the various and colored image of the multiform lands and races over which his sceptre held sway. A short time earlier his old and much tried heart had been deeply moved by a demonstration organized by Dr. Lueger, mayor of Vienna; all the school children of the city came to pay him homage in the great garden of his palace at Schönbrunn. Even more touching to him had been a special act of reverential recognition offered him by Emperor William II, who came to Vienna at the head of almost all the German Princes and a representative of the Free Cities, to congratulate the Emperor on the occasion of his remarkable anniversary. For this gave him back the sense which had been so much to him in the days of his youth—that he was a German Prince. Pain and bitterness must enter in, for him, to any such evocation of the past, with all that it meant of loss for him and his house: yet there was another side to this wholly unique and by no means merely formal homage which William II had devised and carried out. In it Francis Joseph saw a supreme form of recognition of the German-Austrian Alliance as the golden bridge between past and future for the empires it bound together. He knew a moment of grateful respite from the anxious thought of the dangers threatening his realm from within and without.

At this period, too, the Emperor enjoyed a positively astounding health and vigor. He stood the fatigue and strain of these festivities and all the receptions they entailed far better than did his entourage, many of whom were well on in years. In 1910 he suffered a good deal from chills, and consequently often showed the exhaustion

and weakness natural at so advanced an age. But when he
read the Speech from the Throne at the opening of the
new Parliament in 1911, his appearance was that of a
man in full vigor. Actually from this time on his health
was thoroughly satisfactory, although the events that followed the outbreak of the Balkan War were calculated to
tax his mental and moral resistance to the utmost. Those
who saw him holding the manuscript of his address at
the opening of the delegations in Budapest in 1912
could see the painful days he had passed through recorded
in his ravaged features. Yet he continued to retain that
rare natural gift of his, that marvellous equanimity with
which he met whatever came upon him. The few outside
his immediate circle of counselors and his court staff who
saw him on his good days at this time spoke with amazement of the absolute balance of the old man. In summer
he continued, during his period at Ischl, to go up to his
hunting box in his old hunting garb, and enjoy the pleasures of shooting chamois and stags. This enabled him to
support the frightful tension and the grave risks of war
of the days of the Balkan conflagration and the London
Conferences. In every detail he adhered to his wonted way
of life, save that, maintaining only such slight contact
with the world of Vienna as was afforded him by his friend
Frau Schratt, he was now entirely solitary. Since the maintenance of his health was not merely the first professional
care of his excellent physician, but regarded both by Austrian and Hungarian statesmen as being the strongest guarantee of peace at home and abroad, an almost complete
isolation of the Emperor from the world was, as it were,

tacitly established. The object was to spare the aged man all possible excitement. It was also designed to prevent any personal approach to the Emperor on the part of individuals displeasing to the holders of power, whether the elder statesmen or leading parliamentarians, who might then take the opportunity of expressing views contrary to the government's or objections to the policy, at home or abroad, being carried on in his name. Count Stürgkh, above all, dreaded any such criticism, and was for ever speaking of his "dutiful" care in sparing the Emperor any sort of political excitement. In doing so he served his own interest in maintaining himself in power and also promoted his policy of complete passivity on the part of the Emperor and his government towards the conflict of nationalities. For this sterile and sceptical statesman the laming of the parliamentary democracy constituted a complete justification of his tenacious hostility to universal suffrage. In general he quietly carried on the approved tactic of "talking politics" through the administrative machine. From 1913 on Francis Joseph remained completely invisible so far as the public was concerned; living in Schönbrunn, year in, year out, he no longer went to his old workroom in the Vienna Hofburg. His regular contacts with the outer world were confined to the narrow circle of his immediate entourage and his small suite. He no longer gave general audience. As before, he did his vast daily stint of official work, as before he zealously perused all diplomatic reports of importance and followed the world's events with the same steady measure of tranquil interest that his fixed concentration on the troubles and concerns of his various governments had long made habitual to him.

On the classic German-Czech battleground of Bohemia new and hopeful approaches to understanding were visible in 1910 and 1912. But the Emperor had no confidence in his governor there, Prince Franz Thun, who at first eagerly took these efforts up, and Count Stürgkh naturally took no sort of interest in promoting an enterprise whose success would inevitably have cost him his own position. Since German obstruction in the Bohemian Diet had, since 1908, made the constitutional autonomous administration there impossible, Count Stürgkh coolly transplanted the saving institution of the Dictatorship paragraph from the Imperial Constitution to that of the autonomous kingdom of Bohemia—and, to his own mind, satisfactorily. In Galicia, where the Ruthenians had, for years, been struggling in vain against the domination of the Poles, the Vienna government abstained from intervention, even when the new National Democratic party, with the Polish intellectuals as its nucleus, began coöperating openly with its Russian colleague, and a sort of cover was given by the demands of the Austrian general staff, occupied with the idea of a future war with Russia, to the military organization going on among the All-Polish groups. Hardly less menacing was the state of opinion in leading circles in Croatia, and among the Rumanians in Transylvania. Serious disquiet was caused in military quarters by the open propaganda of the Russian Orthodox Church with the masses of the Ruthenian peasants in eastern Galicia, who felt suppressed by the

Polish landlords, their masters. But in Schönbrunn these things were unknown or disregarded. Conditions in the monarchy were certainly at a singular pass. Boundless Magyar pride and self-confidence in the East, embodied in Stephen Tisza; Count Stürgkh's bureaucracy in the West, alike, if by different methods, concerned to give the old Emperor the impression that good order prevailed in all parts of the realm. To all appearance both prime ministers themselves shared the belief that this good order existed! How little Francis Joseph had learned, in sixty years of rule, to value effective personality in politics was conveyed to Count Stürgkh himself when he was compelled to intimate to the Emperor that he had an affection of the eyes which made him doubt his possessing the needful strength for his post for any great length of time. Whereupon, by way of re-assuring and comforting his prime minister, Franz Joseph replied: "Come, if you take things easy, it will be all right. Just take a couple more good Aulic Councillors into your Præsidium to help you."

Those who have followed the account given in these pages of Francis Joseph's life and character will readily understand his attitude in these years, when his ancient realm was entering on its life and death struggle. Too great emphasis should not be laid on the natural effects of his great age on his mental and spiritual powers, although this aspect cannot be left out. By nature, he had, throughout life, been endowed with at least average mental capacity, plus certain peculiar qualities, belonging to the "heredity" of his forefathers, which made him a real

Sovereign in the historic sense. Like almost all the legitimate monarchs of nineteenth century Europe, he was anything but an intellectual, and to attempt to rule by intellectual means was a notion that never entered his head. So, political ideas and problems for him only existed in so far as they were embodied in persons, and such forces behind these persons as his experience had taught him how to measure and assess. He did not see—what must be seen by the creative statesman in our day—the organic connexion of problems of the state with that world of ideas that broke into Europe in 1789, into Austria-Hungary in 1848: a world that, ever since, had been developing progressively under the impetus of scientific advance, technical knowledge, new systems of transport and communication that bound all the peoples of the earth together, and the all-penetrating and irresistible pressure of modern industrialism, not only affecting but transforming the ultimate tissue of thought and feeling, alike in the individual and in the mass. He, Franz Joseph, heir of so long a line of sovereign princes, had, throughout his reign, set himself in opposition to forces he not unjustly designated revolutionary, and did so from a profound consciousness of inalterable antagonism to the whole of this new world. Even when, as in the case of the army, he had a direct interest in modern technique, he had, even in his youth, accepted innovation but slowly and grudgingly. In the single case where he had carried out a fundamental political reform on his own initiative, the harvest had been nothing but disappointment. That universal suf-

[515]

frage, as he was told by Count Stürgkh and others, was a complete failure, he accepted with resignation. In the end he held to his view that Austria-Hungary could not be governed parliamentarily, and let it go at that. That *he* could not govern it otherwise than by a sham parliamentary system he had long ago demonstrated.

From of old Francis Joseph had only been able to grasp political questions by reducing them to their simplest terms. Always he saw only the "immediate" task before him, and sought for "practical" men to find means to solve it. So far as the nationalities problem was concerned, he had long been convinced that such men were not available, and such means did not exist. For that reason he wasted no more trouble upon it. His ministers were, for him, as a rule so many functional instruments which one tried on certain tasks and, if the try failed, dismissed. He ignored now, as he had done throughout most of his reign, that South Slavs, Italians, Ruthenians and Rumanians more and more were accustomed to look over the walls of the Empire and talk with their brothers outside: that the centre of Austrian foreign policy had to be transferred completely to domestic policy. "Nothing is inner, nothing outer, what is inside, that is outside" —it was not given to Franz Joseph to comprehend this apothegm of Goethe's, any more than to his advisers. In his foreign policy, the old Emperor, in contradiction to the restlessness that had characterized him as a youth, had long developed a systematic passivity. He had only agreed to Baron Aehrenthal's plan of annexing Bosnia on his most solemn assurance that there was no risk of warlike complications. Francis Joseph, who had waged so many wars, desired no more war, at any price. He was guaranteed needful protection against Russia by the alliance with Germany, of whose might and of the invincibility of whose army he was profoundly convinced. William II had always shown his best side in his relations, both political and personal, to the old Emperor: in the course of time, despite the antipathy sometimes roused in a genuine Austrian like Franz Joseph by the "Berlinishness" of the Hohenzollern, a really intimate bond had grown up between them, both as men and as allies. He had an absolute —and no doubt justified—confidence in William II as ally, although he would sometimes, among his intimates, pass sharp criticism on his idiosyncracies as a sovereign, his perpetual public speeches, and that odd impetuosity of his, sometimes challenging, sometimes almost overpowering in its expressed friendliness, which was apt to embarrass foreign monarchs. There is no evidence, so far, which reveals his real "view" of the unhappy personal relations between William II and his uncle, Edward VII. The official biographer of the English king, Sir Sidney Lee, apropos of the visits paid by King Edward to the venerable Emperor at Ischl in 1907 and 1908, says that there was no foundation for the report then current in Europe, that Edward VII had tried, on the earlier of these occasions, to detach Francis Joseph from the German Alliance. Lee, however, admits that in 1908 a political discussion did take place between the two monarchs which touched on Germany and its ruler.

[517]

"The Austrian Emperor and King Edward took a drive together one afternoon, and the King afterwards congratulated himself on the freedom with which the old Emperor talked of political matters. But the Emperor was deaf to the King's appeal that he should use his good offices to persuade the Kaiser of the danger of unrestricted naval rivalry between Germany and England. As a matter of fact, the Kaiser had forestalled the King by informing the Emperor of the Cronberg conversation, and had persuaded him that King Edward's real object was sorely disappointed. He had no other purpose than to diminish the tension which was beginning to threaten peace, and Sir Edward Grey could truthfully aver that Britain had carefully avoided anything likely to make mischief between Germany and Austria."

His biographer assures us that King Edward felt a sympathy bordering on affection for the Austrian monarch, and at the same time notes the complete dissimilarity of the two rulers' characters. Both sovereigns, says Lee, understood the difficulties presented by a realm comprising various peoples: each believed that his realm had a special interest in the maintenance of world peace and was clear that no war could bring him any notable advantage. No greater contrast, adds Lee, could be imagined than that between the King, jovial, large-hearted, trustful, charming everyone by his natural bonhomie, and the Emperor, retiring and resigned, with a courtesy in which there was a strong infusion of the cool polish of the grand seigneur. The news of the annexation of Bosnia and Herzegovina but a few weeks after their last meeting in Ischl, produced a positive explosion from Edward VII. Although he replied courteously to Francis Joseph's holograph letter, he was, from that time on, a forthright opponent of Austro-Hungarian policy and a personal foe of Aehrenthal, whom he described as a "slippery man." The hostility of Britain, from 1908 on, distressed Francis Joseph acutely: he had always laid great stress on good relations with the British government. I learned personally how high an opinion the Emperor had of the British people, and its political force, on the occasion of an audience in 1908. In the course of a conversation he himself started, he said to me: "The English are the most intelligent and efficient politicians, for they always manage to get a good compromise between parties. How different from us in Austria!"

Determination to keep the peace was undoubtedly the ruling trait in Francis Joseph's political thinking in this last decade of his reign. He was well aware that, in this, he had against him the leading men among his generals, notably the chief of the general staff, Conrad von Hötzendorf; as well as leading social circles in Vienna and Budapest which, ever since the Annexation crisis, had openly deplored the retreat of Austro-Hungarian policy before the threats of Serbia and its friends as a display to all the world of the Habsburg realm's sense of its own weakness. This view, further, was strongly held in German diplomatic circles, and openly uttered in society.

General Conrad repeatedly laid plans before the Emperor for a preventive war with Italy and Serbia.

Nothing proves better the determined desire of Francis Joseph for preservation of peace in this last truly critical phase of international European politics, which he had gone through since 1908, than the manner in which he decided personally the grave conflict, which developed after 1909 between Count Aehrenthal and the chief of the staff, General Conrad. The former carried on his policy of maintaining the Trïplice and was convinced that Italy in the case of a general embroglio of the great powers would adhere to the alliance which bound her to Germany and Austria. General Conrad knew accurately the extent of the armaments of Italy on the Austrian frontier, the continuous increase of the Irredentist agitation and the steady rising of the hostility of Italian public opinion against the Habsburg monarchy. Therefore he urgently pressed the government to strengthen the army and navy and to make up its mind not to shrink at the possibility of war with Italy. The relations between Aehrenthal and Conrad eventually became strained to a degree which made it necessary to bring the whole conflict before the Emperor. Francis Joseph, in November of 1911, decided against the chief of the staff and at the same time against Franz Ferdinand, who supported the latter. In his memoirs General Conrad gives the most accurate report on the decisive audience which is highly characteristic of the old Emperor's ways and manners of deciding the most fateful problems. After having laid his memorandum before the Emperor, Conrad felt, he says, "that he was in disgrace." Thereupon Francis Joseph replied: "I tell you this from the beginning: I forbid you these continuous attacks against Aehrenthal. These attacks because of the Balkan policy and of Italy, they are *directed* against *me*, for I make this policy, it is *my* policy. My policy is that of peace. To this policy all must adjust themselves. It is possible that this war will come, nay it is probable. But this war will not take place unless Italy attacks us." At a second audience on November 30, Francis Joseph accepted the resignation of General Conrad. Yet twelve months later, after the outbreak of the Balkan War against Turkey and the death of Count Aehrenthal, Francis Joseph reappointed General Conrad as chief of the staff. Events have confirmed many of his positions and have shown how much the international position of Austria-Hungary had been weakened since the Annexation crisis of 1908.

At the end of 1913, Conrad drew the Emperor's attention to the fact that Austria, in the future, would have to count on war on three fronts and that, since the Peace of Bucharest, Rumania must be accounted an enemy. These arguments did not shake Franz Joseph's adherence to a peace policy: he found a certain support in the fact that both in 1908 and again in 1912, the heir apparent refused to hear of war with Serbia. For this reason, a period of tension between Austria and Serbia in 1913 was safely surmounted without the public's being aware of its existence. The new foreign minister, Count Berchtold, was actually by no means hostile to Serbia at the outbreak of the first Balkan War, the less so since he expected a Turkish victory. The success of the Serbs and Bulgars, which went far beyond most people's expectations, caused a perceptible change and stiffening in the attitude to Serbia taken by the leading spirits in the Ballplatz. With the cognizance and sanction of Count Berchtold I journeyed to Belgrade in November, 1912, and there had a conversation of some hours duration with the Prime Minister Pasitch, the topic being the improvement of relations between Austria-Hungary and Serbia and an understanding as to Serbia's aspirations for a harbor on the Adriatic. Count Berchtold, however, neglected to pursue this approach to an understanding with Serbia seriously. Attempts were made at the same time by my colleagues in parliament, the present President of the Republic of Czecho-Slovakia (Dr. Masaryk) and by my friend Dr. Joseph Maria Baernreither,[1] a prominent member of the Upper House and of the Delegations, to induce Count Berchtold to arrange to receive a visit from the Serbian prime minister. They failed, owing to Foreign Office opposition.

After the election of Prince William of Wied to rule over the new state of Albania and his landing at Durazzo, Serbian hostility to Austria-Hungary found more and more open expression in the newspapers. Sazonov and Isvolsky were tirelessly at work tightening the tension of foreign politics: the position of the Dual Alliance grew more precarious, the anxiety of responsible politicians more and more grave. All this gave special political

---

[1] A full account of this will be found in the volume just issued under my editorship of Dr. Baernreither's Recollections, "*Fragmente Eines Politischen Tagebuches*," Verlag für Kulturpolitik, Berlin, 1928.

significance to the report, in April, 1914, that Franz Joseph was seriously ill. There was inflammation of the lung: his life hung in the balance: all night long the special train stood, fully coaled, in the railway station at Konopischt, to bring Archduke Franz Ferdinand with all speed to Vienna. But, to the amazement of his physicians, the iron constitution of the eighty-four-year-old Emperor triumphed once more. Within a few days he was on the way to complete recovery. The doctors naturally pressed him to remove as soon as possible to his summer abode at Ischl, but the Emperor refused. On June 27, however, he did decide to remove from Schönbrunn to Ischl. It has been said that his reason for this was that, being dissatisfied with Franz Ferdinand's organization of the Bosnian Army Corps manœuvres, and displeased that his wife proposed to accompany the Archduke to them, he desired to avoid meeting the heir to the throne on his return thence to Vienna. On June 28, the day after his arrival at Ischl, Francis Joseph took from the hands of his general aide-de-camp, Count Paar, the telegram informing him that the heir to the throne and the Duchess of Hohenberg had been assassinated by shots fired by a Bosnian student of Serbian nationality. It was the last in that long series of bloody catastrophes which had fallen on the Emperor and his house in his sixty years' rule. A darker page was yet to be turned in Francis Joseph's book of life—that which made this catastrophe a catastrophe to the entire world.

CHAPTER XVII

THE WAR AND THE EMPEROR'S DEATH

IT is recorded that, on the evening of this unhappy June 28, Count Paar, the general aide-de-camp, asked how the Emperor had taken the dreadful news, replied: "The Emperor did not say very much about to-day's frightful stroke of fate. He was deeply shaken in the first moment and seemed to be moved by the blow; he closed his eyes for several minutes and stayed wholly lost in thought. Then, however, he spoke—not really to me, but to himself—the words seemed to burst from his breast: 'Horrible! The Almighty permits no challenge! . . . *A higher Power has restored the order that I was unhappily unable to maintain. . .*' Finally the Emperor, with every sign of profound emotion, turned to me and commanded our return to Vienna for the morrow. Otherwise, not a word more." [1]

The words in which Francis Joseph at once summed up the whole train of thoughts suddenly evoked in his mind by the awful deed, show that, always, the first element in his thinking and feeling was the hereditary house, the dynasty and the God-ordained "order of legitimacy" on which it rested. The apprehension that, despite Franz Fer-

[1] General Baron Margutti, "The Emperor Francis Joseph," London, p. 138 *seq.*

dinand's solemn oath, the sacred order of the house might be violated after the Emperor's death, had been lifted from him by the hand of God! The following days were to bring yet another proof of the rigors of legitimism. The Lord High Steward, Prince Montenuovo, prescribed a notably simplified ceremonial for the solemn obsequies of Franz Ferdinand and his wife, because, by the Emperor's command, the murdered pair were to be laid out and interred together. Therefore the dead heir might not have the full military and court honors otherwise due to him. So much resentment and open criticism of the Lord High Steward was caused by what the nobles and many officers regarded as a slight on the dead, that the Emperor was moved to write a holograph letter to Prince Montenuovo, expressing his special confidence in him!

After Francis Joseph's return to Ischl, the common government had to discuss the necessary political consequences of the bloody events of June 28. The leading statesmen, with Count Berchtold, as minister for foreign affairs, at their head, entered on these discussions possessed by the view that the consideration and yielding temper shown by Franz Joseph, notably towards Serbia, in recent years, must not be evidenced this time. The official minutes of the sessions of the cabinet on July 7 and 19, which have long been open to the public, plainly show this frame of mind, as well as the fact that it was shared by German, Slav, and Magyar statesmen alike. It was a mood widely reflected in society and among great sections of the population of Vienna. If Count Tisza was opposed to an immediately aggressive policy against Serbia, which was regarded straightway as guilty of complicity in the crime of Serajevo, the reason may well have been that he was personally cognizant of the fact that Francis Joseph, even at this moment, was ready for peace. It was actually being said, in political circles, that the Emperor had remarked that, however appalling the crime committed in Serajevo, it was impossible to contemplate war because of the death of one human being, even if he were an archduke. This makes it the more astonishing that Francis Joseph should have sanctioned the Ultimatum, drawn up in the Foreign Office on the basis of the deliberations of the cabinet, which most statesmen believed Serbia could not accept. According to the scanty evidence we have had hitherto on the personal reactions which the great events of those fateful days produced in Francis Joseph, it seems, that, when the Emperor was informed that the Austro-Hungarian minister in Belgrade had characterized the Serbian reply as unacceptable and at once left Belgrade, he heard this intelligence with great perturbation of spirit, and, after reading the telegram, said, loudly and distinctly, as though talking to himself, "Well, breaking off diplomatic relations does not necessarily mean war." This leaves the question, insistent as ever, how did it come to pass that, a week later, Francis Joseph signed the declaration of war on Serbia? It is said that the Emperor was brought to this tremendous decision by certain reports, subsequently proved to be false, of Serbian raids in Bosnia and southern Hungary. This explanation is certainly not at all satisfactory. Actually our present knowledge of the events of this time in Vienna and Ischl does not permit of any exhaustive or entirely convincing account of the specific motives that acted on the Emperor's mind. Although the diplomatic notes and other official material bearing on the action of the Austro-Hungarian government in the crucial days has been fully published, we have practically no documentary material on the personal attitude taken by the Emperor during the various phases culminating in the declaration of war on Serbia. Nor has any real light been, so far, cast on this aspect by the men responsible for the action. It appears that the Emperor was definitely given to understand that war against Serbia would be localized and that he was induced to believe that a brief punitive expedition against Belgrade would not involve European complications. If this assumption be correct, a complete change must have taken place in the venerable monarch's mind in the six days after July 25. True, an assurance on the part of Count Berchtold that an Austrian attack on Serbia would remain purely localized, may have powerfully influenced him. On the other hand, however, it is hard to assume that the Emperor can have taken such an assurance seriously, knowing as he did, that at the time of the conflict with Serbia in 1913 over the Albanian frontier, the risk of warlike conflagration had only just been averted by the aid of the London Conference; knowing, too, as he did, the extreme tension that had developed in the last few years between the Central Powers and the Western-Russian Entente. On the top of this comes the further question—Why did not Francis Joseph, whose desire for peace is certainly not open to doubt, seize on and support with all his might the opportunity of keeping peace between the great powers despite the declaration of war, which was offered in Sir Edward Grey's suggestion of mediation of July 29?

This is no place for the full discussion of such questions; they are part and parcel of the great problem of the origins of the war and the so-called question of war guilt, on which so much has already been published and written and no answer satisfying all the canons of justice yet been disclosed. It is certain, anyway, that Francis Joseph entered on war with a very heavy heart and, from the beginning, with but the smallest hope of a happy issue.

At his advanced age he could not command his armies in person. Absolute real control must be assigned to General Conrad von Hötzendorf. So much was clear. If he gave a member of the imperial house, Archduke Frederick, the nominal command, the explanation lies in the over-estimate of dynastic considerations that had become second nature with him. At all events, a confidential rescript deprived this nominal commander-in-chief of all real power and expressly provided that all decisions of the chief of the general staff were to take effect subject to no cavil and be clothed with imperial authority.

The appalling losses of the first battles round Lemberg against immensely superior Russian forces, and still more the defeats undergone by the armies operating in Serbia under General Potiorck, hit the Emperor very hard indeed. His worst fears seemed to be justified by these events. He had never had complete confidence in General Conrad von Hötzendorf, whom he regarded as a sort of military ideologist lacking sufficient sense of military economy or sufficient ability of using men and resources at his disposal to advantage. Whether it is right, as has been said, that Francis Joseph was prepared, from the start, to place his entire army under the German High Command, but failed, owing to General Conrad's violent opposition, is not yet proved. One must remember that the pulmonary attack which the old Emperor had overcome in the spring of 1914 had taken much of his physical strength and undoubtedly had weakened his courage and to a certain extent his mental capacity. Yet after some time he recovered but never regained his former strength. The second great phase of the war on the eastern front, with the break through at Gorlice, carried through under German leadership but in accordance with Conrad's plans, temporarily raised Francis Joseph's spirits a little: and then followed the great success of the campaign against Serbia under General von Mackensen, which put the whole of the western Balkans, Albania and Montenegro, in the hands of the Central Powers. When William II visited him in Vienna on November 19, 1915, he could not, so a witness records, help feeling a certain embarrassment, because he knew that the achievements of the Austro-Hungarian forces had not come up to expectation—an incident that aptly characterizes his sense of honor.

Admiration of the extraordinary courage and self-sacrifice of his troops and their subordinate officers Francis Joseph certainly expressed, but he no longer had much confidence in many of his generals; and after the failure of Conrad's attack on the Italian armies in the Tyrol, and the surprising break through of the Russians on the eastern Galician front, he relapsed into a profound pessimism, hardly relieved by the invincible and unexampled courage shown in the defence of Trieste and along the line of the Isonzo. He never took any part in the strategic decisions of Headquarters, located, during his lifetime, at Teschen in eastern Silesia. His loyal old head of the military chancery, General von Bolfras, kept him regularly informed on everything to do with the conduct and policy of the war. He was deeply incensed by the confidential reports that began to reach him rather early, of desertions from Czech, Ruthenian and Italian regiments, but does not seem to have realized anything like their full political significance. It was, anyhow, not until 1917 that the effects of the systematic propaganda carried on, notably by England and Italy, among the non-German and non-Magyar peoples and their troops in the field really began to be felt. He seems to have disapproved, personally, of the often stupid and even senseless political plans and deplorable actions of the High Command behind the front, which roused increasing excitement among the Slavs, but he took no steps to interfere, even in such a case as the indictment and condemnation, for high treason, of the Czech parliamentary leader, Dr. Karl Kramarz. Francis Joseph believed that, in handing over all his powers to the High Command, he had deprived himself of any possibility of action in matters affecting the conduct of the forces and the measures of high state police in the interior of the Empire.

During these two years the Emperor stayed throughout at Schönbrunn. As had been his regular practice for decades, he received his ministers and generals and the director of his cabinet. Foreign visits he seldom received. It caused him particular pleasure that the German field marshal, Mackensen, waited on him at Schönbrunn before the opening of the campaign against Serbia. The masculine beauty, martial bearing and genuinely Teutonic type of the most attractive and successful of German generals pleased him greatly; he at once invited him to dine, and spent many hours with him, saying later to his aide-de-camp: "With men like that one never goes wrong."

During the first months of the war he had placed the heir apparent, Archduke Charles, at the disposition of the High Command; in spring, however, he caused him to return to Vienna and take up his abode with his family at Schönbrunn. The presence of Archduchess Zita and her children gave the old monarch some degree of distraction and friendly intercourse. He liked his young heir, whose modest bearing and reverent attitude to himself caused the Emperor much satisfaction. "He is a good fellow," he would often say to his intimates. He did not bring this third heir into official business any more than he had his predecessors; at the same time he ordered the head officials in the various ministerial departments to talk to him about their branch of administration so that he might gain some sort of insight into it.

Late in the autumn of 1916 an event occurred at home which must have perturbed him—the assassination of the prime minister, Count Stürgkh, by Dr. Friedrich Adler, son of Dr. Victor Adler, the old founder and leader of the Austrian Social Democratic party. Francis Joseph at once called on Dr. von Koerber, who had in February, 1915, become common minister of finance in place of Baron Burián, on the latter's succession to Count Berchtold at the Foreign Office. On the day of his entry into office as prime minister, Dr. von Koerber, so he related to me, found the Emperor, bent by age and oncoming suffering, in a state of high excitement over the difficulties and disagreements between the German and Austrian High Commands and the two governments, on the question of the future of Poland. The Emperor exhorted Dr. von Koerber to accept the proclamation issued by the German army and about to be promulgated by the two Emperors, solemnly promising the Poles the future unity and independence of their state in union with Austria-Hungary and Germany. Von Koerber drew his attention to the contradiction involved in such an action and, particularly, to the grave dangers likely to accrue. But when, as he was beginning to refuse, he observed the frightful excitement of the aged Emperor who implored him, with uplifted hands, to give way, he was positively terrified and consented. At the same time he entered one small proviso, of which no one took any notice, whose effect was to destroy any future effect of the whole scheme planned by General Ludendorff and his colleagues.

On this day the Emperor was already suffering from a bronchial catarrh, but his constitution was still resisting it. He was still following events in the theatre of war. The last good news he was able to take in, and did, with full appreciation, was that of the victories gained by General Falkenhayn's German and Austrian troops, who after throwing the Rumanian armies out of Transsylvania, were pressing on to occupy Wallachia and Bucharest. His condition grew steadily worse. From about November 10, his immediate entourage faced the probability that the inflammation of the lungs which had supervened might end fatally. On November 20, Franz Joseph exerted his last strength in a vain effort to deal with the papers that had that morning been brought to him. He was not to leave his bed again. An agonizing cough robbed him of sleep and he sank hour by hour. On November 21, at 9 o'clock in the evening, he was released from his suffering. In these last hours, the heir to the throne, the Emperor's daughters, and his old and faithful servants stood around him. On November 30, 1916, the body lay in state in the Cathedral of St. Stephen, whence the funeral cortege, led by the young Emperor Charles and Empress Zita, with their eldest son Otto, proceeded on foot to the Capuchin Church where, for nearly three hundred years, the Habsburgs and Habsburg Lorrainers had found their last resting place. A vast crowd stood in reverent silence along the route of the funeral procession. Genuine popular sorrow was not called out in Vienna by the death of Francis Joseph: frightful losses in the war, that still raged, suffering and the permanent under-feeding of millions in the capital had produced a sort of apathy there. The Emperor's death did not make any great difference to the people, the less that, since the beginning of the war,

Francis Joseph had personally disappeared altogether from their vision.

In Francis Joseph the last real Emperor of Austria-Hungary was entombed. In his Treasury lay the crown with which, for many centuries, German Emperors of the Holy Roman Empire had been crowned: in him, the last of the last line of German Emperors, beginning with the coronation of Charlemagne in Rome, and extending since over more than a thousand years, passed away.

EPILOGUE

NO one who casts a retrospective glance over the entire life and reign of this last monarch of the "Old School" of European sovereigns can resist the impression of its essentially tragic character. Francis Joseph's life was tragic—but not according to common parlance, which constantly assigns the term tragic to what is merely sad. Of a surety, Emperor Francis Joseph was called upon to endure all that a man may, both personally and politically. But a human destiny becomes tragic only when, to employ Hermann Keyserling's admirable phrase, it is inevitable. Inevitability belongs to destiny only when its fulfilment contains within itself a conflict between the individual's inner being and implicit desires and the mental and spiritual forces of the age in which he lives. Conflict of this type is not confined to the actor on the social and political stage: it is but too often the lot of the artist, the poet, or any man of developed mind. But it is in the statesman and ruler, the man of will par excellence, that tragedy, in this strict sense of the word, finds its fullest exemplification, and is understood even by those from whom comprehension of the deeper connection of historic events is more or less hidden. So, with the years' mounting toll, the authentic tragedy of Francis Joseph's life was, almost instinctively, apprehended by succeeding generations among the peoples over whom he held sway. Here, too, lies no small part of the explanation of the unmistakable change in public opinion in the wider sense, both within and without his realm, on his personality—a change sensible to all those who passed the greater part of their lives under his reign. Despite his almost shy withdrawal from the public eye, and his contemptuous rejection of every art, great or small, which might have popularized monarchical activity, Francis Joseph, the old man who had been so sorely tried, did indubitably possess both popularity and the confidence of his people.

His inevitable destiny arose out of the fact that, steeped by temperament, education, and inherited surroundings in the monarchical consciousness of the preceding period, he saw the maintenance of the realm he had inherited and of its historic power as his single mission upon earth, and subordinated everything to that vision and the sense of duty that, for him, flowed out of it. Thus, for Francis Joseph, the maintenance of his imperial power constituted the Tables of the Law of his life.

Not that he was in any way under the spell of the mystic aura that had surrounded the dignity of the German Emperor ever since the days of Charlemagne, whose throne his ancestors had occupied in almost unbroken succession for well-nigh five hundred years. Anything of that sort was wholly alien to his matter-of-fact mind. Yet, in the depths of his consciousness, he always felt himself in solitary elevation as head of the hereditary house, and therefore as all the more bound in duty to maintain his position undiminished. The 1848 Revolution gravely threatened both his own power and that of the dynasty. In the bloom of his youth, he nevertheless succeeded, by the strength of his army, in re-establishing and maintaining imperial power for a full decade, in its integrity, throughout his realm. This achievement established the monarchical idea, already part of his blood and of his inheritance—powerfully strengthened, too, by his earliest counsellors—into the inalterable object and driving force of his entire life. Nothing shows more plainly how deep-rooted and genuine this sense was than the manner of Francis Joseph's adjustment to the modern world, its ideas and aspirations, when the struggle for survival compelled him to make terms with these views and forces. Never did he yield either to liberalism or to nationalism, the basic forces in the age in which he grew up. His attitude to the forces which he must recognize if he was not to jeopardize his life's task of maintaining the hereditary house and the Empire was like that of the Roman Church, never really abandoning a position, though it may have to evacuate it, never abating fundamental doctrines and tenets, even when compelled to promulgate a "tolerari posse." He became a constitutional monarch in Hungary and in his Austrian hereditary realm, and henceforward acted as such. In Austria he found there were men and there were circumstances which enabled him to work the constitution he had granted in such fashion that, to his own sense, everything signifying the reality of imperial power remained intact under this same constitution.

Each decade was to demonstrate more plainly the contradiction between this constitution and the true nature of the Austrian state, and to show the Magyar oligarchy exploiting its parliamentary ascendency in order to nullify any political rights on the part of millions of non-Magyars. He saw all this, at last. Yet he gave no serious support to efforts at federalization in Austria, since, not wholly without reason, he dreaded the consequent weakening of imperial authority and central control. He imposed no veto on Magyar arrogance, encouraged by the 1867 Compromise, until Hungarian nationalism began laying hands on the common army. For Francis Joseph, the political freedom granted to the people under the constitutional principle was admissible and binding only in so far as it did not endanger the prerogatives guaranteed him by the said peoples and their parties in relation to the army and to foreign policy. For, to his mind, these prerogatives did actually fully safeguard the Empire and the dynastic power. For this reason, the progressive degeneration of parliamentary institutions in both halves of the monarchy did not greatly perturb him, though he did resent the slur thereby cast from time to time on Austria-Hungary in the eyes of the outer world. Throughout the period when a solution of the Austrian problem might still have been found in an extension of national autonomy —which had undoubtedly proved its vitality and capacity as an instrument—and a modern way might have been devised of settling the ridiculously exaggerated difficulty of the official language, through the use of his own imperial authority, he made no effort in either direction. When it was too late, his light-hearted grant of universal suffrage threw wide the doors for nationalist democracy, which swarmed in to the old governmental machine and under-mined its strongholds. Francis Joseph was painfully aware of the degeneration of the bureaucracy, but by then he felt too old to contemplate major reforms.

Archduke Franz Ferdinand used, among his intimates, often to compare his relation with his uncle and emperor to that of a trustee who can only look helplessly on while the veteran owner of the estate lets the woods rot, the fields go to seed, and false stewards squander his substance. His comparison was only too apt, although it is open to doubt whether the new régime, for which Franz Ferdinand stood, could have saved the inheritance from ruin. Any-how, to his last day on earth, Francis Joseph remained sovereign in the old sense, the monarch of the old school which he felt himself to be. He was spared seeing with his own eyes the final turn in his tragedy. So it may be said that, at the last, he did, by sheer force of will, suc-ceed in emerging master in the inevitable conflict with the ideas and forces of his own age in which he had been involved from the start. Actually, he remained victorious over the new age. It was not till two years after his death that the Empire and the imperial idea, for whose main-tenance alone he had borne the heat and burden of his long life, collapsed completely. The tragedy of his nature and of his destiny was only to be posthumously revealed, in all its fulness. To the end, he stood faithful to himself and to the one idea that, for him, had any real existence. The mighty forces stirring within the peoples of Austria, the ideas of nationality and of democracy, were not able to win the upper hand over the old idea of a unifying sovereignty, so long as that idea stood over against them, incorporated in the figure of Francis Joseph. Not till war and the will of the Allied Powers to destroy the Central Powers had ripened these ideas to full fruition among the nationalities did the conflict between the old Habsburg realm and its last ruler issue against the Emperor—and by then Francis Joseph had been two years dead.

Thus it seems that tragedy in the full sense belongs not so much to Francis Joseph as to the imperial idea, in the old Austrian sense, as embodied in him. If he himself once voiced the complaint, "Nothing in this world has been spared me," his biographer must reply that the last blow was spared him—the downfall of his realm. On the ancient idea of a union of nationalities, as realized in this realm for centuries, in a form whose very age was causing it to decompose, events serve to pass judgment insofar as Francis Joseph's life proves that in the form at least in which he sought to maintain this supernational state—that of a dynastic inheritance—it was impossible of maintenance. Why and how, with powers which in themselves cannot be rated meanly, he succeeded only in maintaining what existed so as to be a burden to his successor, his biographer may claim to have shown. In so far as he has done so, he has fulfilled the task he set before himself. The problems presented by the new states of central, north- and southeastern Europe, risen out of the ruins of Francis Joseph's realm, lie entirely outside its limits. They usher in a new period in the history of Europe.

INDEX OF NAMES

INDEX OF NAMES

INDEX OF NAMES

INDEX OF NAMES